Praise for *Clinton's Elections*

"While not bringing out a true realignment in American politics, the two presidential victories by Bill Clinton reshaped the politics of the nation in terms of its electoral balance of power, a new norm in the operation of the federal government, and how campaigns operated. As he has done in so many previous works, Michael Nelson tells the story of those campaigns and their ramifications in a clear manner, making the meaning of the Clinton era understandable for generations of students born after the 1990s."

Jay Barth, M. E. and Ima Graves Peace Distinguished Professor of Politics, Emeritus, Hendrix College

"With a cast of political actors as fascinating and flawed as any since the 1850s and a backdrop of cultural warfare, Michael Nelson delivers an absorbing narrative with a timely theme: how divided governance hardened into dysfunctional governance. More than a decade of renewed Democratic presidential competitiveness, the 1990s marked the emergence of institutionalized partisan loathing and automatic, strident opposition by the minority party. Anyone who wants to know what happened to 'the presidential honeymoon,' 'comity,' and other bygone political courtesies will find the answers—and much more—in *Clinton's Elections*."

David Courtwright, author of *No Right Turn: Conservative Politics in a Liberal America*

"The Democratic Party is divided; some believe the party can win only with a moderate presidential candidate who appeals to the interests of the middle class, and others argue that a full-throated tack to the left is needed to regain the White House. Moderately educated white voters move toward the Republicans. The parties are polarizing in Congress and in the country. Politics in 2020? No: this is Michael Nelson's fascinating account of the Bill Clinton presidential terms of the 1990s. Nelson's new book uncovers the roots of the current era, in which presidential elections are highly competitive but states are increasingly one-party, inter-party hostility keeps growing, and the federal government seems unable to respond to a variety of new and age-old challenges."

Marjorie R. Hershey, author of *Party Politics in America*

"Clearly and cogently written, Michael Nelson has produced the definitive book about the electoral politics of the 1990s. Students, scholars, and political junkies will all profit from this outstanding read."

Marc Joseph Hetherington, Raymond Dawson Distinguished Bicentennial Professor of Political Science, University of North Carolina

"The author of nearly two dozen books analyzing recent American political history, Michael Nelson of Rhodes College is one of the nation's most distinguished American political scientists. His latest work, *Clinton's Elections: 1992, 1996, and the Birth of a New Era of Governance*, will only add to this reputation. In a careful analysis of congressional and presidential elections going back to the election of 1968, Nelson argues that until 1992, Congress was partially or completely controlled by the Democrats while the Republicans mostly controlled the White House. This led to an increase in political partisanship. In 1992, Clinton was elected president, but in the 1994 midterm elections the Republicans took control of Congress for the first time since 1952 and held it throughout the remaining six years of his administration. Although Clinton was reelected in 1996, the result of divided government has been 'de facto divided government' and partisan polarization ever since. An absorbing and well-written analysis of a crucial development in American political history, this book should be of great significance to anyone interested in the modern age of US politics."

Burton I. Kaufman, author of *The Post-Presidency from Washington to Clinton*

"Michael Nelson brings his distinctive blend of narrative verve and political science acumen to the story of Bill Clinton's two electoral victories. Just as in his prize-winning volume on the presidential election of 1968, Nelson's tale of how the Clinton years ushered in our current era of divided government and bitter partisanship makes for a fascinating read."

Bruce Miroff, author of *Presidents on Political Ground: Leaders in Action and What They Face*

"Renowned presidency scholar and award-winning author Michael Nelson has penned a captivating analysis of Bill Clinton's two presidential election victories, situating them in the arc from the turbulent 1960s to the divisive age of Trump. Nelson masterfully argues that Clinton's centrism—the very core of his electoral successes—ironically resulted in the polarized extremism of twenty-first-century American politics."

Barbara A. Perry, author of *Jacqueline Kennedy: First Lady of the New Frontier* and *The Michigan Affirmative Action Cases*

CLINTON'S ELECTIONS

American Presidential Elections

MICHAEL NELSON

JOHN M. MCCARDELL, JR.

1992

CLINTON'S ELECTIONS

1992, 1996, AND THE BIRTH OF
A NEW ERA OF GOVERNANCE

MICHAEL NELSON

UNIVERSITY PRESS OF KANSAS

Published by
the University
Press of Kansas
(Lawrence,
Kansas 66045),
which was
organized by the
Kansas Board
of Regents and
is operated
and funded by
Emporia State
University,
Fort Hays State
University,
Kansas State
University,
Pittsburg State
University, the
University of
Kansas, and
Wichita State
University.

© 2020 by the University Press of Kansas

Library of Congress Cataloging-in-Publication Data

Names: Nelson, Michael, 1949– author.

Title: Clinton's elections : 1992, 1996, and the birth of a new era of
    governance / Michael Nelson.

Description: Lawrence : University Press of Kansas, 2020. | Series:
    American presidential elections | Includes bibliographical
    references and index.

Identifiers: LCCN 2019034813

    ISBN 9780700629176 (cloth)

    ISBN 9780700629183 (epub)

Subjects: LCSH: Clinton, Bill, 1946– | Presidents—United States—
    Elections—1992. | Presidents—United States—Elections—1996.
    | Democratization—Government policy—United States. | United
    States—Politics and government—1993–2001.

Classification: LCC E886 .N45 2020 | DDC 973.929092—dc23

LC record available at https://lccn.loc.gov/2019034813.

British Library Cataloguing-in-Publication Data is available.

Printed in the United States of America

10 9 8 7 6 5 4 3 2 1

The paper used in this publication is recycled and contains 30
percent postconsumer waste. It is acid free and meets the minimum
requirements of the American National Standard for Permanence of
Paper for Printed Library Materials Z39.48-1992.

For friends from every generation

Faithful friends are a sturdy shelter:
whoever finds one has found a treasure.
Faithful friends are beyond price;
no amount can balance their worth.

Ecclesiasticus 6:14–15

Joe Birch

Austin Bridgforth

Andy Cates

George Cates

Steve Ceccoli

Dan Cullen

Brad DeWees

Bill Haltom

Erwin Hargrove

Tim Huebner

Jay Mason

Raj Menon

Sid Milkis

Tommy Parker

Don Sweeney

Evan Tucker

D. J. Westbrook

CONTENTS

Millennials and postmillennials may find this difficult to believe, but there was a time in the not-so-distant past when Democrats were resigned to voting for losers in presidential elections. As a late baby boomer, I cast my first presidential vote for a loser in 1980 (Jimmy Carter) and my second for an even bigger loser in 1984 (Walter Mondale). The third time certainly wasn't the charm, as once again, in 1988, my vote went to a surefire loser (Michael Dukakis). None of the election results were even close. The three Democratic nominees won an average of about 10 percent of the Electoral College vote against their Republican opponents, Ronald Reagan and George Bush. To put that record of humiliating futility into historical perspective, Democrats won a smaller share of the Electoral College vote over those three elections than any party in any three consecutive presidential elections in American history. Admittedly, Democrats in the 1980s could take some solace in congressional and state elections, where they continued to perform well. In fact, at the time I voted for Dukakis as a twenty-something in 1988, the Democrats had controlled the House of Representatives for my entire lifetime, and they would continue to hold the House throughout George Bush's presidency.

How different politics looked thirty years later. A millennial turning twenty-four in 2018 would have experienced a House of Representatives controlled by the Republicans for all but four years of her life. She would also have become accustomed to a political universe in which Republicans typically control most state legislatures and governorships. Yet that new political universe was also one in which Democrats had gained the upper hand at the presidential level. In the seven presidential elections following the Dukakis debacle (1992–2016), Democrats won the popular vote in all but one (2004), a feat that no political party has achieved since the Democratic Party's inception in the 1820s. Of course, in two of those contests winning the popular vote was not enough for the Democratic candidate (Al Gore in 2000 and Hillary Clinton in 2016) to win the presidency, but it is nonetheless remarkable that Democrats in short order went from historic presidential losers to (more often than not) presidential winners.

How did this inversion of American politics happen? Some will point to demography, but populations change slowly, and the shift in party fortunes was sudden. In 1992, Bill Clinton won the presidency—the first Democrat to do so since Jimmy Carter in 1976. In 1994, Republicans won a majority in the House of Representatives for the first time since the election of 1952. Then in 1996 Clinton won reelection, becoming the first Democrat since Franklin D. Roosevelt to win a presidential election twice. And Clinton won resoundingly, securing 70 percent of the electoral votes and prevailing in more than three-fifths of the states.

Clinton's electoral victories were certainly not realigning elections in the classic sense. They did not usher in a dominant new political regime in the manner of Andrew Jackson's victories in 1828 and 1832, Abraham Lincoln's in 1860 and 1864, and Franklin Delano Roosevelt's in 1932 and 1936. Indeed, Clinton's two elections were followed by the two-term Republican presidency of George W. Bush. A voracious reader of presidential history, Clinton was only too aware that his position in political time frustrated his aspiration to be a transformative leader who might boldly reconstruct American politics and policy. He lamented that his presidency lacked the kind of extraordinary crisis or challenge, or even "a big, clear task," that could enable him to rally the country behind a unifying cause. Perhaps because Clinton's presidency was hobbled by six years of divided government, ended in a sex scandal and impeachment, and was sandwiched between twenty years of Republican presidents (twelve before, eight after), we have tended to miss the pivotal part that Clinton's two elections, and the intervening 1994 midterm election, played in ushering in a new era of American politics, one in which the two political parties were frantically competitive at the presidential level, even while the country increasingly sorted itself into red and blue states.

Fortunately, that neglect ends here with Michael Nelson's absorbing account of Clinton's two elections. Nelson brings to life an achievement that many Democrats today no longer remember or seem eager to forget: namely, that Bill Clinton revived a presidential party that had become nearly moribund. Indeed, but for Gore's campaign missteps, Ralph Nader's misguided zeal, and a poorly designed ballot in Palm Beach County (not to mention a Republican-dominated Supreme Court that was itself a product of the Democratic Party's futility in presidential races during 1980s), we all might have been quicker to recognize Clinton's elections for the watershed moment they were in modern American politics.

At one level, Clinton's elections seemed to change little. They swapped divided government of one invariant form—from 1969 to 1992 it was always Republican presidents and a Democratic House—for divided government of more variable forms, with occasional bursts of unified government. But at another level, as Nelson shows, they helped to usher in a new era of governance marked by intense partisan loathing and antagonism. The old divided government before 1992 had frequently been effective government (*Divided We Govern* was the sunny title of David Mayhew's influential book, published in 1991), but the new divided government was often, Nelson writes, "dysfunctional bordering on corrosive," marked by government shutdowns, constitutional hardball, threats of impeachment, and the erosion of long-established norms of governance. Routinization of the filibuster—specifically the expectation that sixty votes are required to pass nearly all legislation in the Senate—meant that even unified government in form became dysfunctional divided government in fact.

Clinton's Elections offers an apt bookend to Nelson's award-winning account of the 1968 election, *Resilient America: Electing Nixon in 1968, Channeling Dissent and Dividing Government*. In *Resilient America*, Nelson recounted the famously tumultuous year of 1968 in terms of a nation "holding together" rather than "coming apart," of divided government that paradoxically unified a nation. *Clinton's Elections* marks the end of that era and the beginning of our own. In Clinton's two seemingly run-of-the-mill elections—"it's the economy, stupid," Clinton strategist James Carville famously remarked during the 1992 campaign—Nelson finds a pivotal turning point and the birth of a new era of political divisiveness and dysfunction. After the 1968 election, the center resolutely held. After the 1996 election, in which President Clinton tacked relentlessly to the center, the extremes increasingly held sway. None of us know how and when our current era of dysfunctional governance will end, but every citizen who wishes to understand how this divisive era began will want to read Michael Nelson's engagingly written and endlessly fascinating history of Clinton's elections.

Richard J. Ellis

For better *and* worse, Bill Clinton loomed over the landscape of American presidential politics for a third of a century.

For better, he was the first Democrat to win two terms since Franklin D. Roosevelt and, at the time, one of only four Democrats ever to have done so (Andrew Jackson and Woodrow Wilson were the others). Clinton's victories in 1992 and 1996 broke a Republican winning streak that encompassed five of the six previous elections, four of them by landslides. Clinton also was arguably the most effective advocate for the fifth two-term Democrat, Barack Obama, when he ran for reelection in 2012.

For worse, Clinton was a near candidate in 1988 who backed off (almost literally at the last minute) in the face of unprecedentedly intense media scrutiny of politicians' conduct outside marriage and went on to give an embarrassingly bad nominating speech for his party's candidate at the Democratic convention. In 2000, the challenge of dealing with the uncertain political consequences of Clinton's sexual misconduct in office so rattled his vice president, Al Gore, that Gore fumbled his way to defeat in an eminently winnable presidential election. In 2008 and 2016, Clinton was at best a rusty campaigner for his wife, Hillary Clinton, in her two failed bids for the presidency, the first time by making racially awkward remarks about Obama, her rival for the Democratic nomination, and the second time when his sexual misbehavior came back to haunt him in a way that distracted voters from the egregious conduct of her Republican opponent, Donald Trump.

As its title suggests, *Clinton's Elections* focuses on his two victories in 1992 and 1996. As the book's subtitle indicates—*1992, 1996, and the Birth of a New Era of Governance*—the book embeds these elections in a larger historical framework that both precedes and flows from Clinton's two victories.

In 1992 Clinton defeated incumbent Republican president George Bush less than two years after Bush's job approval rating soared to 89 percent, higher than any of his predecessors. En route to victory in the general election, Clinton won a spirited contest for the Democratic nomination with a campaign aimed at moving his long-forlorn presidential party closer to where most voters were. He accomplished this even though he had to compete with another politically effective new voice, that of independent candidate Ross Perot.

Along the path to reelection in 1996, Clinton did something just as unusual as winning the first second term for a Democrat since 1936. In the 1994 midterm elections Clinton and his party lost Congress to the Republicans for the first time since 1952. Both congressional chambers remained forfeit to the GOP for the rest of his time in office. Not since 1928 had a Republican Congress been reelected even once.

The larger narrative of *Clinton's Elections* is of partisan control of the federal government that has been divided across party lines, united, and then redivided along different lines such that whether or not divided in form, it has become divided in fact. "De facto divided government," as I call it, aggravates and is aggravated by the rising partisan polarization that has come to shadow contemporary governance.

After nearly two centuries in which united party government—that is, same-party control of the presidency, the House of Representatives, and the Senate—was the normal governing situation in Washington, voters began opting for divided government in 1968, the election chronicled in my previous book, *Resilient America: Electing Nixon in 1968, Channeling Dissent, and Dividing Government.*

For the first quarter century of the new era—from 1968 until Clinton was inaugurated in 1993—divided government invariably took the form of a Republican president and a wholly or at least partially Democrat-controlled Congress. Clinton broke this pattern, first with a united party victory in 1992 and then with a variation on the theme of divided government in which Democratic presidents are as likely to face a Republican Congress as Republican presidents are to face a Democratic Congress.

Scholars have debated how much difference divided government makes. But one thing is clear: when both parties anticipate that they may win any combination of the presidency, House, and Senate in the next election, de facto divided government furthers stalemate in Washington and polarization among the voters. No matter what the pattern of partisan control in Washington may be, both parties act as if the other party must be conquered, not just defeated. Only Clinton's productive fourth and fifth years as president—the last year of his first term and the first year of his last term—offer mild reassurance that "normally" need not mean "always."

This book begins with the 1988 election and its aftermath. Chapter 1 focuses on the Democrats and chapter 2 on the Republicans. Both chapters include political profiles of the major figures to emerge from this election with their sights on 1992 and 1996.

Chapter 3 is about President George Bush's first three years in office as head of a divided government, including his difficult relations with the Democratic Congress and his own congressional party, as well as with a rising independent challenger, Ross Perot.

Chapter 4 tells the story of Bush's successful but wounding bid for renomination in 1992, during which he suffered attacks from both Perot and Republican rival Pat Buchanan. Chapters 5 and 6 offer an account of Clinton's own troubled but ultimately triumphant nomination through the strategies, debates, and campaigns of the three-way general election battle, along with an analysis of the results for both the presidential and congressional elections.

Clinton's election, joined with that of the Democratic Congress, created a united party government but not an untroubled one. His struggles with both parties on Capitol Hill, the Democrats' loss of Congress in 1994, and Clinton's remarkable rebound in 1995 are the subject of chapter 7.

Chapter 8 offers an account of the 1996 election: Clinton's adroit efforts to fend off opposition within his party, the Republican contest that resulted in Bob Dole's nomination, Perot's second candidacy, and the campaign that led to the president's convincing reelection. Nineteen ninety-six was also the election in which voters reelected both a Democratic president and a Republican Congress, perpetuating divided government but in a new partisan configuration.

In chapter 9 I explore what the new-style divided government ushered in by Clinton's elections entails for politics in our time—de facto divided government even when, as has been the case during parts of the administrations of all of Clinton's successors, the president's party maintains nominal control of Congress.

In the course of researching and writing this book, I incurred debts too great to pay with words of thanks—but here goes anyway. Press directors Fred Woodward and Chuck Myers and acquiring editor David Congdon supported this project every step of the way. Richard Ellis, Bruce Miroff, and Brad DeWees offered detailed and expert commentary on the manuscript, and Ellis wrote the discerning foreword. Managing editor Kelly Chrisman Jacques, copy editor Susan Ecklund, and project editor Jane Raese saved me from many small errors. My participation in the William J. Clinton

Oral History as a senior fellow at the University of Virginia's Miller Center afforded me invaluable insights into the president and his campaigns, and I have drawn extensively on both the Clinton Oral History and the Miller Center's George H. W. Bush Oral History in this volume. Rhodes College supported my work with a timely sabbatical and research funding from the Fulmer professorship in political science. Rhodes students Sam Holder, Michael Combs, Ted Hall, and Harley Chapman were helpful research assistants at various stages of the research. To all of them, and to the friends listed in the book's dedication who, along with my wife, Linda, have so enriched my life, I offer my deepest thanks.

THE VIEW FROM 1988
THE FIELD OF DEMOCRATS FORMS

Vice President George Bush's landslide victory in the 1988 presidential election seemed to confirm, if anyone still needed confirmation, that the American presidency had become a Republican preserve during the final third of the twentieth century. To the extent that this assessment was accurate, it was also remarkable. As recently as the century's middle third, the GOP had seemed a recrudescence of the nineteenth-century Whig Party, which won just two of seven presidential elections against the Democrats before expiring after 1852. The Whigs' victories came only when they were able to nominate a victorious general (William Henry Harrison in 1840, Zachary Taylor in 1848) whose postwar popularity transcended the party's own more limited appeal. The Republicans' record against the Democrats in presidential elections from 1932 to 1964 was similarly dismal: two victories and seven defeats, with the two won by the transcendently popular Dwight D. Eisenhower, the supreme commander of the victorious Allied forces in World War II. In the last of these nine midcentury elections, the Republican nominee, conservative senator Barry Goldwater of Arizona, lost so massively to President Lyndon B. Johnson that many astute political observers wondered if the party was in its death throes.[1]

Starting in 1968, however, the Republicans won five of the next six elections. Former vice president Richard Nixon's victory in 1968 was narrow, but the other four were overwhelming: his reelection in 1972 by a 520 to 17 electoral vote majority; former California governor Ronald Reagan's two victories in 1980 and 1984, the first by 489 to 49 electoral votes (the largest margin ever against an incumbent president) and the second by 525 to 13; and Bush's own 426 to 111 vote triumph in 1988.[2] In these four elections, the Republican nominee's margin in the national popular vote never fell below 8 percentage points and reached as high as 23 points. Cumulatively, from 1968 to 1988 the GOP outpolled the Democrats by 264 million to 215 million in the popular vote and by 2,501 to 678—79 percent to 21 percent—in the Electoral College. Republican nominees carried twenty-one states with 187 electoral votes in all six elections in this period and won another fourteen states with 157 electoral votes in every election but one. In contrast, their hapless Democratic opponents carried only the District of Columbia and its three electoral votes in all six elections and just one state, Minnesota (10 electoral votes), in five of them. No major party in history—not even the fading Federalist Party of the early 1800s—received a smaller share of the electoral vote in three consecutive elections than the Democrats did in 1980, 1984, and 1988: 11 percent.

Although Bush's majority in 1988 was 5 percentage points and 99 electoral votes smaller than Reagan's in the previous election, it was in some ways even more impressive. Bush was the first incumbent vice president in a century and a half—since Martin Van Buren in 1836—to be elected president. In winning a third victory in a row for his party, the first time this had happened since 1948, Bush overcame the roughly 4-point "time for a change" handicap that political scientist Samuel Popkin assigns to nominees whose party has held the presidency for the previous eight years—a handicap that would grow to 6 points when he sought a fourth Republican term in 1992.[3] "We're close to becoming a one-party presidential country," said former vice president Walter F. Mondale, the defeated Democratic nominee in 1984.[4] That said, in 1988 Bush did not have to run against a southern governor like the one who earned the single Democratic victory of this era, Jimmy Carter of Georgia, a narrow victor over President Gerald Ford in 1976.

Bush's Democratic opponent in 1988 was not southern, but he was a governor: Michael S. Dukakis of Massachusetts. With Reagan leaving office at the end of his constitutionally limited two terms, Democrats were optimistic about their chances of recapturing the White House. In contrast to Mondale, Dukakis was not a Washington insider or an old-school liberal. Instead, his national reputation was as a nonideological technocrat whose austere state budgets and pro–business development policies earned him credit for the "Massachusetts Miracle," which supporters claimed had transformed the declining Rust Belt state into a booming economic powerhouse.

Because in 1988 the Democratic nomination seemed more likely than usual to lead to victory in the November election, Dukakis was opposed for his party's nod by a strong and varied field of contenders. These included Rep. Richard Gephardt of Missouri, the Democratic caucus chair in the House of Representatives; Sen. Paul Simon of Illinois; Sen. Al Gore of Tennessee; Sen. Joseph Biden of Delaware; civil rights leader Jesse Jackson; and former senator Gary Hart of Colorado, the strong runner-up for the Democratic nomination in 1984. Hart was the clear early front-runner after New York governor Mario Cuomo announced in February 1987 that he would not run, but he dropped out in May amid media allegations that he had engaged in sexual dalliances with women other than his wife. Other potential candidates, notably Gov. Bill Clinton of Arkansas, who was himself the subject of widespread rumors about adulterous activities, came close to entering the race but chose not to run.

Most of these candidates fell by the wayside when their campaigns failed to catch fire in the early primaries and caucuses. Along with Dukakis, who won the New Hampshire primary, Jackson and Gore survived into the spring in part by refusing to compete seriously in either New Hampshire or the preceding Iowa caucuses. Their strategy was to keep their powder dry for "Super Tuesday." On March 8, twenty states held their contests, most of them in the South and border states where black voters (Jackson's main constituency) and conservative whites (Gore's presumed base) were concentrated. Gore won four Super Tuesday primaries in Outer South and border states, and Jackson won five, mostly in the Deep South, where African Americans made up at least one-third of the Democratic primary electorate. But Dukakis won the two largest southern prizes—Florida and Texas—and swept nearly all of the contests held that day in other regions, including those in Maryland, Washington, and Hawaii.

Gore dropped out after running a distant third in the April 19 New York primary. Jackson, who enjoyed united support from African American voters and, in contrast to his previous run for the Democratic nomination in 1984, from African American political leaders, stayed in, hoping to leverage his second-place finish into the second spot on the ticket as Dukakis's running mate. Sure-footed as Dukakis was in uniting most of his hungry-for-victory party members behind him at the Democratic National Convention in July, he alienated Jackson by choosing Sen. Lloyd Bentsen, a conservative Texan, and then, with uncharacteristic carelessness, letting Jackson find out about the choice from reporters rather than from Dukakis himself.[5]

The battle for the 1988 Republican nomination was equally spirited. Although Bush served as Reagan's loyal lieutenant for eight years and was, as recent vice presidents Nixon, Mondale, and Hubert H. Humphrey had been, the presumed front-runner for his party's presidential nomination, he had to fend off a number of rivals to win it. Other candidates challenged Bush's claim to be the popular president's true political heir, seeking to discredit the vice president by casting doubts on his conservative bona fides as Reagan's moderate rival for the 1980 Republican nomination. (Bush famously branded Reagan's supply-side tax cut proposal as "voodoo economic policies.") Senate Republican leader Bob J. Dole of Iowa lay claim to the Reagan mantle by arguing that he, not Bush, had gotten the president's legislative program through Congress. Rep. Jack Kemp of New York argued that he was the author of and only true believer in Reagan's supply-side tax cuts. Rev. Pat Robertson, a prominent television evangelist and the founder of the highly successful Christian Broadcasting Network, staked his claim to Reaganites' loyalties as the field's sole Christian conservative. Others offered their own Reagan-related credentials, including Gen. Al Haig, the president's first secretary of state, and Pete DuPont of Delaware, who like Reagan was a conservative state governor before seeking the presidency. Reagan remained officially neutral, but most of his chief supporters favored Bush, whose unflagging loyalty as vice president they and the president appreciated.

Bush stumbled out of the gate in the first contest, finishing third in Iowa behind not just Dole from neighboring Kansas but Robertson as well. With strong support by Gov. John Sununu, he bounced back in New Hampshire and essentially ran the table from that point on, sweeping the Super Tuesday primaries and caucuses and winning every subsequent event. Haig and DuPont received hardly any votes, Kemp dropped out before Super Tuesday, and Robertson, who pinned his hopes on besting Bush among the evangelical Christians who dominated the southern Republican electorate, lost even them to the vice president. Most southern white Christians were Baptist, Methodist, or Church of Christ members made uncomfortable by the Pentecostal Robertson's ease with faith healing and speaking in tongues. Dole hung on the longest in hopes of becoming Bush's running mate or, if political lightning struck, somehow winning the nomination himself. But Bush was reluctant to serve as president in harness with the acerbic Dole (or the verbose Kemp). He chose a young vice presidential candidate who would, as Bush had, function as a grateful, loyal lieutenant in the administration, Sen. Dan Quayle of Indiana.

Dukakis left his convention with a double-digit lead in the polls, which the Bush campaign demolished in the run-up to and, especially, during the August Republican convention, where Bush gave an uncharacteristically forceful acceptance speech. The endlessly rebroadcast sound bite from the speech reassured Reagan's supporters that if Congress tried to increase revenues, Bush's response would be "Read my lips—no new taxes." The speech undid some of the damage caused by Bush's selection of Quayle, whose perceived shallowness in comparison with Bentsen cost the ticket several points in the November election.[6] Even more effective during the summer and fall campaign was the GOP's rebranding of Dukakis as a soft-on-crime, less-than-patriotic liberal, charges that Dukakis mistakenly thought voters would not take seriously. Bush pulled ahead in polls taken right after the convention and never fell behind. Apart from running a slashingly effective campaign, he benefited enormously from the strong economy and his association with the popular president.

In previous eras of American political history, a party's extended command of the presidency was accompanied by a similar hold on Congress. With only occasional exceptions, united party government had long been the normal governing situation in Washington. In the pre-1968 era of the New Deal Democratic majority, for example, Democratic presidents Franklin D. Roosevelt, Harry S. Truman, John F. Kennedy, and Lyndon B. Johnson governed with a Democratic Congress for twenty-six of twenty-eight years—93 percent of the time. When the GOP was the majority party from 1896 to 1932, Republican presidents William McKinley, Theodore Roosevelt, William Howard Taft, Warren G. Harding, and Herbert Hoover served alongside a Republican Congress for twenty-four of twenty-eight years: 86 percent of the time. Divided government, in which the opposition party controls one or both houses of Congress, usually arose only when a president of the minority party such as Woodrow Wilson (a Democrat in the pre–New Deal Republican era) or Dwight Eisenhower (a Republican when New Deal Democrats were ascendant) was in office—and even then, not during his first two years.

Beginning in 1968, divided government became the rule in Washington, no longer the exception. Nixon was the first newly elected president in 120 years—since Taylor in 1848—to confront a Congress controlled by the other party. Reagan brought in a Republican Senate on his coattails in 1980 and 1984, but not a Republican House. He lost the Senate in the 1986 midterm election. In 1988 Bush became the first candidate in history to be elected president even as his party—already in the minority except for the

White House—was losing additional seats in the accompanying House, Senate, gubernatorial, and state legislative elections. Never did a new president have fewer fellow partisans than Bush did in Congress, where Democrats enjoyed a 260 to 175 majority in the House and outnumbered Republicans by 55 to 45 in the Senate. He faced a Democratic Congress during his entire tenure as president, as had Republican predecessors Nixon and Ford.

Why, to a historically unprecedented extent, did divided government in the form of Republican presidents and a wholly or partially Democratic Congress prevail during this period?[7] Different public expectations of the president and members of Congress offer part of the explanation. From the late 1960s to the late 1980s most voters usually regarded Republican presidential candidates—more confident in their political ideology, more nationalistic in their approach to Cold War foreign policy, and less associated in the public mind with "special interests" such as labor unions, feminists, and racial minorities—as the best guarantors of national well-being. But because voters had their own states and districts in mind when judging candidates for Congress, it was pragmatism, not ideology, that they valued in House and Senate elections; localism, not nationalism, that preoccupied them in these contests; and their constituency's particular special interests, not special interests in general, that they felt were at stake. The Democratic Party, with its enthusiastic embrace of domestic federal spending, came out ahead on all counts according to most voters' preferences in congressional races.

The nature of the two parties also helps to explain their contrasting success in presidential and congressional elections. The Republican Party was fairly homogeneous—white, middle-class or higher, Christian, and conservative. The Democrats, in contrast, were raucously diverse—white, black, and brown; liberal and conservative; Christian and Jewish; undereducated and professionally educated. As the Democratic speaker of the House, Tip O'Neill, observed, "In any other country we'd be five splinter parties."[8] When fielding candidates for Congress, diversity served the Democrats better than homogeneity served the Republicans. Depending on the character of each state or congressional district, Democrats usually had little trouble fielding a candidate who was ideologically, ethnically, and personally suitable: liberal in the North, conservative in the South; pro-gun in rural constituencies, pro–gun control in the cities; black or brown in majority-minority districts, white everywhere else; and so on. Republican congressional candidates, in contrast, seemed almost everywhere to be cast from roughly the same mold.

But the Democrats' heterogeneity haunted them in presidential elections. Ideologically and otherwise, by the late 1960s Republicans usually did not have to worry about how to define their party's identity when writing the platform or choosing the presidential candidate who would represent them to the nation. In contrast, the Democrats, who thrived on being many different parties in House and Senate elections, faced the challenge of deciding which one party they would be when nominating their candidate for president. Often the decision was contentious, producing unhappy losers and a divided party, thereby projecting to the voters an image of vacillation and incompetence at the convention. And when unity was achieved, it was often by making such sweeping concessions to the party's most vocal constituencies (a vice presidential nomination for Rep. Geraldine A. Ferraro of New York to please feminists in 1984, a remarkable share of the convention spotlight for Jesse Jackson to placate African Americans in 1988) as to alienate a substantial number of other voters.

Despite the Republicans' recent success in presidential elections, in the view from 1988 leading figures in both parties saw a political future for themselves. Among Republicans, it was taken for granted that in 1992 Bush would seek a second term, as every elected president had since Rutherford B. Hayes in 1880. It was also widely assumed that Quayle would again be Bush's running mate and (probably) would pursue his party's presidential nomination in 1996. No elected vice president had been replaced on the ticket since FDR dropped Henry A. Wallace in 1940, and starting soon after the adoption of the Twenty-Second Amendment in 1951 vice presidents typically were front-runners within the party when, freed from possible charges of disloyalty during a president's second and constitutionally final term, they began their own presidential campaigns. Not just Quayle but other Republicans who figured prominently in the 1988 election also cast their presidential ambitions on 1996, especially Dole and Kemp. Still others, notably the former Nixon and Reagan White House aide and conservative cable television pundit Patrick J. Buchanan, could at least imagine becoming candidates in the not-too-distant future. Buchanan had flirted with running in 1988.

Democratic politicians were no less ambitious than their Republican counterparts, but they also were more uncertain. The Democrats' seemingly secure hold on Congress and most governorships made these offices a safer haven than the presidency, which their party had such a poor recent record of winning. Clearly victory in 1992 or 1996 would require some serious party-wide thinking about how to become competitive again. Gore and Jackson, both of whom sought but lost the Democratic presidential nomination in 1988, seemed likely to consider running again in 1992 or later, and each had his own ideas about the form that a reimagined party should take. The same was true of Clinton, who nearly ran in 1988 and, even more than those who did enter the race, already was devoting serious thought to how to reorient the Democratic Party. Meanwhile, the ever-ambivalent Cuomo, whom many Democrats looked to with longing, was forging ideas of his own.

The leading contenders in the Republican Party, still riding high after winning the presidency once again in 1988 and confident of its nominee in 1992, are the subject of chapter 2. The rest of this chapter treats the Democrats, both their disappointing experience in recent presidential elections and the lessons some of them derived from that experience. The chapter then devotes considerable attention to each of the party's major figures heading into the elections of the 1990s: Clinton, Gore, Jackson, and Cuomo.

As in 1988, the Democrats felt no sense of crisis when they approached the 1984 election. Most party leaders did not think that Reagan won in 1980 as much as that Carter lost through a combination of inadequate leadership and unfortunate circumstances. By 1982 Reagan's job approval rating among voters had sunk to 35 percent. The economy was shrinking (the gross domestic product fell by 5.5 percent in the six months straddling January 1). In the midterm election Democrats added twenty-six seats to their majority in the House and picked up one seat in the Senate. Surely, many prominent Democrats concluded, a traditional Democratic campaign would win back the White House in 1984.

The nomination went to Walter Mondale, an old-school liberal who proudly sought and won the support of "the unions, the teachers, environmental groups, [and] women's organizations."[9] Challenged in a primary debate by his main rival, Gary Hart, to "cite one major domestic issue in the last three or four years where you have disagreed with [the] AFL-CIO or organized labor," Mondale demurred.[10] In choosing his running mate, he publicly invited "a black candidate, a Hispanic candidate, a female candidate, and so on" to visit him in Minnesota.[11] He thought his vice presidential selection process—which resulted in the choice of Ferraro, the first woman ever nominated for national office by a major party but a relatively junior member of the House—was sending "a message about opening doors," Mondale recalled after losing to Reagan in a forty-nine-state landslide.[12] "Others saw a cliché about the Democratic Party"—what the *New Republic* called "a cartoonist's caricature of interest group clamoring."[13] As for his strategy to win the election by assembling a coalition of liberal constituency groups, Mondale wrote, "It made me look like old politics, as if I were trading away the public interest for the special interests."[14]

Mondale's one departure from the well-worn Democratic path in 1984 was his prominent pledge, featured in his acceptance speech at the national convention, to raise nearly everyone's taxes in the interest of reducing the federal budget deficit. Less surprising than the pledge's political tone deafness in the midst of what by then was a strong economic recovery (Reagan "was selling Morning in America and I was selling a root canal," Mondale remembered) was that a traditional "big-spending liberal Democrat" chose to embrace deficit reduction at all.[15] The reason had much to do with the Democratic Party's new reliance on financial contributions from big business. Influenced by a 1971 Chamber of Commerce–sponsored memo from corporate lawyer (and soon Supreme Court justice) Lewis Powell urging corporations to ramp up their political activism, and facilitated by the 1974 Federal Election Campaign Act's encouragement of political action committees (PACs), the number of corporate PACS rose from 89 in 1974 to 1,204 in 1980.[16] Soon after the 1980 election, the chair of the Democratic Congressional Campaign Committee, Rep. Tony Coelho of California, said, "Business has to deal with us whether they like it or not because . . . we are going to be the majority party in the House for many years."[17]

For Democrats as well as for business, this was an alliance of convenience born of necessity. The accelerating decline of organized labor (the United Auto Workers alone lost 20 percent of its membership between 1979 and 1981) meant that the party no longer enjoyed either the amount of funding or the extent of grassroots campaigning that unions traditionally provided.[18] Liking it or not, business responded to Coelho's demands. The share of money the Democratic Party raised from the "top 0.01 percent of the voting population" rose from 7 percent in 1980 to 10 percent in 1984 to 12 percent in 1988 and, eventually, to 22 percent in 1996.[19] Mondale's newfound fiscal austerity manifested the new, business-friendly direction of his party, which for the first time had a section in its platform called "Controlling Domestic Spending" and featured a promise to attack "Republican mega-deficits."[20]

Senator Hart's strong second-place finish in the 1984 Democratic nominating contest and Jesse Jackson's surprising third-place finish were evidence that at least some Democrats were more convinced than Mondale that the party was already in deep trouble entering 1984. Hart was a leader of the so-called Atari Democrats, the early video game label attached to a group of younger officeholders whose plan for national prosperity rested on encouraging the burgeoning computer-based high-tech sector of the economy rather than on trying to revive traditional, union-intensive smokestack industries. "We're not a bunch of little Hubert Humphreys" who think that "if there is a problem, create an agency and throw money at the problem," Hart said.[21] In contrast, viewing both Mondale and Hart as too responsive to business interests, Jackson urged the party to move to the left, where he thought more votes could be found among previously unregistered African Americans and Latinos if only the Democrats would promise to enact new and expanded social programs focused on poor and minority city dwellers. "This is a national campaign growing out of the black experience and seen through the eyes of a black perspective," Jackson declared, while arguing that similar experiences and perspectives marked "the rejected" of every race and ethnicity.[22]

Meanwhile, white southern Democratic leaders who recently had seen the party's fortunes decline in their region began organizing out of frustration that the national party was too beholden to the agendas of feminist, civil rights, peace, and environmental groups. Carter, who won ten of eleven southern states in 1976, lost ten of eleven in 1980. Mondale did not come within 20 points of winning a single one in 1984. After the 1980 Reagan landslide, House Democratic Caucus chair Gillis Long of Louisiana formed the Committee on Party Effectiveness within the caucus, with Al From as executive director. Its purpose was "to reassess our Party's direction and redefine our message."[23] After Reagan was reelected in 1984, Long encouraged the formation of the Democratic Leadership Council (DLC). He died of a heart attack in January 1985, but the DLC was launched the following month, with From continuing as executive director and membership expanded to include interested governors and senators, mostly from the South and border states.

The new organization's purpose was to further reorient the Democratic Party toward the middle class and business sector with an agenda that was pro–free trade (the party's historic position, but one that it had abandoned in response to union pressure), pro–economic growth, pro–universal national service, and, in From's phrase, pro–"mainstream American values" such as "work, family, responsibility, individual liberty, and faith."[24] Prominent liberal Democrats recoiled. Historian and Democratic activist Arthur M. Schlesinger Jr. labeled the new organization "a quasi-Reaganite formation."

Jackson quipped that DLC stood for "Democrats for the Leisure Class" and comprised the "Rhett Butler Brigade.[25] In response, the DLC broadened its eligibility rules to include state legislators and local officials, which enabled it to diversify with at least a few prominent minority and women members such as Mayor Tom Bradley of Los Angeles and Gov. Ann Richards of Texas.

As political scientist (and Democratic House member) David Price has shown, parties that consistently lose the White House feel the greater need to develop new approaches, and those approaches come more easily from unofficial groups.[26] The Democrats' official body, the Democratic National Committee, was slow to acknowledge the deep-seatedness of the party's problems. In 1985, for example, the Michigan state party commissioned public opinion specialist Stan Greenberg to find out why Macomb County, 96 percent white and mostly working class, went from being the most Democratic suburban county in the country in 1960 to voting two-to-one for Reagan in 1984. In focus groups of "Reagan Democrats," Greenberg learned that in these voters' opinion "the party and government were preoccupied with the needs of minorities," so much so that when Mondale proposed to raise taxes and fund $30 billion in new programs to "promote fairness," Macomb's white voters took for granted that the money would come out of their pockets and be given to blacks.[27] National Committee chair Paul Kirk branded Greenberg's findings "inflammatory" and destroyed all copies of a DNC-sponsored nationwide study by the marketing firm CRG that reached the same conclusion.[28] He also tried, unsuccessfully, to convince Governor Clinton not to join the DLC.

Dukakis was not a DLC member, but his candidacy in 1988 initially seemed to have qualities that would appeal to the group's supporters. Unlike Mondale, Dukakis did not promise to raise taxes and create new spending programs to appease every organized Democratic constituency group. Like the two most recent presidents, Carter and Reagan, he was a governor who balanced the budget and oversaw growing prosperity in his state, not a member of the increasingly distrusted Washington establishment. As his running mate, Dukakis chose Bentsen, an economic conservative from Texas, not a liberal ideologue. "This election is not about ideology," Dukakis declared in his acceptance speech at the Democratic convention; "it's about competence."[29]

Bentsen's selection as the Democrats' vice presidential candidate, especially after he demolished Quayle in the October 5 vice presidential debate, turned out well, although the ticket never did have a realistic chance of carrying Texas against the Texan Bush. (Bentsen himself, running simultaneously for vice president and a fourth term as senator from Texas, was re-elected handily.) But Bush and the Republicans, with unwitting assistance from Dukakis, shredded the Democratic nominee's other apparent advantages. Dukakis was a liberal in disguise, they charged. The indictment stuck, with some basis in fact. To be sure, on economic issues, Dukakis was fairly moderate. But civil liberties were a different matter. When Bush attacked him for vetoing a Massachusetts bill requiring public school teachers to lead students in the Pledge of Allegiance, Dukakis said, "It's hard for me to believe it's going to be a big deal." "I told him it is a big deal," said Clinton. "Words matter, values, symbolism matters."[30]

At the start of the second presidential debate on October 10, invoking Republican ads that attacked Dukakis for strongly supporting a prison furlough program in his state that allowed convicted murderer William Horton, who was serving a life sentence without parole, to torture a Maryland couple while on a weekend pass, CNN anchor Bernard Shaw asked the governor whether he would favor "an irrevocable death penalty for the killer" if the victim were Kitty Dukakis.[31] Dukakis gave a bloodless response detailing the problems with capital punishment, never mentioned his wife, and realized only afterward that "I answered it as if I'd been asked it a thousand times."[32] "I'm not a liberal," Dukakis said on October 25, only to say five days later, "I am a liberal" after campaign aides persuaded him that the only way to win was to forfeit the national popular vote and weave an electoral vote majority by threading together the eighteen most winnable states for a liberal candidate.[33]

As a Democrat whose faith in government ran deep, Dukakis was befuddled by Bush's acceptance speech tribute to the "thousand points of light" that symbolized the many volunteer programs in which Americans participated. "I don't know what that means," he said.[34] "This is the problem I have with these big-spending liberals," charged Bush. "They think the only way to do it is for the federal government to do it all."[35] Clinton agreed. Democrats like Dukakis, he lamented, "feel like the only legitimate action that a politician takes . . . is what he does in terms of a program or a bureaucracy."[36] In general, voters preferred Bush to Dukakis on domestic issues, according to political scientist Martin Wattenberg.[37]

As for Dukakis's claim to superior competence, it never was politically persuasive against an opponent who had been Central Intelligence Agency director, ambassador to the United Nations, liaison to China, and vice president for eight years. But Dukakis compounded his problems on September

13 when, in response to pictures of Bush, a former naval pilot, sitting in the cockpit of an F-16, he rode around in an M1 Abrams tank at the General Dynamics proving ground in Sterling Heights, Michigan, with his helmeted head poking out of the turret. Bush's advertising team stockpiled film of the event and one month later ran a spot showing the inadvertently comical tank ride with a voice-over listing all the weapons programs Dukakis opposed. Viewers saw "that guy doesn't belong in a tank," recalled Dukakis's campaign manager, Susan Estrich, "which is to say, that guy doesn't belong running the national security of our country."[38] The spot's tag line—"America can't afford to take that risk"—not only raised doubts about Dukakis's ability to protect the United States from foreign enemies but also reinforced existing concerns about his willingness to protect Americans from criminals. Having lost on ideology despite his effort to neutralize it as a political issue, Dukakis's inept campaign caused him to lose on competence as well. Competence was judged by voters to be Dukakis's weakest personal trait—and Bush's strongest by far.[39]

Dukakis's loss sent Democrats into even deeper despair. Although his 46 percent of the national popular vote surpassed that of every other Democrat presidential candidate since 1964 except Carter in 1976, and his 111 electoral votes nearly doubled those won by Carter and Mondale combined in the two most recent elections, the party's third consecutive landslide defeat against a Republican nominee whom it regarded as weak was especially disheartening. Dukakis won 86 percent of the black vote, but turnout among African Americans was down 11 percent from 1984. Even his 57 percent of union members and their families was less significant than it seemed.[40] In the past, when as much as 35 percent of the nation's workforce was unionized, a majority that size would have brought the Democratic nominee within range of victory. But the national economy's loss of factory jobs, the movement of many remaining positions to the union-unfriendly South, and President Reagan's anti–organized labor policies had reduced the unionized share of the private workforce to 12 percent, the smallest level since 1915.

Despite their disappointment, defeat did not represent complete demoralization for Democrats. They were still the majority party in both houses of Congress and in most states. Two candidates who chose not to run for president in 1988—Clinton and Cuomo—were among those who resolved to keep their powder dry for 1992 or 1996. So did the two runners-up for their party's nomination: Gore and Jackson.

BILL CLINTON

For Bill Clinton and his party, 1988 was the year of what might have been. Clinton came to the brink of seeking the Democratic nomination before backing off at the last minute. His decision was temporary. If Dukakis lost the election, Clinton planned to run in 1992; if he won, Clinton would run in 1996.

Clinton was born and spent his first five years in Hope, a small town in rural southwest Arkansas whose name he later invoked to brand himself as "The Man from Hope." But he grew up in Hot Springs after his mother and stepfather, Virginia and Roger Clinton, moved the family there in 1952. Hot Springs not only offered his nurse anesthetist mother and erratically employed stepfather more opportunities but also placed their son in the first of what turned out to be a series of increasingly cosmopolitan environments. Despite its remote location, Hot Springs contained a rich mixture of native Arkansans and northern retirees, Democrats (the Arkansans) and Republicans (the northerners), blacks and whites, and Southern Baptists and gamblers at the town's many churches and illegal casinos, respectively.

Clinton's parents liked to party on Saturday night, but as a boy he would get himself up and dressed on Sunday mornings and walk nearly a mile to Park Place Baptist Church, where he accepted Christ as his savior at age nine. He drew inspiration three years later from evangelist Billy Graham's insistence that his 1958 Little Rock crusade, which Clinton attended, be racially integrated. In giving the benediction at his high school graduation, Clinton prayed, "Sicken us at the sight of apathy, ignorance, and rejection so that our generation will remove complacency, poverty, and prejudice from the hearts of free men."[41] Clinton left Arkansas to attend Georgetown University in Washington. He had already experienced Catholic education in elementary school in Hot Springs and on one occasion, at age sixteen, visited the nation's capital, where he famously fast walked his way into position for a handshake with President John F. Kennedy during a White House reception for participants in Boys Nation. Coming home from that trip, Clinton decided that he "wanted to be in public life as an elected official. . . . I knew I could be great in public service. I was fascinated by people, politics, and policy."[42]

The face Clinton showed the world while growing up was energetic and exuberant. The reality was more complicated. His often-drunk stepfather was at times physically abusive toward his mother. Once he was big enough, Clinton intervened to defend his mother several times, as he testified in an affidavit when she filed for divorce. But he also called Roger

Clinton "Daddy" and changed his surname from Blythe, inherited from the father who died in a car crash three months before his son was born, to Clinton so that he and his younger brother Roger would not have different names. His mother then remarried Roger Clinton, who remained occasionally abusive. Their elder son concealed all of this from others and developed what he later described as a dual persona: happy and outgoing in public, worried and secretive in private. He never talked about "the secrets of our house" to anyone—"not to a friend, a neighbor, a teacher, a pastor."[43]

Clinton went to Georgetown because he wanted to be in Washington. He spent summers in Arkansas because he knew that the path to elective office ran through his home state. In summer 1966 he campaigned for Judge Frank Holt, who was the establishment candidate for the Democratic gubernatorial nomination against the segregationist Jim Johnson. Clinton admired Holt because "he refuses to attack his opponents" but also learned from Holt's defeat in the primary that "politics is a contact sport."[44] During the school year that began in the fall he worked for J. William Fulbright, the Arkansas senator who as chair of the Senate Foreign Relations Committee was the leading early critic of the Vietnam War. Like Fulbright, Clinton did not "embrace the lifestyle or the radical rhetoric" of the rapidly growing antiwar movement. "I just wanted to end the war," he said.[45] In the 1968 election Clinton lamented the Richard Nixon– and George Wallace–style "conservative populism [that] replaced progressive populism as the dominant political force in our nation," as well as the Democrats' growing "associat[ion] with chaos, weakness, and out-of-touch, self-indulgent elites."[46]

Clinton won a Rhodes Scholarship to attend Oxford University after graduating from Georgetown in 1968. He was unusually popular with his high-achieving, self-absorbed peers, mostly because he was a great listener. "Curiosity about the people around him was one of his strongest traits," biographer David Maraniss has written, "the main intersection of his gregarious, empathetic personality and his political ambition."[47] As his fellow scholars became actively involved in opposing the war abroad while seeking not to be drafted into the army at home, so did Clinton, but with the additional complication of not wanting to jeopardize his future "political viability."[48] Arkansas was a conservative state (its voters tossed out Fulbright in 1974) and, more generally, military service was a long-established credential for nationally ambitious political leaders.

"I searched my heart, trying to determine whether my aversion to going [to war] was rooted in conviction or cowardice," Clinton later wrote. "Given the way it played out, I'm not sure I ever answered the question for myself."[49] In any event, in ways that became politically problematic when he sought the presidency in 1992, Clinton avoided being drafted in summer 1969 by promising his local draft board to enroll in the Reserve Officer Training Corps (ROTC) at the University of Arkansas law school if he was allowed to complete his studies at Oxford. In December he drew a high number in the new draft lottery, which made him all but immune from conscription. He returned to the United States in 1970, enrolling not at the University of Arkansas and in ROTC but at the Yale University Law School.

While at Yale, Clinton met and then moved in with a fellow law student, Hillary Rodham, who grew up in suburban Chicago in a politically conservative family but, like Clinton, was moved by her Christian faith to embrace liberal positions on civil rights and, later, the war. In 1969, speaking at her Wellesley College graduation, Rodham ad-libbed an attack against politicians—including the invited commencement speaker, Republican senator Edward Brooke, who had just completed his remarks—for treating "politics as the art of the possible. And the challenge now is to practice politics as the art of making what appears to be impossible possible." Her speech was featured in *Life* magazine.[50]

Clinton had long been attracted to beauty pageant–style women, but with Hillary, he wrote, he was choosing "brains and ability rather than glamour" (he meant this as a compliment).[51] In fall 1972 he and Rodham worked for the antiwar Democratic presidential candidate George McGovern against President Nixon. Assigned to Texas, Clinton learned how to deal with contentious Democratic factions, including many conservative Democrats who ended up voting against their party's nominee. After the summer's chaotic national convention, he rued, "we were in even worse shape" than in 1968, "looking both too liberal and too inept."[52]

Finished with his legal studies at Yale in 1973, Clinton returned to Arkansas to teach at the law school he had avoided attending. In 1974, at age twenty-eight, he ran for Congress against four-term incumbent John Paul Hammerschmidt, the first Republican in history from an Arkansas district. Hammerschmidt, a likable man who tended the district's interests assiduously, had been reelected in 1972 with 72 percent of the vote. But Clinton campaigned tirelessly and, doing his best to tie his Republican opponent to the recently resigned Nixon, came within 4 percentage points of beating him, closer than any Democrat before or after. Rodham, who had been working for the House Judiciary Committee on Nixon's impeachment, married Clinton in Fayetteville in October 1975. She joined him on the law school faculty, envisioning a short stay before returning to Washington as the wife of a senator while pursuing a professional career of her own. Having emerged from his near victory in 1974 as the rising star of his state's Democratic Party, Clinton was easily elected state attorney general in 1976. Unopposed in the fall, he worked hard for the party's presidential candidate, Jimmy Carter. He did not dislike President Ford, he told a friend, but, referring to Ford's running mate, Sen. Bob Dole of Kansas, said, "the biggest prick in Congress is on the ticket."[53]

Attorney general was an excellent launching pad in Arkansas politics. The job put Clinton in close touch with the Democratic courthouse crowd in every county and served as a platform to crusade for popular causes, notably opposition to utility rate increases. Clinton wanted to run for senator in 1978 when the incumbent, John McClellan, retired; he had always "thought Washington was where the action was" and for years had "no interest" in being governor.[54] But the vastly popular Gov. David Pryor wanted the seat, and "the competition wasn't as stiff" for governor.[55] Clinton brushed aside a weak primary field and ran unopposed in November, becoming at age thirty-two the youngest governor in the country and the first from the post–World War II baby boom generation.[56]

Clinton regarded his victory as a mandate to move Arkansas in the leftward direction he embraced during his years at Oxford and Yale. His leading aides—dubbed the "Three Beards"—were even more liberal than he was. Several other staff members were from out of state and, as one of them later put it, "sort of smart ass."[57] Clinton's wife kept her maiden name, her full-time job with Little Rock's Rose Law Firm, and her frizzy-haired, makeup-free, goggle-glasses appearance—none of which bore any relation to what culturally conservative Arkansans expected of a first lady. Clinton's main policy initiative was to fund improvements in the state's roads with a steep increase in the annual "car tag" fee that vehicle owners had to pay. Clinton wanted the tax to be proportional to the value of each vehicle, but after lobbyists persuaded the legislature to keep it based on vehicle weight, he signed the bill anyway—"the single dumbest mistake I ever made in politics."[58] Every month one-twelfth of the state's car and truck owners, the poorest of whom drove old and heavy vehicles, were freshly outraged when they saw how much more they had to pay to renew their tags. County clerks would respond to their complaints by pointing to the governor's picture on the wall and saying, "Call him."

President Carter added to Clinton's woes when he deployed 18,000 newly arrived Cuban refugees, many of them criminals or mental patients whom the dictator Fidel Castro expelled from his country, to Fort Chaffee in western Arkansas. When several hundred broke out of the camp on May 26, 1980, and rampaged through nearby streets, Carter promised not to send any more. But on August 1 he closed the refugee camps in Wisconsin and Pennsylvania—two swing states in the upcoming presidential election—and moved them all to Arkansas. "The guy screwed me and never tried to make amends," Clinton fumed.[59] Still, he thought his reelection was secure against a relatively weak Republican opponent, Frank White, and did not bother to respond to attack ads that singled out the car tax and Cubans. When Reagan carried the state against Carter by 9 points, Clinton was swept out of office with the Republican tide, running ahead of the president but still losing by 4 points. Speaking to a group of Florida Democrats after the election, now the youngest former governor in the nation's history, Clinton passed along one lesson he learned from his defeat: "If your opponent picks up a hammer at you, you need to pick up a meat ax and cut off his arm."[60]

The other lesson Clinton earned from his defeat, once he overcame the "self-pity and anger" that immobilized him for a time, was "to be more sensitive to the political problems inherent in progressive politics."[61] "If I ever get the chance again," he told a reporter, "I'm not going to try to force people to do what's good for them."[62] He brought in a consultant, Dick Morris, who worked for both Democrats and Republicans. Morris recommended that Clinton launch his campaign to regain the governorship with an ad apologizing for the car tax increase. On February 8, 1982, Clinton aired one with the tag line, "My daddy never had to whip me twice for the same thing."[63] That same day Hillary Rodham, whom the Wellesley alumni magazine had celebrated in 1979 as "the nation's only first lady to have retained her maiden name"—became Mrs. Bill Clinton, complete with dyed hair, makeup, contact lenses, and a new wardrobe.[64] No governor in the history of the state had ever been elected, defeated, and then elected again, but Clinton pulled it off. In a fierce primary campaign against Rep. Jim Guy Tucker, his main generational rival in Arkansas politics, Clinton prevailed by 42 percent to 23 percent; he then won the runoff against former lieutenant governor Joe Purcell. In a midterm election that went almost as strongly Democratic nationally as 1980 had gone Republican, Clinton won in November by 8 points against Governor White. He never lost a general election again.

Clinton was reelected easily in 1984 and 1986, the latter to a four-year term born of a change in the state constitution that gave him "space to move into the national political arena," giving speeches in thirty-four states during the first six months of 1987 alone.[65] He built alliances with the Arkansas business community, especially national corporations Walmart, Tyson Foods, and Stephens, in service of his new emphasis on education reform as a vehicle for economic development. Arkansas ranked fiftieth in per-pupil spending, and its population included the smallest percentage of college graduates of any state in the country. "Even Mississippi is ahead of us now," Clinton lamented.[66] After sending Hillary Clinton on a listening tour of all seventy-five counties, he proposed smaller classes, more science and foreign language courses, and higher teacher pay. These three measures were part of the standard liberal Democratic package, but not the fourth: competency testing for teachers. The main message Hillary Clinton had heard from parents around the state was "raise teachers' salaries, yes, but first get rid of incompetent teachers."[67] The Arkansas Education Association went ballistic over teacher testing, which made Clinton's proposal even more credible with parents and business leaders.

In Clinton's view, education reform lay squarely at the intersection of two core values: opportunity, which he wanted to provide more of, and responsibility, of which he wanted to demand more. In recent decades public employees—civil servants of all kinds, not just teachers—had steadily become a larger share of the nation's unionized workforce and of the Democratic Party, especially its activist base. But "how they think, how they talk, how they view things is much different [from] the way most taxpayers do," said Clinton.[68] He carried the same blend of liberalism and conservatism into welfare reform and other measures in his state, as well as into national policy discussions with fellow governors in the National Governors Association and fellow Democrats in the DLC, which he joined in 1987. Young as he was, as the 1980s unfolded Clinton's longevity in office made him the most senior governor in the country. His gregarious personality, avid interest in public policy, and creatively centrist position on the political spectrum made him the most respected by his colleagues as well. A *Newsweek* survey of the nation's governors ranked Clinton "the most effective" in the country.

Clinton was also someone with a wandering eye, so much so that Betsey Wright, his gubernatorial chief of staff and a friend of both him and Hillary dating back to the McGovern campaign in Texas, "insisted that he not go on jogs alone," lest he stray into one of any number of paramours' apartments.[69] Rumors about Clinton's infidelity were rampant in Arkansas, as they long had been about other politicians in Washington and elsewhere. But the long-standing tradition in journalism was to overlook what reporters regarded as purely personal misbehavior. As recently as 1984, for example, political reporters kept their knowledge of Gary Hart's two marital separations out of their stories, even when Hart bunked at investigative reporter Bob Woodward's apartment for several weeks.

Reporters' growing doubts about this tradition, spurred by feminist criticisms of male politicians' "boys will be boys" attitude toward women as disposable sex objects and Hart's seemingly open path to the presidency in 1988, caused them to treat his reckless sexual behavior differently as the presidential election campaign approached. On May 3, 1987, a profile of Hart appeared in the *New York Times Magazine* in which the candidate, irritated that reporter E. J. Dionne pressed him on the matter, said, "If anybody wants to put a tail on me, go ahead. They'd be very bored."[70] Coincidentally, the *Miami Herald*, responding to a tip, was tailing Hart that very weekend. *Herald* reporters discovered that a strikingly attractive woman named Donna Rice was with Hart in his Washington townhouse after sailing with him on an overnight cruise to Bimini in March. The newspaper's front-page stories to that effect on May 3 and 4 caused a sensation. When Hart claimed in a May 5 speech that he "absolutely did not . . . do anything immoral," *Washington Post* reporter Paul Taylor publicly asked the candidate if he had committed adultery. Hart refused to engage. The paper's editors then quietly showed him the report of a private investigator who recently tailed him to the home of a well-known female lobbyist. The woman confirmed the affair. Hart dropped out of the race to forestall publication of the report.[71]

The restraints were off. "The old rules had changed, and the new rules guaranteed scrutiny by the press if they got wind of any ongoing extracurricular escapades," wrote Ben Bradlee, the *Post*'s editor.[72] News organizations began investigating rumors of infidelity concerning Vice President Bush ("The answer to the Big A question is N-O," his son George told *Newsweek*, referring to adultery) and Jesse Jackson, whose wife angrily declared that this was nobody's business but hers.[73] Reporters claimed that their interest was not in Hart's unfaithfulness but rather in what David Broder, the fabled dean of political journalists, said was "the fundamental character questions" of "Hart's truthfulness, his self-discipline, his sense of responsibility to other people."[74] But it was the sex that led readers and viewers to hang breathlessly on every new revelation, including a cover photo in the *National Enquirer* that displayed a grinning Hart with Rice sitting on his lap.

The Hart affair gave pause to Clinton, especially when two lawyers portraying him and Hart sang a duet of "To All the Girls We've Loved Before"

Bill Clinton's debut on the national stage as the speaker who nominated Gov. Michael Dukakis at the 1988 Democratic National Convention started out well but ended poorly. Courtesy of the Associated Press.

at the Little Rock bar association's biennial Gridiron show.[75] Clinton was planning to announce his candidacy for president on July 15. Hillary Clinton's parents bought a condominium in Little Rock, expecting to babysit their young granddaughter Chelsea while Bill and Hillary were off campaigning. Friends were invited from around the country to witness Clinton's announcement. Columnist Robert Novak touted Clinton as the "DGA [Democratic Governors Association] candidate"—just "what the governors want: attractive, Southern, moderately liberal, nonconfrontational."[76]

A few days before the planned launch of his campaign, Wright sat Clinton down with a list of names and asked him to speak frankly about "all the women he'd been with, when and how often." "I was horrified because I thought I knew everybody," Wright said. "And he came up with these people I didn't know about." She then went through the list a second time, asking which women he thought would tell their story to the media.[77] At the end of the discussion Wright urged Clinton not to run, echoing advice he already had received from consultant Dick Morris and others. Morris told him that in the immediate aftermath of the Hart revelations "this was a terribly inhospitable environment in which to tread."[78] On the eve of his scheduled announcement, Clinton explained to his gathered friends that for the sake of spending more time with Chelsea he did not think the time was right to run. But wait for another day, he added, "because it's coming."[79]

In August, Clinton told Arthur Schlesinger privately that of the candidates seeking the Democratic nomination, "Dukakis was the only one he could really envisage as president."[80] He refused to endorse anyone, including Gore of Tennessee, who was his natural rival for the mantle of up-and-coming leader of the party's southern wing. When Dukakis asked Clinton, who had given a crisp, well-delivered prime-time address at the 1984 Democratic convention, to nominate him at the 1988 gathering, Clinton eagerly agreed—and then proceeded to deliver a speech so long and boring that CBS showed delegates giving him the cut sign. But Clinton was nothing if not resilient. The next night he appeared on *The Tonight Show* with Johnny Carson, played "Summertime" on the saxophone, and joked that Dukakis not only liked his speech but wanted him to nominate Bush as well.

JESSE JACKSON

Bill Clinton was not the only Democratic leader to emerge from challenging childhood circumstances. Jesse Jackson was born into poverty in racially segregated Greenville, South Carolina, in 1941. His father abandoned the family soon afterward. Like Clinton, Jackson took the surname of his stepfather, Charles Jackson, who adopted him at age sixteen. A student leader and star football player in high school, Jackson went to North Carolina A&T State University. As part of the emerging civil rights movement on historically black southern campuses, he participated in sit-ins in nearby Greensboro. After graduating Jackson enrolled at Chicago Theological Seminary at age twenty-four while working as the youngest staff member of the Southern Christian Leadership Conference (SCLC). Sinking roots in Chicago, Jackson ran Operation Breadbasket, which threatened to boycott businesses unless they signed "covenants" pledging to employ more African Americans. He became nationally famous on the morning of April 5, 1968, when he appeared on the *Today* program wearing a shirt soaked with the blood of Rev. Martin Luther King, who was assassinated the previous day in Memphis. Jackson had been there with King and other SCLC leaders to help lead a sanitation workers strike.

Jackson's eye for personal publicity (he portrayed himself as much closer to King than he really was) led to a falling-out with the SCLC and a move back to Chicago in 1971 to form People United to Save Humanity (PUSH). The new organization was basically Operation Breadbasket plus some social programs. Jackson's entry into Democratic politics came the following year, when he helped lead a successful effort to unseat the Illinois delegation to the party's 1972 national convention headed by Mayor Richard Daley. Although the mayor was by far the most influential Democrat in the state, his unwillingness to open up the delegate selection process in full conformity with new party rules was treated as a cardinal sin by Jackson and most other supporters of Senator McGovern.

Problems with PUSH, rechristened as People United to *Serve* Humanity but deeply in debt and in trouble with the Internal Revenue Service because of lax accounting procedures, preoccupied Jackson during much of the decade that followed. The result was another reboot of the organization as PUSH-Excel, which he formed to motivate black students, with ample funding from the Ford Foundation, Merrill Lynch, and the Department of Health, Education, and Welfare. "I'm a tree shaker, not a jelly maker," said Jackson, defending his emphasis on oratorical inspiration rather than organizational follow-through.[81] Starting in 1980, he spent time every two years leading national voter registration campaigns designed to bring more African Americans into the electorate. The path to success for the Democratic Party lay not in moving toward the center in pursuit of Reagan Democrats, Jackson argued, but rather toward the left with programmatic appeals that would motivate blacks and Latinos to become politically active.

Concerned that none of the candidates for the 1984 Democratic presidential nomination shared his vision, and seeking an even brighter national spotlight for himself, Jackson declared his own candidacy for president. "When I win," he grandiosely announced, "justice wins."[82] Nearly all African American big-city mayors, members of Congress, and other elected officials, whose ranks had been growing rapidly, shunned Jackson in favor of former vice president Mondale. "Who does he think he is?" said Gary, Indiana, mayor Richard Hatcher, summing up the view of many of his colleagues, including the black mayors of two of the country's three largest cities, Harold Washington of Chicago and Tom Bradley of Los Angeles. "He hadn't even been elected dogcatcher."[83] They felt vindicated when *Washington Post* reporter Milton Coleman reported on a conversation in which Jackson, after telling the African American Coleman, "Let's talk black talk," described Jews as "hymies" and New York City as "Hymietown."[84] Their unease with Jackson grew after the February 13, 1984, story appeared and militant black leader Louis Farrakhan, who provided security at Jackson's rallies, vowed to Coleman, "We will punish you with death."[85]

Jackson's lack of support among black political leaders had little effect on black voters. He won the primaries in Louisiana, Mississippi, and the District of Columbia and ran strongly in several other southern contests, taking advantage of changes in the region's electorate that had seen many whites flee the Democratic Party, leaving African Americans with a strong voice in intraparty affairs. Overall Jackson finished third in the presidential nominating contest behind Mondale and Hart, drawing 21 percent of the overall primary vote based on his 80 percent support among black voters.[86]

The "Hymietown" remark and his refusal to disavow Farrakhan aside, Jackson acquitted himself well in 1984 in the eyes of the larger political community. In debates with the other Democratic contenders, he was "strikingly composed and knowledgeable, almost *presidential* in demeanor."[87] In one debate with just Mondale and Hart, Jackson stood out as the voice of reason, chastising his two opponents for the "rat-a-tat-tat" character of their heated exchanges.[88] Jackson also enhanced his stature with a foreign policy breakthrough, personally convincing the Syrian government to release a downed American pilot to his custody.

In 1988 Jackson ran again, this time with two related advantages that he had not enjoyed in 1984: the absence from the field of a white candidate with strong black support like Mondale and unified backing from black political leaders, who paid a price with their constituents for opposing him in his previous campaign. Jackson's goal in 1988 was to forge a "rainbow coalition"

VOTE JESSE JACKSON '84

For President

Now Is The Time...
VOTE
MAY 1, 1984
D.C.Primary

Authorized by Jesse Jackson For President D.C. Committee, Charlotte Chapman, State Treasurer

A campaign poster for Jesse Jackson, a prominent civil rights leader making his first bid for the Democratic presidential nomination in 1984. Courtesy of the Library of Congress.

that included not just African Americans and Latinos but also white feminists, environmentalists, and, especially, factory workers and small farmers whose economic security was in jeopardy. In a year when many Democrats were running away from what Republicans called "the L-word," Jackson offered a full-throated defense of liberalism. "Moses, Jesus—they were the liberals," he declared. "And Pharaoh, Herod, Pilate, ol' Nero—they were the conservatives."[89] Chastising Democrats who wanted the party to move toward the center, he said, "If people have to choose between the authentic and an imitation, they'll choose the authentic every time."[90] Even in the South, Jackson argued, it was his most recent voter registration drive in 1986 that provided the margin of victory for white Democratic Senate candidates in North Carolina, Louisiana, Alabama, and Georgia.

Campaigning against Dukakis and Gore, Jackson showed particular strength in two kinds of states: small, overwhelmingly white states like Maine, Alaska, and Vermont (where he had the active support of Burlington mayor Bernie Sanders) that chose their delegates in lightly attended, liberal-dominated caucuses and, more important, primary states with large black electorates, especially in the South. Remarkably, on the day after Super Tuesday, with thirty-one states by then having voted, Jackson had more delegates than any other candidate. He carried his campaign from the South to Illinois and Michigan, outpolling Dukakis and Gore in both large midwestern states in March. "Jesse Jackson has become the frontrunner," CBS Evening News anchor Dan Rather announced after the Michigan caucus results were in.[91]

The peak of Jackson's candidacy precipitated its downfall. As his campaign manager Jerry Austin said, "Winning in Michigan basically doomed us because people who would be voting for Jesse as a protest said, 'Wait a minute, this guy could be president.'"[92] In every subsequent primary, starting with the April contests in Wisconsin, New York, and Pennsylvania, Democratic voters cast a majority of their ballots for Dukakis, convinced that only he was sufficiently credentialed and moderate to win the general election. Still, by the time the last results were tallied in mid-June, Jackson had won 6.6 million votes, more than any other second-place finisher in history and more than all the other runner-up candidates in 1988 combined. About 2 million of these votes came from whites, among whom he earned 12 percent support, triple the 4 percent he received in 1984.[93]

As was the case with other recent second-place finishers such as Lyndon Johnson in 1960 and George Bush in 1980, Jackson thought he had earned the right to become the Democrats' vice presidential candidate in

1988. "The office of the vice president can carry out significant missions," Jackson said, and after eight years, he would be on track to become the party's presidential nominee in 1996.[94] In truth, Dukakis had no intention of choosing Jackson, whom he regarded as too liberal, too dynamic, and too independent. His mistake was stringing Jackson along, pretending that he was giving him "very serious consideration" when he really was not.[95] Jackson's strong finish in the nominating contest did make it politically impossible for Dukakis to choose Gore or any of the other contenders whom Jackson outpolled in the primaries. He chose a different southern centrist, Senator Bentsen, instead.

Dukakis left the convention with a strong lead in the polls, but when that evaporated he turned to Jackson to campaign on his behalf in the inner cities, where black voters seemed distinctly unenthusiastic about the Democratic nominee. "Santa Claus running into heavy weather, and he calls for Rudolph," Jackson ruefully commented. "Course, no promotion, no equity, no vice presidential nomination. But don't worry—your name will 'go down in history.'"[96] Political scientist Tali Mendelberg found that when anti-Dukakis television commercials featuring William Horton (the name he went by, transposed during the election to the more racially stereotyped Willie) began airing, Democratic politicians and mainstream journalists treated them as issue ads about crime, downplaying their racial element. To be sure, rising rates of crime in the 1980s, especially violent crime, were a serious concern in the minds of voters, and support for capital punishment, which had been declining, was steeply increasing.[97] But when Jackson attacked the ads as racist, the coverage changed.[98]

Jackson ended 1988 stronger than ever. He was the undisputed political leader of black America yet had shown a growing ability to make inroads among white voters. Dukakis's failed candidacy, like Mondale's in 1984, did nothing to disprove Jackson's argument that to become competitive in presidential elections the Democratic Party needed to embrace its liberal identity. Between 1988 and the next presidential election in 1992, Jackson would have more options than ever to explore.

AL GORE

Like Bill Clinton, Al Gore was a baby boomer, born in 1948, less than two years after Clinton, to southern parents. Unlike Clinton, Gore's birth occurred in Washington, DC, where his father, Albert Gore Sr., represented middle Tennessee's rural Fourth District in the House of Representatives until 1952, when he was elected to the Senate. The Gores spent most of the year in the Fairfax Hotel on Embassy Row, a "world of old people and bellhops," and Al attended the elite St. Albans School before enrolling at Harvard in 1966.[99] He spent summers on the family farm in Carthage. In contrast to Clinton, who grew up deeply rooted in Arkansas before going to Washington for college, Gore straddled the two worlds of Tennessee and the nation's capital during all of his formative years.

Gore's time in college coincided with steeply rising opposition to the war in Vietnam at Harvard and on other campuses, a stance that he and Senator Gore—but not most Tennesseans—shared. Of the 234 sons and grandsons of members of Congress eligible to serve in Vietnam, at a time when only men were drafted, only 28 did.[100] Gore was one of them. He enlisted in the army in 1969, right after graduation. "The most effective way to express my opposition to the war," he said, "was to go, and help my father," who faced a tough reelection in 1970.[101] Although a Gore campaign commercial featured father and son (the latter in uniform) as fellow patriots, Senator Gore was defeated by his Republican opponent.[102]

Returning in 1971 from Vietnam, where he worked as a reporter for an army publication, Gore spent the next several years in Nashville writing for the state's leading Democratic newspaper, the *Tennessean*, and taking classes at Vanderbilt University's divinity and law schools. He earned degrees at neither, mostly because a rare vacancy occurred in his father's old congressional district in 1976 and Gore decided to seek the Democratic nomination, which at the time was tantamount to election. Running against the liberal state House Democratic leader J. Stanley Rogers, Gore tacked right on issues such as abortion, gun control, and welfare, surprising friends with these positions just as Clinton was surprising his own friends that year with his pro-right-to-work law campaign for attorney general of Arkansas. Running as Al Gore Jr. (in future campaigns he dropped the suffix), Gore was narrowly elected.

Gore was a diligent representative both in the district, where he solidified his political standing by conducting town hall meetings nearly every weekend, and in the House of Representatives, where he dug deeply into neglected issues that he knew would attract media interest, such as the safety of infant formula and contact lens solutions. In 1982, with an eye toward higher office in the future, Gore extended his reach into national security. He became the leading advocate of adding "Midgetman" missiles to the nation's nuclear arsenal, relatively inexpensive single-warhead weapons so numerous that it would be impossible for the Soviet Union to destroy them all in a first strike. Gore parlayed his growing professional reputation in Washington and popularity back home into a successful campaign for a Senate seat in 1984, when Senate Republican leader Howard Baker retired. He was unopposed for the Democratic nomination and won easily against his Republican opponent.

A glowing *Washington Monthly* profile of Gore in November 1986 created buzz about his political future that showed up in a March 15, 1987, *New York Times* column by James Reston, which in turn caught the eye of leading Democratic fund-raiser Nathan Landow.[103] After serving as Mondale's finance chair in 1984 and grown tired of losing, the Maryland real estate developer formed IMPAC 88, a group of forty-five fellow Democratic fund-raisers from around the country whose purpose was to unite their financial support behind a candidate who was politically moderate enough to win in 1988. Not Clinton but his fellow Arkansan Sen. Dale Bumpers was their first choice. When Bumpers decided not to run and Gore appeared before the group on March 19, four days after the Reston column, Landow and his deep-pocketed colleagues were impressed. They met with Gore again on March 25, and seventeen of them promised to raise at least $250,000 each if he entered the race.[104]

Bidding at age thirty-nine to be the youngest major party nominee for president since William Jennings Bryan in 1896, Gore announced his candidacy on April 11, 1987. His strategy was to sweep the fifteen southern and border state primaries on Super Tuesday (March 8) and then persuade the rest of his party's primary voters that only a southern centrist could be elected in November, mostly by winning back a majority of the ten states in Gore's home region that Carter carried in 1976 but Reagan swept in 1980 and 1984. Lending luster to Gore's appeal, he thought, was his youth. Mimicking John F. Kennedy, Gore said in his announcement speech, "Americans may well feel as they did in 1960 that it is time to turn to youth, vigor, and intellectual capacity."[105]

After the announcement, nothing in the Gore campaign went as well as planned. Most of the IMPAC 88 pledges failed to materialize, even as the group's endorsement left Gore with "the lingering image that he had been bought by a small group of rich guys."[106] His solemn, hypermature demeanor in public appearances undermined the Kennedy-style appeal. He was often described as an old person's idea of a nice young man. Such energy as Gore displayed tended to come in the form of severe attacks on his opponents for the Democratic nomination. He blistered them on defense issues, charging that they opposed every proposed weapons system on the naive assumption that the president could "go into negotiations with the

Soviet Union on the basis that we get something for nothing."[107] In an April 12 debate, Gore criticized Dukakis for supporting the Massachusetts prison furlough program. Both the national defense and prison furlough attacks planted seeds for the Republicans' defenestration of Dukakis in the fall campaign. Indeed, Bush's opposition researcher, James Pinkerton, only learned about the furlough program after Gore mentioned it in the debate.[108]

Gore's centrist appeal was authentically grounded in much of his record. But he downplayed his deeply held concerns for the environment and arms control when audiences failed to respond to his discussion of these issues in speeches. This left him reeling from one theme to another—"put the White House on the side of working families" one day, uncritical pledges of support for Israel the next. In an Iowa debate, Gore said "there should not be any public subsidy for tobacco at all." The next day, in North Carolina, he said that "the money that is earned growing tobacco should go to the small family farmers."[109] He emerged from Super Tuesday as one of the three remaining contenders from the original field of nine, but far from sweeping the southern primaries, he did slightly less well than Jackson and Dukakis. In the April 19 New York primary, Gore tethered his campaign to New York City mayor Ed Koch, who overshadowed him with statements such as "Jews would be crazy to vote for Jackson."[110] On primary day, Gore ran third with only 10 percent. He withdrew right afterward. With little reason to think he would be offered the vice presidential nomination, he dismissed the office as "a political dead end."[111] Gore was barely visible at the Democratic convention while embarrassingly telling John F. Kennedy Jr., who gave a riveting prime-time speech, that they needed to get together because they were both "American royalty."[112]

Although his campaign ended badly, Gore emerged from the 1988 election battle-hardened with only political flesh wounds. At forty-three he would still be young in 1992, barely older than Kennedy when he was elected. He had run a yearlong national campaign, an experience that few potential rivals had. His candidacy made him the best-known southern Democrat in the country. Most of all, the hugely disappointing landslide defeat of the Massachusetts governor whom the Democrats did nominate made the party even more open to the possibility of nominating a southern centrist in 1992 than it was in 1988.

MARIO CUOMO

In 1974 Mario Cuomo, like Bill Clinton, made his first bid for elective office and lost, in his case for the Democratic nomination for lieutenant governor of New York. Unlike Clinton, who at age twenty-eight was fresh out of law school when he ran for Congress in Arkansas, Cuomo was forty-two. For him, as for Gore and Jackson, a political career was a late, not a lifelong, ambition.

Cuomo grew up in Queens County, one of the outer boroughs of New York City, in a first-generation Italian American family. His parents, with help from their children, ran a small grocery store, above which Mario was born in "an urban log cabin," in journalist Sidney Blumenthal's apt phrase.[113] Andrea and Immacolata Cuomo were largely apolitical, so much so that when Cuomo was appointed New York's secretary of state in 1975, his father wondered why his lawyer son wanted to be a secretary.[114] Emerging into adulthood, Cuomo was a scholar-athlete in every sense of the word. He earned academic scholarships to St. John's Preparatory School, St. John's College, and St. John's Law School, all in Queens (richer students seeking a Catholic education went to Georgetown or Notre Dame). He was a good enough center fielder that the Pittsburgh Pirates signed him for their Class D Brunswick, Georgia, team in 1952, but injuries ended his promising baseball career.

As a young lawyer, Cuomo was intent on building his practice and supporting his growing family (including sons Andrew, a future New York governor, and Chris, a future CNN anchor). "Mario slept through the sixties," said New York journalist Jack Newfield.[115] He was largely uninterested in the controversies roiling the country during that decade, except in the Catholic Church, whose post–Vatican II emphasis on "the concerns of the world" inspired him. Cuomo placed his faith at the center of his life. "I am a governor, I am a Democrat, but I am a Catholic first," he later said—baffling and sometimes alienating liberal political reformers in his city and state who reflexively viewed religious commitment in general and the Catholic Church in particular as retrograde obstacles to progress.[116]

Cuomo's entry into public life came when he skillfully negotiated compromises between the New York City government, which wanted to build large public housing projects in previously white outer-borough neighborhoods, and the bitterly opposed, tight-knit ethnic communities that already lived there. As his reputation for defusing conflict grew, politics seemed the logical next step, an endeavor that fulfilled not just Cuomo's faith-inspired commitment to serve but also his personal desire to compete and excel.

Throughout most of the 1970s Cuomo competed in politics but did not excel. He ran for the Democratic nomination for lieutenant governor in 1974 and lost; ran for mayor of New York City in 1977 and lost twice, once in the Democratic primary and then, still on the ballot as the Liberal Party nominee, in the general election; and ran President Jimmy Carter's reelection campaign in New York, losing again in both the April primary and the November election. But Cuomo's one victory, as Democratic gubernatorial nominee Hugh Carey's running mate for lieutenant governor in 1978, was enough to position him for a long-shot bid for the party's nomination for governor in 1982, when Carey decided not to seek a third term. Cuomo's opponent was Mayor Koch, who had beaten him in 1977 and later aligned himself with President Reagan. Koch's decision backfired in 1982, when Reagan's popularity reached its nadir. Cuomo defeated Koch in the Democratic primary and the self-financed Republican nominee, Lewis Lehrman, in the general election.

It was during the 1982 campaign that Cuomo developed his distinctive vision of New York (and soon America) as an extended family. Republicans had seized on family values as a way of appealing to Christian conservatives, but the language came just as naturally to Cuomo, who was raised in the intensely family-centric Italian American community. "We must be the family of New York," he declared in his 1983 inaugural address, "feeling one another's pain; sharing one another's blessings, reasonably, equitably, honestly, fairly."[117] During the 1980s (he was reelected in 1986), Cuomo governed as a "pay-as-you-go liberal," practicing fiscal austerity in pursuit of traditional liberal goals and then, when the mid-decade economic boom began, cutting taxes while increasing social spending.[118] He embraced labels such as "progressive pragmatism" to distinguish himself from conventional liberals. Unlike many other ambitious Democrats, he did not respond to Reagan's popularity by moving rightward.

Cuomo's moment in the national spotlight came during his keynote speech at the 1984 Democratic convention. Mondale may have been "polenta," which he said was his mother's description of the blandly midwestern nominee, but not Cuomo.[119] Invoking the "family of America," Cuomo electrified the delegates and the national television audience by doing what Reagan did so well: articulating the values of his party in an inspiring way.[120] "Cuomo in '88" buttons appeared on delegates' lapels the next day. Later that year, unsettled by New York archbishop John J. O'Connor's statement that he "did not see how a Catholic in good conscience could vote for a candidate who explicitly supported abortion," Cuomo deepened his growing ties to liberal Democrats with a thoughtful and widely reported speech on the subject at Notre Dame.[121] He said that although he accepted "the Church's teaching on abortion," he could not endorse measures to outlaw

Gov. Mario Cuomo of New York, a favorite of Democratic liberals, considered seeking his party's presidential nomination in 1988 and 1992 but decided not to both times. Courtesy of the Library of Congress.

the procedure unless there was "a consensus . . . shared by the pluralistic community at large."[122] Running for lieutenant governor in 1974, Cuomo had been, like many Democratic politicians at that time (including Gore), on the other side of the issue.

Cuomo emerged from the 1984 election as the preferred candidate of most white liberal Democrats for the 1988 presidential nomination. Four previous governors of New York, ranging from Martin Van Buren in 1836 to Franklin D. Roosevelt in 1932, had been elected president, and three others were nominated by a major party. None was elected governor by as large a majority—64 percent to 32 percent—as Cuomo in 1986, who by then was already consulting with experts and traveling abroad to shore up his foreign policy credentials—essential political groundwork at the time for a presidential candidate without Washington experience. But none of Cuomo's predecessors in Albany were as beset by self-doubt as he was concerning his motives, worthiness, and ability to function simultaneously as governor and candidate. The question, fellow New York Democrat Mark Green wryly asked, was, "Will Mario Cuomo throw his halo into the ring in 1988?"[123]

Cuomo's answer, which he announced at the end of his monthly radio talk show *Ask the Governor* on February 19, 1987, was no, which surprised those who knew him less than those who thought he would be the odds-on favorite to win the Democratic nomination in what initially promised to be a strong Democratic year. Cuomo hated raising money for his campaigns—"it killed him—it actually killed him" to go to fund-raisers, an associate said.[124] He did not like approaching voters to shake hands ("These people worked all day. . . . They're tired; they want to go home").[125] He was "against debates," which he regarded as superficial.[126] He disdained the "fire in the belly" required to keep a candidate going through the long campaign. Who wants a president "sitting down next to the phone with the red button with fire in his belly?" he asked.[127] Having spent only his few months as a ball player outside New York a third of a century earlier, Cuomo could not imagine devoting months to retail campaigning in Iowa and New Hampshire. Indeed, his long-standing practice when giving out-of-town speeches, far from using these occasions to learn about other parts of the country, was to fly in, give the speech, and immediately fly home.[128] Lurking underneath all of these overt concerns was the Italian question, which plagued the unfamiliarly named, earnestly ethnic, thoroughly New York governor. When media consultant David Garth asked voters who did not know much about Cuomo what came to mind when they thought of him, he found that a large percentage assumed (baselessly) he was connected to organized crime.[129]

Cuomo endorsed no candidate for the 1988 Democratic nomination. Some were surprised by this, assuming that as a liberal, intellectual, ethnic, northeastern governor he would support his fellow liberal, intellectual, ethnic, northeastern governor, Michael Dukakis. But for all their obvious similarities, Cuomo and Dukakis were different in ways that made their relationship awkward. Cuomo embraced his ethnicity and religion. His liberalism was passionate. Dukakis downplayed his ethnicity and religion, and his liberalism was technocratic. What's more, a Dukakis victory in 1988 would close the door to a Cuomo candidacy in 1992, when, after four more years of national exposure, the New York governor would be better known, less stereotyped, and in his own mind more qualified to be president.

2

THE VIEW FROM 1988
THE FIELD OF REPUBLICANS FORMS

Republican success in presidential elections was a consistent feature of American politics from the late 1960s to the late 1980s. But this pattern of stability masked two important developments. By 1988 the Republican Party was much more conservative than it had been as recently as a decade before. Simultaneously, the meaning of conservatism as a political force underwent some important changes. As chapter 1 did for the Democrats, this chapter surveys the Republican Party and its leading national figures heading into the presidential elections of the 1990s: George Bush, Bob Dole, Jack Kemp, Dan Quayle, and Pat Buchanan.

The Republican presidents of the twentieth century's middle decades were at most moderately conservative, as evidenced by the liberal policies they mixed into their broadly conservative agendas. Dwight D. Eisenhower, when chastised by his brother Edgar for not trying to repeal the New Deal, replied: "Should any political party attempt to abolish social security, unemployment insurance and eliminate labor laws and farm programs, you should not hear of that party again in our political history."[1] Ike launched the largest infrastructure program in history, the interstate highway system, and resisted calls to intervene against communist revolutionaries in French Indochina. Richard Nixon's generally conservative policy agenda nonetheless included wage and price controls, a 20 percent increase in Social Security benefits, and the creation of the Environmental Protection Agency and the Occupational Safety and Health Administration, along with diplomatic openings to Cold

War enemies China and the Soviet Union. Gerald Ford extended Nixon's policy of détente with the communist powers, supported the Equal Rights Amendment (ERA) to the Constitution, and appointed liberal Republican icon Nelson A. Rockefeller as vice president.

Moderate conservatism was also the modal position of Republicans in Congress during this period, albeit with considerable ideological diversity. Their leaders in each chamber—Everett Dirksen of Illinois, followed by Hugh Scott of Pennsylvania and Howard Baker of Tennessee in the Senate, and Gerald Ford of Michigan followed by John Rhodes of Arizona and Bob Michel of Illinois in the House—ran the spectrum from moderately liberal (Scott) to moderately conservative (the others). With only a handful of southern members in their ranks, Republicans in Congress supported the Civil Rights Act of 1964 and the Voting Rights Act of 1965 by greater margins than congressional Democrats did.

Ronald Reagan's strong run for the Republican nomination against President Ford in 1976 and his two terms as president in the 1980s marked a clear turn to the right in Republican presidential politics. Indeed, in 1988 every candidate tried to package himself as Reagan's true heir. In Congress, the systematic data on roll call votes compiled by political scientists Keith Poole and Howard Rosenthal demonstrate that the steady trend toward greater centrism and growing ideological overlap between the parties that had prevailed since 1900 shifted into reverse in the mid-1970s, The House Republican caucus "moved sharply to the right," and its Democratic counterpart "became somewhat more liberal than the Democratic Party of the 1960s."[2] Starting in 1973, ideological polarization between the conservative Republican and liberal Democratic caucuses increased in every subsequent Congress.[3]

Conservatives were hardly absent from Republican ranks prior to Reagan, any more than moderates and liberals were. Sen. Barry Goldwater of Arizona, an ardent conservative, won the party's presidential nomination in 1964. As political scientist Sam Rosenfeld has argued, conservatism's rise within the Republican Party during the 1950s and early 1960s was in part a reaction against Eisenhower's active efforts to remake the GOP as a "modern," centrist party. New or newly energized institutions arose on the right to further this cause, notably the Young Republican National Federation, the previously skeletal southern state party organizations, and *National Review*, a magazine dedicated to fusing the long-separate strands of conservatism into a unified political force.[4] But the themes that dominated conservatism in the 1950s and 1960s were different from those that marked it afterward.

As evidence of how much conservatism changed starting in the 1970s, consider Goldwater's best-selling book *The Conscience of a Conservative* (1960), which at the time was a near-scriptural text for those on the right.[5] In it Goldwater called for ending farm subsidies, making Social Security voluntary, reducing the federal budget by 10 percent, affirming states' rights, and lifting the restraints on Cold War–era containment policy toward the Soviet Union. Not a single mention was made of abortion, homosexuality, gun control, prayer in public schools, or women's rights. For Goldwater and other Republican conservatives of the 1950s and 1960s, cutting taxes ran a distant second to cutting spending in the service of a balanced budget. In 1967, when Rep. George Bush of Texas said, "We must have a tax increase" to help reduce "exorbitant projected deficits," he was taking an orthodox conservative position.[6] Even as late as 1976, Reagan ran not on a platform of tax cuts or social issues but rather on a plan to devolve power from Washington to the states. By most contemporary accounts the social conservative in that election was Democratic presidential nominee Jimmy Carter, who as a self-described "born-again Christian" said that from a moral standpoint "abortion is wrong."[7] Carter won the votes of most Southern Baptists against Ford, as well as the endorsement of the popular Pentecostal television host Pat Robertson.[8]

The changes within conservatism that already were beginning to take place as the 1970s unfolded—specifically, a new emphasis on tax reduction, a tougher line in foreign policy, traditional stances on social issues, and resistance to further expansions of civil rights—help to account for the GOP's growing identity as the party of the right and its expanding electoral appeal to white voters across economic lines.

The power of the tax cut issue became apparent in June 1978, when California voters passed Proposition 13 by an almost two-to-one margin. The measure, which was opposed by nearly every leading figure in the state except former governor Reagan, reduced property taxes by $6 billion and made future tax increases extremely difficult to enact. That November the voters in twelve of the sixteen states that had ballot measures to reduce or limit taxes passed them, joined two years later by Massachusetts. "It was a little bit like dumping those cases of tea off the boat in Boston harbor," said Reagan.[9] A bill sponsored by Rep. Jack Kemp of New York and Sen. William Roth of Delaware to cut federal income taxes by 30 percent won the official endorsement and active support of the Republican National Committee. Never before had tax cuts been an issue that divided the parties. In 1976 it was Carter who branded the tax code "a disgrace to the human race."[10] After his efforts to reform it failed, Republicans seized the issue and never let go.

Support for Kemp-Roth became a central appeal of Reagan's campaign for president in 1980. Its grounding in a new "supply-side" economic theory, which held that tax cuts would pay for themselves by rapidly accelerating economic growth, relieved him and like-minded conservatives of having to propose substantial reductions in popular entitlement programs, especially Social Security, Medicare, and Medicaid, on which many of the blue-collar voters whose support Republicans were wooing depended. Journalist Jude Wanniski and economist Arthur Laffer not only developed the theory but promoted it successfully among Republican writers, activists, and members of Congress, with Kemp as their most ardent and influential convert.[11] Starting in 1986, a new group called Americans for Tax Reform began demanding that Republican candidates sign the Taxpayer Protection Pledge promising to oppose any increase in taxes.

Conservatism's second rising strand in the 1970s was a small but influential movement of previously liberal, mostly eastern public intellectuals away from the Democratic Party and toward—sometimes into—the Republican Party. In the aftermath of the Vietnam War, which ended badly in 1975, many leading Democrats became less willing than in the past to support American efforts to use force to contain communism by preventing its spread into new countries.[12] In the mid-1970s, as Soviet-aided governments came to power in, among other places, Angola and the newly consolidated Vietnam, congressional Democrats and the Carter administration were loath to intervene. Democratic leaders also tended to deny or downplay the threat posed by the Soviets' dramatic expansion of their nuclear arsenal.

Dissatisfied Democratic national security conservatives, soon labeled "neoconservatives," criticized Carter and their party's other leaders for overlearning the noninterventionist lessons of Vietnam. They responded positively to Reagan's promise to abandon Nixon- and Ford-style détente and not just contain Soviet expansion but seek to roll it back through increased defense spending and a more assertive approach to the Cold War. Several neoconservatives, including Jeane Kirkpatrick, Richard Perle, and Irving Kristol, either entered the Reagan administration or joined the ranks of its most articulate defenders.[13]

In addition to tax cutters and neoconservatives, the Republican Party attracted support from Christian conservatives. Since the nineteenth century, most white evangelical and fundamentalist Protestants had been Democrats, a consequence of their generally working-class status and geographic concentration in the then solidly Democratic South. They also tended to eschew political activity beyond voting as excessively worldly and potentially corrupting.[14] All that changed starting in the 1970s. In 1972 Congress endorsed the ERA and sent it to the states. The following year the Supreme Court legalized most abortions in *Roe v. Wade*. Phyllis Schlafly, a prominent Catholic conservative activist, organized a campaign eponymously named STOP-ERA (STOP stood for "Stop Taking Our Privileges") that mobilized Catholic and evangelical women who shared her commitment to preserving traditional feminine roles. Schlafly's group stopped ERA dead in its tracks after all but three of the required thirty-eight states voted to ratify it.[15]

Catholics forged an additional alliance with evangelicals in a campaign to roll back abortion rights through both a constitutional amendment overturning *Roe* and judicial appointments that would shift the Supreme Court in a conservative direction. In 1979 the Southern Baptist Convention, newly captured by theological and (increasingly) political conservatives, voted to change its stance on abortion rights—which it previously regarded as a "Catholic issue"—from acceptance to opposition.[16] As recently as 1971, two years before *Roe*, the convention had urged Baptists "to work for legislation that will allow for the possibility of abortion" under most circumstances, including the loosely defined "likelihood of damage to the emotional . . . health of the mother."[17] Both the new activism and the new alliance with the Catholic bishops, whom evangelicals had long despised, represented dramatic departures from previous practice for most conservative Protestants. Meanwhile, southern and Catholic Democratic political leaders, who once were the main opponents of abortion, began altering their position in response to pressure from feminists within the party for whom protecting *Roe* was a defining issue. Among prominent Democrats whose stance shifted from pro-life to pro-choice were Jesse Jackson, Edward M. Kennedy, Joseph Biden, John Kerry, Al Gore, and Mario Cuomo—all of them with presidential ambitions.[18]

Conservative Christians admired Carter in 1976 as one of their own but during his presidency were outraged when he refused to overturn an Internal Revenue Service ruling that private schools created in the post–*Brown v. Board of Education* era would have to meet minority enrollment benchmarks or lose their tax-exempt status. The great majority of these schools were Christian academies in the South, which attracted parents and students who were angry about racial integration as well as about "sex education or the lack of classroom prayer" in public schools.[19] Nearly all of these schools were created by white churches. The short-lived IRS ruling provoked several hundred thousand letters of protest, fueled by a sense of betrayal by Carter, who had already disappointed evangelicals with his generally liberal policies once in office.

Capitalizing on all of these developments, in 1979 Jerry Falwell, a Baptist minister in Lynchburg, Virginia, with a large television following, organized the Moral Majority. He grounded it in local congregations to promote a variety of conservative causes, including opposition to abortion, which he equated with women "caught up in the ERA movement [who] want to terminate their pregnancies because it limits their freedom and their job opportunities."[20] Falwell had preached against Christian political activism during the civil rights era. "Preachers are not called to be politicians, but soul winners," he said then. Now he declared, "The idea of 'religion and politics don't mix' was invented by the devil to keep Christians from running their own country."[21]

The Republican Party, seeing an opportunity, abandoned its support for the ERA and indifference to abortion and Christian schools and rode the rising tide of evangelical activism.[22] "I know you can't endorse me," Reagan told an evangelical gathering in August 1980, "but I want you to know that I endorse you and what you are doing."[23] In the four years between Reagan's two elections, Southern Baptist ministers swung from a 41 percent to 29 percent preference for Democrats (already a major shift toward the GOP by this group) to a 66 percent to 25 percent preference for Republicans.[24] Around 80 percent of them—and nearly 100 percent of Assemblies of God ministers—began voting Republican for president.[25] Once engaged in the political process, these ministers and their congregants were able to use the organizational and communications skills they formed within their churches on behalf of Republican candidates who shared their values. Evangelical churches not only were doing the grassroots work for the GOP that labor unions did for the Democrats but also were growing in membership even as the unions were shrinking. An interesting consequence of the rising tide of Christian conservatism was that it enabled the GOP to broaden its economic base among white voters without having to make working-class-based economic appeals. As political scientists Jacob Hacker and Paul Pierson found, "An evangelical with $50,000 in annual income is as likely to be a Republican as a nonevangelical with $100,000 in annual income."[26]

Undergirding both the rising conservative influence within the Republican Party and the changes in what conservatism meant was the regional transformation the GOP was undergoing, with consequences for the Democrats as well. In 1960, as in most previous presidential elections, none of Republican nominee Richard Nixon's fifteen strongest states was in the South. By 1988, seven of the eleven southern states were among George Bush's fifteen best. In 1960, 35 of the 174 Republican House members were from New England or New York; only 8 were from the South. In 1988 the nearly identical 175-member House Republicans contingent included 40 southerners (a number that would continue to rise steeply in coming years) and only 22 (a number that would continue to fall) northeasterners. None of the South's 22 senators were Republicans in 1960, but half of them were by 1988.

The reason for the regional transformation of the GOP is that as the Republican Party became more conservative, its northern liberal and moderate officeholders either converted to the Democratic Party, like Rep. Don Riegle of Michigan and Mayor John Lindsay of New York City; were defeated by conservative challengers in party primaries (Clifford Case of New Jersey, Jacob Javits of New York); or lost to equally liberal Democrats in a general election (Edward Brooke of Massachusetts, Margaret Chase Smith of Maine.) In New England, where he ran especially well, the independent presidential campaign waged in 1980 by Rep. John Anderson of Illinois, a liberal Republican, served as a way station on the road to the Democratic Party for many Republican liberals disenchanted with the party's southern and rightward turn.

Alabama governor George C. Wallace's independent campaign for president in 1968 already had performed a parallel function for many white segregationist Democrats seeking a psychologically comfortable way to break with their party before reaffiliating with the Republicans. In a mirror image of what happened with the liberal Republican officeholders in the North, some conservative Democrats in the South either lost primaries to more liberal candidates or were defeated by Republicans in their reelection bids. Even more common were the loss of Democratic seats to Republicans when incumbents retired and the decisions by Democratic officeholders to switch parties, as Rep. Phil Gramm of Texas did in 1983 and Sen. Richard Shelby of Alabama did in 1994, along with hundreds of state and local officials throughout the South.

During his first term as president, Nixon labored to bring Wallace's supporters into his 1972 reelection coalition. His efforts to use racially charged issues such as law and order and opposition to school busing to graft southern white support onto the traditional midwestern Republican base were rewarded on Election Day. Nixon swept the South, carrying every state in the region, with majorities ranging from 65 to 78 percent, and won the rest of the country with more than 55 percent, nearly all of them white voters.

One of the southern Republicans who rode Nixon's 1972 coattails into Congress was Jesse Helms, the first member of his party elected to the Senate from North Carolina since Reconstruction. Helms beat back the previously dominant moderate business wing of his state's GOP and relocated his party's base among blue-collar cultural conservatives, most of them erstwhile Democrats who voted for Wallace in the 1968 presidential election and the 1972 Democratic primary. He played a major role in rousing white evangelicals to organize in opposition to the proposed withdrawal of tax-exempt status from Christian schools. In the early 1980s he strenuously fought the creation of the Martin Luther King national holiday. Helms's most famous election came in 1990 when he was challenged by the African American mayor of Charlotte, Harvey Gantt. Trailing in the polls, Helms ran a television ad showing a white man's hand crumpling a rejection letter from an employer. "You needed that job and you were the best qualified," the announcer intoned. "But they had to give it to a minority because of a racial quota." As a measure of how successful Helms's campaign strategy was, he won stronger support from the state's poorest and least-educated white voters—long the mainstay of the southern Democratic majority—than from any other group.[27]

The growth of the Republican Party in the South was more than a response to the Democrats' embrace of civil rights or the efforts by Helms, Sen. Strom Thurmond of South Carolina (an early convert to the GOP in 1964), and other regional figures to lead blue-collar whites out of the Democratic Party. It already had begun in the early 1950s, before civil rights became a major political issue. Many northern businesses and their Republican executives moved south after World War II in search of a nonunionized labor force, milder winters, and, with the spread of air-conditioning, bearable summers. The Republicans' embrace and the Democrats' rejection of conservative positions on largely nonracial economic and moral issues also drove many white voters toward the GOP. In a region dotted by military installations, the party's commitment to a strong national defense even as Democrats were becoming hesitant about the use of force added still more voters to the party's southern ranks.

Clearly, however, race had much to do with the growth of the Republican Party across various parts of the country, but especially the South. The Voting Rights Act of 1965 brought millions of previously unregistered black southerners into the electorate, nearly all of them Democrats because of

President Lyndon B. Johnson's support and Senator Goldwater's opposition to the landmark Civil Rights Act of 1964. White southern conservative Democrats grew increasingly uncomfortable sharing the state and local parties they previously dominated with liberal African Americans. And as the South became more Republican and the Republican Party more southern, the pace at which many longtime northeastern and Pacific Coast Republican voters headed for the exit and reentered politics as Democrats accelerated. Among the states Bush carried in 1988 that went Democratic in every subsequent election were California, Connecticut, Delaware, Maine, Maryland, New Jersey, and Vermont.

"In its grand outlines," wrote V. O. Key in his classic book *Southern Politics in State and Nation* (1949), "the politics of the South revolves around the position of the Negro."[28] Republicans built their southern-based presidential majority on more than just race. But one thing did not change as the region's partisan composition did: the South's dominant political party, Democratic in Key's time, Republican starting in the 1970s, remained essentially all white.

As the twentieth century approached its final decade, GOP leaders with national ambitions—Bush, Dole, Kemp, Quayle, and Buchanan, all of them middle-aged—would have to take account of a Republican landscape different from the one in which they grew to maturity.

GEORGE BUSH

George Bush was both an old northern and a new southern Republican. Born in 1924 and raised and educated in, at various times, three of the six New England states, Bush was the son of Prescott Bush, who became one of nine Republican senators from the then-staunchly Republican region when Connecticut voters elected him in 1952 after two failed attempts. George Bush absorbed his father's teaching that upon securing financial stability for one's family, which Prescott Bush did as a member of the elite investment firm Brown Brothers Harriman, a man's life should be devoted to public service. He also learned from his father that losing elections may be a step along the way toward winning them.[29]

After returning from World War II, in which he earned the Distinguished Flying Cross for leading fifty-eight missions as the youngest naval aviator in the Pacific theater, to finish his education at Yale, George Bush joined the postwar migration of ambitious young northern businessmen to the South. Alone among Prescott Bush's four sons, he did not follow his father into a career in finance. Moving his wife, Barbara Bush, and their growing family to Odessa and Midland, Texas, in pursuit of success in the independent oil business, Bush achieved financial security. He settled in Houston in 1959 after taking ownership of the offshore component of Zapata Petroleum, the company he cofounded a few years earlier with financial backing from family and friends. In 1962 he was elected chair of the Harris County Republican Party, winning enough support from other northern migrants in the business and professional community to beat back a fierce challenge from the extreme right-wing John Birch Society—"the meanest political battle of his life," according to Barbara Bush.[30] From that springboard Bush launched his first political campaign in 1964 as the Republican nominee for senator against the incumbent Democrat, Ralph Yarborough.

An old northern and new southern Republican, Bush was also an old-style and a new-style conservative. As political scientist Hugh Heclo rightly observed, the midcentury conservatism that prevailed during Bush's formative years was "a disposition more than an ideological package of doctrines."[31] Its essence was prudence, incrementalism, and an aversion to statism. The conservatism Bush encountered in Texas was more an ideology than a disposition. Adapting to the era and setting in which he began his political career, Bush tied his Senate campaign to Goldwater's hoped-for presidential coattails in the state, which vanished when Johnson became president after the regionally less popular John F. Kennedy of Massachusetts was assassinated in November 1963. Following Goldwater's lead, Bush opposed the nuclear test ban treaty with the Soviet Union, the Civil Rights Act of 1964, Medicare, and the "left-wing spending programs" that constituted Johnson's War on Poverty.[32] Bush-style conservatism was, like Goldwater's, centered on balanced budgets and a strong national defense. After overcoming a far-right challenge for the Republican nomination from an opponent who tried to tar him with his father's supposed complicity in "the whole diabolical scheme of creating a ONE-WORLD FEDERATION of socialist states under the United Nations," Bush lost to Yarborough by 56 percent to 44 percent in November while running 7 percentage points ahead of Goldwater.[33]

Bush came out of the 1964 defeat with regrets that morphed into resolve. Invited to contribute to a postelection forum in the National Review, Bush condemned the right-wing "'nut' fringe" that "pounced on" undecided voters, "pushed their philosophy in Goldwater's name, and scared the hell out of the plain average non-issue-conscious man on the street."[34] He ran for and was elected to the House of Representatives in 1966 from a new, mostly Republican district in Houston.

At a time when his party's liberal wing still was large (nearly every one of Johnson's Great Society bills enjoyed at least 25 percent support from Republican representatives and senators), Bush's voting record in the House was consistently conservative.[35] His average "Liberal Quotient," as measured by the liberal Americans for Democratic Action, was 5 percent. One year it was the most conservative of anyone in the twenty-three-member Texas delegation. Yet Bush's reputation in later years as a moderate Republican was forged at this stage of his career.[36] The origin of this reputation lay mainly in his intense interest in issues related to population control—so intense that Rep. Wilbur Mills, the chair of the Ways and Means Committee on which Bush served, referred to him as "rubbers."[37] Bush, like his father—but also like Senator Goldwater and many other conservatives of the era—was a strong supporter of Planned Parenthood at a time when that organization was mostly interested in promoting birth control as a way to reduce childbearing by poor and single women.[38]

The Republican nominee for president in 1968, Richard Nixon, elevated Bush's prestige in Texas by circulating his name as a possible vice presidential running mate in response to advice from Texas businessmen, younger Republican congressmen, former president Eisenhower, and even Rev. Billy Graham.[39] Nixon "confirmed that he gave it very serious consideration," Bush wrote after Nixon chose Gov. Spiro Agnew of Maryland instead, "but decided against it because of my short service in the House."[40] Nixon did not want to invite the charge of inexperience that was leveled at Goldwater's running mate, Rep. William Miller of New York, four years earlier.[41]

Despite encouragement from Texas Republicans to run for governor in 1968, Bush instead ran unopposed for reelection to the House. "Pop really would like to be president," Barbara Bush wrote in her diary.[42] The conventional view at the time, shared by her husband but soon to be overturned when voters began looking outside Washington for their presidents in the mid-1970s, was that a gubernatorial career was a dead end for someone with presidential ambitions.[43] Instead Bush prepared for a rematch against Yarborough in 1970.

Bush's strategy for victory in his second Senate race was clear: build a coalition consisting of Republicans and conservative Democrats by attacking Yarborough from the right. Almost certainly this strategy would have succeeded. But Bush's plan was thwarted when former representative Lloyd Bentsen—a banking and insurance millionaire whom *New York Times* columnist Tom Wicker described as "at least as conservative as the Republican George Bush, and probably hawkier, fat cattier, and oilier"—challenged and defeated Yarborough in the Democratic primary.[44] Bush was flummoxed by Yarborough's loss, especially when Bentsen attacked him from the right as "a liberal Ivy League carpetbagger." On Election Day he lost to Bentsen by 46 percent to 54 percent.[45]

Having forsaken his House seat to seek the Senate, Bush spent the remaining years of the Nixon presidency representing the United States at the United Nations (Nixon's consolation prize for losing in 1970, ironic considering how harshly Bush criticized the UN during his 1964 Senate campaign) and then, starting in December 1972, chairing the Republican National Committee (RNC). Although the party job was "no fun at all" after the Watergate crisis hit in spring 1973, it allowed Bush to connect with hundreds of local Republican leaders around the country. Like every other prominent Republican, he was slow to accept Nixon's culpability, but at an August 6, 1974, cabinet meeting, speaking up even though he had not been called on by the president, Bush urged Nixon to resign based on all he had been hearing from local Republican leaders around the country.[46]

Nixon's resignation three days later elevated Vice President Gerald Ford to the presidency, creating a vacancy in the vice presidency that Ford needed to fill under the terms of the recently enacted Twenty-Fifth Amendment. More than in 1968, Bush was a finalist for the second spot, along with former governor Nelson Rockefeller of New York and White House chief of staff Donald Rumsfeld. Ford's survey of congressional Republicans found that House members favored Bush over Rockefeller by 101 to 68 and that Rockefeller outpolled him by only 14 to 12 in the Senate.[47] But Ford chose Rockefeller, whom he regarded as "an international figure. He was a major national figure."[48]

Adding to Bush's disappointment, when Ford nominated him as director of the Central Intelligence Agency (CIA) in October 1975, congressional Democrats demanded that he promise not to put Bush on the ticket in 1976.[49] As a matter of duty, Bush felt he had no choice but to do what the president wanted, but he was convinced that the appointment meant "the total end of any political future."[50] When Carter defeated Ford in 1976, he replaced Bush, the first new president to fire an incumbent CIA director since 1953.[51]

Out of government and "bored silly" back in Texas, Bush decided to run for president in 1980. He grounded his candidacy in his résumé with the slogan "A President We Won't Have to Train."[52] In the span of barely a half decade, Bush had been UN ambassador, RNC chair, liaison to China, and CIA director. Yet, as historian Jeffrey Engel has written, he was experienced rather than "accomplished," having held "positions of greater and greater responsibility without changing any one of them along the way."[53] Nor was any of these positions a traditional stepping-stone to the presidency—indeed, none had been held by any previous president or major party nominee. But Bush calculated that voters' disappointment with Carter, a former governor, would turn them against other Washington outsiders vying for the Republican nomination, including Reagan.[54] Bush also jogged a lot in public to illustrate that he was energetic and Reagan, at age sixty-nine, was old.[55]

Bush ran as a conservative; when shown the text of a Bush campaign speech, Sen. Orrin Hatch of Utah guessed that its author was Illinois representative Phil Crane, the most conservative candidate in the race.[56] But Bush's Goldwater-era brand of conservatism had yet to catch up with the changes in the conservative movement that occurred during the 1970s. His opposition to abortion was less than absolute. (He wanted to allow it in cases of "rape, incest, or when the life of the mother is endangered.") Invoking the traditional but no longer regnant conservative orthodoxy that reductions in spending must accompany reductions in taxes, Bush offhandedly decried Reagan's tax cut proposal for the "economic madness" of its "voodoo economic policies."[57]

Unlike Reagan, Bush campaigned heavily in Iowa, whose caucuses had never been important in Republican nominating contests, and won a narrow victory. Claiming to have the "Big Mo" based on polls showing him surging in New Hampshire, Bush assumed that momentum alone would carry him to victory in the state's primary, and after that "there's no stopping me."[58] Overconfidence meant "he wasn't quite as responsive as we hoped" to staff recommendations that he offer the voters clear stands on the issues, said campaign manager James Baker.[59] Reagan ramped up his campaigning; grounded his speeches in the new conservative emphases on tax cuts, greater defense spending, and social issues; routed Bush in a televised debate; and soared to victory in the primary by 50 percent to 23 percent.

After losing New Hampshire, Bush won a few northern primaries, but Reagan won everything else, clinching the nomination on May 20 even as Bush was winning that day's Michigan contest. Although Bush wanted to fight on, Baker convinced him that "he would blow any chance of getting on the ticket if he ran a hopeless campaign much longer."[60] Reagan already resented Bush for disparaging his tax cut proposal and implying that he was too old to be president, and Bush disdained any interest in being vice president. "Take Sherman and cube it," he said, referring to Civil War general William Tecumseh Sherman's oft-quoted declaration that he would not run for president if nominated and would not serve if elected.[61] But, politically secure on his right flank, Reagan wanted a moderate conservative on the ticket, preferably someone with the foreign policy experience he lacked. The only suitable running mate who polled better than Bush was former president Ford. After negotiations at the Republican convention to bring Ford onto the ticket as a kind of "co-president" foundered when Reagan realized what a bad idea sharing executive power would be, Reagan called Bush, who by now was eager for the invitation.[62] The night before, when it appeared that Ford was a sure thing, a shaken Bush had said, "That's it. I'm getting out of politics."[63] Instead he was offered the vice presidential nomination on the condition that he pledge to support the entire Republican platform, including tax cuts and the proposed pro-life constitutional amendment. "Enthusiastically," Bush replied.[64]

The vice presidency suited Bush. All of his jobs since leaving Congress in 1970 had been appointive positions whose purpose was to serve a president faithfully. During the campaign and as vice president, Bush staunchly supported Reagan and never tried to outshine him. "I'm for Mr. Reagan—blindly," Bush said in 1984.[65] The president genuinely valued the expert advice Bush was able to offer—always in private—based on his experience with international issues and wide acquaintance with foreign leaders. Reagan especially appreciated Bush's discretion after the president was shot by a would-be assassin on March 30, 1981. According to Baker, the White House chief of staff, Bush's refusal to seize the spotlight while Reagan underwent emergency surgery prevented "two negative and inaccurate messages" from being sent to foreign governments—"that the president was no longer in charge and the vice president was." "After the first three or four months" of the first term," Baker added, "Ronald Reagan developed total confidence in George Bush."[66]

Service as vice president is a useful credential for someone seeking his party's nomination for president, as Bush began doing as soon as he and Reagan were reelected in 1984. The two-term limit imposed by the Twenty-Second Amendment in 1951 makes it possible for the vice president to step forward as a presidential candidate during the president's second and final term without alienating the president. In addition, the many trips around the country that vice presidents make as state and local party builders (campaigning during election years and raising funds between elections) and as public advocates of the administration and its policies uniquely situate the vice president to win friends among the party activists who influence presidential nominations.[67]

Just weeks after the 1984 election, Reagan's political director, Lee Atwater, wrote a long memo to Bush offering a strategy for winning the presidential nomination in 1988. It knitted together "country club" Republicans, who already were inclined to support him, with "Populists—generally middle class and lower middle class—across the country [who] are . . . anti–Big Government, anti–Big Business, anti–Big Labor," and "hostile to the media."[68] Atwater arranged meetings between the vice president and southern party leaders as well as prominent Christian conservatives to lock in their support, hoping to create a "fire wall" so that no matter what happened in Iowa and New Hampshire, Bush would win the nomination by sweeping the South on Super Tuesday, which Atwater called "the pig in the python."[69] The booming economy already made it easy for Bush to embrace the idea that the president's tax policies, far from being "voodoo," were exactly the medicine the country needed. Bush's viewing of the movie *Silent Scream* (1984), which showed what happens to a fetus as it is being aborted, lent fervor to his pro-life position, as did some of his adult children's decisions to adopt children of their own.[70]

Atwater also made sure that Vice President Bush missed no opportunity to campaign for and with Republican candidates in the 1986 midterm election, with a particular focus on the thirty-six gubernatorial contests. Because governors are leaders within their states rather than in Washington, Atwater knew, they could do more good for the presidential candidate they supported in their local primaries and caucuses than the senators who favored Sen. Bob Dole of Kansas or the representatives who endorsed Rep. Jack Kemp of New York, Bush's main rivals for the nomination. The midterm was disastrous for Republicans campaigning for Congress, but the party gained eight additional governorships. Bush was able to secure the support of big-state governors such as George Deukmejian of California, Mel Martinez of Florida, and John Engler of Michigan, as well as governors in states that had important early nominating contests, notably John Sununu of New Hampshire and Carroll Campbell of South Carolina.[71] "Governors live among the constituents and dispense all the patronage," said Sununu.[72]

Perversely, vice presidents who are nominated by their party for president carry certain disadvantages into the fall campaign that are as surely grounded in the office as the advantages they bring to the nominating contest.[73] Indeed, some of the activities of the modern vice presidency that are most appealing to the party activists who influence nominations may repel members of the broader electorate that decides the general election. Days and nights spent fertilizing the party's grass roots with fervent, sometimes slashing political rhetoric can alienate voters who look to the presidency for leadership that unites rather than divides.

Certain institutional qualities of the modern vice presidency also handicap the vice president who becomes a presidential nominee. Vice presidents must work hard to gain a share of the credit for the successes of the administration, but they can count on being attacked by the other party's presidential nominee for all of the administration's shortcomings. Such attacks allow no good response. A vice president who tries to stand apart may alienate the president and cause voters to wonder why the criticisms were not voiced earlier, when they might have made a difference. Vice presidents can always say that loyalty to the president forecloses public disagreement, but that course is no less perilous. The public that values loyalty in a vice president values other qualities in a potential president. Strength, independence, and vision are what most voters look for—the very qualities that vice presidents almost never have an opportunity to display.[74]

Bush had to overcome all of these challenges. During election week in 1984, the popular *Doonesbury* cartoonist Garry Trudeau lampooned him for having placed his "manhood in a blind trust."[75] In January 1986 the widely read conservative columnist George F. Will described Bush's placatory speeches to conservative groups as "a thin, tiny 'arf'—the sound of a lapdog."[76] On the eve of the 1988 campaign, *Newsweek* ran a cover story on Bush, "Fighting the Wimp Factor," that noted the widespread perception that he was not "strong enough or tough enough for the challenges of the Oval Office," based in part on his having served for nearly two decades in subordinate positions.[77] And starting on November 3, 1986, when it became known that the Reagan administration had secretly sold weapons to Iran and illegally diverted the profits to Contra rebels fighting to overthrow the elected Marxist government of Nicaragua, Vice President Bush faced serious questions about how deeply involved he was in the ongoing Iran-Contra scandal. As always, he refused to reveal anything about what he told the president in confidence while maintaining that, in this case, he was "out of the loop."[78]

Fortunately for Bush, opportunities arose early in the campaign to "fight the wimp factor." In a televised Republican debate on October 28, 1987, ten days after the *Newsweek* story appeared, Bush was the only candidate to forthrightly defend Reagan's Intermediate-Range Nuclear Forces treaty as an "agreement that takes out 1600 Soviet warheads for 400 of ours." He also told "Pierre"—the self-styled Gov. Pete DuPont—that his proposal to make Social Security voluntary was "nutty" and "dumb."[79] More dramatically, three months later Bush escaped an ambush on live television by *CBS Evening News* anchor Dan Rather, a liberal villain in the eyes of conservatives. When Rather pressed him relentlessly about his role in the Iran-Contra scandal, Bush fired back, "It's not fair to judge my whole career by a rehash on Iran. How would you like it if I judged your whole career by those seven minutes you walked off the set in New York?," which Rather recently had done (for six minutes) when his program was delayed by a tennis match.[80] Rather "stepped on his own dick" was Reagan's private assessment of the confrontation.[81] The anchor functioned as "high priest in the ceremonial de-wimping of George Bush," according to ABC News anchor Ted Koppel.[82]

De-wimped or not, Bush stumbled out of the gate in the February 8 Iowa caucuses. A suffering farm economy under Reagan made it the worst state in which to be the president's political heir. Bush compounded the problem by running a lazy campaign even after his third-place finish in the informal September 12, 1987, Iowa straw poll clearly indicated how much work he needed to do. Senator Dole of neighboring Kansas won the caucuses, and Reverend Robertson took advantage of the high concentration of charismatic Christians in the Iowa Republican electorate to finish second, his high-water mark as a presidential candidate.[83]

Bush ran an embarrassing third in Iowa, raising the stakes in New Hampshire, which voted eight days later. Governor Sununu, Bush's ally from the 1986 midterm election, took the chastened and now fully engaged candidate under his wing. Bush shook an estimated 50,000 hands, operated heavy equipment for the cameras when a blizzard struck, and, reluctantly, approved an ad attacking Dole for being unreliably opposed to tax increases. In contrast to Iowa, Robertson found few evangelicals in the state, and Reagan was popular among New Hampshire (and almost all other) Republicans. Another Bush ad played on his close association with the president: "When President Reagan wanted a vice president he could count on, he didn't call Bob Dole. He called George Bush." Bush won New Hampshire by 38 percent to 29 percent for Dole and swept to victory in nearly every remaining contest. He wrapped up the nomination earlier than anyone had in the modern era of primaries and caucuses.

Even so, Bush trailed his presumed Democratic rival, Michael Dukakis, by more than 15 percentage points when the primary season ended in June.

Senate Republican leader Bob Dole was Vice President George Bush's leading rival for the party's 1988 presidential nomination. Courtesy of the Dole Archive at the University of Kansas.

Adding to his distress was that his wife, Barbara Bush, portrayed in drag by comedian Phil Hartman, was being regularly mocked on *Saturday Night Live* for her appearance.[84] Bush's aides were convinced he would fall even further behind if he waited until after the Democratic convention in mid-July to begin his general election campaign. On April 25 Bush wrote in his diary, "gut issues" will dominate: "neighborhood, family, death penalty, and even abortion and prayer."[85] "We're going to strip the bark off the bastard," Atwater reportedly said of Dukakis.[86] Seven years earlier, in an interview with political scientist Alexander Lamis, Atwater had observed, "By 1968 you can't say 'nigger.' That hurts you. Backfires. So you say stuff like forced busing, states' rights, and all that stuff."[87]

Atwater assigned opposition researcher James Pinkerton to develop lines of attack. Pinkerton struck gold when he discovered that in 1976 Governor Dukakis vetoed a bill to end weekend furloughs for first-degree murderers and never apologized to the victims after inmate William Horton invaded a Maryland home, raped a woman twice, and then stabbed and pistol-whipped her fiancé in 1987. Dukakis also vetoed a 1977 bill requiring public school teachers to lead their students in the Pledge of Allegiance. When two focus groups of Reagan Democrats in Paramus, New Jersey, who initially regarded Dukakis as a moderate, competent governor, were told about these actions, "their mouths fell open."[88] On June 8, two weeks after the focus groups were conducted, Bush attacked "unsupervised weekend furloughs to first-degree murderers" in a speech; two weeks later, he mentioned Horton.[89] He later campaigned at a flag factory.

Bush also decided to distinguish his message ever so carefully from Reagan's, more to establish himself in voters' minds as a leader in his own right than to break with the president in any serious way. In May, having privately disagreed with Reagan about dropping federal drug charges against Panama's Manuel Noriega if he resigned from office, Bush publicly expressed his determination to prosecute the dictator.[90] In even more subtle ways, Bush's promises to take a "hands-on managerial approach" to the presidency, to be the "education president" and the "environmental president," and to bring about a "kinder, gentler America" were all designed to differentiate him—mildly—from the president. "Kinder and gentler than whom?" First Lady Nancy Reagan sniffed.

In every other way, Bush embraced Reagan in his acceptance speech at the Republican convention in mid-August, just as Reagan embraced him for having "played a major role in everything we've accomplished."[91] "When you have to switch horses in midstream," Bush declared, "doesn't it make sense to switch to the one who's going the same way?" Famously, he laid out a scenario in which Congress repeatedly came to him demanding more taxes. "I'll say no," Bush said, and "I'll say no . . . again." When Congress still doesn't get the message, "I'll say to them, 'Read my lips: No new taxes.'"[92]

Richard Darman, Bush's chief economic adviser, had tried, unsuccessfully, to get the "read my lips" line out of Bush's acceptance speech and "was livid," according to White House chief of staff John Sununu, when it stayed in.[93] "It was fine," Darman said, "to be against raising taxes. But it was imprudent to be absolutist" and "lock himself into a box."[94] Politically, however, Bush was already locked in. Months earlier, he had signed the Taxpayer Protection Pledge. As for the line, it helped make the speech the best—and best-delivered—of Bush's career. Doubts that he could pull it off without looking silly—"read my lips" was a well-known tough-guy quote from the film *Dirty Harry*—were assuaged when media coach Roger Ailes assured the rest of the staff, "I can make him say any line right."[95] Ailes's confidence was not misplaced. "Bush for the first time looked presidential," Arthur Schlesinger conceded in his diary.[96] Postconvention polls showed Bush in the lead.

From August through November, Bush never trailed. A typical campaign day involved him attacking and Dukakis defending on matters such as the Pledge of Allegiance, furloughs, high taxes in Massachusetts, national defense, Dukakis's liberalism (which Republicans treated as an obscenity, the "L-word"), and his membership in the American Civil Liberties Union ("ACLU" became another four-letter word when Bush spoke it). Bush even attacked Dukakis on the environment, a seeming strength of the Democrat until the Bush campaign featured the polluted Boston Harbor in a campaign ad. From late September to early October, two prison furlough–related commercials ran on television: one by an independent group called Americans for Bush that featured a scary picture of Horton and the other a Bush campaign ad filmed in Utah that showed convicts (nearly all of them portrayed by white students from Brigham Young University) coming in and out of prison through a revolving door.[97] The campaign's ad did not show or mention Horton, but Bush regularly did in speeches. An angry Susan Estrich, Dukakis's campaign manager, charged, "You can't find a stronger metaphor, intended or not, for racial hatred in this country than a black man raping a white woman."[98]

Both Bush and Dukakis were experienced, well-mannered, and intelligent public servants. Dukakis campaigned that way and Bush, who believed that politicking is the intrinsically squalid rite of passage one must undergo in order to do the real work of governing, did not. The share of voters who thought Dukakis was a liberal rose from 27 percent in May to 56 percent in November, and they broke two-to-one for Bush.

Bush's greatest strengths as a candidate lay well beyond his brutally effective and Dukakis's ineffective campaigns, important as they were to the outcome of the election. The economy was strong. During the eight years Bush served in the Reagan administration, inflation fell from 12.0 percent to 4.4 percent, unemployment from 7.2 percent to 4.4 percent, and interest rates from 20.0 percent to 9.3 percent. Eighteen million jobs were created, and the gross domestic product doubled. In addition, President Reagan was both popular and, more than any other departing incumbent in history, willing to share credit for his achievements with the vice president. He regularly praised Bush's work on regulatory relief, drug enforcement, and arms control in thirty-five campaign speeches in sixteen states.

On Election Day, Bush prevailed by 53.4 percent to 45.6 percent in the national popular vote and by 426 to 111 in the Electoral College, carrying all but a handful of states in the Pacific Northwest, the Upper Midwest, and the Northeast. He swept the South with a record 81 percent of the white evangelical vote but lost about 500 counties that Reagan had won elsewhere in the country.[99] Although his victory was convincing—neither his electoral vote nor his popular vote majority has been exceeded in any subsequent election—Bush secured no mandate. The Republicans lost ground in the House, the Senate, the governorships, and the state legislatures—the first time this ever had happened to a winning presidential candidate's party. Not having proposed much in the way of new policies during the campaign, Bush could not plausibly claim strong public support for even a modest legislative agenda. The voter turnout rate in 1988 was 50.2 percent, the lowest since 1924, and 68 percent of Americans agreed that the "presidential campaign has been one of the worst in history."[100] "That's history," Bush said of the campaign shortly before his inauguration. "That doesn't mean anything anymore."[101]

BOB DOLE

Bob Dole was of the same generation as George Bush, born in 1923, just a year earlier. Like his rival for the Republican presidential nomination in 1980 and 1988, Dole was a political figure who grounded his career in Washington in the old-style conservatism that focused on economic issues in general and fiscal prudence in particular. Like Bush, too, Dole was often prone to speak in seemingly disconnected sentence fragments rather than soaring oratory and eschewed the "vision thing" in favor of the daily grind of political campaigning and policy enactment. Both men had been young athletes, and both fought valiantly in World War II. In the 1980s both dutifully and then enthusiastically aligned themselves with Reagan, and each claimed credit for helping the president to enact the major elements of his agenda.

There the similarities between Dole and Bush ended and the differences, which struck both of them as more important, began. Unlike Bush, Dole said resentfully, "I didn't have rich and powerful parents."[102] He grew up during the Great Depression in small-town Russell, Kansas, where his mother and father rented out their house to bring in income while the family lived in the basement. A strapping letterman for Russell High School in football, basketball, and track, Dole planned to play basketball for the legendary Coach Phog Allen at the University of Kansas en route to medical school and a career as a doctor. These plans were interrupted and then ruined by the war. In 1945 Dole was severely wounded in Italy, causing paralysis from the neck down and hospitalizing him for the next two years. He grittily fought his way to recovery, regaining nearly everything but the use of his right arm and hand. His ambitions turned from medicine to law and politics.

Dole was elected to the Kansas state legislature in 1950 and served there while earning a living as county attorney for Russell County. Rising up the party's ranks in his heavily Republican state, he was elected to Congress in 1960 at age thirty-seven and to the Senate in 1968 when the incumbents retired. Dole also served as Republican National Committee chair starting in 1971. He deeply resented the way the 1972 Nixon reelection campaign "treated the Republican Committee like a poor cousin" (Dole is the one who branded the Committee to Re-elect the President as CREEP).[103] He also felt badly used both by Nixon, who replaced him as RNC chair with Bush in 1972, and by Bush for pretending in a meeting with Dole that he did not know he was taking the job when he actually did.

Dole's deep competitiveness and partisanship sometimes burst unattractively through his dryly witty public demeanor. Facing a tough Senate reelection campaign in 1974, a strong Democratic year, against popular congressman and doctor Bill Roy, Dole lashed out at the end of a debate: "Why do you do abortions? And why do you favor abortion on demand?"[104] Dole won and, in 1976, seeing an opportunity for Republicans in the Democratic platform's rejection of a pro-life constitutional amendment, persuaded the GOP to add a plank endorsing a proposal to "restore protection of the right to life for unborn children."[105] President Ford tapped him as his vice presidential running mate, counting on Dole to carry the attack to Carter so that Ford could take the high road. "You're going to be the tough guy," Ford told him.[106] In the first-ever vice presidential debate, tough lapsed into harsh when Dole said he did not think it was fair to make Watergate an issue any more than "Democrat wars," a reference to the "1.6 million . . . killed and wounded" in World Wars I and II, the Korean War, and the Vietnam War— all begun under Democratic presidents. Dole suffered by comparison with his Democratic opponent, Walter Mondale, but he may have helped offset Carter's appeal as a farmer in the normally Republican farm states of the Great Plains.

Dole launched a barely organized bid for the Republican presidential nomination in 1980, which ended quickly when he received only 597 votes—less than one-half of 1 percent—in the New Hampshire primary. During the Reagan years, Dole rose in the Senate, becoming majority leader after Howard Baker retired in 1984. He was a loyal but undogmatic supporter of Reagan's tax-cutting, supply-side economic policies, sometimes persuading the president to raise taxes when the annual budget deficit exploded. His true feeling emerged when he quipped, "Good news is that a bus full of supply-siders went over a cliff last night. Bad news is there were three empty seats."[107] Approaching the end of Reagan's second term, Dole regarded himself as the logical heir based on his effectiveness promoting the president's agenda on Capitol Hill.

Like Bush, the well-connected Dole was able to raise plenty of money for his 1988 nomination campaign. Overlearning the lesson of his failed 1980 bid, however, Dole spent way too much on organization, building a top-heavy, burdensomely expensive campaign structure riddled with ego and conflict. He won a solid caucus victory in neighboring Iowa on the theme "He's one of us" and headed into New Hampshire as the front-runner. On the Friday before the primary, Dole's veteran pollster, Richard Wirthlin, told him he was all but certain to win.[108] But Bush ran a frenetic weekend campaign in the blizzard-bound state, leaving Dole to lament, "Maybe I could have done that . . . if I was whole."[109] In the final debate on Sunday night, Governor DuPont handed Dole the written pledge that he and the other candidates had already signed to oppose any increase in the "marginal income tax rate for individuals and business" as well as any "reduction or elimination of deductions and credits" unless matched by lower rates.[110] "Sign it," DuPont said, but Dole, who despite promising again and again during the campaign that he would not raise taxes, replied, "Give it to George. I'd have to read it first."[111] By dismissing the matter on live television in the famously tax-averse state, Dole unwittingly reinforced the message of Bush's final-weekend commercials, which labeled him "Senator Straddle" for taking "both sides" on taxes and other issues.

Republican presidential nominee George Bush announced his controversial
choice for a running mate in 1988, Dan Quayle, on the eve of the Republican
National Convention. Courtesy of the George Bush Presidential Library.

Dole lost New Hampshire to Bush by 9 points. Asked that night by NBC News anchor Tom Brokaw if he had a message for the vice president, he snarled, "Tell him to stop lying about my record."[112] It was all downhill from there. Bush swept the Super Tuesday primaries; Dole came within 10 percentage points of him in only three states. Dole withdrew soon afterward, hoping to secure a second vice presidential nomination. He was one of the finalists on Bush's short list and, like Bush in 1980, had a claim based on having been the runner-up in the primaries. In addition, Dole's stature as a senior Washington figure promised to offset any advantage Dukakis gained from putting Senator Bentsen on the Democratic ticket. But Dole's personal dislike of Bush was reciprocated. Dole has a "bitter, jealous, and class conscious hatred for me," Bush wrote in his diary after Super Tuesday.[113] Nor did Bush trust the temperamentally independent Dole to be as loyal to him as Bush had been to Reagan.

Bush's decision to pass on Dole left the senator disappointed but unbowed. Although he had hoped to parlay the vice presidency into a presidential nomination in 1996, he could run then anyway. In the meantime, Dole's stature as Senate Republican leader was undiminished by Bush's decision not to put him on the ticket.

JACK KEMP

Jack Kemp was the closest thing to a Republican rock star during the decade preceding the 1988 election. A Los Angeles native, born in 1935, Kemp was sufficiently impressive as the country's leading small-college quarterback at Occidental College that he was drafted to play professionally in the newly formed American Football League (AFL). Starting with the Los Angeles (soon San Diego) Chargers in 1960, he spent most of the decade with the Buffalo Bills, leading them to two league championships. He also cofounded the AFL's Players Association and led it for five years, using his position to fight against discrimination by, for example, persuading teams to pair roommates across racial lines. Interested not just in union affairs and racial integration but also in politics and economics, Kemp was called "the Senator" by his teammates. Few were surprised in 1970 when, after working on the staff of California governor Ronald Reagan during the 1967 off-season, Kemp ran for Congress as a Republican in New York's Thirty-Ninth District, composed mostly of Buffalo's working-class suburbs. Kemp's popularity as a winning quarterback and ebullient campaigner transcended his party's appeal in the mostly Democratic district, along with his union leadership and growing reputation as a self-described "bleeding-heart conservative."[114]

Kemp's "bleeding heart" was manifest in his concern for people downtrodden by prejudice and poverty. His "conservative" identity was grounded in his belief in the power of the free market to foster economic growth and thereby create jobs and opportunities for those who lacked them. He became the leading champion in congressional and Republican circles of supply-side economics, with its promise that steep tax cuts would do more good for the economy than budget deficits would do harm. More than anyone else, Kemp shifted his party's center of gravity from a preoccupation with reducing federal spending to a newfound emphasis on cutting federal taxes. A corollary to his theory was that tax cuts would fuel so much economic growth that higher revenues born of lower marginal rates on much greater incomes eventually would cause deficits to disappear—not that Kemp really cared about deficits. In 1978, the year of the "tax revolt" spurred by the passage of California's Proposition 13, Kemp persuaded the Republican National Committee to endorse his proposed Kemp-Roth tax bill. As the GOP's presidential nominee in 1980, Reagan picked up and ran with the Kemp-Roth proposal to reduce federal income taxes by 30 percent over three years.

Kemp was one of eight prospective vice presidential nominees whom Reagan considered, but as biographers Morton Kondracke and Fred Barnes have written, "A Reagan-Kemp ticket would have paired a former movie actor with a former football player"—an overdose of celebrity when what Reagan needed was a running mate with established governing credentials.[115] Kemp was instead reelected to his sixth congressional term and, in preparation for the new Congress, was chosen by his Republican colleagues as conference chair, the party's third-ranking House leadership position.

Kemp championed Reagan's 1981 tax cuts but disagreed with his subsequent tax increases. Arguably, Kemp "was more loyal to his idea of Reagan's basic beliefs than to particular policies Reagan might be advancing"—in contrast to Vice President Bush's down-the-line support for whatever the president's agenda happened to be.[116] Kemp sought the Republican presidential nomination in 1988, claiming (like Bush and Dole) to be the true heir to Reagan's antitax fervor and sunny optimism. The House of Representatives was an unlikely launching pad for a presidential campaign, but so were the offices occupied by Bush and Dole. No incumbent vice president had been elected president since 1836, and no incumbent party leader in the Senate had ever been elected. Kemp could at least point to 1880, when Rep. James A. Garfield won the presidential election.

Kemp was a youthful (even at age fifty-three), energetic, and, for many younger Republicans, inspirational candidate. But his campaign was seriously flawed, not least by what he later described as his own "ego, pride, and conceit that I was the only 'true believer.' What nonsense!"[117] Kemp was an undisciplined orator whose speeches "made twenty-two points badly instead of three points memorably and well."[118] All too often those points were about Malthus, Maimonides, Treasury bills, and other obscure topics. He eschewed the boring but necessary tasks of a national campaign. "He didn't want to make his fund-raising calls or practice for debates, for instance," wrote Ed Rollins, the Kemp campaign's national chairman.[119] Above all, as appealing as Kemp's devotion to low taxes was to Republican voters, his disregard for fiscal restraint—"the politics of root canal," he called it—struck many of them as a bridge too far.[120] In his announcement speech on April 6, 1987, Kemp opposed reductions in federal spending on Social Security, Medicare, food stamps, Head Start, and other familiar conservative targets. He dismissed as irrelevant the campaign for a balanced-budget amendment to the Constitution, an enormously popular cause within the party. Kemp opposed state right-to-work laws, describing himself as part of "the

Lane Kirkland wing of the Republican Party."[121] In truth, there was no such wing. Kemp alone, it seemed, chose to identify with the ardently Democratic head of the AFL-CIO.

Kemp ran third or fourth in most Republican caucuses and primaries in 1988, trailing not just Bush and Dole but also Pat Robertson before dropping out on March 9, the day after Super Tuesday. Like Dole, Kemp made it onto Bush's short list for the vice presidential nomination and hoped to use it as a springboard to another presidential campaign in 1996. Like Dole, too, he was rejected by Bush as too independent-minded to serve as a reliably loyal lieutenant, as well as (unlike Dole) too verbose for Bush to want to deal with every day. When it came to both Kemp and Dole, Bush was unwilling to do what Reagan did when making Bush his running mate in 1980: get over his personal discomfort with a highly credentialed party leader and put him on the ticket.

DAN QUAYLE

In 1968 George Bush was excited by the prospect that Richard Nixon might choose a young, attractive, conservative member of Congress as his vice presidential candidate in the presidential election—him. Nixon decided to go in a different direction, but the approach apparently still made sense to Bush twenty years later when, as the Republican nominee for president, he chose the young, attractive, conservative member of Congress Dan Quayle to run with him.

Quayle was a forty-one-year-old senator from Indiana when Bush tapped him for vice president. He was born in Indianapolis and, after growing up in Arizona, returned to his native state for high school, college at DePauw University, and law school at Indiana University. He married fellow law student Marilyn Tucker, whose conservative political and religious views were more developed than his own. Between college and law school, Quayle worked family connections (his maternal grandfather, Eugene Pulliam, owned the *Indianapolis Star* and several other newspapers) to secure a place in the Indiana National Guard rather than be drafted into the army and, it seemed likely at the time, deployed to fight in Vietnam. Quayle's first job out of law school was as associate publisher for another of his family's papers, the *Huntington Herald-Press*, in the northeastern part of the state.

In 1976, at age twenty-nine, Quayle was elected to Congress, winning the Republican nomination because no one else thought the eight-term Democratic incumbent could be beaten. Two years later Quayle was easily reelected. In 1980 he challenged another seemingly invulnerable Democratic incumbent, Birch Bayh, and was elected to the Senate. "I pretty well knew at that time that I would someday try to figure out how to run for president," Quayle said.[122] His early success as a candidate was remarkable. At age thirty-three, he was the youngest newly elected senator in Indiana history. His reelection margins to the House in 1978 and the Senate in 1986 were the largest ever recorded in the district and state, respectively.

Quayle was a reliably conservative member of Congress, specializing in issues related to national defense. But he was willing to reach across the aisle on certain matters, including the Job Training Partnership Act of 1982, a bill he cosponsored with the liberal Democratic senator Edward M. Kennedy whose passage is chronicled in a closely observed and generally admiring study of Quayle by the eminent congressional scholar Richard Fenno.[123] On the eve of his reelection to the Senate, Quayle told Fenno, "I haven't had many failures. So I just keep going on the theory that when you're hot, you're hot. . . . I never earned my spurs as they say. And I guess I'm still flying high."[124] Quayle later wrote, "My win in 1986 was so lopsided, and the Reagan-Bush administration found itself in such hot water over Iran-contra, that I briefly contemplated making a run for President myself in 1988."[125] Instead, after Bush won the New Hampshire primary, Quayle launched a quiet campaign to be chosen as his running mate, writing op-eds and giving speeches to enhance his public profile.

"Still flying high" and "never earned my spurs" turned out to be revealing phrases when Bush chose Quayle in 1988. The process was intensely secretive. Bush disliked the approach taken by Carter in 1976 and Mondale in 1984 of publicly inviting prospective candidates to his home for lengthy interviews. Nor did he much admire Dukakis's practice of campaigning with potential running mates in 1988. Regarding those approaches as undignified and humiliating for the losers, Bush swung to the opposite extreme in making his own choice. He asked attorney Robert Kimmitt to compile background material on prospective candidates and, James Baker recalled, "nobody saw the material that the potential candidates supplied except the vice president."[126] Nor did Bush interview any of them himself, even privately. Working alone, Bush distilled the list to six names: Dole, Kemp, Quayle, former secretary of transportation Elizabeth Dole, and Senators Alan Simpson of Wyoming and Pete Domenici of New Mexico. (Domenici withdrew from consideration).[127]

Bush decided that he wanted a vice president in his own image, one who would be loyal, self-effacing, and grateful for the honor. When it came to Quayle, he loved that "I'm sixty-four and he's forty-one."[128] Choosing the young Hoosier as the first baby boomer on a national ticket "would make a generational difference," Bush wrote in his diary.[129] He also thought, inaccurately, that Quayle's youth would appeal to young voters and his good looks would attract support from women. Kimmitt told Bush about Quayle entering the national guard to avoid the draft but may not have appreciated the political implications of that decision. In any event, George W. Bush had done the same thing, and his father was unlikely to think it disqualifying.[130] Because Bush did not tell any of his campaign aides whom he intended to choose, none of them was in a position to advise him differently. Close advisers Baker, Craig Fuller, Robert Teeter, and Roger Ailes had a betting pool on the choice. No one bet on Quayle. As a result, no one bothered to arrange for Republican senators who knew Quayle to praise him to the media or even to compile briefing materials that they could use to explain the decision on interview programs. "Nobody was lined up," fumed Marilyn Quayle.[131]

Instead, Bush revealed his choice only when he arrived at New Orleans's Spanish Plaza on the SS *Natchez* riverboat on August 16, the Tuesday of convention week, making Quayle the last vice presidential nominee to be unfurled that late in the process. Bush's aides were so desperate for information about Quayle that James Pinkerton sent a junior staffer racing to a local bookstore to buy a copy of *The Almanac of American Politics*. Quayle himself wrote that when, beaming ecstatically and sweating heavily after rushing from the hotel to the plaza, he and Bush appeared together for the first time, "I looked like the guy on the game show who'd just won the Oldsmobile."[132] Others compared the excited Quayle to "a puppy let off his leash."[133] Still worse, at Quayle's first press conference, "I sounded as if I had joined the Guard to escape the war." "I did not know in 1969 that I would be in this room today," he told the press. At the end of convention week, Bush wrote in his diary, "It was my decision and I blew it, but I'm not about to say I blew it."[134]

The Bush campaign assigned veteran handlers Stuart Spencer and Joe Canzeri to monitor Quayle, who resented their lack of confidence in his abilities. Although they sent him to obscure locations until November to shore up support from Republican voters, there was no hiding a major party nominee for vice president. In the twelve days after Quayle was nominated, the three broadcast networks' evening news programs aired ninety-three stories about him, more than they had done on Dukakis during the entire primary season.[135] Nor was there any avoiding the vice presidential debate with Bentsen. Quayle's own verdict on his debate performance—"I

George Bush and Michael Dukakis, the Republican and Democratic candidates for president in 1988, faced off in two debates. Courtesy of the George Bush Presidential Library.

was awkward and stiff"—marked the least of his problems.[136] The worst came when, hounded repeatedly by the debate panel about his qualifications, Quayle said, "I have as much experience in the Congress as Jack Kennedy did when he sought the presidency." To devastating effect, Bentsen replied, "I served with Jack Kennedy. . . . Senator, you're no Jack Kennedy."

In truth, Quayle was at least as accomplished a senator as Kennedy had been, but the Kennedy whom voters remembered was not the senator but the president. The Dukakis campaign quickly aired an ad with the Bentsen put-down followed by: "President Quayle?"

For all its flaws—including trimming several points off Bush's victory margin in November—the Quayle nomination was not an unmitigated disaster.[137] "We got Kemp without Kemp," said Lee Atwater sunnily: youth and enthusiasm without unmanageable independence.[138] Evangelicals liked that the Quayles belonged to a theologically conservative Presbyterian church.[139] Although polls showed that twice as many people thought Quayle lost the debate to Bentsen as won it, his "qualified-unqualified" ratio immediately rose from 37 percent to 52 percent negative to a more neutral 47 percent to 48 percent as Republican voters rallied to his defense.[140] And, Estrich observed, Bush's willingness to stand by Quayle "with strength and conviction" contributed to the effort to undermine his image of "weakness and of not being a stand-up guy."[141]

Curiously, although in choosing Quayle Bush adopted Eisenhower's approach in 1952 by pairing a senior presidential candidate with a junior running mate, he did not assign Quayle to carry the attack to the Democrats while staying on the high road himself, the role Ike assigned to Nixon. Instead Bush, still determined to remove the last traces of the "wimp" image, served as his own attack dog against Dukakis. Quayle ended the year wounded but still very much alive politically. He was vice president of the United States, with a large staff, an office in the West Wing, a seat in Oval Office meetings, and a budding protégé-mentor relationship with the president. No incumbent vice president had been dropped from a ticket since 1940, which was reassuring as Quayle looked ahead to 1992. The price for Bush of admitting a mistake and alienating whatever support the vice president developed within the party would be too high. And, with 1996 in mind, Quayle surely did not overlook that six of the eight most recent vice presidents had been nominated to run for president themselves.

PAT BUCHANAN

Despite his later claim to be leading "peasants with pitchforks" against "King George" and the rest of the political establishment, Patrick J. Buchanan was a Washington figure born (in 1938) and bred. Buchanan was raised in Georgetown, an Irish and German American middle-class neighborhood before it became posh in the early 1960s, by his ardently anticommunist father, an accountant, and his mother, a former nurse. Both parents were strong Catholics and sent their son to Gonzaga High School and, for college, to Georgetown University. In the mid-1950s Buchanan became an early subscriber to *National Review*. Reading the magazine inspired him to be a writer. In 1962, after earning a master's degree from the Columbia University journalism school, Buchanan began working for the conservative *St. Louis Globe-Democrat* as a sharply polemical editorial writer. He caught Richard Nixon's eye and joined him as an advance man and speechwriter during the 1966 midterm election. The Republicans made dramatic gains that year and, as Nixon had hoped, he received much of the credit. The campaign launched Nixon into his campaign for the presidency in 1968 as a winner, not the tarnished political loser of his failed bids for president in 1960 and governor of California in 1962.

Buchanan followed Nixon to the White House as one of three talented and, reflecting Nixon's own eclectic views and uneven temperament, politically diverse speechwriters: the liberal Ray Price, the moderate William Safire (both of them elegant writers whom the president relied on for statesmanlike rhetoric), and the conservative Buchanan, whose specialty was capturing Nixon's "rock 'em, sock 'em" style of partisan oratory. "Divide the country, sir, and we'll get the larger half," Buchanan counseled Nixon, disdaining advice from other aides who thought the country was divided enough over the Vietnam War and racial issues.[142] Along those lines, Buchanan wrote the address in which Nixon claimed to represent the "great silent majority" of Americans, as well as several highly publicized speeches in which Vice President Spiro Agnew attacked various liberal critics as "an effete corps of impudent snobs" and a new-style "4-H club: hopeless, hysterical, hypochondriacs of history."[143] After Nixon was reelected in 1972, basically by adding the 14 percent of the national popular vote received by Wallace in 1968 to the 43 percent Nixon himself won in that election, Buchanan told Nixon: "Our future is in the Democratic working man, Southern Protestants and Northern Catholics."[144]

Buchanan prided himself on being a brass-knuckles fighter with a blue-collar style. He was one of the last in Nixon's orbit to accept that the president had to resign in 1974 when White House tape recordings (which Buchanan urged Nixon to burn) revealed that he obstructed justice in the Watergate case. Nixon's successor, Gerald Ford, did not appreciate Buchanan's pugnacious, hard-edged, and strongly conservative persona and cut him loose from the White House staff. Ford also vetoed a recommendation from his first chief of staff, Al Haig, that Buchanan be appointed ambassador to the all-white government of South Africa. Returning to the

Globe-Democrat as a syndicated columnist with a national audience, Buchanan supported Reagan's campaign to displace Ford as the Republican nominee in 1976. When Ford won the nomination, Buchanan urged Reagan to run as an independent candidate.

Along with liberal columnist Tom Braden, Buchanan extended his audience in 1978 by cohosting a radio talk show, which four years later became the nightly *Crossfire* program on CNN. *Crossfire* created a new cable television genre: loudly polemical debates between a host and guest "on the right" and a host and guest "on the left." Buchanan, who praised *Crossfire* as "a no-B.S. show," was also a feisty regular on another popular new fight club–style political talk show, *The McLaughlin Club*. The "training" he got on these shows, Buchanan said, was "extraordinary for a candidate. Almost nothing catches you off guard. You are able to articulate your views clearly, sharply, and briefly."[145] As Steve Kornacki has pointed out, "Without ever running for office, Buchanan had become one of the best-known conservatives in America."[146]

Reagan's second-term chief of staff, Donald Regan, brought Buchanan into the White House as communications director, where he served from 1985 to early 1987. But Buchanan's brand of conservatism placed him farther right than Reagan, whom he subsequently criticized as "a president of the Order for Peaceful Coexistence" because of his insufficiently anti-Soviet views, as well as for allowing the "continued socialization" of the United States to "proceed apace."[147] Politically, Buchanan was convinced that "the greatest political vacuum in American politics is to the right of Ronald Reagan."[148] In truth, Buchanan's brand of conservatism—isolationist in national security matters, protectionist in trade, and restrictionist toward immigration—had more in common with his party's pre–World War II ideology than with Reagan's open and optimistic version.[149]

On January 14, 1987, one month before Buchanan left the White House, two dozen leading activists who shared his opinion that the president was not conservative enough and regarded Bush and Dole as even less orthodox, gathered in Buchanan's living room. The group, which included Phyllis Schlafly, Howard Phillips, Richard Viguerie, and Paul Weyrich, urged him to seek the Republican nomination for president in 1988. Buchanan eventually decided not to, saying that he did not want to divide the right and thereby jeopardize Kemp's chances.[150] But his decision not to run came only after he gave serious consideration to doing so and was more a matter of "not now" than "never."[151] In the meantime, Buchanan regained his public platform by resuming his syndicated column and returning to *Crossfire*,

The McLaughlin Group, and a new weekly shoutfest that began on CNN in 1988, *The Capital Gang*.

Another potential candidate who, like Buchanan but unlike most other prominent Republicans, viewed the United States as endangered by its allies as much by its enemies was a young New York businessman, Donald J. Trump, who recently had gained notoriety by publishing a best-selling book, *Trump: The Art of the Deal*. Speaking to a rally organized in 1987 by a group of supporters in New Hampshire, Trump declared, "I'm here because our country is being kicked around."[152] Singling out Japan and Saudi Arabia, Trump vowed to balance the federal budget by making these and other countries pay their debts. After briefly flirting with a candidacy, Trump, like Buchanan, decided not to run, later claiming that Bush considered him for the vice presidential nomination. In truth, Trump offered himself to Bush, who described the approach in his diary as "strange and unbelievable."[153]

The 1988 election answered one question—who would be president and vice president for the next four years?—but left others left hanging. On the Republican side, would Bush be readily nominated for a second term in 1992, or would he face the same sort of challenge for renomination faced by two of his three most recent predecessors, Ford and Carter? If the latter, who from a roster that included Dole, Kemp, and Buchanan would emerge to challenge him? If the former, would Bush keep Quayle on the ticket? And whether or not the president was reelected, who from this cohort of national Republican figures would run in 1996?

Even more questions faced the Democrats, whose choice of a presidential nominee in 1992 was unforeseeable. Would the party try to break its twelve-year losing streak by moving toward the center and nominating a Clinton or Gore? Or would it move even farther left in hopes of energizing its base and expanding the electorate by choosing a Jackson or Cuomo?

And with many voters dissatisfied with both major parties, would a popular independent candidate emerge, as had happened in two of the six most recent elections: George Wallace in 1968 and John Anderson in 1980?

Much would depend on how things went during the four years that would begin when George Bush was inaugurated on January 20, 1989.

3

DIVIDED GOVERNMENT
GEORGE BUSH AND THE DEMOCRATS
(AND ROSS PEROT), 1989–1991

Time magazine's sole criterion for choosing its Person of the Year was simple: Who in the previous twelve months had the biggest effect on the world "for better or worse"? At the end of 1990 its answer was President George Bush, both for better (his "resoluteness and mastery" of foreign affairs) and for worse (his "truly embarrassing" conduct of domestic affairs).[1] "I must say I hate dealing with Congress and these budget matters," Bush confided to his diary. "I much prefer foreign affairs."[2] White House aide Thomas Scully recalls "sitting in the Roosevelt Room with a bunch of veterans' groups one day and [Bush] was bored to tears about VA [Veterans Administration] stuff. Somebody asked about Israel and boom! It was like somebody hit him with a cattle prod. He woke up and shot into an incredibly cogent half-an-hour explanation of what was going on in Israel at that time."[3]

Bush became president by discrediting his Democratic opponent, Michael Dukakis, and by riding the crest of Ronald Reagan's transformational presidency. Reagan stood "second to none among presidents of the second half of the twentieth century," wrote the liberal historian Sean Wilentz, in "reshaping the basic terms on which politics and government would be conducted long after he left office."[4] He was a "reconstructive" president who built a new and enduring governing coalition out of the ashes of the old New Deal regime, according to political scientist Stephen Skowronek.[5] Without offering many ideas of his own before taking the oath as Reagan's successor in January 1989,

Bush declared, "We're coming in to build on a proud record that has already been established."[6] He embraced the role of "orthodox innovator," in Skowronek's phrase, a president who "came to power affiliated with a set of governing commitments that he affirmed forthrightly."[7]

As Skowronek also has shown, no orthodox innovator since James Monroe in 1820 was reelected to a second term. The same is true of another category of presidents into which Bush fit: "understudies." The five presidents whom Walter Dean Burnham identified as having been elected to conserve the transformational changes in public policy wrought by their immediate predecessor saw their share of the national popular vote fall from an above-average 55.0 percent when they first were elected to a catastrophic 38.8 percent when they ran for a second term—portentous numbers for Bush, who received 53.4 percent in 1988.[8] For both orthodox innovators and understudies, the challenge of holding together the majority coalition forged by a powerful predecessor has been too formidable to overcome.

For most of his tenure, Bush seemed likely to defy these historical patterns. His job approval rating remained above 60 percent during nearly all of his first two years as president, soaring to a then-record 89 percent after the collapse of the Soviet empire (and soon the Soviet Union itself) and the American victory in the Gulf War against the Saddam Hussein regime in February 1991. In the spring season of the "invisible primary"—the year before any votes are cast when candidates typically lay the foundation for a presidential campaign if they plan to run—multiple leading Democrats decided that Bush probably would be unbeatable in his bid for reelection in 1992. Most of them were young enough to wait until 1996, when Bush no longer would be on the ballot. But a few others, seeing that the path to the Democratic nomination was less crowded than usual and, like the president himself, anticipating a decline in Bush's political standing as the nation's attention turned to domestic affairs, began the hard work of assembling an organization, raising money, wooing party activists in the early primary and caucus states, and developing policy ideas and visionary themes that could undergird a successful candidacy.

Among those who eventually (and reluctantly) decided to stay on the sidelines were the two runners-up in the 1988 nominating contest, Sen. Al Gore of Tennessee and Rev. Jesse Jackson, along with Gov. Mario Cuomo of New York. All of them trailed Bush in a March 1991 trial heat poll by about 50 points.[9] The candidates who did run were generally thought of as constituting a weak field: two small-state Midwestern senators, Tom Harkin of Iowa and Bob Kerrey of Nebraska; former senator Paul Tsongas of

Massachusetts and former California governor Jerry Brown, both of whom had been out of office for about a decade; and two incumbent southern governors, Douglas Wilder of Virginia and Bill Clinton of Arkansas. (Their stories are told or, in Clinton's case, resumed later in this chapter.) Meanwhile, as Bush's standing declined throughout mid- and late 1991 among conservatives who still regarded him as a closet moderate, commentator Pat Buchanan emerged as a challenger for the Republican nomination. In addition, dissension within the GOP, along with growing public unhappiness about politics in general, created the conditions in which a significant third-party candidacy could arise, with public fascination growing in the Texas businessman Ross Perot.

THE BUSH PRESIDENCY: FOREIGN AFFAIRS

By experience and interest, George Bush was strongly oriented toward foreign policy. Although international affairs was not a prominent theme of his election campaign in 1988, it was in a sense the theme of his career, culminating in eight years as the most widely traveled vice president in history. Over time, Bush cultivated a broad personal acquaintance with world leaders. As president, he spent hours each day touching base with his fellow presidents and prime ministers by telephone. He also chose strong foreign policy advisers: former Reagan chief of staff and secretary of the Treasury James Baker as secretary of state, former Ford chief of staff Richard Cheney as secretary of defense, former air force general Brent Scowcroft as national security adviser (a position he also held in the Ford administration), and former Reagan national security adviser and army general Colin Powell as chairman of the Joint Chiefs of Staff. Equally important, the president forged his advisers into a cohesive team.

Bush's accomplishments in foreign policy nearly spanned the globe. He inherited two simmering problems in Latin America from the Reagan administration: one in Nicaragua and the other in Panama. In 1989 Bush was able to work out an agreement with Democratic congressional leaders on Nicaragua. The civil war in that country was the most acrimonious issue dividing Reagan from Congress, spurring White House aides to engage in the ill-advised secret sale of weapons to Iran and the illegal, under-the-table diversion of the profits to the Contra rebels—the Iran-Contra scandal. Although Bush and Secretary of State Baker were Contra supporters, they understood that the Democratic Congress could not be persuaded to approve new military assistance to the anticommunist rebel army. Determined to find a bipartisan solution that would end the long and enervating interbranch conflict over Contra aid, Baker and congressional leaders struck a deal to provide nonlethal assistance to the rebels for a limited period. The administration then roused sufficient pressure from Europe, the Soviet Union, Latin America, and Democratic members of Congress to persuade the Marxist Sandinista government to conduct a fair election in February 1990. To Bush's delight, the Sandinistas lost.

Bush acted militarily rather than diplomatically to accomplish his main objective in Panama, which was to remove from power the once pro-American, now anti-American dictator Gen. Manuel Noriega well before the scheduled transfer of the Panama Canal from the United States to Panama in 2000. In Bush's view, Noriega's offenses were legion: election fraud, money laundering, clandestine arms trading, and drug trafficking. (The Panamanian leader was indicted on the latter charge by a federal grand jury in Miami in 1988.) Matters came to a head when Noriega annulled the results of a presidential election. On December 15, 1989, the servile national legislature accorded him "maximum leader" status in a self-declared "state of war" with the United States. Five days later, Bush responded by sending 12,000 troops to the Canal Zone to join the 12,000 already stationed there. Their mission was to capture Noriega and return him to American soil to stand trial. Guillermo Endara, the winner of the annulled election, was sworn in as president. Operation Just Cause, as Bush named the Panama invasion, was the largest American military effort since Vietnam and was considerably more successful. Panama changed "the mindset of the American people about the use of force in the post-Vietnam era," according to Baker, and thereby "established an emotional predicate" for future interventions.[10]

In Eastern Europe, Bush oversaw the disintegration of the Soviet empire and, soon after, of the Soviet Union—a dream of presidents since Harry S. Truman that no one until Reagan imagined would come true. The Soviets "cannot vastly increase their military productivity because they've already got their people on a starvation diet," Reagan wrote in his diary in 1981, vowing to "go forward with an arms race and they can't keep up."[11] Bush was encouraging but not intrusive in 1989 and 1990 when first Poland, then East Germany, and then the other Soviet-dominated governments of Eastern Europe dissolved, followed in 1991 by the dissolution of the Soviet Union. With support from Bush overcoming British and Russian reluctance, Germany reunited on West German terms. Critics variously charged that the president was either too reticent in publicly celebrating communism's fall or too willing to interfere in other countries' affairs. In truth, Bush adroitly avoided both extremes. A more triumphant policy of "jump[ing] up and down on the Berlin wall," as some figuratively encouraged Bush to do, may well have provoked a defensive, even military, response from the Soviets.[12] "My mind kept racing over a possible Soviet crackdown," Bush wrote in his diary.[13] A less supportive stance could have turned the newly free and democratic governments of Eastern Europe away from the United States.

Although the near-half-century-long Cold War with the Soviet Union was over, it was far from clear what the world would be like without it. The president hoped to forge a "new world order" in which the United States, as the only remaining superpower, would foster free trade and peaceful relations among the nations. But the Bush administration did not view the end of the Cold War as marking the removal of all imperial ambitions from the globe. Instead, historian Jeffrey A. Engel has written, Bush envisioned a new international regime that was "bonded across Cold War lines, that would unite against aggression."[14] In the Middle East, his ambition faced— and passed—its first test.

The test came on August 1, 1990, when Iraq's brutal leader, Saddam Hussein, launched an invasion and occupation of Kuwait, a neighboring oil-rich state. Saddam believed that since losing the Vietnam War the United States had lost its stomach for serious military action in distant parts of the world, especially in a region where it had never fought a war. "This will not stand, this aggression against Kuwait," Bush declared. He quickly assembled a large and diverse multinational coalition to support and finance his Operation Desert Shield campaign. Knowing that it was important that this not just be a coalition of westerners, he worked the phone to rally the leaders of China, Japan, Europe, several Arab nations, and even the crumbling Soviet Union to support his strategy of diplomatic, economic, and military pressure on Iraq. By not humiliating the Soviets as their empire fell, he made possible their willingness to join the coalition against a traditional ally. Bush also dispatched nearly half a million soldiers to Saudi Arabia, overcoming its government's doubts about American resolve, and persuaded the other members of the coalition to pay $54 billion of the operation's $61 billion final cost.

When Hussein remained adamant in refusing to withdraw from Kuwait, Bush won strong approval from the United Nations on November 29, 1990, and narrow approval from Congress on January 12, 1991, to force out Iraq if it did not leave voluntarily by January 15. After the deadline came and went, Operation Desert Shield became Operation Desert Storm. On January 16, American and other allied bombers began a thirty-eight-day air

In a moment of triumph after the First Gulf War in 1991, President Bush surveys the scene with Gen. Norman Schwarzkopf, who commanded the coalition forces. Courtesy of the George Bush Presidential Library.

campaign to cripple Iraq's military and communications infrastructure. On February 23 the ground invasion was launched, and in four days, with fewer than 150 Americans killed in action, the allies' military offensive drove Iraqi forces out of Kuwait and severely weakened Saddam Hussein's capacity to threaten neighboring countries and dominate the world's petroleum market. Nevertheless, Hussein remained in power, much to Bush's surprise and disappointment. The president had expected that military defeat would lead to Hussein's overthrow by the Iraqis themselves.

Substantively and politically, the victory over Iraq was the high point of the Bush presidency. The patriotic fervor aroused by the Gulf War served to conceal long-standing differences about foreign policy between the Republican president and the Democratic Congress.[15] Not since the War of 1812 had Congress been so divided when approving the use of military force. Although Republicans lined up solidly in favor of the president (42–2 in the Senate and 165–3 in the House), Democrats voted against authorizing military action by large margins: 45–10 in the Senate and 179–86 in the House. Among congressional Democrats with presidential ambitions, Gore voted for the use-of-force resolution and House Democratic leader Richard Gephardt of Missouri and Senators Bill Bradley of New Jersey, Bob Kerrey of

Nebraska, and San Nunn of Georgia voted against it. Nunn's standing as a defense expert made his leadership of the opposition especially significant. Cuomo suggested "a deal with the Iraqis" that "gets them out of Kuwait for the most part, leaves them maybe a little bit on the water, leaves them a little bit of the oil."[16] Two days after the congressional vote, Gov. Bill Clinton of Arkansas muddled, "I guess I would have voted with the majority if it was a close vote. But I agree with the arguments the minority made."[17] The Bush administration issued a statement denying that the president needed legislative approval to implement the UN resolution authorizing the use of force.

Bush had already dodged a foreign policy–related political and perhaps legal bullet in August 1988 when Judge Gerhard Gesell decided to postpone the trial of White House national security council staffer Oliver North from mid-September until after the presidential election. In April 1989 the government's admission of facts in the case revealed that then vice president Bush knew more about the illegal funneling of funds to the Contras than he ever admitted. But the new president was still enjoying his honeymoon period and was not pressed on the matter to the extent he would have been during the campaign. Nor was the collapse of the Soviet empire free of complications. When Yugoslavia, which had been held together for decades by adroit leadership from Josip Broz Tito in the face of Soviet pressure, dissolved into warring ethnic states, brutally violent ethnic hatreds were unleashed. Bush was criticized for remaining aloof from the conflict on the grounds that, as Baker said, "we don't have a dog in this fight."[18]

Although he was not able to resolve every global issue or transcend every partisan difference over foreign policy, Bush displayed a deft and steady hand in the international arena throughout his tenure as president. One consequence was to create a false sense of security about his reelection. "Do you think the American people are going to turn to a *Democrat* now?" asked George W. Bush.[19] Office of Management and Budget director Richard Darman told Bush, "Mr. President, you could go out there and tell them that a depression is upon us and no one would even notice."[20] The president was doubtful. In March, just weeks after victory against Iraq, he noted in his diary that although the "common wisdom is I'll win in a runaway, I don't believe that. . . . The economy will make that determination."[21]

THE BUSH PRESIDENCY: DOMESTIC AFFAIRS

The collapse of the Soviet empire and the defeat of Iraqi aggression solidified Americans' opinion that President Bush was a maestro of foreign policy. His job approval rating not only soared to 89 percent in late February 1991 but remained above 70 percent well into the summer.²² Ironically, however, the widespread perception that, for the first time since the Japanese attacked Pearl Harbor in 1941, the world was peaceful enough that the country could turn its full attention to domestic affairs did not augur nearly as well for Bush's reelection. In the same poll in which nine in ten Americans approved his overall performance in office, fewer than four in ten said the same about his handling of the economy, the budget deficit, health care, or poverty.²³ During the summer the unemployment rate rose to 7 percent. Over time voters came to resent what they saw as Bush's concentration on the world's problems at the expense of their own, especially when after six boom years under Reagan a recession slowed economic growth from 2.5 percent in 1989 to 1.0 percent in 1990 and a negative 0.7 percent in 1991.²⁴ "What do these people have to do to get the president's attention?" Gephardt said of the unemployed. "Move to Kurdistan?"²⁵

In the 1988 presidential campaign, Bush portrayed himself as Reagan's true heir in domestic policy, albeit a "kinder, gentler" version of his conservative predecessor. Bush's "no new taxes" campaign pledge solidified his conservative Republican base even as his promises to be the "education president" and the "environmental president" and to do "whatever it takes to make sure the disabled are included in the mainstream" attracted support from moderate independents.

Once in office, Bush took the latter pledges more seriously than the former. In 1989 he hosted an "education summit" of the nation's governors at the University of Virginia. In 1990 he helped secure passage of the Americans with Disabilities Act and the Clean Air Act Amendments. The following year, after vetoing as a "quotas bill" a civil rights measure that placed the burden of proof on employers in discrimination lawsuits, he signed the Civil Rights Act of 1991, which was only cosmetically different from the version he vetoed. Bush signed it on November 21, just weeks after the stormy Senate confirmation hearings for Supreme Court nominee Clarence Thomas, an African American man who was charged by an African American woman, Anita Hill, with sexual misconduct when he was her boss at the Department of Education and the Equal Employment Opportunity Commission. Ominously, during the previous eight months, when the civil rights bill was being considered in Congress, frequent references to "Willie" Horton began appearing in related news stories that typically treated Bush's invocation of Horton in the 1988 election as an exercise in racism.²⁶

President George Bush, flanked by Democratic and Republican congressional leaders, faced politically difficult budget negotiations in 1990. Courtesy of the George Bush Presidential Library.

In every case the major legislation approved by Bush involved issues that voters traditionally associated with the Democratic Party and that, in the hands of a solidly Democratic Congress, ended up more liberal than Bush would have preferred. By putting up any resistance at all, Bush guaranteed that congressional Democrats, not he, would be credited with the bills' passage. By signing them, he revived conservative Republicans' suspicions that he was not one of them.

Bush's main challenge as president was to continue his predecessor's generally successful economic policies while smoothing out their rough edges, especially the huge budget deficits that had caused the national debt to grow more during the eight years of the Reagan administration than in the nation's previous 192 years combined—from about $1 trillion to $3 trillion. In March 1989 Darman, who had tried very hard to soften Bush's antitax pledge during the election, told the new president that he would need to "raise revenues" no later than the following year.[27] "I'm not going to be held up by campaign rhetoric," Bush wrote in his diary, offhandedly dismissing what for conservatives was his most important pledge and for voters in general his most explicit one.[28]

On June 26, 1990, congressional Democratic leaders agreed to enter negotiations to reduce the deficit after extracting from Bush a statement that "tax revenue increases" were necessary. "Read My Lips—I Lied!" was the headline in the next day's *New York Post*. On September 26 a five-year, $502 billion deficit reduction agreement was reached that included $134 billion in new revenue (mostly from increased federal taxes on gasoline, alcohol, and tobacco) and $368 billion in spending cuts. It was a solid win for the president, who got nearly $3 in Democratic concessions on spending for every $1 he made on taxes, with no increase in income tax rates. Yet conservative House Republicans, led by minority whip Newt Gingrich, rebelled at the tax hike—exactly the sort of thing Bush had feared when he moved Cheney from the House GOP whip position to the Defense Department.[29] On October 5 the agreement was voted down by 254 to 179, as Republicans sided with Gingrich over their president by 105 to 79. Democratic leaders then rammed through the Omnibus Budget and Reconciliation Act, a bill that raised the highest income tax bracket from 28 percent to 31.5 percent, which conservative Republicans liked even less. "Newt nuked the first deal," said Scully, "and we ended up with a much worse deal."[30] Bush swallowed hard, called it "a good plan," and signed it into law. A month later, after enduring serial barrages of outrage from conservatives who blamed the president for the tax increase while ignoring the spending cuts, Bush announced that the agreement made him "gag."[31] A "new norm" had arisen among conservatives, according to journalist E. J. Dionne, and "opposing all tax increases became the single most important test of philosophical loyalty."[32]

In March 1991, riding high politically after the triumph of Operation Desert Storm, Bush enjoyed a rare opportunity to mobilize Congress in support of a domestic legislative agenda. But he had no such agenda. As Sununu told a conservative audience in November 1990, "There's not a single piece of legislation that needs to be passed in the next two years for this president. In fact, if Congress wants to come together, adjourn, and leave, it's all right with us."[33] A cobbled-together "Domestic Desert Storm," which Bush sent to Congress on March 6, consisted of a transportation bill and a crime bill, neither of which excited anyone enough to persuade Congress to pass them.

"We didn't do that," lamented Baker, referring to Bush's failure to introduce a legislative agenda "around which we could build his [reelection] campaign. . . . That was our fault."[34] Opposition within the White House from Sununu and Darman smothered in their cradle a host of "New Paradigm" proposals to mobilize free market forces to address the problems of the poor, in part because the ideas were inspired by the endlessly talkative secretary of housing and urban development Jack Kemp, "Bush's least favorite member of the cabinet."[35] More generally, Bush "was sort of dismissive" of ideas, says James Pinkerton, Kemp's main ally on the White House staff. "He said, 'It's what's in my heart that matters,' and 'if you know me, you'll like me,' and things like that. That's a great argument if you're Henry V, but it's not such a great argument if you're trying to get demotic people to vote for you."[36] Bush instead endorsed a series of proposed constitutional amendments, six in all, most of them aimed at overturning liberal Supreme Court decisions on abortion, school prayer, flag burning, and other social issues. Conservative leaders recognized that none of these amendments had much chance of running the constitutionally arduous obstacle course to enactment any time soon and that, as with Bush's successful effort to rouse them by talking about the Pledge of Allegiance and prison furloughs in his 1988 campaign, their emotions were again being played.

Bush's economic advisers kept telling him that the recession ended in March 1991 and that economic growth would accelerate by the end of the year, in plenty of time for voters to change their minds about how successful the president's domestic policies had been. Yet the economy remained sluggish. Real economic growth averaged about 1 percent per year during the Bush administration, the lowest rate in any four-year period since the Great Depression. Americans' real per capita income fell, unemployment rose to 7.8 percent, and more businesses failed than during any presidential term since Herbert Hoover's. Because of the weak economy, tax revenues decreased even as government expenditures increased to meet the rising demand for unemployment insurance, food stamps, and other forms of public assistance. And so, despite the tax increase and spending cuts that Bush paid such a high political price to secure in 1990, the deficit continued to rise, eventually adding another trillion dollars to the national debt, raising it to $4 trillion by the time he left office.

Even while Bush was soaring in the polls, an event occurred in May 1991 that revealed another potential political liability. He collapsed while running and was taken to the hospital with an irregular heartbeat. The diagnosis proved relatively benign: a thyroid condition that was treatable with prescription medicine. But any presidential health crisis draws attention to the vice president who would succeed him in the event of his death or disability. Polls showed that about two-thirds of Americans still regarded

Vice President Dan Quayle as unqualified to be president, raising questions about his political fate when Bush decided whether to keep him on the ticket in 1992.

THE BUCHANAN INSURGENCY

Pat Buchanan's decision to challenge Bush's 1992 renomination was in some ways unsurprising. Starting with Alabama governor George C. Wallace's entry into three presidential primaries against President Lyndon B. Johnson in 1964, every reelection-seeking president except Reagan in 1984 faced at least one challenger within his own party. Two Republican House members opposed Richard Nixon's renomination in 1972, Rep. Pete McCloskey of California from the president's left and Rep. John Ashbrook of Ohio from his right, but neither reached 20 percent of the vote in any state contest. After both parties opened up the presidential nominating process by requiring that delegates from every state be chosen in a primary or caucus, the next two presidents were nearly unseated by their party's voters. Reagan in 1976 and Sen. Edward M. Kennedy of Massachusetts in 1980 fought incumbent presidents Gerald Ford and Jimmy Carter, respectively, all the way to the convention.

As the 1992 nominating contest approached, enough conservative Republican activists were unhappy with Bush to make a challenge possible.[37] For Dole, the Senate minority leader, and Kemp, a cabinet member, the cost of making such a challenge was too high. Buchanan, who considered running in 1988, had much less to lose. He was mad at the president for reneging on his "main commitment" as a candidate by raising taxes, launching the Gulf War against a country that Buchanan did not regard as a threat to the United States, and signing the 1991 Civil Rights Act, a "cave in" to what he regarded as no less a "quota bill" than the one Bush vetoed the previous year.[38] "I don't believe he is a conservative," Buchanan said of Bush. "He campaigns as Ronald Reagan but he governs as Jimmy Carter."[39] With virtually no money and a campaign organization consisting mostly of his sister Bay Buchanan, Buchanan announced his candidacy in Concord, New Hampshire, on December 10. "We are nationalists," he declared. "We will put America first."[40]

Buchanan had several things going for him in New Hampshire, starting with strong support from the *Manchester Union-Leader*, which urged him to run in a November 15, 1991, front-page editorial headlined "Go Pat, Go." The Bush campaign was totally unprepared for a contest. "We didn't think Pat was going to run," said Bush campaign consultant Charlie Black.[41] In

December, Bush cut loose his main political connection in the state by firing former governor Sununu as chief of staff, partly out of growing irritation within the White House at the chief's high-handed ways and partly because Sununu was found using government aircraft for personal trips. Most important, New Hampshire's economy, more than that of most states, suffered a deep recession after booming during the 1980s.

Even if, as seemed almost certain, Buchanan did not win the Republican nomination, three positive outcomes were possible for him that made running worthwhile. First, he might weaken Bush enough that the party would nominate a different conservative, one who had sought and won public office in previous elections. Second, said Bay Buchanan, he "might actually move the president, force him to keep to the issues that we felt were right and proper for the Reagan legacy."[42] And third, Buchanan almost surely would raise his public profile, no small consideration for someone who made his living as a media commentator. Buchanan loved thinking of himself as the movie boxer Rocky, a loser all the more beloved for taking on the champ and not going down without a fight.[43]

THE DEMOCRATS

During nearly all of 1991, the main story in the Democratic Party was about the candidates who announced they were not going to run. Gephardt, favored by House Democrats, declared he was not running in July. Gore, who emerged from the 1988 campaign as the party's most prominent southerner, made his declaration of noncandidacy in August. Jackson, whom many African American voters hoped would elevate his runner-up status in 1988 by securing the nomination this time, announced in November that he would not be a candidate. Cuomo followed in December, once again leaving the hopes of liberal Democrats unrequited.

The reasons these much-longed-after Democratic leaders offered for passing up 1992 varied. Since 1989, Gephardt had settled into his new role as House majority leader. Gore was focused on his family (a son recovering from a serious accident and a wife experiencing depression) and on the book he had immersed himself in writing about the environment, *Earth in the Balance*. Jackson, still dealing with the financial and family strains of his two previous campaigns, was about to begin hosting a weekly program on CNN called *Both Sides Now*.

Cuomo took the longest to decide and came the closest to running. But on December 20, with a chartered plane standing by to fly him from Albany to Concord in time to meet New Hampshire's primary filing deadline,

Cuomo announced that with his state's budget unresolved, "It's my responsibility as governor to deal with this extraordinarily severe problem."[44] What Cuomo, Gephardt, Gore, and Jackson knew was that in four years Bush, who still appeared to be unbeatable, would not be on the ballot and that the Republicans would be in the difficult position of trying to win their fifth consecutive presidential election. All of them—Gephardt, who would turn fifty-five in 1996; Gore, who would turn forty-eight that year; Jackson, also fifty-five; and Cuomo, sixty-four—would still be young enough to launch a campaign. So, for that matter, would others who gave some thought to running in 1992 but decided not to, including Senators Bradley (fifty-three in 1996), Nunn (fifty-eight), and Jay Rockefeller of West Virginia (fifty-nine).

BILL CLINTON

"Dream On, Democrats" was *Newsweek*'s advice to Democratic politicians thinking of challenging Bush in its March 18, 1991, issue. But even though Clinton, at fifty, would also be plenty young in 1996, he made a different calculation concerning 1992. No one from Arkansas had ever been nominated, much less elected president. Nor had the governor of any small state won the White House since Franklin Pierce of New Hampshire in 1852, nearly a century and a half before. But the absence of strong candidates, especially after centrist rivals Gore and Gephardt begged off, offered Clinton a clearer path to his party's nomination in 1992 than in the field that already was forming for 1996. No other white southern governor was running, even though the Democrats' only recent victory had come when, acknowledging its shrinking southern base and the voters' growing estrangement from Washington, the party nominated former Georgia governor Jimmy Carter in 1976. As for beating Bush, Clinton overcame his initial post–Gulf War belief that the president's victory had put a "no vacancy" sign on the White House and decided that with the Cold War won and Iraq defeated, domestic issues would soon return to their usual centrality in presidential elections, tilting the playing field in the Democrats' favor.[45] Others were less optimistic. When George Stephanopoulos joined Clinton's campaign, for example, he "thought this was practice" for 1996.[46]

First things first, though: Clinton needed to be reelected as governor in 1990 to confirm his political stature and preserve his fund-raising base in Arkansas. Another option—having Hillary Clinton run in his stead—was abandoned after private polling demonstrated how unpopular the idea was.[47] Clinton succeeded, but paid a price for his victory. During a debate he impulsively promised—"You bet!"—that if he won he would serve his full four-year term.[48] Afterward he feared that breaking that pledge—a pledge "he had to make—polling indicated that he did"—to win reelection, according to campaign aide Gloria Cabe, might finish him in Arkansas politics if a bid for the presidency fell short. Clinton solved the problem by touring the state in 1991.[49] Speaking before audiences that aides secretly seeded with supporters urging him to abandon his 1990 pledge, Clinton was pleased to conclude that Arkansans would be proud rather than angry if he ran for president.[50]

In addition to securing his home-state base, Clinton knew that he would also have to persuade the Democratic Party to remake itself to free it from its losing ways. He found national homes in the National Governors Association, of which his long tenure leading Arkansas eventually made him the senior member, and the Democratic Leadership Council (DLC), the group formed in 1985 to help make the party more acceptable to middle-class voters by proposing innovative centrist policies that transcended orthodox conservatism and liberalism.[51] Four years later, after the Democrats lost their third landslide presidential election in a row, political scientists William Galston and Elaine Kamarck wrote an influential paper for the DLC's think tank, the Progressive Policy Institute, on "the politics of evasion." The evasion they spoke of was the harsh reality that neither a return to "liberal fundamentalism," a focus on mobilizing nonvoters, nor an expectation that the party's losing streak was a fluke would win back the White House. Instead, Democrats must do what Republicans did during the 1970s: "endure a frank internal debate on political fundamentals." Galston and Kamarck were confident that if their party did so, it would nominate a candidate in 1992 who embraced "middle-class values—individual responsibility, hard work, and equal opportunity—rather than the language of compensation."[52]

As a "New Democrat," Clinton became the leader of both the DLC and the governors association, a natural pairing because as his chief domestic policy adviser, Bruce Reed, pointed out, "The DLC essentially represented the governors' wing of the Democratic Party." In contrast to congressional Democrats, governors "had to solve problems all the time. . . . They actually had to balance a budget every year, make progress on schools and health care. . . . And as it turned out, the governors after whom we modeled ourselves had figured out pretty much what the country wanted: a less ideological, more pragmatic approach to policy and politics that appealed because it worked."[53]

The DLC's emphasis on winning presidential elections rather than appeasing the party's varied and conflicting constituency groups was consistent with this approach. "We had done a whole lot of work on a whole bunch of ideas," said executive director Al From: "national service, charter schools, welfare reform, community policing, reinventing government, our [nonprotectionist] position on trade."54 The "watchword" for Clinton and the DLC, according to Clinton's media consultant Frank Greer, was "new common sense solutions, putting aside false choices, being different in the sense of having values, having religious faith, and having a sense of patriotism and love of country," all of which "Democrats have too often run from."55 "Liberal passions, but conservative governing values" (Reed) and "a shift of Democratic economic policy from redistribution to growth" (From) were hallmarks of the DLC approach.56 Coming from a Democrat, "traditionally the party identified with rights, not responsibilities," Clinton's support for an ability-to-pay student loan program tied to national service set him apart and emerged as one of his most effective applause lines in campaign speeches.57 In addition, Galston observed, after Clinton became DLC chair in 1990, he reaped a collateral benefit: he "could move around the country on somebody else's dime in the guise—a legitimate guise—of establishing chapters in various states, but also plant his own political flag."58

The highlight of Clinton's time at the DLC's helm came at the organization's May 1991 convention in Cleveland. A showcase for several better-known potential candidates for the 1992 Democratic nomination, including Gore, the convention became a pep rally for Clinton, who gave a stunningly effective keynote address. "He put 'opportunity, responsibility, community' into the lexicon on that day," said From. "What he convinced a lot of people of is that you could be a centrist with passion."59 "Democrats have been talking about opportunity since Roosevelt, if not longer," added Reed, "and community since Johnson. But they'd gone a long time without talking about responsibility, and that was Clinton's obsession." At the DLC convention not just the delegates but also "the national press corps was blown away," Reed recalled. "In that speech he laid out the basic themes of his [1992] campaign: that for too long Democrats had failed to represent the economic interests, defend the values, and stand up for the security of the forgotten middle class."60 "Too many of the people that used to vote for us," Clinton argued, "the very burdened middle class that we are talking about, have not trusted us in national elections to defend our national interests abroad, to put their values into our social policy, or to take their tax money and spend it with discipline."61

Clinton's decision to seek the Democratic nomination in 1992 was not an easy one. He "pointed out to me," said Greer, "that a sitting president who had won a war had never lost an election" (true, but other than William McKinley, no sitting president who won a war was reelected either).[62] He worried, as he had when declining to run in 1988, that rumors about adulterous relations with women might sink his candidacy, as they sank Colorado senator Gary Hart's bid in 1988, or at a minimum embarrass him before his family. Already, in his 1990 reelection campaign, Clinton's aides had to work hard to steer local media away from covering a press conference at which a former state employee, Larry Nichols, announced a lawsuit alleging that the governor used state funds to pay for his affairs with five women.[63] Clinton counted on political reporters being so chastened by adverse public reaction to the "feeding frenzy" they engaged in against Hart that they would tread lightly on similar matters in the coming election.[64]

What decided the matter for Clinton was his certainty that a campaign based on ideas for reforming domestic policy would overcome all obstacles against a president whose post–Gulf War, post–Cold War glow would wear off by November 1992. "He had a better idea of what he wanted to do as president," said Reed, which offered "a good contrast with Bush, who didn't have much of an agenda, and with the other Democrats, who hadn't thought it through."[65] In his October 3, 1991, announcement speech and in three subsequent policy addresses at Georgetown University, Clinton built his campaign on a work-centered platform. Under the "New Covenant" he proposed, government would foster opportunities for people seeking employment and those without jobs would be responsible for taking them. At the heart of this appeal was the promise to "end welfare as we know it" by limiting welfare payments to two years at a time and five years in a lifetime.[66] As Clinton said in his announcement speech, "Government's responsibility is to create more opportunity. The people's responsibility is to make the most of it."

"Welfare was the best example of what Clinton would prove to be a master of," said Reed: "taking an issue that Republicans had demagogued for years and turning it into an affirmative political and substantive agenda for Democrats."[67] Although Clinton's agenda placed him at odds with many traditional Democrats, who thought more in terms of public than private sector jobs and resisted any change in welfare policy, he counted on them caring more about breaking their long losing streak in presidential elections than about preserving ideological purity. He also hoped that congressional Democrats who had grown comfortable with their majority status in Washington would overlook gibes such as "Congress raised its pay and guarded its perks while most Americans were working harder for less money."[68]

Clinton won the pre–election year "invisible" primary and emerged from 1991 as the front-runner for his party's nomination. His campaign's ideas-based rationale, deep pockets (with Arkansas business leaders a particularly strong source of funds), and effective organization surpassed those of any other Democratic candidate.[69] Success bred success: Clinton was able to use his early strength to recruit an all-star team of campaign operatives: pollster Stan Greenberg, fund-raiser Robert Farmer (who turned out to be less valuable than his deputy, Rahm Emmanuel), campaign manager David Wilhelm, communications director George Stephanopoulos, and—fresh from managing Pennsylvanian Harris Wofford's upset victory in the November 1991 special Senate election—strategists James Carville and Paul Begala.

National political reporters were strongly impressed by all of these successes, as well as by Clinton's intelligence, political skill, and understanding of the issues.[70] Their major doubts concerned his personal life, with its potential for scandal. In an effort to dissuade journalists from pursuing allegations of marital infidelity, Clinton, accompanied by Hillary, met in September 1991 with the "Sperling Breakfast"—described by Greer as "a kind of political reporter insider group"—to declare, "What you need to know about Hillary and me is that we've been together nearly twenty years. It has not been perfect or free from problems, but we're committed to our marriage."[71] As a consequence, the issue vanished from the mainstream media for several months.

PAUL TSONGAS

Paul Tsongas was, by most measures, an unlikely contender when he became the first declared candidate for the Democratic nomination on April 3, 1991. He was, in the words of his campaign manager, Dennis Kanin, "Greek, Massachusetts, . . . [and] out of office for seven years"—among other political liabilities in the aftermath of Massachusetts Greek American Dukakis's defeat in 1988. These included "a perceived charisma deficit, which ultimately was to his advantage."[72]

In 1978, at age thirty-seven, Tsongas defeated the incumbent Republican senator from Massachusetts, Edward Brooke, after serving two terms in the House of Representatives. His national ambitions were stymied when he was diagnosed with cancer of the lymph nodes in 1983 and told that he had perhaps eight years to live. Tsongas chose not to seek reelection in 1984, focusing instead on spending time with his family and making money to assure their financial security. "No one on his deathbed said, 'I wish I had spent more time at the office,'" Tsongas explained.[73] Through the rest of the decade he represented business clients as a lawyer and lobbyist and served on several corporate boards, less time-consuming activities than office holding. Tsongas became convinced that in order for the Democratic Party to achieve its goal of helping poor and working-class people, the government had to encourage, not rein in, the businesses that create jobs. When he was found to be cancer-free, Tsongas decided to reenter politics as a candidate for president in the 1992 election.

Tsongas, along with Jerry Brown and Douglas Wilder, was written off by the national press corps as a "second-tier candidate" with much less chance of winning the nomination than Clinton, Harkin, or Kerrey. But his experience in the world of commerce had given Tsongas a distinctive perspective on the issues facing the country. He was a self-described "pro-business candidate" opposed to the "old Democrats who are into giveaway, giveaway, giveaway, antibusiness corporate bashing."[74] Competing with Clinton for centrist support within the Democratic Party, Tsongas attacked him for pandering to voters by promising a middle-class tax cut. He also competed with Clinton as the candidate of ideas by publishing a short book titled *A Call to Economic Arms* and eventually distributing 250,000 copies.

Tsongas's appeal was grounded as much in character as in issues. He presented himself to voters as a courageous truth teller unafraid to challenge his party's orthodoxies, a intellectually and morally serious leader whose lack of charisma was a mark of authenticity, and a survivor who beat cancer and became a competitive swimmer, the theme of the one early ad he could afford to run on television. Tsongas was not able to raise much money in 1991. "The 14,000 Greek contributors to the Dukakis campaign" did not come through as hoped, said Kanin. As Tsongas himself foresaw when Dukakis ran, "Being the first person in the Greek community running for the presidency is an obvious advantage."[75] "The next Greek that runs for president will not have this success because the fervor will not be there." Offsetting this disadvantage, Tsongas was already a familiar figure to New Hampshire voters who got their television from Boston.[76] He also lived in Lowell, five miles from the New Hampshire border, which allowed him to campaign in the first primary state virtually full time.

JERRY BROWN

The once (1975–1983) and future (2011–2019) governor of California, Jerry Brown was between jobs in 1991. After leaving the governorship and losing a Senate election in 1982, Brown spent several years in Japan at a

Buddhist monastery and in India working with Mother Teresa at the House of the Dying. He returned to California to become chair of the state Democratic Party from 1989 to 1991 as a way of getting back into politics. The essence of the state chair's job was to raise money from wealthy donors. The disgust Brown developed with the fund-raising process became the basis of his presidential campaign in 1992.

Brown's dislike of conventional politics was deeply rooted, dating back to his experience growing up as the son of a decidedly conventional politician, California's two-term Democratic governor Pat Brown. Brown benefited from his father's name when he entered politics after abandoning study for the priesthood. But he departed from Pat Brown's official style when he was elected governor of California in 1974 at age thirty-four after serving four years as secretary of state. Substantively, Brown separated himself from his father's enthusiastically pro-growth policies, focusing instead on energy conservation and environmental protection as the hallmarks of the politics of limits he embraced. Stylistically, Brown drew a sharp contrast with Richard Nixon's "imperial presidency," which was desperately unpopular in the year after Nixon's resignation. He disdained the governor's mansion and slept instead on a mattress on the floor of his apartment.

On an impulse, Brown brought his "era of limits" theme into presidential politics in 1976 by making a late entry into the Democratic nominating contest. Carter was close to locking up the nomination when Brown declared as a candidate in March, but Brown ran off a string of primary victories in the late spring by appealing to Democrats who, for varying and conflicting reasons, had doubts about Carter. Brown drew on a coalition of the unlikely that included Maryland's most conventional party operatives as well as ardent environmentalists. In 1980, bearing the derisive nickname "Governor Moonbeam" that Chicago columnist Mike Royko had recently attached to him, Brown challenged Carter again, this time running on a platform that emphasized space exploration. He lost badly to the president and his main opponent, Senator Kennedy of Massachusetts. Brown drew less than 3 percent of the primary vote.

Brown's single theme entering the 1992 election was disgust with the "unholy alliance of private greed and corrupt politics" that he said infected both political parties.[77] His distinctive promise, repeated endlessly, was to accept no donation larger than $100. Brown declared his candidacy on September 3, urging voters to call his toll-free 800 number (a major innovation in campaign technology at the time) to make their small pledges.

DOUGLAS WILDER

The last of the three "second-tier" candidates to enter the Democratic race was Gov. Douglas Wilder of Virginia, who declared that he was running on September 13. On the face of it, Wilder was not second-tier at all: he was the fiscally conservative governor of an important southern state, having overcome Virginia's then-strong Republican inclination to be elected in 1989. But, according to Wilder, the national media and the Democratic Party failed to take his bid seriously because they did not think that an African American candidate had a realistic chance of being elected president. "I don't think I'm being overly sensitive," Wilder wrote, "when I suggest that I was being judged by a different standard."[78]

Wilder was surely right. Focus groups run by his own campaign in monochromatically white New Hampshire found that Democratic voters liked hearing about his record as governor—until they saw his picture.[79] Of the first eleven state primaries and caucuses in 1992, only Maryland's would take place in a state with a significant black population.

But Wilder's problems launching a presidential campaign extended beyond the racial prejudice he encountered. He offered himself even to black voters as, in effect, the antithesis of Jesse Jackson, who announced he would not run on November 2. Unlike Jackson, who built his national reputation as an activist rather than an office holder, Wilder pursued a conventional political career. In 1969, at age thirty-eight, he was elected to the state senate from a newly created majority-black district in Richmond. He served in that office for sixteen years before being elected lieutenant governor in 1985 and governor four years later. Wilder was the first African American since Reconstruction to win any of these offices in Virginia. His growing responsibilities in government, the statewide trajectory of his career, and his gradually developing fiscal conservatism (the three were intertwined) led Wilder to regard Jackson as a mere agitator, which alienated Jackson's many supporters in the Democratic primary electorate. In a sentence one could not imagine Jackson uttering, Wilder said, "I don't believe that you can afford the things that some of us call 'niceties' for programs to help people unless you have fiscal responsibility."[80]

Wilder also feuded publicly with other Virginia Democrats who, like him, were fiscal conservatives and might have been expected to support him for president. These included his predecessor as governor, Gerald Baliles, and Sen. Charles Robb, with whom he publicly traded charges of improperly investigating each other's personal lives. In the end, Wilder's best hope was to run well enough in 1992 to stake a claim for a vice presidential nomination. An African American governor, he calculated, would be a much more attractive running mate to his party's presidential nominee than Jackson was to Dukakis in 1988. But to approach even that goal Wilder would need to raise enough money and build a strong enough organization to compete effectively in at least some primaries, neither of which he was able to do.

TOM HARKIN

Second-term senator Tom Harkin of Iowa announced his candidacy on September 15, about two weeks before Kerrey and three weeks before Clinton. Harkin was the first of the three first-tier contenders in the eyes of national political reporters to enter the race, all of them at risk of demotion to the second rank if either Jackson or, especially, Cuomo became a candidate, which neither did. Being judged first-tier meant that reporters and their editors devoted more coverage to a candidate and that potential donors and campaign professionals looking to back a winner were more willing to sign on. Harkin raised about $2 million in 1991, not as much as Clinton (about $3 million) but approximately the same as Kerrey and considerably more than Tsongas, Brown, or Wilder.

Most of Harkin's money came from labor unions, whose champion he was in the field of candidates that was forming. An Iowa coal miner's son who, while rising through the political ranks, never forgot his roots or abandoned his class-based resentment of the wealthy, Harkin was, like Nixon and Dole, a kind of "[Horatio] Alger with attitude."[81] He graduated from Iowa State University in 1961 and served five years as a naval pilot before earning a law degree at Catholic University in Washington. In 1974, at age thirty-four, Harkin defeated the incumbent Republican congressman from Iowa's Fifth District and ten years later beat an incumbent Republican senator. His Senate years coincided with the presidencies of Reagan and Bush, both of whom he regularly excoriated as enemies of the working class.

Harkin spent most of 1991 speaking to labor audiences, who reveled in his red-meat rhetoric and old-time political religion. "I'm a real Democrat," he would proclaim, not "a warmed-over Republican."[82] Embracing the liberal label, he vowed to bring down "every double-breasted, scab-hiring, union-busting employer in America."[83] The contrast Harkin drew was with all of the other announced candidates, and if the election had continued to look hopeless for the Democrats well into 1992 the party may have embraced him in order to go down with flags flying. Labor unions represented a declining share of American workers—down from more than one-third in the early 1950s to little more than one-tenth in the early 1990s—but were still a major force in the Democratic Party. Indeed, as the number of votes unions could deliver shrank, they worked to preserve their influence in party councils by increasing their financial contributions. But by spending so much time with the labor wing of the party, Harkin immersed himself in an echo chamber in which the traditional class-based rhetoric that resounded there did not speak to other Democrats, many of whom wanted above all to find a way to break their party's losing streak in presidential elections.

Harkin's popularity in Iowa guaranteed victory in its January 1992 caucuses, but the political significance of that usually important first-in-the-nation contest was severely diminished by the unwillingness of the other candidates to compete with him in his home state. More telling was the straw vote that took place at the Florida Democratic convention on December 15, 1991. Harkin made a major effort with strong support from labor. He lost to Clinton by 54 percent to 31 percent. Harkin missed another opportunity after Cuomo, his main competitor for liberal Democratic support, announced five days later that he was not running. Harkin's campaign organization was in disarray at the time. "Not really knowing what to do" when Cuomo dropped out, recalled Harkin campaign press secretary Lorraine Voles, "we went on vacation."[84]

BOB KERREY

On paper, Bob Kerrey had everything going for him when he declared for president on September 30. He was an authentic war hero whose award of a Congressional Medal of Honor and loss of a leg in combat as a Navy SEAL during the Vietnam War immunized him against any Republican effort to question his toughness or patriotism. He was a successful entrepreneur, having partnered with his brother-in-law to build a chain of restaurants and health clubs in his native Lincoln, Nebraska. He was undefeated in his political career despite running as a Democrat in a strongly Republican state. He had experience as both a governor and a senator, offices he won by defeating the incumbent Republican governor in 1982 and an incumbent Republican senator in 1988. Divorced by the time of his governorship, Kerrey was attractive enough at age thirty-eight to have a romantic relationship with the much younger actress Debra Winger when she was in Lincoln to film *Terms of Endearment*. United Press International ranked him first on its list of the World's Top 10 Eligible Bachelors.[85] In Washington, Kerrey was regarded by the national press corps as a presumptive first-tier candidate for the Democratic presidential nomination, perhaps the front-runner, if he decided to run.

Kerrey did decide to run, but in a way that left him blinking when he stepped into the bright media spotlight that immediately shone on him. "Early in the year [1991] I didn't seriously consider it," Kerrey said of a candidacy.[86] But when he saw who was and was not running, he thought, if the path to the nomination is that uncluttered, why not?—almost that casually.

Kerrey paid the price for his late and impulsive decision to enter the race in the currency of preparations not made. The closer a candidate comes to the start of the election year—especially one who begins the race near the front of the pack—the greater the scrutiny he or she will receive from party activists, donors, campaign operatives, and the national media. All of them are in the business of judging whether the candidate has an effective organization, an appealing rationale for being elected and, in service of that rationale, well thought-out positions on the issues and a basic stump speech that can be given again and again to hammer home the campaign's vision and substance.

Kerrey's haste once he decided to run, joined with the improvisational temperament that had served him so well in smaller-scale endeavors throughout his life, meant that he stood up to scrutiny on none these things. His organization was forming on the fly, which left him unprepared to respond to news stories about the use of child labor in his restaurants and the lack of health insurance for many of his employees. His vision—"building for greatness"—was airily free of content. Even the exception, his promotion of national health insurance, was undermined by the news accounts of his business practices. Kerrey disdained honing and repeating a stump speech because saying the same thing over and over bored him. Instead, he improvised his speeches in ways that sounded disjointed. "He's an inch away from Moonbeam," said one of his veteran campaign advisers, John Reilly.[87]

ROSS PEROT

Bush, Buchanan, and the Democrats completed the roster of major party candidates for president in 1991 but not the roster of all serious candidates. Conditions were ripe for a third-party (more accurately an independent) candidacy in 1992. According to the model developed by political scientist Steven J. Rosenstone and colleagues, there was a 97 percent chance that a "nationally prestigious third-party candidate" would emerge to challenge the major party nominees in that election, based on measures of dissension within the incumbent Republican Party and voter dissatisfaction with the status quo. Historically, such candidates were public officials elected to office as major party nominees who then broke with their party, such as former president Theodore Roosevelt in 1912, Gov. Strom Thurmond of South Carolina and former vice president Henry A. Wallace in 1948, Rep. John Anderson of Illinois in 1980, and former governor George Wallace of Alabama in 1968.[88]

In 1992, however, the independent candidate who emerged did not fit the traditional profile of a "nationally prestigious" public official. Nor did he look or sound the part. Ross Perot was short, jug-eared, and twangy, clothed in what appeared to be a fifty-dollar suit and trimmed up with a fifty-cent haircut. Yet for all that, it was not altogether surprising that a serious independent candidate would arise from a different lane of American society. For years, a certain *Mr. Smith Goes to Washington*–style romance had attached to the idea of finding a president outside the usual political channels with none of the blow-dried, blue-suit-and-red-tie polish of a traditional politician. The October 1967 issue of *Esquire* magazine, for example, featured a large photograph of industrialist J. Irwin Miller on the cover with the heading "This Man Ought to Be the Next President of the United States." The accompanying article offered a long list of corporation, university, and foundation leaders who were said to have the "honesty, high purpose, and intelligence to be elected president of the United States."[89] In 1984 Lee Iacocca, the burly president and public face of the revived Chrysler Corporation, was a much-discussed potential candidate. Three years later celebrity real estate developer Donald J. Trump flirted with a run for the Republican nomination; he took a more serious look at the Reform Party nomination in 2000 and was elected president as a Republican in 2016.[90]

Ross Perot was, like Trump, a businessman with a broad and well-established public reputation when interest began to be expressed in his running for president in 1992. Without knowing what the other was doing, retired Florida financial planner Jack Gargan and longtime lawyer-politician-businessman John Jay Hooker of Nashville beseeched Perot to enter the race in multiple flattering phone calls. Gargan, who ran an anti-incumbent organization called Throw the Hypocritical Rascals Out, persuaded Perot to speak at THRO's annual gathering in Tampa in November. The event turned into a "Run, Ross, run!" rally.[91] Public disgust with politicians was at a peak in the early 1990s, with strong movements under way both nationally and in many states to limit the number of terms legislators could serve.

Perot grew up in the 1930s in the nation's heartland, the son of a cotton broker in Texarkana, Texas. He changed his middle name from Ray to Ross in memory of a brother who died when a toddler, and then used it instead of his Christian name, Henry. An Eagle Scout, paperboy, and bronco buster as a youth, Perot secured an appointment to the US Naval Academy, where he was elected class president in his third and fourth years. After four years in the navy, he took a job in 1957 with International Business Machines (IBM) in Dallas. As a sales representative dealing with Texas Blue Cross, Perot concluded that IBM was much better at selling computers than at helping customers make the best use of them with software and technical support. He started his own company, Electronic Data Systems (EDS) and, drawing on what he learned working with Blue Cross, became the leading outside contractor for Medicare and Medicaid, both of which were created in 1965. Two years after taking EDS public in 1968, Perot's shares were worth more than $1.5 billion.

Perot first gained a national reputation in 1969 by sending planeloads of food, medicine, and Christmas presents to American prisoners of war in North Vietnam. He got a second wave of publicity when the North Vietnamese refused to accept them. In 1979, after two EDS employees were trapped in revolutionary Iran, Perot formed a team to free them and then hired author Ken Follett to write an account of the rescue. *On the Wings of Eagles* was a Perot-glorifying best seller and a popular television miniseries.

In 1984 Perot's reputation grew when he headed an educational reform commission in Texas that, like Clinton's in Arkansas, championed small classes and teacher competency but, unlike Clinton's, took on high school football as an obstacle to learning. "No pass, no play" was controversial in Texas but enhanced Perot's national stature as a no-nonsense, plain-talking reformer. Later that year he sold EDS to General Motors for $2.5 billion and a seat on GM's board, a platform he used to publicly criticize the company's top-heavy management. "The first EDSer to see a snake kills it," Perot complained. "At GM, first thing you do is organize a committee on snakes."[92] In truth, EDS did at least as well as part of GM as it had when Perot ran it.

In 1986, two years after GM bought out Perot to end their short and unhappy association, he founded Perot Systems, which grew into another multibillion-dollar health care information technology corporation by the time he sold it in 2009. He also returned his attention to service members who were prisoners of war or missing in action. North Vietnam freed all captured Americans in 1973, but Perot was convinced that it was still holding many more with the assistance of drug-running CIA agents. He pestered the Reagan administration until the president called him off, assigning Vice President Bush the task of showing Perot all of the relevant

Defense Intelligence Agency files because he was tired of dealing with him and knew that Bush and Perot had crossed paths over the years in Texas. (Bush even remembered Perot offering him a job after Carter replaced him as CIA director.)[93] None of the evidence supported the theory that the North Vietnamese were still holding any Americans prisoner. Unconvinced, Perot blamed Bush for trying to deceive him.[94] Bush "had known Perot for years [and] thought he was a nut case," according to Scully.[95]

When Bush became president, Perot took to the television talk show circuit to oppose the Gulf War as an effort "to erase our errors with human lives" and, striking a more resonant chord, to criticize him for raising taxes while running up the deficit. This attracted the attention of Gargan, Hooker, and a large viewing audience.[96] Lines that would become familiar during the 1992 campaign, such as that the budget deficit was being ignored like "a crazy aunt we keep in the basement" and "It's our country, we own it. . . . We've got to start acting like owners," began appearing in Perot's speeches—even as he maintained that he had no interest in running for president.[97] In 1991 Perot appeared three times on CNN's *Larry King Live* to criticize Bush's policy toward Iraq both before the war (when plenty of opposition voices clamored for airtime) and after the victory, when only Perot and Buchanan spoke out in opposition.[98]

THE BATTLE FOR THE 1992 REPUBLICAN NOMINATION AND THE RISE AND (TEMPORARY) FALL OF ROSS PEROT

Few things affected President George Bush's bid for reelection in 1992 more than the decisions made nearly a quarter century before by the Democratic Party's Commission on Party Structure and Delegate Selection, better known as the McGovern-Fraser Commission. The commission spurred both major parties to transform the way they choose their candidates for president. As late as 1968, that decision was largely in the hands of state party leaders. The relatively few primary elections played at most a secondary role, so much so that Vice President Hubert H. Humphrey was able to win the Democratic presidential nomination without entering a single primary. The McGovern-Fraser Commission not only opened up the nominating process to include the voters but actually placed them in the driver's seat. Most important, the commission required that delegates to the quadrennial presidential nominating conventions be chosen in primaries or caucuses in which any interested supporter could participate. No longer could party leaders screen out undesirable candidates or anoint a winner.

One consequence of the open process that took effect in the 1970s was to make it easier for dissident candidates from the president's own party to oppose him for renomination. Both Republican president Gerald Ford in 1976 and Democratic president Jimmy Carter in 1980 were forced to spend more than half of the election year facing down serious intraparty challengers in a series of acrimonious, expensive primaries—the first time this had happened to an incumbent since 1912. As such, each faced a "pincer movement" of opposition, having to fend off foes from both the opposition party and his own party.[1] Weakened from within, Ford and Carter were defeated in their bids for reelection.

Ford and Carter were less-than-popular presidents facing serious challenges from well-known political leaders with strong followings. In contrast, Ronald Reagan was renominated in 1984 without opposition. Throughout much of 1991 Bush was even more popular than Reagan had been. Nor did there seem to be any reason to take seriously the two individuals who were hoping to unseat him. Neither Pat Buchanan nor David Duke, an openly racist state representative from Louisiana, had credentials to rival those of Ford's opponent in 1976, former California governor Reagan, or Carter's opponent in 1980, Sen. Edward M. Kennedy of Massachusetts.

In addition to expecting an easy renomination, Bush simply didn't want to start campaigning. "It's just a two-month sprint," he said in August 1991, thinking the general election was the only battle he would have to fight.[2] "He wanted to run a Rose Garden campaign"—that is, a campaign that did not require leaving the White House for long stretches—"like Reagan did in 1984," said Vice President Dan Quayle.[3] One reason was Bush's health. According to his son George, after developing Graves' disease in May 1991, Bush "never had quite the same energy level again."[4] In that same month, Barbara Bush wrote in her diary, "George has talked privately like a man who is not running for office."[5] Bush told Joint Chiefs of Staff chairman Colin Powell that he "didn't have the mental energy to cause change." Powell himself observed "a passive, sometimes detached George Bush."[6]

Even more important, Bush simply dreaded the day when he would have to put aside governing and statesmanship, which he loved, and turn to speech making and campaigning, which he merely endured. Resisting the idea that the modern presidency requires both forms of leadership, "the president saw 'campaign mode' and 'governing mode' as two separate and unrelated activities, two apparently contradictory habits of mind," wrote White House domestic policy adviser Charles Kolb.[7] Because all of Bush's major political campaigns, not just the one that earned him the presidency in 1988, had been negative, he came to regard campaigning as intrinsically degrading. The president "detested what he perceived to be name-calling and ugliness," according to Dan Quayle. Bush transposed his own harsh approach, which he regarded as a necessary evil, onto electioneering itself. Not surprisingly, he told nagging advisers, "I want to postpone politics 1992."[8]

And why not? Bush had been a faithful "party builder" before and after becoming president. As political scientist Daniel Galvin has shown, because of Bush's efforts, "his party organization was in strong shape. Its physical assets—including its computer technologies, voters lists, and state party infrastructures—had received continual upgrades over the course of Bush's four years."[9] Eight states canceled their Republican primaries, reducing the opportunities for a challenger to Bush's renomination. His economic advisers—Council of Economic Advisers chair Michael Boskin, secretary of the Treasury Nicholas Brady, and Office of Management and Budget director Richard Darman—told him that the recession was mild by historical standards (unemployment never exceeded 7.8 percent) and in any event had ended in spring 1991, setting the stage for the economy to grow throughout the election year without the president having to do anything to stimulate it. They later claimed to be right, just a bit off on the timing: after anemic first and second quarters, economic growth rose to 2.7 percent in the third quarter and soared to 5.7 percent during the final quarter of 1992. But politically, that was too late to do Bush much good.

So unworried was Bush about an intraparty challenge from the right that he moved left in an effort to preempt the Democrats, the only opponents he expected to face. Throughout 1990 and 1991, he signed relatively liberal legislation concerning the environment, disability, taxes, and civil rights. In February 1992, White House personnel director Chase Untermeyer sent a memo to all of the administration's political appointees saying that "only a very few" campaign operatives would be hired, and even then not until "two months before the [Republican] Convention." His explanation: "There is no reason to believe we need to run a national campaign in 1992 in order to keep hold of the Executive. Our Commander in Chief has seen to that!"[10]

Even in 1991, however, Bush had reason to be apprehensive about the election. His approval rating fell steadily throughout the year, from 89 percent in February to 46 percent in early January 1992.[11] At its peak, Bush's handling of foreign policy, not the economy or other domestic concerns, was the basis of his support. The same polls that marked his sky-high overall rating showed no increase in approval of his handling of the economy, which remained mired at about 40 percent.[12] Yet foreign policy mattered less to voters after the Cold War was won and Iraq defeated. As James Baker observed, "Unless the country is about to go to war or suffered casualties or something like that, the foreign issues don't cut it in our domestic politics. People vote their pocketbooks."[13] Because the promised upturn in the economy did not quickly materialize, Bush was plagued by rising public unhappiness about his handling of this issue at the very time it was becoming more salient to voters. In the so-called Christmas Massacre, for example, General Motors announced in December that it was closing twenty-one plants and laying off 74,000 employees, the latest in a series of corporate downsizings. Not just assembly-line workers but, to an extent unmatched in previous downturns, white-collar managers were affected. More businesses failed than during any administration since the Great Depression. The White House was forced to acknowledge that the economy might be in recession after all.

Apart from that, many conservative Republicans were still mad at Bush about the tax increase and, most recently, the Civil Rights Act of 1991, which they regarded as a thinly disguised quota bill and which fed the long-standing narrative that he was a closet liberal at heart. "Because we had no stake in his presidency," said conservative activist Richard Viguerie, "it was easy to oppose him." "The last year has been the worst of my political career," Bush lamented—not knowing how much worse the next year would be.[14]

With Bush's chief campaign advisers from 1988 out of the picture— Lee Atwater because he died of a brain tumor in March 1991 and Baker because he was secretary of state—no one whose voice Bush respected on political matters was there to make him understand how precarious his position was. Authority within his reelection team, which was headed by a troika of pollster Robert Teeter, fund-raiser Robert Mosbacher, and former Nixon campaign aide Frederick Malek, was fragmented. None of them had ever run a presidential campaign or shown much interest in the day-to-day business of doing so.[15] Moreover, they and their counterparts in the White House were bound by a legal opinion issued by White House counsel C. Boyden Gray that campaign discussions had to be kept separate from governing discussions. Only Malek and Teeter were allowed to communicate with White House chief of staff Samuel Skinner, who was in any event the farthest thing from a take-charge leader. As a result, campaign aide Mary Matalin recounted, in order to get "the vet[eran]s' issue" into a campaign speech in Georgia, for example, "in every single instance I'd have to write a memo, go to Teeter, explain what we needed and why we needed to speak directly [to a presidential speechwriter]. Teeter would have to go to Skinner, Skinner would have to go to Boyden. Boyden would have to consider it, give the permission," and send word back down the chain to Matalin. Even worse, "The attitude at the White House [was] that the campaign were monkeys, and at the campaign we thought the White House couldn't walk and chew gum."[16] Ultimately, however, the fault for Bush's slow start lay with the president himself. As Baker said, "He waited too long to gear up and get going," even as he was telling interviewer David Frost in December that he would "do anything" to be reelected.[17]

At last, in a ham-handed move to take control of the economic issue, Bush led a delegation of American business leaders on an early January trip to South Korea and Japan, whose exports of cars and consumer electronics to the United States were putting domestic manufacturers out of business. Far from underscoring the advantage Republicans derived from foreign policy when the danger was the Soviet military during the Cold War, the new-style economic threat posed by Japan made the GOP's long-standing defense of free trade politically problematic. Bush's effort to play the international statesman who could secure jobs for Americans foundered. He won few concessions from the Asians, provoking critical public comments from the "Big Three" auto executives who accompanied him. On January 8, 1992, in a cruel twist of fate, Bush's diplomatic weakness seemed to take physical form. Sick with flu and with cameras rolling, he passed out at a banquet, vomiting in the lap of the Japanese prime minister. By unhappy coincidence, immediately on his return to the United States the Bureau of Labor Statistics announced that the unemployment rate had risen to 7.1 percent.

Bush's next opportunity to regain the initiative was the January 28, 1992, State of the Union address, a nationally televised prime-time speech to Congress that reliably draws tens of millions of viewers. But with few ideas queued up within the White House for launch, the address became a lost opportunity to "propose a domestic economic program around which we could build a campaign—call it a Domestic Storm, okay?" said Baker: "'I've taken care of Saddam Hussein and Desert Storm. I'm going to turn my attention now to the domestic problems facing this country.'"[18] Bush adopted the "storm" rhetoric: "We can bring the same courage and sense of common purpose to the economy that we brought to Desert Storm."[19] But his proposals were modest and familiar, most of them retreads from earlier in his presidency such as cutting the capital gains tax.

FENDING OFF BUCHANAN

As Bush's approval rating continued to slide, Buchanan's campaign began resonating with many Republican voters in New Hampshire, the first of the thirty-eight primary states in which three-fourths of the party's convention delegates would be chosen. New Hampshire offered fertile soil for a protest candidate. When Bush took office, its jobless rate was 2.5 percent, one of the lowest in the country. Unemployment had since quadrupled to 10 percent, one of the highest. Personal bankruptcies in the state had sextupled since 1988, 10 percent of the state's jobs disappeared, and all five of its largest banks closed.

Buchanan offered himself to New Hampshire voters as a protest candidate. "Send Bush a message" was the tagline of his commercials, including the first negative ad of the year, which charged the president not only with raising taxes but also with deceit. "We believed George Bush . . . when he promised, 'Read my lips: No new taxes,'" the announcer intoned. "Then he hit us with the largest tax increase in history." More than running ads, however, the cheerfully pugnacious Buchanan canvassed New Hampshire nearly every day for ten weeks, lambasting "King George" and offering at least one irresistible sound bite per news cycle. "Pat *was* a sound bite," said his sister and campaign manager, Bay Buchanan.[20] Asked if there were any guns he thought should be regulated, Buchanan paused a beat and said, "If it requires a truck to pull it, it should be banned."[21]

Buchanan also was a regular on talk radio. Since the Federal Communications Commission repealed the fairness doctrine in 1987, the AM dial had become a talk redoubt. From 1987 to 1992 alone, the number of stations with a talk format nearly quadrupled, from about 240 to 900.[22] Equally important, these stations found an audience by reviving an earlier era of American journalism in which the press, instead of striving for objectivity, was avowedly partisan. Because this audience was concentrated on the political right, whose adherents were seeking refuge from mainstream media that they thought were tainted by liberal bias, talk radio was dominated by conservative programming.[23] Buchanan, at home in the world of broadcast badinage, used the medium artfully to convince many voters that he was the true Reaganite in the race, despite his distinctly un-Reagan-like positions favoring protectionist trade policies, severely limited use of force to deter international aggression, and a 200-mile-long "Buchanan Fence" along the Mexican border to keep out immigrants. "We will put America first," he vowed.[24]

In late 1990 and early 1991, Buchanan joined Democrats in opposing the Gulf War. As the months passed after the war was won but with Hussein still in power, this position became steadily less toxic even among Republican voters. Indeed, in many ways, Buchanan did the Democrats' job for them. Attacks on Bush as being out of touch with the voters and more concerned with the world's problems than their own were more effective coming from a fellow Republican than from Democrats, whose criticisms

Conservative commentator Pat Buchanan waged a persistent campaign for the 1992 Republican presidential nomination against incumbent George Bush. Courtesy of the Associated Press.

could be written off as simple partisanship. New Hampshire's only state-wide newspaper, the archconservative *Union-Leader*, endorsed Buchanan.

Bush was flummoxed about how to respond to Buchanan: "leave him alone, not offend him," thereby allowing his attacks to go unanswered, or "stick your nose in there and hit back," elevating him as a serious rival and perhaps alienating his supporters.[25] Never a surefooted campaigner—"his natural instincts were to sort of talk about nothing, to acknowledge everybody in the audience," according to White House aide James Pinkerton—and rusty after three years off the campaign trail, Bush was saddled by schedulers with multiple appearances on January 15, his first of only three days in the state.[26] He began the day by saying, "Look, the economy is in free fall," failing to specify that he meant New Hampshire's economy, not the national economy, which he refused to concede was in a recession.[27] Later he read aloud an instruction in his speech notes to improvise some compassionate remarks as if it were the speech itself: "Message: I care." Quoting a lyric in a popular Nitty Gritty Dirt Band song—"If you want to see a rainbow, you've got to stand a little rain"—he attributed it to the "Nitty Ditty Nitty Gritty Great Bird."[28] In an attempt at modesty, wanting to convey that his problems were as nothing compared with those faced by Abraham Lincoln, he began bafflingly: "I'm okay, I'm in good health. Don't cry for me, Argentina," an oddly esoteric reference to the Broadway show *Evita*.[29] Local and national news media naturally broadcast what Bush said, not what he meant. The cable television news channel CNN, a rising force in a rising medium, did so around the clock. Another round of mocking stories followed Bush's comment on January 27 that "American families should be a lot more like *The Waltons* and a lot less like *The Simpsons*," especially after Bart Simpson said in the episode that aired three days later, "We're just like the Waltons. We're praying for an end to the depression too."[30]

When the votes were tallied on February 18, New Hampshire handed Bush a reasonably clear victory: he outpolled Buchanan by 53 percent to 37 percent. But the media reported the results as a defeat for the president. In addition to wanting to keep the contest alive so they would have something to cover, journalists were deceived by the exit polls, which initially showed that the race was a dead heat. "I think a lot of reporters started writing their leads" based on these early results and then felt locked in to their interpretations, Buchanan observed.[31] CBS interrupted its regular evening programming with an inaccurate announcement that "Buchanan gets well over 40 percent of the Republican primary vote."[32] Knowing from his time in journalism that the media would jump the gun, Buchanan had urged his supporters to vote in the morning.[33] Bush contributed to the early evening gloom among his own supporters by prematurely saying, "This election was far closer than many had predicted."[34] With his defeat widely characterized as a victory, Buchanan joined the ranks of what political scientist Larry Bartels has called "losers treated like winners" in New Hampshire, including Eugene McCarthy in 1968, George McGovern in 1972, and, in the Democratic primary held the same day, Bill Clinton in 1992.[35] Buchanan rushed on air to claim that "we are going to make America great again, because there is nothing wrong with putting America first."[36] (See appendix A for the results of the 1992 Republican primaries.)

Were Republicans endorsing Buchanan for president or merely registering a protest against Bush? The 31 percent vote for an uncommitted slate of delegates in the February 25 South Dakota primary, along with polls that showed Buchanan drawing support evenly from liberals, conservatives, and moderates, suggest the latter. Either way, after New Hampshire voted donations poured in to the Buchanan campaign. Although Bush raised more money than his rival, $10.7 million compared with $5.2 million, it was mostly in the form of large contributions. Buchanan's donors outnumbered Bush's by 166,000 to 142,000. Because nearly all of them gave small amounts, the federal government matched their donations almost dollar for dollar under the Federal Election Campaign Act.[37]

The Buchanan campaign was organized only in New Hampshire, but it was able to outspend Bush on television by nearly two to one in their next confrontation in Georgia's March 3 primary. Bush continued to blunder, clumsily renouncing his tax increase in an interview with the *Atlanta Journal-Constitution* not on its merits but for "political reasons" because of "all the flak it's taking."[38] In doing so, the president forsook any claim he may have had to putting politics aside to do the right thing for the country. But his campaign stopped ignoring Buchanan and went on the attack. In one ad, retired marine commander P. X. Kelley charged, "When Pat Buchanan opposed Desert Storm, it was a disappointment to all military people."[39] More important, unlike in New Hampshire, Georgia's economy was booming, with an unemployment rate of only 4 percent.

Buchanan won 36 percent in Georgia, about the same as in New Hampshire. But Bush's 64 percent nearly doubled his margin of victory over the challenger from 16 percentage points in New Hampshire to 28 points, slowing Buchanan's momentum. One week later, Bush swept all eight of the mostly southern Super Tuesday primaries by margins ranging from 31 points to 46 points. Although four-fifths of Christian Coalition founder Pat Robertson's television audience initially had indicated that they favored Buchanan, he and other conservative Christian leaders cast their lot with Bush in order to keep their influence with the White House alive. Their support was especially valuable in the South.[40] In the aftermath of Super Tuesday, Buchanan's vote in subsequent primaries fell into the 20s and then into the teens. He lost every remaining contest and never matched his losing totals in New Hampshire and Georgia.

With an eye toward another presidential candidacy in 1996, Buchanan toned down his attacks on Bush while staying in the race so that he could continue to expand his list of small donors. He also wanted to keep his leverage in negotiations with the Bush campaign for a prime-time speaking slot at the national convention in return for his eventual endorsement. In one way, Bush actually benefited from Buchanan's continuing candidacy. As long as Buchanan was on the ballot, he displaced former Ku Klux Klan leader Duke, who entered the Republican race six days before Buchanan, as a potentially embarrassing vehicle for Republican protest against the president. Duke won no delegates in any contest and, his candidacy largely unnoticed, he dropped out of the race on April 22.

But even as Buchanan kept losing, Bush wasn't really winning, despite outpolling his opponent in all thirty-eight primaries by a total of 73 percent to 23 percent. Because most Republican contests were winner-take-all, Bush secured about 96 percent of all convention delegates. But "a 40-point win isn't considered a victory" by the media, Bush complained. "I've got to know what the hell [victory] is because I want it."[41] Fending off Buchanan not only meant taking serious rhetorical hits from his sound bite–savvy opponent but also kept Bush from carrying the fight to the Democrats. His approval rating, which fell below 50 percent in January 1992, sank to the low 40s during the primary season and the mid-30s by season's end, when California voted on June 2.

The media narrative continued to feature an out-of-touch president who seemed slow off the mark when sixty-three people died in race riots—the most destructive of life and property in American history—in late April in Los Angeles after a jury acquitted four police officers in the beating of a black man, Rodney King. Bush was then portrayed as unwilling to concede that new economic policies were needed even as the unemployment rate rose toward 8 percent. "Far better than doing something bad for the economy is doing nothing at all," he said—but who was listening?[42] On one occasion, when the president marveled at a new supermarket scanner that could read a badly torn price tag, the *New York Times* fed the prevailing narrative by inaccurately reporting that it was the first time he had ever seen a scanner. (The front-page headline of its story read, "Bush Encounters the Supermarket, Amazed.")[43] Soon after, when asked if he would make the sort of nontraditional television appearances Clinton was making on entertainment programs, Bush demurred. "You have to draw the line somewhere and I am not going to be out there being a teenybopper."[44]

PEROT FOR PRESIDENT

One reason that both Buchanan's vote and Bush's approval rating fell throughout the spring was the emergence of Ross Perot as an independent candidate. Perot drew support from Buchanan as an alternate outlet for protest. He also kept Buchanan's remaining voters from uniting behind Bush by attacking the president with particular fervor.

Serious talk by Perot about running for president began in the medium in which he was most comfortable: call-in cable television shows, especially CNN's prime-time program *Larry King Live*, which Perot inadvertently transformed from an entertainment venue into a major election-year forum for presidential candidates. The idea of an independent seeking the office was already in the air. In 1990 a governor, a senator, and a congressman had all been elected in various states by running as independents.[45] On February 20, pressed by King to declare that he would enter the race, Perot told the viewing audience, "If you're that serious—you, the people, are that serious—you register me in all fifty states" by filing petitions with enough signatures to place his name on the ballot.[46] He also said, "I wouldn't be temperamentally fit for it," referring to the "political process."[47]

Perot offered viewers no toll-free 800 number but, at a time when long-distance calls still cost money, they flooded in anyway to the corporate offices of Perot Systems in Dallas, sometimes exceeding 2,000 per hour. Perot assigned two high-ranking business associates, Tom Luce and Mort Meyerson, to tend his budding political operation. In March they rented 1,200 toll-free phone lines from cable television's Home Shopping Network and began compiling a database of those who called to volunteer. When Perot mentioned his new 800 number on *Donahue*, a syndicated daytime television talk show, a quarter million people phoned within the hour.

Perot's timing was excellent. In the past, candidates had to rely on "paid media" (that is, advertising) and "earned media" (coverage by news organizations) to get their message to the voters. Perot needed little of either. The rapid rise of cable and syndicated talk shows hosted by entertainment figures provided all the forum he required. Perot also benefited from recently eased ballot regulations. In 1980, when the last serious independent candidate, John Anderson, ran, he needed a total of 1.2 million valid signatures to get on the ballots of all fifty states. Changes in election law, often spurred by court orders, reduced that number to 716,000 by 1992.

Perot's appeal was grounded less in issues and experience dealing with them than in his seeming authenticity and businessman's commonsense approach to solving problems. Bush's claim that he had "spent 50 percent of my adult life in the private sector" fell flat because for the previous quarter century he had held one public office after another.[48] He and his major party rivals could not compete with Perot's outsider status and snappy aphorisms. "In plain Texas talk, it's time to take out the trash and clean out the barn," Perot often said. People "want a guy to get under the hood of the car and fix it."[49] Above all, Perot promised to replace the special interests, foreign lobbyists, and party politicians that he thought ran Washington with a new style of leader who would spend his time with other "leaders . . . listening, listening, listening to their ideas. . . . We then take these ideas to the people, present them to the people. The people say let's do it and now we have a system out of gridlock and a system that works."[50] How taking "these ideas" to the people, ascertaining their views, and handling the inevitable clashes of opinions and interests would work in practice was less clear, but Perot had no doubt he could do it. "In my sleep I'm a better consensus leader than anybody who's up there now," he said.[51] As for critics "accusing me of buying the election, . . . my reply to them is, that's right. I made that deal with you because you can't afford it. It's that simple."[52]

To the extent that Perot did talk about issues, his focus was on the budget deficit—"the crazy aunt you keep down in the basement—all the neighbors know she's there but no one talks about her." He wanted to cut spending by taking Social Security and Medicare from rich people, eliminating "waste, fraud, and abuse" (a common and, in practice, elusive target for generations of office seekers), and trimming back the defense budget.[53] But he also endorsed liberal positions on abortion, gay rights, and gun control and refused to rule out a tax increase, stating, "I don't know yet."[54] And when asked if he would say, "Read my lips: no new taxes," Perot replied, "You can't ever quote me as saying something that stupid."[55]

Perot took aim at both political parties, tapping into the general revulsion with Washington that arose not just from Bush's reversal on taxes and apparent indifference to the recession but also from scandals on Capitol Hill: a House bank that allowed members free overdrafts and criminal abuses of the Congressional Post Office that involved embezzlement and money laundering by some members and employees. Perot's special ire, however, was reserved for Bush, at whom he remained furious for conveying President Reagan's unwillingness to cooperate with Perot's quest to find imagined still-captive prisoners of war in Vietnam. "I will not go to war to prove my manhood," he said, a veiled criticism of Bush's conduct of the Gulf War that became explicit when he added: "For ten years his fingerprints were all over creating Saddam Hussein and putting billions of dollars in taxpayer-guaranteed loans in Hussein's pocket."[56]

"Perot never opened his mouth without trashing Bush," said Mary Matalin with only slight exaggeration.[57] For his part, Bush underestimated Perot, regarding him as a "crackpot" based on their long acquaintanceship in Texas.[58] "He's on a massive ego trip," Bush wrote in his diary, regardless of whether Perot's true purpose was "winning the election or, if not that, bringing me down."[59] But for several months both Bush and the Democrats gave Perot a free ride, sparing him from criticism. Neither side wanted to alienate his supporters, who both parties hoped would eventually abandon him in favor of either the president or his Democratic opponent. Thinking

Perot "an eccentric," the Bush campaign "didn't take him quite as seriously as we probably should have," according to White House chief of staff Sam Skinner.[60]

Perot surged in Gallup polls taken throughout spring 1992, rising steadily from his 24 percent benchmark against Bush and Clinton in the first three-way trial heat survey taken in late March.[61] But success brought challenges that Perot was not prepared to confront. In order to get on the ballot in about half the states, he was required to identify a vice presidential running mate. Lacking connections with suitable nominees, on March 30 he asked a friend, former admiral James Stockdale, if he could use his name as a placeholder. The apolitical Stockdale agreed, but only if Perot promised to find someone else before the election.[62] He promised but never did.

Perot also blundered when pressed on issues, saying that despite his support for gay rights he would not choose a gay person for his cabinet because to do so would be a "point of controversy with the American people" that "would distract from the work to be done."[63] Addressing the convention of the National Association for the Advancement of Colored People, he predicted a "long, hot summer" in which "you people" would "get hurt first."[64] On May 3, pressed insistently by *Meet the Press* host Tim Russert to be specific about how he would erase the budget deficit, Perot floundered, telling aides afterward, "The hell with this. I don't need this."[65] He went back on the entertainment talk show circuit but could not prevent news organizations from investigating his record, as they do all candidates who become serious contenders for the presidency. Perot was especially infuriated by an Associated Press account of his efforts to get out of the navy two years early because it was a "fairly Godless organization" in which "I constantly hear the Lord's name taken in vain" as well as a *Washington Post* story that claimed he had two of the president's sons investigated.[66]

Luce and Meyerson eventually told Perot that his rising political status meant he needed to hire political professionals to run his campaign. Perot accepted and even briefly embraced the idea. "Let's assume you're going to try to build a world-class NFL team," he said. "You'd probably want someone who's played football before, right?"[67] On June 3 Perot announced that he had recruited two successful presidential campaign veterans, Republican Ed Rollins and Democrat Hamilton Jordan. The political world took notice. But when they told him that running a successful race would cost about $150 million, Perot balked. Despite his earlier pledge on March 20 that he would spend from his fortune whatever it took to give his supporters a "first-class" $50 to $100 million campaign, Perot's talk show–fueled rise to first place in the polls, which cost almost nothing, convinced him that he knew more about politics than the professionals. For as long as he was a new and interesting phenomenon, Perot did. But early and rapid success sent him into uncharted waters that he was unprepared to navigate. He clearly needed advisers with national political experience to prepare him for the day when his candidacy's novelty wore off. All Perot could see, however, was how clear the sailing was, not the boat-crushing rapids that lay ahead. Weeks before quitting the campaign, Rollins told his wife, Sherrie Rollins, that Perot "is nuts and wouldn't make a good president."[68] The candidate did not help matters. "I've got a theme song for our campaign," Perot declared at a rally, at which point the loudspeakers played it: "Crazy," a Patsy Cline classic written by Willie Nelson.[69]

Temperamentally, Perot was as ill-suited to the political process as he told Larry King he was in February. He was especially sensitive to criticism from either the news media or his opponents. Bush's "dirty tricks crowd," Perot was convinced, was behind the critical news coverage he began receiving in May.[70] It wasn't, but that didn't mean that Bush administration officials did not take off the kid gloves when they saw Perot's rise in the polls coming at their expense. In the late March Gallup poll, Perot's 24 percent trailed Bush's 44 percent by 20 points. Most Buchanan supporters, whose candidate conceded on March 20 that Bush would be the Republican nominee, were ready to come home to their party in plenty of time for the general election. It even seemed possible that Perot would actually split the anti-Bush vote with Clinton, who continued to poll at 25 percent, thereby allowing the president to sail to a landslide victory in the Electoral College.

By mid-May, however, Bush's hopes for this kind of victory seemed forlorn. He fell 9 points and Perot rose by 10 points in the Gallup poll, leaving them tied at 35 percent. By early June Bush lost an additional 4 points and Perot gained the same amount, earning him a 39 percent to 31 percent lead over the president, with Clinton still trailing. Because every rise in Perot's standing was matched by an equal decline in Bush's, the president's advisers unsurprisingly deduced that all of Perot's gains were coming from their candidate.

Perot's easy ride soon ended. For months neither Bush nor Clinton had wanted to be the first to attack him. But the Bush campaign reluctantly concluded that it had no choice but to publicly place Perot's obvious weaknesses in sharp relief. Press secretary Marlin Fitzwater accused him of being a "dangerous and destructive . . . monster." Vice President Quayle ("Perot is a temperamental tycoon who has contempt for the Constitution") and his wife Marilyn (Perot is trying to "buy an election without standing for anything") joined in the assault.[71] At that point "we thought Clinton was gone," recalls Bush White House aide Thomas Scully. "We all thought we were running against Perot, which screwed up the summer because everyone kept taking shots at Perot and at the same time Clinton was building strength."[72]

Republican charges reinforced the ongoing media revelations. They had their intended effect, along with Perot's own testy reactions to them. By July 10, his support was in steep decline. He not only abandoned his candidacy on July 15, the day of Clinton's nomination by the Democratic convention, but in dropping out of the race took his revenge on Bush. "Now that the Democratic Party has revitalized itself, I have concluded that we cannot win in November," Perot announced. Two days later, already on the ballot in twenty-one states with petitions submitted for ten more and efforts under way everywhere else, he nonetheless urged his supporters to continue their state petition drives "so that everybody running for president will know the names and addresses of all the people who are unhappy with the way things are today."[73] Uncharacteristically, Clinton's immediate reaction to news of Perot's withdrawal—"Damn!" he told Carville, "Ross Perot is my main man"—was politically off the mark.[74] In truth, the combination of Perot's implicit endorsement and a successful convention launched Clinton, who had trailed both Bush and Perot all year, into a 56 percent to 34 percent lead over the president in mid-July.

KEEPING QUAYLE

The loss of Bush's lead, first against Perot and then against Clinton, roused growing pressure to replace Quayle on the ticket with a more widely respected running mate. Former presidents Richard Nixon and Gerald Ford urged this course, offering Gen. Colin Powell and Sen. Bob Dole as better choices for Bush.[75] Campaign pollster Fred Steeper found in July that replacing Quayle "with someone of neutral stature" potentially would add 10 points to Bush's total while costing it 6 points—a "net gain of 4 percentage points."[76] Quayle himself worried that Bush might choose James Baker or Secretary of Defense Cheney, who had earned a positive national reputation during the Gulf War.[77] Cheney was George W. Bush's suggestion, one that he took eight years later.[78]

The vice president had presidential ambitions of his own that hinged on serving a successful second term. He did not want to do "the biggest favor he could have done for the president—and the country, in my opinion," said Baker: namely, "to graciously take himself off the ticket."[79] Bush also hoped Quayle would volunteer to leave, especially after the vice president attacked a popular television character, Murphy Brown, in a May speech for "mocking the importance of fathers by bearing a child alone," prompting Fitzwater to publicly commend the fictional Brown for "demonstrating pro-life values" by not aborting the child.[80] (Quayle apparently had not learned from the president's own bad experience attacking *The Simpsons*.) Bush and his aides were further exasperated when, feeding the false but long-standing narrative that Quayle was not intelligent, the vice president corrected a student's accurate spelling of "potato" at an elementary school spelling bee in June by insisting that he add an "e" to the end of the word.

In the end, Quayle remained on the ticket because there was no way to push him off without making things worse. Like most modern vice presidents, Quayle had spent much of his time in office cultivating the party's grass roots with campaign and fund-raising appearances, for which local Republican activists around the country were deeply grateful.[81] Conservatives regarded him as one of the few people in the White House who were sincerely committed to their cause. "I could never get away with taking Quayle off the ticket," Bush told his diary. "I wouldn't look strong . . . and the hue-and-cry would rise up, particularly from the right."[82] Indeed, dumping Quayle would reignite the anger that fueled the Buchanan campaign, and, as Baker pointed out, "The press would say, 'Hey, you dummy, the problem is not the vice president. It's you.'"[83] Besides, Quayle had been exactly the sort of loyal and helpful vice president Bush was during the Reagan years and Bush, unlike most presidents, was the sort of person who regarded loyalty as a two-way street. After meeting privately with the president on July 24, Quayle decided to force Bush's hand by telling the *Washington Post* that his place on the ticket was secure. "There weren't any such discussions," Bush fumed in his diary, "but I have concluded that he should."[84]

THE REPUBLICAN CONVENTION

Conjecture concerning Quayle dominated much of the news coverage about Bush and the GOP during the week after the Democratic convention ended on July 16. It was soon replaced by stories speculating about whether Buchanan would endorse Bush at the Republican convention, which was scheduled to gather in Houston during the week of August 17, as well as whether the party would replace its previously undiluted pro-life platform statement on abortion with a "big tent" plank saying that the party welcomed people with other views on the issue. None of these stories did anything to advance Bush's prospects, but the president was giving reporters little else to write about. He conspicuously went fishing during the Democratic convention, then remained in governing mode as much as possible until he had no choice but to do otherwise. As Quayle complained, "In the month between the conventions . . . , our campaign remained inexplicably complacent."[85] To the extent he was right, this was the same mistake Dukakis, not Bush, made in 1988.

Oddly, on the eve of the Republican gathering, Bush somehow ended up on the less popular side of a foreign policy dispute with the internationally inexperienced Clinton, who charged that the administration was taking an unconscionably passive approach to the genocide that Serbs were inflicting on Bosnian Muslims in the former Yugoslavia. Then, on August 11, during a joint news conference with the prime minister of Israel, Bush was forced to deny a *New York Post* story ("it's a lie") that he had conducted an affair with aide Jennifer Fitzgerald.[86] "Why does the press shy away from investigating rumors of George Bush's extramarital life with Jennifer and all these other people?" Hillary Clinton complained.[87] "I just wish it were over," Bush told his diary, referring to the election.[88]

For years, the Republicans had run famously scripted, politically effective conventions, which may have contributed to their complacency in 1992. But the complacency had no basis in reality. Bush's approval rating had been in relentless decline for more than a year. Not a single week of polling, a single major event, or a single significant bit of news had gone his way in months. Perot's abandonment of the race was working completely to Clinton's advantage, as he and Al Gore campaigned vigorously and successfully on bus tours across the country. The conservatives who dominated the GOP never regarded Bush as one of their own, and those who voted in the primaries either for Buchanan or against the president (it still was not clear how many fit each category) needed to be wooed and won, lest they sit out the November election.

Effective political conventions both unite a party and broaden its appeal. Bush's team decided that, more than anything else, it had to placate the right, first on the platform and then from the podium. Although the Clinton campaign briefly considered running a "34 percent strategy" when Perot was still a candidate—that is, focus on mobilizing the left to unite Democrats and win a plurality of the popular vote en route to an electoral vote majority—it decided not to take that course.[89] Now, with Perot out of the race, the Republicans were the ones who seemed to embrace the strategy, not in name but in practice.[90] Until Bush gave his acceptance speech on the final night of the convention, the focus among the event's planners was on running to the right to unite the party rather than broadening the base with appeals to moderate and independent voters. The rationale, as explained by Matalin, was that "we had to get the Buchanan Brigade back in the tent as well as appease the more significant, antitax, anti–big government segment that was still ticked off over the 1990 budget deal."[91]

Bush's treatment of the abortion issue got him the worst of both worlds: platform language that was unyieldingly pro-life in supporting a "human rights amendment" to the Constitution to overturn *Roe v. Wade* and secure for the unborn all the protections afforded by the Fourteenth Amendment's "due process" and "equal protection" clauses, but public comments that renewed long-standing conservative doubts about the sincerity of his commitment. Asked in an NBC interview what he would do if one of his granddaughters wanted an abortion, Bush said that he "would encourage her not to do that. But of course I'd stand by my child." Asked in a follow-up, "So in the end the decision would be hers?" Bush responded, "Well, who else's could it be?"—a fair approximation of the pro-choice position that the Supreme Court upheld in late June in the case of *Planned Parenthood v. Casey*.[92] The ruling further stirred conservative anger, especially since the majority opinion was joined by Bush's first appointee to the Court, David Souter. Social conservatives were in no mood to adopt the big tent approach favored by the president.[93] Meanwhile, fiscal conservatives on the platform committee inserted a plank stating that "the tax increases of 1990 should ultimately be repealed," and Buchananites added a promise to "equip the Border Patrol with the tools, technologies, and structures necessary to secure the border." Both additions were not-too-veiled rebukes of the president.[94]

The Bush managers' handling of Buchanan was equally maladroit. So determined were they to gain his full-throated endorsement that they moved Reagan's speech out of prime time on Monday, the first night of the convention, and handed that slot to Buchanan. They did this despite concluding as early as mid-March that "Pat Buchanan is unimportant" compared with the "non-ideological protest vote on the economy and government inaction."[95] Campaign officials and Bush himself combed through the speech draft Buchanan submitted, found the passages in which he showered praise on the president, and apparently stopped reading. The rest of the speech was a full-throated assault against "abortion on demand, . . . homosexual rights, discrimination against religious schools, women in combat," and the "cultural war" and "religious war going on in our country for the soul of America."[96] For the first major address at the Republican convention to portray in such apocalyptic terms a country led for the previous twelve years by Republican presidents was especially jarring to voters. Buchanan's speech was "a polarizing event," Bush despaired in his diary after gauging the public reaction.[97] "We ended up repeating the Democrats' mistake in 1984 and 1988," Quayle lamented, referring to Jesse Jackson's prominent role at those conventions. "We showcased the candidate who had been repeatedly rejected in the primaries, and in the process we scared off the party's moderates and some independent voters."[98]

Yet, two nights later, Marilyn Quayle's red-meat rhetoric overshadowed Barbara Bush's conciliatory speech just as Buchanan's had Reagan's. "Liberals are always so angry . . . because most women do not wish to be liberated from their essential natures as . . . mothers and wives," Quayle charged.[99] "Her speech did not convey her warmth or caring," wrote Mrs. Bush with customary delicacy.[100] But Dan Quayle chose to double down in his own speech on the final night of the convention, just before the president's. Renewing Buchanan's "religious war" theme, Quayle charged that the difference between the parties was in truth a "cultural divide . . . between fighting for what is right and refusing to see what is wrong."[101]

Bush had his work cut out for him when he stepped into the spotlight. As in 1988, he needed to give an uncharacteristically great speech. Above all he had to convince Americans that he was more concerned about their economic problems than about taking sides on cultural and religious issues, and that his second term would offer more solutions than his first. But the problems that had afflicted the Bush campaign all year afflicted it once again. As the convention week unfolded, "you might wonder," Matalin wrote, "how, between three mega-organizations—a campaign, a White House, and a convention operation—we had no acceptance speech for the President of the United States. Well, we had no speech precisely because . . . no one and everyone was in charge."[102] In the end, Bush's speech was well delivered but long (fifty-four minutes, longer than Clinton's) and themeless, an admixture of attacks on Clinton and the Democratic Congress and familiar promises from the first term.[103] As election chroniclers Peter Goldman and colleagues observed, "It was as if he had emptied a truckload of bricks on the podium and said they were a house."[104] Implausibly, given his broken pledge of four years earlier, Bush raised the tax issue and asked, "Who do you trust in this election?"

George W. Bush lamented that the "chaotic process" of writing Bush's convention speech explains why, "unlike the 1988 speech, which soared and presented a positive vision, the 1992 speech was defensive and relatively flat."[105] So did the absence of speechwriter Peggy Noonan, another star player in the 1988 campaign who was no longer involved. But the deeper problem was neither organizational nor rhetorical. It was, as Quayle's chief of staff, Bill Kristol, observed, that the president "didn't want to make a fundamental statement, at any point in 1992, that, 'My second term would be fundamentally different than my first term,'" with "'a whole new attitude on domestic and economic policy.'"[106]

The Republican convention achieved its modest goal of uniting the party behind Bush. The postconvention Gallup poll showed him trailing Clinton by 49 percent to 40 percent. But because the convention had done so little to broaden the president's appeal, that 40 percent was a ceiling rather than a floor. Bush never was able to raise it in the months that followed, even after he persuaded the highly reluctant Baker to return to the White House as chief of staff and overseer of both politics and policy. Baker, masterful and deeply satisfied in his role as secretary of state, agreed to come back out of friendship and because he realized that if, as seemed likely, Bush lost the election he would be out of office too. Baker's appointment was announced on August 13, but he chose not to assume his new duties until ten days later, after the convention ended. He quickly smoothed out the organizational tangles in the White House and campaign and adroitly jettisoned the convention's culture war theme, throwing a scare into the Clinton camp. Baker was "larger than life," said James Carville, "the Babe Ruth of political operatives."[107] But even Babe Ruth never batted one thousand.

THE BATTLE FOR THE 1992
DEMOCRATIC NOMINATION

Bill Clinton's quest for the 1992 Democratic nomination
was shadowed by the aftermath of the 1968 election in a
different way than was George Bush's battle for renomination by the GOP. In Bush's case, the shadow was cast
by the postelection adoption of a reformed nominating
process that made intraparty challenges to the incumbent
more possible. In Clinton's, it was his party's defeat in four
of the next five presidential elections, all of them by landslides—including the 426–111 electoral vote victory by the
incumbent president Clinton was trying to unseat. For a
quarter century the Republicans had worked hard, steadily,
and successfully to attract groups of voters who previously
were either Democratic (southern and blue-collar northern
whites) or politically dormant (evangelical Christians) to
their national coalition using a host of racial, religious, cultural, and economic appeals.[1] The Republicans' perceived
toughness on national security issues, which historically
had little effect in elections, also was important during the
height of the Cold War between the United States and the
Soviet Union.

The Democratic Party usually played into the GOP's
hands by nominating candidates for president whom most
white voters regarded as more concerned about racial minorities than the white majority; squeamish on matters of
security, whether against communism abroad or criminals
at home; insufficiently respectful of religion and traditional
values; and determined to protect every domestic federal
program regardless of its effectiveness or cost. The lesson
from the Democrats' shrinking vote in recent elections,

Clinton speechwriter David Kusnet said, "was that if all the groups in the Democratic coalition, including labor, liberals, minorities, and women's rights advocates, were in the same tent, we could still get clobbered."[2]

Aware of these trends, as well as of the fact that their party's only victorious nominee since 1968 was the politically moderate southern governor Jimmy Carter, even liberal Democrats were tired enough of losing that they looked favorably on Clinton's candidacy as he and his rivals entered the 1992 primary season. Clinton clearly won what campaign manager David Wilhelm called the "pre-primary primary" and emerged from 1991 as the front-runner for his party's nomination.[3] His campaign's ideas-based rationale, deep pockets, and effective organization surpassed those of any other Democratic contender. His vast network, dubbed "Friends of Bill," from Yale, Oxford, the McGovern campaign, and gatherings of big thinkers at annual "Renaissance Weekends"—along with Hillary Clinton's own network from Wellesley, Yale, the Children's Defense Fund, and the Watergate investigation—helped make his candidacy palatable to many liberals in the national party. Yet so determined was Clinton to prove that he was a "different kind of Democrat" from the capital punishment–averse Michael Dukakis that, having already pledged to add 100,000 officers to the nation's police forces, he flew back to Arkansas during the New Hampshire primary campaign to oversee the execution of a convicted murderer who was brain-damaged to the point that he told the guards taking him to be lethally injected that he was saving the dessert from his last meal "for later." "It never even occurred to any of us to use the word 'liberal,'" said Clinton campaign aide Paul Begala, because voters had come to associate it with someone "more concerned with minorities than the majority" and "about the rights of criminals more than crime victims."[4] Clinton also counted on the ending of the Cold War to dilute the national security–based component of the Republican advantage in presidential elections.

In a seemingly successful effort to dissuade national political reporters from pursuing allegations about marital infidelity, both Clintons met with the "Sperling Breakfast" in September 1991 to erase doubts about their commitment to each other, even as he admitted in general terms that in the past he had caused "pain in my marriage."[5] As a consequence, the issue vanished from the mainstream media for several months. Reporters barely acknowledged a January 16, 1992, story that appeared in the *Star*, a supermarket tabloid, with the headline "DEMS' FRONT RUNNER BILL CLINTON CHEATED WITH MISS AMERICA AND FOUR OTHER BEAUTIES." Indeed, nothing seemed to slow Clinton's early momentum, including Sen. Tom Harkin's victory in the February 10 Iowa caucuses. Because Harkin's home state was Iowa, Clinton and the other candidates conceded the contest to him, which meant that Harkin gained little and they lost nothing when he defeated "uncommitted," his nearest rival among caucus-goers, by 76.4 percent to 12.0 percent. Not having to campaign in Iowa, whose left-leaning Democratic electorate typically encouraged candidates to take extreme positions that later haunted them in the general election, came as a relief to Clinton and his staff.

Although Clinton faced another local favorite, former Massachusetts senator Paul Tsongas, in New Hampshire, that did not discourage him or his other rivals—Harkin, Sen. Bob Kerrey of Nebraska, and former California governor Jerry Brown—from going all in. Kerrey was the only other contender besides Clinton whose prospects major donors and the national media took seriously, mostly because of his Medal of Honor status as a navy SEAL in the Vietnam War and his repeated success as a Democrat in solidly Republican Nebraska. Clinton himself, in a phone call with paramour Gennifer Flowers, said, "I might lose the nomination to Bob Kerrey because he's . . . got all the Gary Hart/Hollywood money, and because he's single, looks like a movie star, won the Medal of Honor, and since he's single, nobody cares if he's screwing."[6] Harkin, well funded like Clinton and Kerrey but chiefly by labor unions, hoped that he could win by being the only traditional liberal in the race. Brown was praying that lightning would strike, as it soon did for Ross Perot, because of his attacks on big money in politics and use of a toll-free number to encourage small donations. But Brown, unlike Perot, was a longtime politician, not a fresh face on the political scene. In the end, including matching funds from the federal government, Brown raised $9.4 million from 84,600 donors. This was more than any of Clinton's other Democratic rivals, an artifact of Brown's staying in the race long after they dropped out. Clinton had twice as many donors as Brown—169,200—and their larger average gifts meant that he ultimately raised four times as much money for his nomination campaign: $37.6 million.[7]

NEW HAMPSHIRE

Neither Kerrey, Harkin, nor Brown gained much traction with New Hampshire voters. Tsongas did. In addition to being familiar to them, he impressed many as a straight shooter, unafraid to tout his pro-business, anti–deficit spending agenda even though it might be unpopular. Truth-telling about politically sensitive issues was the lane Clinton hoped to dominate, but his espousal of a middle-class tax cut enabled Tsongas to attack him as just another politician making irresponsible promises. Although both candidates stood out from the field by having a well-developed economic plan, Tsongas's tough medicine initially seemed more curative than Clinton's, which was sweetened with the tax cut. Nevertheless, polls showed Clinton with a healthy lead as late as January 23, one month before the February 23 primary.

January 23, however, turned out to be an especially difficult day for Clinton. One week after running its widely ignored sex story about him, the *Star* ran another, its front-page blaring, "THEY MADE LOVE ALL OVER HER APARTMENT." Ignoring this story was impossible because it was based on public testimony from Little Rock lounge singer Gennifer Flowers, generally supported by excerpts from fifteen taped telephone conversations. Flowers claimed that she "was Bill Clinton's lover for twelve years" and that he told her, "If everybody is on record denying it . . . no problem."[8] Six years later Clinton admitted the affair under oath, but for now denial was the watchword. James Carville told a group of Clinton fund-raisers, "This is nothing but a trollop and we are going to smash the shit out of her in the news media"; he also said, "If you drag a hundred-dollar bill through a trailer park, you never know what you'll find."[9] Hillary Clinton dismissed Flowers as "some failed cabaret singer" and formed a "defense team" headed by longtime Arkansas aide Betsey Wright to stifle "bimbo eruptions" from Flowers and any of the other nineteen women mentioned in various tabloids. Wright pressured them to sign affidavits denying they had sex with Clinton.[10]

In the meantime, both Clintons decided they once again must address the infidelity charge, this time in public. They did much to defuse it when they appeared before a massive television audience—perhaps the largest for any news program in history—on CBS's *60 Minutes*, which aired right after the January 26 Super Bowl between the Washington Redskins and the Buffalo Bills. "You're looking at two people who love each other," Bill Clinton declared. "This is a marriage."[11] Even as she denied "sitting here, some little woman standing by my man like Tammy Wynette," Hillary Clinton sat there standing by her man. The next day Wynette, whose classic country song "Stand by Your Man" inspired Clinton's comment, angrily declared that the singer was not her song.[12] "I believe you have offended every person who has made it on their own with no one to take them to the White House," Wynette added.[13]

Eight days later, on February 6, a different allegation was published in the widely respected *Wall Street Journal* recounting Clinton's efforts to avoid military service in Vietnam. In 1969 Clinton promised to enroll in ROTC at the University of Arkansas law school but then reneged when he drew a high enough number (311 out of 366) in the newly instituted draft lottery to make certain that he would not be conscripted. Clinton "was able to manipulate things so that he didn't have to go in," said Col. Eugene Holmes, the ROTC commander who handled Clinton's case in Fayetteville. On February 7 ABC News broadcast an anguished letter Clinton sent to Holmes two days after he learned he was immune from the draft that included the unfortunate phrases "maintain my political viability" and "thank you for saving me from the draft."[14] In 1988, Clinton had criticized Dan Quayle for joining the National Guard to avoid serving in Vietnam, saying, "What matters is not what it is that you did. What matters is just level with us and tell us exactly what you did."[15] Campaign pollster Stan Greenberg told Clinton that in New Hampshire his support suffered an immediate "melt-down," dropping "like a turd in a well" (Clinton's phrase) from 37 percent to 17 percent in his surveys after the *Journal* story and draft letter were published.[16] "All I've been asked about by the press are a woman I did not sleep with and a draft I did not dodge," Clinton lied.[17] In Washington, Al Gore "bet me Clinton would not be the nominee," recalled Gore's chief of staff, Roy Neel.[18]

What enabled Clinton to survive the Flowers and draft controversies with a solid second-place finish behind Tsongas? He won 24.7 percent compared with Tsongas's 33.2 percent, with roughly 10 percent each going to Kerrey, Harkin, and Brown, who finished in that order.

For one thing, Clinton took a page from previous surprise runners-up, going on national television early on primary night before the magnitude of Tsongas's victory was apparent to proclaim joyously that "New Hampshire has made Bill Clinton the Comeback Kid." (Republican Pat Buchanan was saying essentially the same thing about his own showing.) A second part of the answer is personal. "He had the tenacity and the courage to stand up and take it," said media adviser Frank Greer, "when a Gary Hart or somebody—I mean the tradition in American politics has been, 'Let's just collapse, let's walk away.'"[19] Clinton translated his own adversity into the idiom of a small state whose economy was suffering. "That's when he said [to the voters], 'The hits I've taken are nothing compared to the hits that you've taken,'" policy aide Bruce Reed pointed out. "They loved that about him."[20] "If you'll give [this election] to me," Clinton vowed in a memorable speech at the Elks Club in Dover, New Hampshire, "I'll never forget who gave me a second chance, and I'll be there for you until the last dog dies."[21]

A third reason Clinton survived Flowers and the draft was organizational. His campaign's strong funding meant he was able not only to propose a detailed, centrist economic plan but also to publicize it widely in multiple ads and televised town meetings, which gave him "the strength to withstand two major bits of scandal, largely on the strength of his plan," according to Greer. "Even the national press corps said, 'We may be a little carried away with this,'" fearing that they might be engaging in the same sort of "feeding frenzy" that drove Gary Hart from the race in 1987 and therefore backing off for a couple weeks.[22]

In the modern history of presidential elections, almost no one has earned a party's nomination without winning in either Iowa or New Hampshire. But after losing both states, Clinton was well on his way to doing so.

VICTORY IN MARCH

Like Buchanan on the Republican side, Clinton emerged from second place in New Hampshire with the wind at his back. Unlike Buchanan, Clinton had the money and organization to fight through the long primary campaign that lay ahead. Tsongas might win isolated contests in the Northeast and elsewhere, as he did the Massachusetts primary and Delaware caucuses. Kerrey might prevail in a small western state like South Dakota, which he did on February 25. Brown could compete successfully in scattered low-turnout caucus states like Maine (February 23) and Nevada (March 8). But when multiple primaries were scheduled for the same day, only Clinton had the resources to compete everywhere. And with Gov. Mario Cuomo not in the race and Harkin no longer a viable contender, Clinton did not have to worry about guarding his left flank. Indeed, because Tsongas had emerged as his main rival, Clinton could move even further toward the center, where he was most comfortable anyway. Nor were any of his rivals experienced at campaigning among black voters, enabling Clinton (who as a southerner was) to win a strong majority of their support without having to make too many overt appeals.

The first multiple-contest day was March 3—dubbed "Junior Tuesday" because it preceded the even larger Super Tuesday by one week—when seven states held their primaries and caucuses. In one sense it was the high-water mark of the Tsongas campaign. Tsongas won caucuses outside his home region in Utah and Washington State and a much higher-visibility primary in Maryland. But when he narrowly lost the Colorado primary to Brown, Tsongas was denied the sort of sweeping victory that could have made him the co-front-runner. Still worse was his landslide defeat by Clinton in the delegate-rich Georgia primary, despite the endorsement of the state's leading newspaper, the *Atlanta Journal-Constitution*. Clinton took off the gloves in advance of the contest, declaring that he was "tired of what is cold-blooded being passed off as courageous"—a slap at Tsongas's pro-business austerity campaign.[23] Drawing on support from Georgia's popular conservative Democratic governor, Zell Miller, as well as from prominent liberal African American Democrats such as Rep. John Lewis and Atlanta mayor Maynard Jackson, Clinton won by 57.2 percent to 24.0 percent. Explaining his endorsement of Clinton, Lewis said, "In the communities I deal with, . . . they want to see a Democrat in the White House. They understand that in order to win, it's necessary to bring back those individuals who had left the party."[24]

Kerrey and Harkin, who ran badly everywhere on Junior Tuesday, dropped out of the race the following week rather than accumulate further debt by trying to compete in the March 10 Super Tuesday primaries. Five of the eight primaries held that day were in the South, and Clinton swept them easily. Florida, with its dense concentration of migrants from the Northeast and Midwest, was the only southern state that Tsongas contested. Even there, Clinton won by 50.8 percent to 34.5 percent. For the first time, southern Democratic leaders' purpose when creating Super Tuesday in 1984—to boost a candidate who could compete against the Republican nominee in their conservative region—was fulfilled. One week later, on March 17, Clinton easily disposed of Tsongas in two industrial midwestern states, Illinois and Michigan, defeating his rival by margins of two to one and three to one, respectively. In a further demonstration that Clinton was not a traditional liberal Democrat, the campaign's deputy communications director Robert Boorstin recalled, "We went to an AFL-CIO hall in Flint and we said we are for NAFTA [the North American Free Trade Agreement]. Heretical. We went to [white working-class] Macomb County and we talked about race. Heretical. Then the next morning we went to the black church [in Detroit] and we gave the exact same talk."[25]

Eager for a nominee to emerge from the primaries as early in the year as possible, Democratic National Committee chair Ron Brown told Clinton that the nominating contest was essentially over after Illinois and Michigan and began mobilizing the party's resources behind him.[26] Tsongas, like Kerrey before him, dropped out on March 19, but not before both inflicted rhetorical wounds on Clinton. Kerrey said that Clinton "will not win in November" because he is "going to be opened up like a soft peanut" by the Republicans.[27] Tsongas called Clinton a "panderer" because of his promise to cut taxes and willingness to "say anything to get elected," even holding up a stuffed animal and saying, "This is my opponent—pander bear."[28] Unlike Clinton's two serious rivals, however, Brown reprised the role he played in 1976, when he became the ABC candidate—Anybody But Carter. He stayed in the race after the presumptive nominee's other rivals dropped out so he could claim part of the national media spotlight while gathering the votes of all the Democrats who remained dissatisfied.

In 1992, ABC meant "Anybody But Clinton." When the *New York Times* ran a complicated front-page story on March 8 with the headline "CLINTONS JOINED S & L OPERATOR IN AN OZARK REAL ESTATE VENTURE" called Whitewater, all that most readers could remember was the vague aroma of another Clinton scandal and the fact that Hillary Clinton, in addition to being an investor in the venture, did some legal work for the savings and loan institution when she was with the Rose Law Firm in Little Rock.[29] A week later the *Washington Post* reported that the Rose firm had done considerable business for the state when Clinton was governor, downplaying Hillary Clinton's claim that she did not personally profit from that share of the firm's income.[30] Brown picked up these news stories and ran with them. In a March 15 debate he charged that Clinton "is funneling money to his wife's law firm for state business." Both Clintons took the bait. The red-faced candidate told Brown, "You're not worth being on the same platform with my wife."[31] His wife testily told a reporter, "I suppose I could have stayed home and baked cookies, and had teas. But what I decided to do was to fulfill my profession."[32] Throughout the campaign, Clinton had often said that with his brilliant, politically experienced spouse at his side, voters would get "two for the price of one" if they elected him.[33] Now that seemed like less of a bargain, especially to women who had chosen homemaking over the workforce.

LOSING WHILE WINNING

To his dismay, just when Clinton hoped that his March 17 victories in Illinois and Michigan meant that the battle for the nomination was over, Brown narrowly won the March 24 Connecticut primary. With the New York primary scheduled for April 7, this meant that Clinton had to endure Brown's "scandal-of-the-week" and "prince of sleaze" accusations for at least fourteen more days in the highly charged media environment of New York City.[34] At a time when marijuana was everywhere illegal, Clinton stumbled when pressed in a debate by local media to say whether he had ever smoked it. "A time or two" in England, he grudgingly admitted, then opened himself to mockery by adding, "I didn't inhale."[35] But the more Clinton campaigned in New York, the more surefooted he became. He adroitly deflected the popular drive-time radio host Don Imus, who usually referred to him as "Bubba." In Arkansas, Clinton said, "Bubba" meant *mensch*, the Yiddish term for a solid guy. He stared down syndicated television talk show host Phil Donahue, who pressed him repeatedly about Gennifer Flowers. Clinton said the "story is not true," then told Donahue that if he didn't move on to the "real issues, . . . we're going to sit here a long time in silence, Phil. I'm not going to an-swer any more of these questions."[36] Donahue's normally adoring studio au-dience cheered Clinton loudly. Meanwhile, Brown was repeating Al Gore's mistake in 1988, when he awkwardly attached his campaign to the city's controversial mayor, Ed Koch. Brown made the equal and opposite error of embracing Koch's nemesis, declaring that Jesse Jackson—who had called New York City "Hymietown"—would be his vice presidential running mate.

Clinton won New York handily and then beat Brown everywhere else, including in his home-state California primary on June 2, where Clinton prevailed by 47.5 percent to 40.2 percent. A month earlier, he had outraced Bush to Los Angeles in the aftermath of the Rodney King riots, showing sympathy as he walked though poor black neighborhoods while making clear, "I have a good law-and-order record and I condemn the violence as well as the [jury] verdict" that acquitted the police officers who severely beat King.[37]

Overall, Clinton won twenty-eight of his party's thirty-five primaries, vindicating his campaign's decision to bypass the caucus states, where he was victorious in only five of twenty-one. (See appendix B for the results of the state primaries and caucuses.) His support among African American voters was as crucial to victory as his support among more conservative whites. Clinton won 52.0 percent of the total Democratic primary vote— 10.5 million out of 20.2 million cast—but he carried about 70 percent of the black vote, which made up a large share of his party's primary electorate in southern and industrial states.[38] Like Carter in 1976, Clinton benefited from being the only candidate in the race who had long experience cam-paigning not just among white voters but also among African Americans, visiting with them while governor at funerals, at schools, and in church, and dealing with their leaders.

Clearly the absence of Jackson from the contest—and even Gov. Douglas Wilder's decision to drop out, which Clinton thought earned him whatever votes Wilder might have gotten—was to Clinton's advantage.[39] As James Carville pointed out, for a southern white to win the Democratic presidential nomination, as Carter had in 1976 and 1980, "there was no path to victory unless you have southern blacks in there."[40] Clinton also was able to work around Jackson in a way that Walter Mondale and Michael Dukakis were not in 1984 and 1988. He didn't need Jackson to be "the emissary for validation to the black community," said Rep. Mike Espy, a Congressional Black Caucus member from Mississippi. "He could go himself. He was very comfortable already."[41] In one highly publicized incident, Clinton implicitly rebuked Jackson at a June 13 gathering of the Rainbow Coalition. The night before Clinton spoke to the organization, rapper Sister Souljah, who recently had said, "If black people kill black people every day, why not have a week and kill white people?," was on the event's stage. When it was Clinton's turn, he said that these words were "filled with a kind of hatred you do not honor."[42] Jackson was upset afterward and, even more, when Clinton made clear that he was not considering him for vice president because they were "too incompatible." According to Carville, Clinton's message was: "I'm not going to insult you the way that Mondale and Dukakis did and pretend that you're being seriously considered. Those guys never seriously considered you."[43]

Unlike any of his rivals, Clinton was able to appeal to white voters by disrespecting Jackson and taking conservative positions on some issues without jeopardizing his black support. In addition to his personal ease with African Americans, Clinton strongly endorsed affirmative action and had an extensive record of appointing blacks to prominent positions in his gubernatorial cabinet. For black Democrats who had been frozen out of jobs in the Republican-dominated executive branch for twelve years, nominating a racially liberal candidate who was moderate enough on other issues to be elected was an appealing prospect. Another reason for Clinton's success was the way he articulated his more conservative views. Like other conservative Republicans, Ronald Reagan had decried welfare by conjuring an unnamed "welfare queen" who supposedly was raking in "$150,000 a year" under "80 names."[44] When Clinton talked about "ending welfare as we know it," he celebrated a black woman from his state named Lillie Hardin. Hardin "had recently found work as a cook. . . . I asked Lillie what was the best thing about being off welfare. Without hesitation she replied, 'When my boy goes to school and they ask him, "What does your mama do for a living?" he can give an answer.'"[45]

THE MANHATTAN PROJECT

Whether measured by his ideological position within the broad center of the American electorate or by his generally positive relations with his party's victory-starved constituency groups, Clinton emerged from the primaries with an issues agenda that positioned him well for the fall campaign. According to deputy political director Nancy McFadden, "traditional Democratic constituencies," desperately tired of losing presidential elections, accepted that "this election is bigger than them. It is bigger than a labor union. It is bigger than the Sierra Club. It is bigger than the Gray Panthers. It is bigger than the choice issue alone."[46] "The pragmatic sense of wanting to win again was very strong among some labor leaders," according to Greer, including "Jerry McEntee, who was head of the American Federation of State, County, and Municipal Employees."[47] Public employee unions, which already were outstripping traditional trade unions in membership, were exactly the sector of organized labor that Clinton had long experience dealing with as governor.[48] And yet as late as the end of June, only one-fourth of voters polled by Gallup supported Clinton in the general election, leaving him well behind Bush and Perot. Among voters in the California Democratic primary, a plurality chose Clinton over Brown, but more of them said they would have voted for Perot if he had been on the ballot. (The same was true of the state's Republican primary voters, who preferred Perot to Bush).[49] The reason had little to do with Clinton's platform and nearly everything to do with what people thought of him as a man.

This conclusion emerged from the Clinton staff's "Manhattan Project," an effort by a few aides, notably Carville, Greenberg, Greer, and media adviser Mandy Grunwald, to peel off from the day-to-day campaign in April, figure out what voters did not like about Clinton, and develop a strategy to fix it. "After the win in New York we were going to win [the nomination] and it was foolish for the strategic people to be involved in the ongoing primary thing," said Carville.[50] Officially called the General Election Project, it was nicknamed the Manhattan Project "because we thought we were dealing with that scale of a problem," said Greenberg, referring to the government's campaign to develop an atomic bomb during World War II.[51] "This is what people knew"—or thought they did—about Clinton, said Paul Begala: "Yale, Georgetown, Oxford, dodged the draft, smoked pot, cheated on his wife." Stitched together, these perceptions added up to a portrait of a candidate who was "rich, spoiled, never had a hard day in his life."[52] But when aides told focus groups in Allentown, Pennsylvania, and California's

San Fernando Valley about Clinton's hardscrabble origins and upbringing in Hope and Hot Springs, his decision to return home to Arkansas after bootstrapping his way up the educational ladder to work on issues such as jobs and education, and his refusal to use his power as governor to let his brother off a drug charge, their opinions changed to include phrases such as "down to earth," "self-made," "honest, hard struggle," and "no silver spoon."[53] Hence was born the "Man from Hope" strategy of reintroducing Clinton to voters as a man who overcame adversity, rose high, and then committed himself to helping those who grew up in circumstances like his own. If the messenger became credible, the Manhattan Project concluded, the voters would listen to his message.

Closely related to Bill Clinton's image problems were Hillary Clinton's. In many ways, she had been of enormous value to him in winning the Democratic nomination. In what was shaping up at the congressional level to be "The Year of the Woman," during which a record number of mostly Democratic women were elected to Congress, feminists were disappointed that the field of presidential contenders was all male. Some regarded Clinton in particular as a kind of overgrown southern frat boy. But Hillary Clinton's presence by her husband's side went a long way to validate his openness to feminist concerns.

Still, with the nomination won and the general election looming, Greenberg and his pollster partner, Celinda Lake, found reasons for concern in their polling data. They reported in a memo to the Clinton campaign dated May 12 that voters thought of Hillary Clinton as "the corporate lawyer, the political strategist, and the tough political wife," as well as being "too politically ambitious, too strong, and too ruthless"—more like Nancy Reagan, whom "they dislike," than Barbara Bush and Eleanor Roosevelt, whom they liked. As for Clinton's "buy one, get one free" boast about his wife, voters "don't want any suggestion that someone who has not been elected will exercise presidential authority." Greenberg and Lake recommended that Hillary Clinton "pick up one issue to highlight during the campaign, as Barbara Bush chose litereacy" (an odd word to misspell). "Oh man," said the loyal candidate, when presented with such research. "They don't like her hair."[54] In contrast, Hillary Clinton faced the results head-on and, eager for her husband to win the election, accepted the need "to project a softer side—some humor, some informality."[55] For the rest of the campaign, she did "a lot of what presidential candidates' wives traditionally had done," wrote her biographer, Carl Bernstein: "sit demurely on stage through the drone of their husbands' speeches . . . and wave to the cheering crowds at oratory's end."[56]

During the six-week period between the last primary and the Democratic convention, executing the new strategy meant disengaging from reporters, who only wanted to ask Clinton tactical political questions. Instead Clinton appeared on nontraditional television programs, such as the late-night *Arsenio Hall Show* and MTV's *Choose or Lose*. The candidate sported shades and saxophone and played "Heartbreak Hotel" on the former and freely answered a question about his sign (Leo), his favorite musician (Kenny G), and his willingness to inhale marijuana ("Sure, if I could") on the latter.[57] Clinton also made the rounds of *Larry King Live, Good Morning America, Today, CBS This Morning,* and the other talk shows that Perot used to such advantage. The hosts of these programs, as well as their callers, were interested in learning about Clinton the man and in giving him a chance to talk about the issues that animated his candidacy.[58] Realizing that Clinton's wide range of themes and promises—national health insurance; opportunity, responsibility, and community; a pro-choice abortion policy that would keep the procedure "safe, legal" but also "rare"; and a middle-class tax cut—meant that none of them were standing out enough to get through to the voters, he and his advisers arrived at the unifying theme that drove the rest of the campaign: "putting people first." The slogan was shorthand for a program to invest in the nation's human capital with student loans, job training, a work-oriented welfare program, and similar efforts. The program was rooted in friend and Berkeley economist Robert Reich's theory that because other forms of capital, notably factories, were free to move overseas, the federal government should invest in developing the productive capacity of the American people, who were here to stay.

Even with Perot still running first or second in the polls, the Manhattan Project advised Clinton to reject what Carville disparaged as "the so-called 38 Percent Strategy"—namely, win a plurality against Bush and Perot by seeking to "get your core base out. Get the black vote out. Get the liberals out. Work through the unions. That is not a strategy. That is crazy thinking."[59] It wasn't crazy, but Carville and his colleagues were convinced that if voters learned who Clinton was and what he stood for, the Democratic base would turn out and so would many white southern and centrist voters—the so-called Reagan Democrats—who in recent years had shunned the party's presidential candidates. Even so, Greenberg "felt that our best shot was to make sure that our 34 percent showed up," according to Reed.[60]

In some ways the 38 (or 34) percent strategy was a variation on the standard political playbook. Part of the prevailing lore of American politics in 1992 was that to be elected president a candidate must run to his party's ideological extreme to get the nomination, and then tack toward the center to win the general election. If Clinton had run to the left to win Democratic primary voters, he could not have stayed there through November. But Clinton did not do that. From October 1991 to November 1992, his centrist message hardly changed at all. Clinton "kept saying to me, 'I need a new stump speech,'" says Begala. "I would give him one and he would say, 'There's nothing in here that wasn't in my announcement speech.' And I would say, 'That's because on announcement day you knew why you wanted to be president.'"[61] The campaign's "workhorse" ad all year, according to Mandy Grunwald, was "the first spot we did on welfare. . . . It was a really boring spot."[62] But Clinton's promise to move people "from welfare to work" continued to air because the campaign's research showed that it connected with voters.

THE DEMOCRATIC CONVENTION

Good strategy met good fortune when two events broke in Clinton's favor during the early summer, the latter of which was outside his control. First, on July 9, four days before the Democrats gathered in convention, Clinton tapped Gore for vice president. In contrast to Bush, who in 1988 ran a closed process for choosing his running mate in which prospects were first contacted just three weeks before the Republican convention, Clinton began focusing on his choice in early spring.[63] He told campaign chair Mickey Kantor, who along with Warren Christopher, Vernon Jordan, and former Vermont governor Madeleine Kunin helped run the vice presidential search, to "throw out all notions of what the criteria politically had been in the past and think about this from a new perspective."[64] This was not entirely true: all the finalists on Clinton's list were Washington figures, which was the default setting for presidential nominees like Carter and Reagan (and himself) whose experience was in state government. Kerrey made the final cut, along with Rep. Lee Hamilton of Indiana, a foreign policy specialist, and Senators Bob Graham of Florida, Harris Wofford of Pennsylvania, and Gore. Although Clinton and Gore "had been natural rivals" (Reed) and "had virtually no relationship" (Neel), they had a professional respect for each other and hit it off personally in a three-hour, late-night meeting.[65]

Clinton's choice of Gore took the political world by surprise.[66] It defied all the traditional canons of ticket balancing: both men were southerners, Southern Baptists, baby boomers with young families, policy "wonks," and ideological centrists. The day after the forty-five-year-old Clinton announced

An August 1992 campaign rally in Austin, Texas, featuring Democratic presidential nominee Bill Clinton, Hillary Clinton, and vice presidential nominee Al Gore. Courtesy of Larry Murphey, University of Texas Public Affairs Records.

the forty-four-year-old Gore's selection, they went jogging together, borrowing a tactic that Bush deployed during the 1980 nomination campaign to remind voters how much younger he was than Reagan.[67] This time the contrast was with Bush, who had collapsed with an irregular heartbeat while jogging in May 1991. In all the obvious ways—region, religion, ideology, and so on—Gore reinforced rather than offset Clinton's most visible qualities. In more subtle ways, however, Gore did bring balance to the ticket. Clinton's potential vulnerabilities as a foreign policy novice, pro-industry governor (his state's Pollution Control and Ecology Commission was widely known as the Pollution Permission Commission), skirt chaser, and draft avoider were buttressed by Gore's Senate experience, environmentalist credentials, straight-arrow lifestyle, and service in the Vietnam War. To most voters, Gore also provided a welcome contrast to Bush's gaffe-prone vice president. An election year poll found that voters thought Gore was "more qualified to be president" than Dan Quayle by 63 percent to 21 percent.[68]

The break that fell into Clinton's lap came on July 15, the third day of the Democratic convention. Perot, besieged by critical news stories about his naval service, business dealings, use of private investigators, and testy, suspicious temperament, withdrew from the race. Better still for the

Democrats, he halfway endorsed Clinton by saying that "the Democratic party has revitalized itself," while having nothing good to say about Bush and the Republicans.[69] Although Perot urged supporters to continue their efforts to get his name on the ballot in all fifty states, his withdrawal meant that voters who were dissatisfied with the incumbent president now had only one alternative rather than two. As such it contributed to Clinton's emergence from the convention with a strong lead.

So did the Democrats' uncharacteristic display of unity when they assembled on July 13 at New York City's Madison Square Garden. A political party only gets one chance every four years to command the attention of tens of millions of voters. Its four-day-long national convention conveys to the electorate an image of either competence and coherence or ineptitude and discord, with predictable effects on many voters' willingness to entrust the party with control of the executive branch. For nearly a half century, most Republican conventions had conveyed a confidence-inspiring image and most Democratic conventions a doubts-raising one. In 1992 (as at the convention that nominated Carter in 1976, the Democrats' only recent winning year), this pattern was reversed. Buchanan, not Bush, set the tone at the Republican gathering, just as Reagan had in 1976 even as he lost the nomination to Gerald Ford. In contrast, the Democratic convention was all Clinton, all the time. The unity projected by the party's leaders and activists gathered in New York fostered unity among Democratic voters across the country. Their view of Clinton rose from 34 percent favorable before the convention to 64 percent afterward.[70]

Democratic National Committee chair Ron Brown's yearlong effort to unify the party behind its presumptive nominee as early as possible and then design the convention as a weeklong infomercial for him and his running mate contributed to this success. The sort of platform fights, credentials challenges, and rules disputes that plagued previous conventions were snuffed out in advance. Dissident party leaders like Jerry Brown and Jesse Jackson were denied prominent speaking roles on the convention program unless they offered a full-throated endorsement of Clinton. Jackson fell into line and got a prime-time slot, as did most of Clinton's defeated rivals: Harkin, Kerrey, and Tsongas. Brown did not. Neither did Gov. Robert Casey of Pennsylvania, who was denied any podium time at all as punishment for describing the platform's abortion plank as "abortion-on-demand," as well as for withholding his endorsement from Clinton. Because the three broadcast television networks had decided to reduce their coverage of the convention to about an hour per night, the DNC chair worked especially hard to assure that the speakers scheduled to appear during those sixty-plus minutes were all singing from the same songbook and did not exceed their allotted time. "What Ron Brown gave to the nominee was a party united and under control—be good, behave, be quiet, let's get somebody elected, and let's see what it's like to be back in the White House," said Bush political affairs director Dave Carney.[71]

For the Clinton campaign, the convention provided the best opportunity to apply the conclusions of the Manhattan Project. The candidate's lengthy acceptance speech was unmemorable—"a B–," according to Carville—but it did the job. Clinton mixed specific appeals to feminists, environmentalists, gays, and other powerful Democratic constituencies with broader appeals to less partisan voters and Perot supporters—"an army of patriots for change"—whom he invited to "join us, and together we will revitalize America."[72] Working hard to get reporters to pick up the phrase he had introduced the previous fall in his Georgetown University speeches, Clinton declared, "The New Covenant is a solemn agreement between the people and their government based not simply on what each of us can take but on what all of us must give to our nation. We offer opportunity. We demand responsibility. We will build an American community again." Even more appealing than the speech was a seventeen-minute biographical film telling the up-from-nowhere story of "The Man from Hope." The film, whose dramatic high point came when Clinton recalled standing up to his violent stepfather as a teenager and saying, 'Don't you ever, ever lay your hand on my mother again," was shown to the delegates and telecast by all the networks.[73] In telling his life story, it omitted any mention of Georgetown and Oxford and only referred to Yale as the site of his and Hillary's "meet-cute."

In 1988 Dukakis chose to spend the weeks between the Democratic and Republican conventions in Boston, being governor of Massachusetts. The Bush campaign filled the silence with a series of largely unanswered attacks that severely weakened Dukakis before the fall campaign even began. Four years later the governor of Arkansas made a different choice. He and Gore, both of them young, attractive, and energetic, and their equally engaging families hit the campaign trail. Eschewing both air travel, which takes candidates from tarmac to tarmac, and the more traditional "whistle-stop" train tour, which can only go where the tracks take it, the Clintons and Gores boarded buses, overcoming some staffers' objection that "you can't put two southern guys on a bus; they're going to look like hayseeds."[74] For six days the candidates headed west from New York City, drawing ecstatic crowds at multiple stops in New Jersey, Pennsylvania, West Virginia, Ohio, Kentucky,

Indiana, Illinois, and Missouri. In 1988 Bush carried all of these states but West Virginia, outscoring Dukakis by 121 electoral votes to 5. He did so by dominating the states' southern and central areas, outside the big cities, which is why campaign manager David Wilhelm "was absolutely adamant" about going there.[75] The obvious pleasure that Clinton and Gore took in each other's company reinforced the perception that they would function as a dynamic team if they were elected. They "were like two guys at their twentieth reunion who really didn't know each other in school, but just discovered that they have a lot in common," according to Roy Neel.[76] The bus tour worked so well that others were later sprinkled throughout the fall calendar.

Meanwhile, Clinton's campaign team, which had seen how effectively Bush emerged from his convention four years earlier, developed what Greenberg called the "Teeter Project," taking its name from Bush's main strategist. In an effort to "role-play" the Bush campaign's best strategy for exploiting Clinton's weaknesses, Greenberg and colleagues "created ads for them against us and developed the response ads to those ads." They discovered that a frontal assault on Clinton's character did not resonate with focus groups, but that "if you attacked his Arkansas record as a bad record—raising taxes, failed governor—that was much more effective." In fact, they concluded, if Bush first softened up Clinton with attacks on his record, then character attacks would be take root in fertilized soil. Anticipating that Bush would run a smart campaign, the Clinton team developed response ads to mute the expected attacks. "I think we would have won no matter what," said Greenberg, but the Bush campaign made things easier when it "did the opposite"—character attacks first, then attacks on the record.[77]

Clinton's postconvention "bounce" far exceeded the usual 5 to 6 percentage points for a party's nominee.[78] In the first Gallup poll that did not include Perot, taken on the eve of the Democratic convention, Clinton trailed Bush by 8 points, 48 percent to 40 percent. In the first one taken after the convention, Clinton led by 22 points (56 percent to 34 percent), a lead that grew to 25 points after the bus tour. Speaking of the Democratic gathering, Bush campaign aide Mary Matalin ruefully conceded, "Clinton went in there on his knees and sprinted out as America's panacea. It was the most stunning 180 I'd ever seen in politics."[79]

6

UNITING GOVERNMENT
THE GENERAL ELECTION FOR
PRESIDENT AND CONGRESS IN 1992

By Labor Day weekend, historically the starting gun for the general election, both George Bush and Bill Clinton were already vigorously touring the country appealing for votes. Both candidates benefited from organizational changes designed to see them through the next two months, until Election Day on November 3. James Baker's return to the White House as chief of staff after the Republican convention brought an end to the indecisiveness and lack of coordination that had plagued the Bush campaign. The White House ceased to be "the black hole" into which ideas disappeared, said Mary Matalin. "We got all kinds of decisions. There was no wasted time."[1] Although the quality of the strategic and tactical decisions made by Baker and his new team was yet to be revealed, his return worried Clinton's campaign staff, which had seen him lead the charge in 1988 that transformed a 17-point deficit against Democratic rival Michael Dukakis into an 8-point victory for Bush. "In the pantheon of presidential campaign strategists," said senior campaign strategist James Carville, "Jim Baker is the gold standard."[2]

Clinton's organizational response was to create the "war room" at his Little Rock headquarters. Having avoided Dukakis's mistake of wasting the weeks between the two parties' national conventions, he was determined to avoid Dukakis's other major mistake as well: letting attacks, however preposterous, go unanswered. The war room, named by Hillary Clinton, was a twenty-four-hour-a-day rapid response unit whose mantra was "Get hit?—hit back harder."[3] Rapid response was especially valuable to the Clinton campaign because twelve of Bush's campaign ads attacked his opponent, with nine of them focusing on Clinton's character. In contrast, only eleven of twenty-four Clinton ads were negative, and just three attacked the president's character.[4]

By night, war room staffers used new satellite technology to monitor Bush's radio and television ads and fax machines—another innovation—to receive newspaper articles from around the country. A daily 7:00 a.m. meeting open to all headquarters staff was devoted to "setting the agenda for the day," according to pollster Stan Greenberg. "If you're attacked and you fail to respond immediately," said campaign manager David Wilhelm, "the first day the story is attack, the second day is a repetition of the attack with your response, and then the third day is an analysis of the response and so on. If you respond on the same day you're attacked, that's the story of the day."[5] A second daily meeting, this one at 7:00 p.m., was "much more of a pep rally, morale building," and again open to all. The Clintons imbued the staff with the flat-organization "management lessons that they learned from Arkansas corporations," said communication director George Stephanopoulos. "We kept hearing about Walmart."[6]

Meanwhile, Ross Perot, despite dropping out of the race with kind words for the Democrats, was far from inactive. During the seventy days that followed his withdrawal, he spent $11 million to keep his state campaign offices open and his volunteers working to get his name on every state ballot. They achieved that goal on September 18, when Arizona became the fiftieth state to list Perot. His new book, *United We Stand: How We Can Take Back Our Country*, reached the top of the paperback best-seller list on the Sunday of Labor Day weekend, less than two weeks after it was published. Unlike Perot's spring campaign, which centered on his critique of what was wrong with politics and government, his book offered an extensive policy agenda. In April, Perot had said that no tax increase was needed to balance the budget—"we've been taxed to death!" His new plan featured raising taxes by $302 billion, including a fifty-cents-per-gallon gasoline tax, as well as cutting federal spending by $416 billion.[7] Meanwhile, by withdrawing as a candidate, Perot stopped the barrage of critical news stories that preceded his withdrawal.

Scholars in several disciplines have argued that the general election campaigns waged by presidential candidates are largely irrelevant to the outcome.[8] National conditions—economic factors alone according to economist Roy Fair, economic factors plus political metrics such as the president's approval rating early in the year according to political scientists Michael Lewis-Beck and Tom Rice, and an eclectic list of "thirteen keys" according to historian Allan Lichtman—form the basis of models whose preelection predictions claim so much accuracy as to make the candidates' campaigns sideshows. To the extent that this claim may be true in general, it was false in 1992. Fair, who predicted that Bush would get 56 percent of the national popular vote; Lewis-Beck and Rice, who projected a Bush victory with 58 percent of the electoral vote; and Lichtman, who saw eight of his thirteen keys turning in Bush's favor, all predicted in the spring that the president would be reelected.[9]

What happened in September, October, and early November that helped Clinton not just to win, but to win handily? And what happened in the 435 House elections and 34 Senate contests that were decided in the same election, whose outcome would do so much to affect the Clinton presidency?

STRATEGIES

Clinton's strategy for victory in November was grounded in geography. Based on the results of the previous six elections, a theory had arisen that because twenty-one states with 191 electoral votes went Republican every time (and only the District of Columbia with 3 electoral votes was consistently Democratic), the GOP had a "lock" on the Electoral College.[10] Fueling this theory was the transfer of electoral votes between states that occurred as a result of the 1990 census, which subtracted 5 electoral votes from states carried by Dukakis in 1988 and added them to states carried by Bush. The implication was that Clinton would need to "pick the lock," either by winning nearly 80 percent of the remaining 344 electoral votes (as Dukakis had tried and woefully failed to do with an eighteen-state strategy in 1988) or by turning previously Republican states Democratic.

Clinton's substantial lead entering the fall, in both national and state polls, convinced his aides that he could win by taking the fight into Republican territory. To be sure, according to Wilhelm and advertising director Mandy Grunwald, nineteen states were solidly Republican—"*their* states"— and thus not worth the effort because they were either unwinnable for Clinton (Mississippi and Utah) or potentially winnable only at great expense of time and money (Florida and Texas). Another thirteen were "'top end,' which were those states we thought we could win without advertising." These included most of the states Dukakis carried plus five Bush states where the Democratic Party had been gaining and Clinton already had a solid lead: Arkansas, Connecticut, Vermont, and, most important, Illinois and California (which alone gained 7 electoral votes after the 1990 census). That left eighteen "battleground" or "play hard" states "where we thought, 'if we spend money, we can win.'" With the exception of Iowa, Minnesota, and Wisconsin, all of these states voted for Bush in 1988: Colorado, Delaware, Georgia, Kentucky, Louisiana, Maine, Maryland, Michigan, Montana, New Jersey, New Mexico, North Carolina, Ohio, Pennsylvania, and Tennessee. If Clinton could carry all of the "top end" and "battleground" states, he would have 376 electoral votes, 106 more than he needed to be elected. "We did not need to win 500 electoral college votes in order to win the presidency," said Wilhelm. "We needed to win 270."[11]

Running state campaigns was something that Carville, Greenberg, Grunwald, and media consultant Frank Greer were more experienced at doing than their peers in Bush's high command. This showed up in Clinton's advertising strategy, which consisted almost entirely of commercials aired in local markets in battleground states—not just ads for Ohio, for example, but different ads for northern Ohio and southern Ohio.[12] Few dollars—about 10 to 15 percent of their advertising budget, and only in the last two weeks of the campaign—were spent on national ads, which expensively reach tens of millions of voters in noncompetitive states.[13] The same was true of Clinton and Gore's time. Their first bus trip, for example, took them through eight competitive eastern and midwestern states. Their second began in St. Louis, where the first one left off, and went north through three more: Iowa, Wisconsin, and Minnesota.

Running convincing ads and making effective campaign appearances was more than a matter of location. It meant having a persuasive message. The war room took on much of the burden of answering Republican attacks, allowing Clinton to spend less time going after Bush and more time advancing a positive message. It also generated a famously three-pronged agenda in the form of phrases Carville wrote on a dry-erase board:

- Change vs. more of the same
- The economy, stupid
- Don't forget health care[14]

In truth, Clinton mostly did forget health care, whose importance Carville may have overvalued because it was a central issue in the campaign that made his reputation: long-shot candidate Harris Wofford's upset victory over former governor Richard Thornburg in the October 1991 special Senate election in Pennsylvania. As Greer reminded Clinton after he became president, "You didn't get elected on health care. You didn't run one spot on health care."[15] As for the "change vs. more of the same" theme, that is intrinsic to any campaign against an incumbent president, especially when one party has controlled the White House for twelve years.

The economy was a different matter. As political scientist Thomas Patterson has shown, more than 90 percent of the references to the economy on the network evening news programs in 1992 were negative, along with more than 80 percent of the networks' references to Bush's handling of the matter. Indeed, "the networks' portrayal of the economy got worse as the economy improved" over the course of the election year.[16] In two of the previous four elections—1976 and 1980—economic issues headed voters' list of concerns, and the challenger (Jimmy Carter in 1976 and Ronald Reagan in 1980) won both of them.[17] Seeing that the same might be true in 1992, the title of Clinton's campaign book—*Putting People First: How We Can All Change America*—conveyed the theme of his economic plan.[18] Clinton stressed that his strategy was neither "trickle-down economics" (the standard Republican approach) nor "tax-and-spend government" (the traditional Democratic solution). Instead it was "invest-and-grow"—that is, channel federal money into new education, training, and infrastructure programs designed to enhance American competitiveness in an increasingly global economy. Perot's continuing presence on state ballots, especially after *United We Stand* put the focus on balancing the budget and controlling spending, "did help us keep Clinton disciplined," said Progressive Policy Institute scholar Elaine Kamarck: "Don't promise to spend so much; don't sound like an old-fashioned Democrat; you're doomed if you sound like a tax-and-spend Democrat.'"[19]

Clinton's message had other elements. One was a middle-class tax cut. Another was his ongoing emphasis on "ending welfare as we know it." The oft-repeated promise to move people "from welfare to work" by imposing strict time limits on welfare recipients (no more than two years on welfare at a time and no more than five years total) while providing them with the education, training, and child care they needed to enter the workforce continued to air because the campaign's research showed that it connected with voters better than anything else.[20] It was this promise in his announcement speech the year before that set Clinton apart from a generation of losing Democratic presidential nominees as well as from his rivals for the nomination in 1992.

Still another recurring element in Clinton's message was Gore's superiority to Quayle and the synergy between the two Democratic running mates that made the whole greater than the sum of its parts. One oft-aired ad labeled them "a new generation of Democrats" who "don't think the way the old Democratic Party did" about welfare, capital punishment, and "tax-and-spend politics."[21] Less visible but also important was the ongoing effort to keep Gennifer Flowers–style stories from recurring by separating Clinton from the young women whom high-level political campaigns attract. "I told him if I found him having sex on the campaign trail, he was dead," said scheduler Susan Thomases, "that I was leaving and taking everybody with me. I said, 'You're stupid enough to blow this whole presidential thing over your dick. . . . If you don't have enough self-control to keep yourself straight, then it's just dumb.'"[22]

Bush's strategic options were more limited than Clinton's. His record included historic accomplishments in foreign policy. But his campaign's polls showed, in Baker's words, that "it just was not a salient issue. It wasn't a cutting issue."[23] Remarkably, the network evening news programs' 314 references to foreign policy during the ten months leading up to the election were fewer than their 329 references to Clinton's draft history—and most of them were unfavorable to Bush.[24] Yet Clinton's advisers were relieved that Bush's campaign did not make more of its candidate's greatest strength, which might have elevated foreign policy in voters' minds and reminded them of all he had accomplished. "They never raised the issue of foreign policy," Greer marveled—"a terrible mistake," according to Clinton foreign policy adviser Anthony Lake. "If he had been all over us, he could have killed us."[25] Bush's media adviser Sig Rogich agreed. "We had a president with among the greatest records in foreign policy . . . but we didn't do one commercial on the subject. . . . The pollsters said that no one cared about foreign policy," overlooking that "we can create poll numbers" by drawing attention to an issue.[26] To be sure, although emphasizing foreign policy risked feeding the narrative that Bush cared more about the world than the country, not discussing it at all meant his strongest card as president went unplayed.

The decision to downplay foreign policy left Bush with just two alternative strategies. One was to offer the voters a second-term economic agenda. This was intrinsically difficult. As political scientists John Aldrich and Thomas Weko observed, "Why, voters wondered, would Bush change?" and why should they trust someone who "had broken the most important policy commitment of his 1988 campaign, 'no new taxes'"?[27] But Bush gave it a try—and the Clinton campaign a scare—when he delivered an effective speech to the Detroit Economic Club and immediately ran a five-minute ad on all three broadcast networks with highlights from his plan: free trade, capital gains tax cuts, tuition vouchers for private schools, urban enterprise zones, tort reform, and a line-item veto. Greer described it as "one of the most effective spots of the campaign" and was amazed that Bush did not follow it up with subsequent ads and speeches.[28]

Instead, Bush adopted the strategy that worked for him in 1988: overcome his Democratic rival's lead by tearing him down. "I am going to come out and go after that opponent," he said in early August. "He has been on my case for six months, and we are going to define it, and we are going to win the election."[29] But Clinton was no Dukakis. Unlike the Massachusetts governor, his record in Arkansas did not offer easy targets like prison furloughs for convicted murderers or civil libertarian objections to requiring teachers to lead their students in the Pledge of Allegiance. Unlike Dukakis, too, when Clinton was hit, he and the war room hit back. After the Manhattan Project led 84 percent of voters to realize that Clinton had risen from humble origins, he was able to portray Bush as the aloof elitist on the ballot, the opposite of what Bush did to Dukakis.[30] And, unlike in 1988, Bush had a record to defend—not the popular Reagan's but his own. As political scientist William Mayer pointed out, of the seven incumbent presidents who had run for reelection since 1952—three of whom failed—Bush had the worst average election-year approval rating. It started low and fell still lower, from about 40 percent to about 30 percent.[31]

Nevertheless, "trust and taxes"—shorthand for Clinton's character weaknesses and his record in Arkansas—became the message of the campaign. Bush himself was drawn to the trust issue because he simply did not believe that voters would regard Clinton—in his view a womanizing draft dodger who unpatriotically demonstrated against the Vietnam War while attending graduate school overseas—as more worthy of the presidency than himself, a war hero with strong values and a long record of public service. "He just viewed Clinton as so inferior," said Quayle, "that, somehow, by golly, he was going to pull this thing out."[32] "I don't think any of us believed Clinton could win," said White House press secretary Marlin Fitzwater, because never before would a known "philanderer" and "draft dodger" have had a chance.[33] Recalling how much ground he gained against Dukakis in 1988, Bush's attitude toward polls showing Clinton in the lead was, "Big deal. We'll still win," according to White House aide Thomas Scully.[34] But although "we tried to make character an issue," said James Baker, "we were unsuccessful in doing so."[35] Voters had already taken Clinton's measure and decided that his public virtues outweighed his private vices.

Taxes were something else entirely. To be sure, Bush's abandonment as president of his promise not to raise taxes diluted this issue's potency. Yet, astonishingly, after the Bush campaign charged that Clinton raised taxes 128 times as governor, the chief defender of Clinton's Arkansas record, Betsey Wright, compiled a list of 34 tax increases and 93 increases in user fees and gave it to the *Washington Post*. Not surprisingly, the *Post* added the two numbers, came up with 127, and put it on the front page—even though it included irrelevant items such as extending the dog-racing season in West Memphis. "It was a problem," said Carville: "'the failed governor of a small state.' That gave people some pause. It wasn't a bullshit charge, there was something to it."[36] "If they had done a solid six-week campaign attacking Arkansas, we would have been meat," said deputy communications director Robert Boorstin, with some exaggeration.[37] Eventually the Bush campaign did so, but only after wasting weeks chasing the character chimera—exactly the wrong sequence, a relieved Greenberg and his "Teeter Project" had found.[38] And even when Bush and his surrogates went after Clinton's record as governor, they sometimes did so ineffectively. For example, "the way they did the environment was dead wrong because they were arguing two things at the same time," noted Boorstin. "They were saying, 'He's the pits' and then they were saying, 'He's too green.'"[39]

Bush's erratic attempts to settle on a strategy were hindered by the length of the lead he had to overcome. His campaign decided it could win only by, in effect, "drawing to an inside straight"—that is, forfeiting the national popular vote and stringing together twenty-nine mostly small states where it thought it could compete.[40] Desperate to show some progress in the national polls and create a sense of momentum, Bush spent about 80 percent of his advertising budget on spots that ran nationally. By conveying the same message everywhere instead of addressing local concerns that varied from state to state, such ads were less effective than more tailored spots. They also were inefficient, costing more per viewer than local ads and seen by voters in states Bush had no chance of winning or, in some cases, losing. For example, although voters in solidly Democratic Massachusetts saw Bush commercials every day and never saw a Clinton ad, all that Bush could hope to accomplish there was to reduce the margin by which he lost the state's twelve electoral votes.

Clinton's strategic advantages at the start of the fall campaign were formidable. He had a strong lead and a clear plan to protect it. He also had more money to spend than Bush. Although both major party nominees received an identical $55.2 million in public funding for the general election from the federal government and each raised the $10.3 million that the law allowed their national parties to spend on their behalf, Clinton was able to outraise Bush by $73.1 million to $22.4 million in additional funding. Most of the difference was accounted for by the $35.0 million that organized labor—like other Democratic constituencies desperate for even a centrist Democrat like Clinton to win after three consecutive defeats—spent on his behalf in coordination with the Clinton campaign. With these funds, Clinton outspent the president by $130.1 million to $89.9 million. Hedging their bets in advance of Clinton's likely victory, business groups supported the Republican president, but not by much. Campaign chief of staff Eli Segal said that he knew Clinton would win the election when, in each of the five days after the Republican convention, "I got a phone call, direct and indirect, from a prominent Republican leader, announcing that they wanted me to know that they were going to make a six-figure gift . . . to the Democratic National Committee." The list of callers included August Busch of Anheuser-Busch, Ernest Gallo of Gallo Winery, Thomas Watson of IBM, and Dwayne Andreas of Archer Daniels Midland.[41]

SEPTEMBER

To Bush's detriment, the first month of the fall contest was spent in a pointless "debate over the debates," which the president provoked and eventually conceded at the expense of campaign time that could have been used more fruitfully.

Debates between the candidates had not always been a standard feature of presidential campaigns. From 1960, when in the first debates Sen. John F. Kennedy engaged Vice President Richard Nixon four times on national television, until 1980, when President Carter grudgingly debated Governor Reagan just once, debates took place only if both candidates saw an advantage in participating. Challengers always did in order to show that they belonged on the same stage as the president, but incumbents debated only if they were trailing in the polls. Neither President Johnson in 1964 nor President Nixon in 1972 found anything to be gained by debating, but President Gerald Ford did in 1976 and President Carter did in 1980 once they saw how far behind they were. Not until 1984, when President Reagan agreed to debate his opponent even though he was way ahead in the polls, did the expectation take root that participating in debates was something both presidents and challengers have to do as a matter of political necessity. In 1988 Bush and Dukakis debated, as did their vice presidential running mates.

Less institutionalized were the logistics of the debates: how many would take place, as well as where and when; what their format would be; and—most important—who had the authority to make those decisions. In 1987 the Republican and Democratic national party chairs formed a bipartisan Commission on Presidential Debates in hopes of regularizing the process. Even though it was the official sponsor of the 1988 Bush-Dukakis debates, the commission's newness on the scene limited its influence. As in the past, the real negotiations took place between the candidates' campaign organizations, each of which sought the format, number, and timing of debates it thought would help its man. In 1988 Bush's lead in the polls meant that he held all the high cards. Baker, his lead negotiator, swatted away the commission's four-debate proposal and the Dukakis campaign's desire for direct exchanges between the candidates. As in 1984, when Baker also got his own way on behalf of the front-running Reagan, only two presidential and one vice presidential debates took place. In all of them the candidates answered questions from a panel of reporters.

In 1992 things were different. The commission's authority had grown stronger with the passage of time, voters now took for granted that the candidates would debate, and, as the representative of the trailing candidate, Baker's negotiating position was weak. "The further we got behind in the polls, the less leverage we had," said Scully.[42] On June 11 the commission announced that there would be three presidential debates and one vice presidential debate, spread across the calendar from September 23 to October 15. In the interest of more freewheeling exchanges, each would be presided over by a single moderator. Clinton agreed immediately after the Democratic convention confirmed him as its nominee. But even though Baker realized that "you can't refuse to debate at all" without "taking on a lot of water," the Bush campaign prevaricated for nearly two months before rejecting the commission's proposal on September 3.[43] As in 1984 and 1988, Baker and his colleagues wanted two presidential debates and one vice presidential debate, each conducted by a panel of questioners. They also wanted them scheduled later in the fall so that Bush would have more time to shrink Clinton's lead before the candidates appeared on the same stage. And they rejected the commission's presumptive sponsorship, arguing that the candidates should negotiate the terms of the debates and then seek a sponsor.

Unfortunately for Bush, his rejection of the commission proposal was widely regarded as politically unacceptable. A CBS/*New York Times* poll found that 63 percent of voters thought he was unwilling to debate.[44] On September 23, as Bush made stops in all six states that border on Arkansas to attack his rival's record as governor, Clinton went to East Lansing, Michigan—the site of the scheduled first debate on the day it was scheduled—to dare Bush to make his charges face-to-face. He even quoted Bush against himself. In 1980, when running for vice president, Bush said that President Carter "wants to avoid debate because he wants to avoid talking about his economic record."[45] Protesters dressed in chicken costumes began appearing at Bush's rallies with signs saying, "Chicken George won't debate." Bush began responding to the chickens: "You talking about the draft-record chicken or are you talking about the chicken in the Arkansas River?"[46]

Flailing, Bush finally issued a debate challenge of his own on September 29: four Sunday night debates starting on October 11 and continuing until November 1, two days before the election, along with two vice presidential debates. Two days later, after the Conference Board announced that the Consumer Confidence Index had sunk to 56.4 and the Commerce Department reported that second quarter economic growth—an important variable in shaping the outcome of presidential elections—was only 1.5 percent, Bush and Clinton negotiators hammered out an agreement for three presidential debates in nine days—October 11 in St. Louis, October 15 in Richmond, and October 19 in East Lansing—with a vice presidential debate sandwiched in on October 13 in Atlanta.[47] The first debate would feature a panel of reporters asking questions, and the third would be half panel and half single moderator. The second, reflecting Clinton's preference, would be a town hall with undecided voters. "Why'd I agree to this?" Bush asked. As Quayle remembered, "Teeter or someone said, 'Don't you remember in 1988 we had all those "[Ask] George Bush" forums and you were great?' I was thinking to myself, 'Yes, that was in '88. He hasn't done that in four years."[48] Campaign chair Mickey Kantor, negotiating on Clinton's behalf, said that it came as a "surprise" that "the Bush people accepted immediately" when he put the town hall format on the table.[49] Clinton, whose "strong suit" during the nomination campaign was not reporter-led debates with other candidates, according to policy director Bruce Reed, had been doing town hall events comfortably all year.[50]

Clinton's lead over Bush in the Gallup poll was 15 points at the start of September and 15 points at month's end. He held on to all the Perot voters who moved his way when their candidate dropped out in July, even as Bush wasted the month with bootless attacks on Clinton's character and debates with chickens instead of his rival. Less encouraging to Clinton were the noises Perot was making about reviving his candidacy. On September 12 Perot said, with faux resignation, "If the volunteers said, 'It's a dirty job but

Independent presidential candidate Ross Perot revived his flagging candidacy with appearances in the 1992 presidential debates. Courtesy of the George Bush Presidential Library.

you've got to do it,' I belong to them."[51] Three days later, he said he might be "trapped" into running because he wanted to take his economic agenda to the people and the networks "won't sell [time] to me unless I declare as a candidate."[52] Maintaining the pretense that he was his volunteers' suffering servant, Perot invited both the Bush and Clinton campaigns to send high-level delegations to appear before them in Dallas on September 28 and make the case for their candidates. Both campaigns did, to no avail. "Perot stood there with his pants down and his ass in the draft," said Carville, "and everybody was kissing it, and he was clearly enjoying it."[53] On October 1, having determined that the volunteers would settle for no one but him, Perot reentered the race, just thirty-three days before the election.

OCTOBER

Most observers of the major party candidates' teams who appeared before Perot's volunteers in Dallas concluded that Clinton's representatives tried harder than Bush's. To the extent that they were right, it was for good reason. At this stage of the campaign, nearly every voter who moved back to Perot would be leaving Clinton to do so. For a while few of them did. Even before Perot's reentry, he was on every state ballot and was still supported by 8 percent of all voters. That number rose only to 9 percent during the first week of his renewed candidacy. Considering that support for independent candidates usually declines by Election Day, it seemed as if the Clinton campaign's apprehensions were groundless. Even so, Perot's mere presence in the race threatened to dilute Clinton's status as the outsider, the fresh face, the only alternative to the status quo.

Two things changed the situation and sent Perot's support soaring. The first was his new agenda and willingness to spend vast sums of money to advance it. No sooner did Perot resume his candidacy than he bought a half hour of prime time on CBS on October 6 and another half hour on ABC on October 9, time that the networks' policy made him eligible to purchase now that he was back in the race. Playing against type in the modern television age, Perot used a pointer and hand-lettered charts to walk viewers through "The Problems—Plain Talk about Jobs, Debt, and the Washington Mess" on his first show and "Ross Perot Solution: Balancing the Budget [and] Reforming Government" on his second. "The Problems" drew an audience of 16.5 million viewers, more than watched the major-league baseball playoff game airing that night on a different network. The audience for the second also was large.

During the month that followed, Perot bought two more widely viewed half hours, an hour, and multiple commercial spots. His $53 million in spending in October and November, nearly all of it from his own pocket, exceeded that of any independent candidate in history and rivaled Bush's and Clinton's.[54] Although he continued to appear on television talk shows, Perot made few campaign appearances—just six all month, with five more in early November. Significantly, he had no regional strategy, which meant that winning electoral votes, as previous independent and third-party candidates like Theodore Roosevelt in 1912, Strom Thurmond in 1948, and George Wallace in 1968 had done, was beyond his reach.

Working at least as hard in Perot's favor as advertising was his appearance in the debates. In June, while his first campaign was still active, the commission announced that its criteria for including independent candidates were basically the same as in 1988, when there were no politically serious contenders besides the Republican and Democratic nominees. Although the commission stated three criteria, including "evidence of national organization" and "signs of national newsworthiness," they really boiled down to one: "whether a candidate has a realistic chance of election."[55] Perot clearly met the standard in the spring, when his support neared 40 percent, but probably did not meet it in October. But, in a classic prisoner's dilemma, neither major party candidate wanted to be the one to risk alienating Perot's supporters by trying to freeze him out. Both reluctantly agreed to invite him. Perot had every reason to be jubilant: merely to appear on the same stage as Bush and Clinton undermined the classic argument that to vote for an independent candidate is to "waste" one's vote.

Clinton's unhappiness that Perot was back in the race did not mean that Bush was pleased. He and Perot had despised each other for years, and nearly everything Perot said about the president was not just critical but disdainful and dismissive. In addition, Bush, who hated debating under the best of circumstances, especially dreaded being attacked by both Perot and Clinton for ninety minutes at a time. Historically minded campaign advisers were all too aware that in four of the six elections since 1860 that featured strong third-party candidates, the nominee of the incumbent party lost.[56] And even though the softest Clinton supporters were those who recently came over from Perot, Bush could not help but think that his fellow Texan was stealing issues and votes from him by emphasizing traditional Republican themes such as deficits, debt, and "the mess in Washington."

Approaching the first debate, Clinton prepared assiduously, as challengers typically do, and Bush did not, as presidents typically do not. Like Reagan before him and George W. Bush and Barack Obama after him, Bush took for granted that his four years as president equipped him with all the information he needed to win a debate against less experienced rivals. No candidate enjoys practice debates, but presidents have a perfect excuse to avoid or cut them short: they have to run the country. "These 'performances,' played to the handlers, irked him," said Matalin.[57] Overawed by the office, aides were reluctant to confront Bush with the sort of face-to-face charges and criticisms he surely would encounter in debates.

Bush went into the October 11 debate determined to make news by announcing that during his second term, Baker would "be the economic coordinator of all the domestic side of the house." He muffed the line by burying it deep within a rambling answer about small business. Baker himself showed no enthusiasm for the role, saying later, "I would have gone back to State, notwithstanding some of the things he said in the campaign."[58] Clinton went into the debate determined to deflect Bush's expected attack on his draft record and overseas demonstrations against the Vietnam War. He hit the charge out of the park, citing Bush's father, former senator Prescott Bush, who criticized Sen. Joseph McCarthy for attacking people's patriotism. "Your father was right to stand up to Joe McCarthy," said Clinton. "You were wrong to question my patriotism." Bush realized he lost the debate—his attack on Clinton was "a dud," he wrote in his diary, and "the results, let's face it, were not good."[59] The clear winners were Clinton and Perot, whose relaxed demeanor, snappy one-liners ("I'm all ears," the jug-eared candidate said), and rejoinder to a question about his inexperience in government ("I don't have any experience in running up a $4 trillion debt") impressed many voters.[60]

The first presidential debate featured a panel of reporters, Bush's preferred format even though he did poorly in it. The single-moderator vice presidential debate between Gore and Quayle two days later was much more freewheeling. Quayle relentlessly tore into Clinton, and Gore refused to respond in kind. When Quayle said that "Bill Clinton has trouble telling the truth" and Gore was granted a chance to answer, he returned instead to an earlier question about family leave policy. Within the Clinton campaign, "most people thought Gore was too proud to be vice president," said Reed, who had helped persuade them otherwise.[61] In the debate, Gore seemed more concerned about preserving his senatorial dignity than mixing it up with Quayle. Yet if there was a clear loser in the encounter, it was Perot's running mate, James Stockdale, a man of demonstrated courage and intellect but utterly unsuited to the political arena. During the spring Perot promised Stockdale that he would find a replacement for him on the ticket, but by the time he reentered the race after dropping out, it was too late to change the name on the state ballots. The fish-out-of-water Stockdale said little during the debate and, when pressed to comment on health care policy, confessed, "I'm out of ammunition."[62]

The audience for the vice presidential debate was 51 million, not much smaller than the 62 million who watched the first Bush-Clinton-Perot debate (and larger than the audience for the presidential debates in 1996).[63] Stockdale's performance was personally embarrassing but also damaging to Perot. It made voters consider that although Perot might be an appealing protest candidate, he was ill-equipped to be president. The same was true of Perot's second debate performance on October 15, when it became clear that he had emptied his shallow pool of one-liners in the first encounter ("I'm all ears," he repeated).[64] At no point after resuming his candidacy did Perot approach a lead in the polls like the one he achieved in the spring.

The second presidential debate, on October 15, was the first ever with a town hall format. Two hundred Richmond-area voters, chosen by Gallup because they had yet to decide whom to support, constituted the pool of questioners. Still trailing Clinton by about 13 points, Bush knew he needed to sharpen his attack. But about a half hour before the debate began, moderator Carole Simpson of ABC News asked the audience for "an idea of the questions you want to ask."[65] After they responded with the pieties appropriate to the occasion, she began the debate by inviting them to tell the candidates what they had told her. "We want an end to the mudslinging," said one man. "We're tired of negative campaigning."

There went Bush's Plan A, with no Plan B at the ready. In his worst exchange, Bush responded clumsily to a poorly phrased question about how the "national debt personally affected each of your lives." "What she meant to say," according to White House communications director David Demarest, "was, 'How bad is the economy?,'" but Bush "was so much of a literalist, he kept trying to figure out what she was getting at."[66] When it was Clinton's turn, he walked across the stage to face the young questioner ("remote mikes" for the candidates were something Clinton's debate negotiators insisted on) and gave an empathetic answer grounded in his experience knowing many of "the people [who] lose their jobs" in Arkansas "by their names."[67] Bush compounded the impression of insensitivity by looking at his watch, as if he were tired of spending time with all these voters. In truth, he was signaling the moderator that she was letting Clinton go on too long as well as thinking, "only ten more minutes of this crap."[68]

Clinton's lead rose to 18 points after his triumphant appearance in the second debate, raising the stakes dramatically for Bush in their final encounter. The compressed, miniseries-like schedule of four debates in nine days caused the audience to grow from one to the next. Bush rose to the occasion, counterpunching crisply when Clinton said that "the person responsible for domestic economic policy in my administration will be Bill Clinton." "That's what worries me," Bush shot back immediately. Even more significant, Perot redirected his rhetorical fire at Clinton rather than his usual target, Bush. Of Clinton's experience as governor, Perot sniffed, "It's irrelevant. I could say I ran a small grocery store on the corner, therefore I extrapolate that to the fact that I could run Walmart. That's not true."[69] By attacking both candidates—even as they continued to forswear attacking him in hopes of wooing away his supporters—Perot's seeming evenhandedness made his blow against Clinton land more squarely than anything Bush said about his rival.

Postdebate surveys of viewers indicated that Clinton won two of the three encounters and Bush none.[70] Yet Perot and Bush were the debates' main beneficiaries. Perot's hours in the spotlight, side by side with the Republican and Democratic nominees for president, restored some of his stature. His share of the vote doubled from 9 percent in the Gallup poll to

17 percent by debates' end. Because most of his gains involved previous supporters who returned after moving to Clinton in mid-July, the Democrat's lead over Bush narrowed. With two weeks left until the election, Bush's support was not increasing—he still barely cracked 30 percent—but Clinton's support fell to about 40 percent.

Bush doubled down on taxes—his proxy for Clinton's record as governor—during the campaign's home stretch. A widely aired commercial, formally titled "The Arkansas Record" but better known as the "vulture ad," included an image of a vulture in a dead tree overlooking a desolate landscape and concluded: "Bill Clinton wants to do for American what he has done for Arkansas." Clinton's war room hit back immediately by pointing out that Arkansas had the second-lowest taxes and the fifth-highest rate of job growth in the country, but that wasn't enough for Clinton, who long had been convinced that his worst electoral defeat, for reelection in 1980, was the result of leaving charges unanswered. He wanted to go nuclear against the president. Carville, Greenberg, and Stephanopoulos fought back, persuading Clinton that Bush's ad was too late, desperate, and histrionic to do him much good. Clinton grudgingly agreed to stick to the economic, welfare, and tough-on-crime message that had served him well all year.[71]

Bush took his over-the-top rhetoric onto the campaign trail as Election Day neared, swinging wildly in ways that excited partisan crowds but, as Matalin said, undermined the effort "to reaffirm in the voters' mind that our man was more mature, more elevated, more presidential" than his rivals.[72] Attacking Gore on October 29, Bush charged, "You know why I call him Ozone Man? This guy is so far off in the environmental extreme, we'll be up to our neck in owls." The next day, he said, "If I want foreign policy advice, I'd go to [my dog] Millie before I'd go to Ozone and Governor Clinton."[73]

Meanwhile, Perot was reinforcing existing doubts about his temperament and his hold on reality. In a *60 Minutes* interview that aired nine days before the election, he charged without evidence that the real reason he abandoned his campaign in July was that he "received multiple reports that there was a plan to embarrass [my daughter Carolyn] before her wedding, and to actually have people in the church to disrupt her wedding."[74] Perot's support in the Gallup poll fell from a postdebates peak of 20 percent down to 14 percent. To the extent that these defecting voters lost confidence in his suitability to be president but still liked his message, they seem to have taken their cues from his late-campaign attacks on Clinton in deciding whom to support instead. Pointing out that one in five jobs in Arkansas was in the poultry industry, Perot said on one of his thirty-minute programs that "if we take this level of business-creating capability nationwide, we'll all be plucking chickens for a living."[75] His 6-point drop in the polls was matched and exceeded by a 9-point gain for Bush. In an October 27 survey taken by Gallup for CNN/*USA Today*, Bush closed to within 1 point: 40 percent to Clinton's 41 percent and Perot's 14 percent.

On October 30, a shoe unexpectedly dropped in the form of a newly filed criminal court case: *United States v. Weinberger*. For nearly six years, independent counsel Lawrence Walsh had been investigating the Reagan administration's second-term Iran-Contra scandal. Four days before the November 3 election, Walsh indicted former secretary of defense Caspar Weinberger for lying about his involvement in the legal but ill-advised exchange of arms for hostages with Iran. As vice president and president, Bush consistently claimed he was "out of the loop" on this matter. But Weinberger's notes of a January 7, 1986, Oval Office meeting, which Walsh released along with the indictment, seemed to contradict this account: "President decided to go with Israeli-Iranian offer to release our 5 hostages in return for sale of 4000 TOWs [missiles] to Iran by Israel. . . . VP favored."[76]

Baker was furious. The indictment was "clearly timed to try to destroy President Bush." Indeed, it was dismissed by the judge two months later for exceeding the statute of limitations. Baker was also convinced that Walsh's action was a major cause of Bush's defeat in the election. It shattered the president's momentum, undermined his claim to superior trustworthiness and competence, and caused his support to plummet, draining some votes to Clinton and even more back to Perot. Whatever small hope Bush may have had of trying to make something of the economy's 2.7 percent growth rate in the third quarter, which was announced on October 27 and was in any event politically less meaningful than growth during the first half of the year, was gone.[77]

Greenberg's state polls for Clinton challenge the idea that Bush ever drew close to victory. To the extent that national surveys tightened, it was because Bush was gaining unneeded votes in his own electorally secure states and unhelpful votes in Clinton's, where only Bush's ads were running. In the battleground states, where Clinton's more targeted ads dominated the airwaves, Greenberg's polls showed his lead was holding steady. In any event, by election eve Bush knew he would lose. "And so it is, the end of campaign '92, the ugliest period of my life," he wrote in his diary, echoing his previous assessment of 1991.[78] "It hurts," he said afterward. "It really hurts."[79]

It was also the end of twelve years of Republican control of the presidency, which added a degree of difficulty to Bush's reelection campaign simply because voters almost never grant the same party four victories in a row. What political scientist Alan Abramowitz has called the "time for a change" element in presidential elections would have put whoever the Republican nominee was in 1992 at about a 6 percentage point disadvantage—not enough to cost the GOP the election in 1980, 1984, or 1988 but a severe handicap nonetheless. Baker was surely right to sense that in leaving the State Department to take charge of the White House staff and the reelection campaign, he was probably bringing his career in government to an end.

THE RESULTS

Clinton won a solid victory in the Electoral College with 370 electoral votes—nearly double the 188 won by the Democrats' three previous presidential candidates combined—to Bush's 168. He won a clear victory in the popular vote, in which he prevailed by nearly 6 million votes: 44.9 million (43.0 percent) to 39.1 million (37.4 percent) for Bush and 19.7 million (18.9 percent) for Perot. Clinton swept the Northeast and Pacific Coast, as well as border states Delaware, Kentucky, Maryland, and Missouri; carried all of the large states in the Midwest; split the Mountain West evenly with Bush; and made inroads in the South, where he carried his and Gore's home states of Arkansas and Tennessee, along with Louisiana and Georgia. (See appendix C for the state-by-state results.) One-third of Clinton's electoral votes came from states that had voted Republican in every presidential election since 1968, including California, Illinois, and New Jersey. In fact, in the twenty-one previously consistent Republican states, Clinton bested Bush by 118 to 73. (So much for the "electoral lock" theory.) The falloff in support for Bush since 1988—from 53.4 percent of the national popular vote to 37.4 percent and from 426 electoral votes to 168—rivaled that suffered by President Herbert Hoover, who faced reelection in the Depression year of 1932. Just twenty-one months before the 1992 election Bush's approval rating was 89 percent, the highest in history. On Election Day, with well over half of that support gone, he received the lowest share of the national popular vote of any reelection-seeking president since William Howard Taft in 1912.

Demographically, Clinton carried every group that Dukakis won in 1988, in nearly every case by a larger margin: African Americans (+73 points for Clinton over Bush), Latinos (+36), Jews (+69), unmarried women (+17), low-income (+35) and poorly educated (+26) voters, union households, and residents of large cities (+19). He also won several groups that had voted Republican in every recent presidential election: married women (+3), voters in all age-groups (ranging from +1 among fifty- to fifty-nine-year-olds to +13 among eighteen- to twenty-four-year-olds), suburban (+7) and rural (+2) voters, high school graduates (+7) and those with either some college (+5) or a postgraduate (+13) education, Roman Catholics (+9), and voters whose incomes placed them in the working class or middle class (+5).[80] White evangelical Christians (+38) voted strongly for Bush, but mainline Protestants, most of whom still identified as Republicans, went narrowly (+1) for Clinton. Other Republican groups supported their party's nominee but by reduced margins from recent elections. White southerners, for example, gave Bush a 35-point majority in 1988 but only a 14-point plurality in 1992.[81]

With the exception of low support from African Americans, Jews, and older voters, Perot ran fairly evenly among all groups of voters, not deviating more than 5 points either way from his national vote share with any of them. His support, like Bush's, was concentrated among whites. He won 23 percent of the vote in states whose African American population was below the national average compared with 13 percent in states where the black population was above average. Perot also ran better among people who seldom attended church than among people who often did so.[82]

Politically, Perot did exceptionally well among independent voters, earning about 30 percent from those of all ideological stripes: liberal, moderate, and conservative. He also did well among Republicans who considered themselves liberals or moderates. Perot won nearly half again as many of their votes (22 percent) as he won from Democratic conservatives and moderates (14 percent). Following the pattern revealed among the various demographic groups, Clinton ran more strongly than Dukakis among all partisans except conservative Republicans and liberal Democrats, who remained about as polarized in their voting as they were in 1988. Clinton also became the first Democrat since 1964 to win a higher percentage of self-identified Democrats (77 percent) than his rival won among self-identified Republicans (73 percent).

In terms of ideology and issues, although voters were inclined to regard Clinton as slightly more liberal than they had Dukakis in 1988—and farther from themselves on the ideological spectrum—he nonetheless prevailed among moderate voters by 47 percent to 31 percent. The main reason—even more than how voters thought they were doing personally in economic terms—was their assessment of the state of the national economy and the salience they attached to that issue. Seventy-two percent of voters—up from 31 percent in 1988—thought the economy had gotten worse during the previous year. Of the two-thirds of all voters who identified the "economy/jobs" (43 percent) or "U.S. deficit" (21 percent) as the issue that mattered most to them, 47 percent voted for Clinton and only 26 percent for Bush—less than the 29 percent who voted for Perot. Conceding Bush's argument that the economy was improving, Kantor said, "It was the perception of the economy, not the actual."[83] Having impressed the voters in 1988 as far more competent than Dukakis as well as the better choice on domestic issues, Bush had lost both advantages by 1992. Even in the face of evidence to the contrary, voters no longer believed that he could make their lives better. The Clinton campaign's strategy of focusing on "the economy, stupid" was vindicated.

In contrast, the Bush campaign's decision to downplay foreign policy was not. Eighty-seven percent of voters who considered that the biggest issue voted for Bush, but they constituted only 8 percent of the electorate, a number that perhaps could have been driven up if Bush featured it more prominently in his speeches and advertising. His actual appeal—"trust and taxes"—flopped, at least as he and his campaign executed it. Voters were much more likely to identify "bring change" (37 percent) and "best plan" (25 percent) as the qualities they valued in a president than "experience" (18 percent) and "crisis judgment" (16 percent). Those who chiefly valued the former two qualities voted strongly for Clinton, while those—about half as many—who valued the latter two voted for Bush.

Support for independent candidates normally wanes as Election Day draws near and less-attached supporters decide not to "waste" their vote on someone who is unlikely to win. Perot's debate appearances and massive advertising late in the campaign enabled him to mitigate this tendency. His share of the national popular vote exceeded that of any independent or third-party candidates in history except two former presidents: Millard Fillmore in 1856 and Theodore Roosevelt in 1912. Yet in contrast to Fillmore, Roosevelt, and three other contenders who received many fewer popular votes than Perot—Robert M. LaFollette in 1924, Thurmond in 1948, and Wallace in 1968—Perot carried no states and therefore won no electoral votes. With no geographic base and an entirely national campaign strategy, he ran reasonably well almost everywhere, doing best in the Mountain West and worst in the South. But he came close to winning nowhere. Perot's best showing was in Maine, where he won 30.4 percent, 8.3 points behind Clinton. Nor is it clear that his presence on the ballot changed the outcome in any state. Some have argued that Bush would have carried Ohio and perhaps Georgia and New Hampshire in a two-candidate election, but even if he had won all three states, their 38 electoral votes still would have left him far behind Clinton in the Electoral College: 334 to 204.[84]

How the Perot vote affected the election in less obvious ways is a matter of some controversy. Baker and nearly all of Bush's other aides argue that because "about two-thirds of Perot supporters were natural Republicans who would have supported George [Bush] in a head-to-head race, . . . take two-thirds of 19 percent, and we got 51 percent." Lending partial credence to this claim, Perot won, as has been typical of independent candidates, a greater share of votes from members of the incumbent president's party than the opposition party: 21.6 percent from self-identified Republicans compared with 17.3 percent from self-identified Democrats. Throughout the entire election year, Perot added decibels to the chorus of prominent public figures criticizing Bush at every turn, directing his fire at Clinton only at the end.

Yet most of the research concludes that Perot did not cost Bush the election. Surveys showed that somewhere between one-fifth and one-third of those who voted for Perot would not have voted at all if he was not a candidate. Indeed, about half of the increase in turnout from 50.3 percent of the voting age population in 1988 to 55.2 percent in 1992 was because of Perot's presence on the ballot. Of those who would have voted for either Bush or Clinton if those were their only options, the evidence is strong that they would have divided their votes equally between the two major party candidates or, even more likely, turned Clinton's plurality of the popular vote into a majority by breaking strongly in his favor as the only remaining candidate of change.[85] A postelection Voter News Service study of the Perot vote indicated that Clinton would have received 53 percent of the national popular vote if Perot had not been on the ballot, 10 points more than he actually received.[86]

At a minimum, Perot complicated matters for the new president. Most independent candidates "sting and die"—that is, they run one time and then move on with their careers. Perot was different. On election night, he compared himself to "the grain of sand in the oyster that irritates the oyster and out comes a pearl."[87] Perot intended to keep close watch on President Clinton. In addition, federal election laws passed in the 1970s guaranteed public funding in the next election for any third party that received at least 5 percent of the national popular vote, creating an incentive for Perot to create such a party in anticipation of 1996. This newly complicated the efforts of both major parties to woo independent voters—in Perot's case, nearly 20 million of them—into their fold. The challenge for Clinton, in particular, was greater than for Richard Nixon after Wallace won 13.4 percent of the vote in 1968. "Perot had given defecting Republican a place to pause," noted Greenberg, "but the election would only prove historic and realigning, as happened when Nixon worked to incorporate the Wallace voters after the 1968 election, . . . if we accepted the challenge of bringing Perot voters into our coalition."[88]

Perot also undermined Clinton's hopes of winning a mandate to enact the kinds of sweeping legislative changes that might consolidate his hold on the Democratic Party and add new voters to its ranks. Democratic activists did their best to sell an interpretation of the election as a "mandate for activism." Historian and Democratic Party stalwart Arthur Schlesinger said that Clinton's victory augured the coming of a new generation of liberal change like the ones that occurred every thirty years or so throughout American history.[89] Although he lacked any publishing or journalistic experience, John F. Kennedy Jr. was so taken by Clinton's "hipness" that he decided to found *George*, a new magazine at "the intersection of popular culture and politics."[90]

Most scholars and journalists, however, interpreted the election in retrospective terms, as a "defeat for Bush rather than a victory for Clinton."[91] They also noted that Clinton's 23.8 percent of the voting age population was the lowest for any winning candidate since 1924, and his 43.0 percent of the national popular vote was the lowest winning percentage since 1912.[92] In truth, in the history of the modern office, transformational presidencies—notably those of Woodrow Wilson, Franklin D. Roosevelt, Lyndon B. Johnson, and Ronald Reagan—have only been ushered in when three specific conditions were met: a candidate who ran a change-oriented campaign; won in a landslide; and had long coattails in the congressional elections, thereby sending a strong signal to senators and representatives that his standing with the voters might affect their own standing.[93]

Clinton ran a change-oriented campaign. But his victory in the Electoral College fell below the 400 vote standard that usually earns landslide status, as did his popular vote margin—5.6 percentage points rather than 10 points or more. Still worse from the standpoint of claiming a mandate, his party actually lost nine seats in the House elections and only broke even in the Senate. He may have thought, when invoking two of political scientist

James MacGregor Burns's terms in an interview with Burns, that he would be an FDR-style "lion" and "transforming leader" as president.[94] But any president with his mixed mandate would have to overcome long odds to do so.

THE ELECTIONS FOR CONGRESS

The modest swing toward the Republicans in the 1992 congressional elections—and, at least as important for Clinton, the lack of significant gains for his own party—seemed out of keeping with the dominant mood in the country. Clinton took office with fewer Democrats in the House of Representatives than any Democratic president since Harry Truman: 258. The results in the Senate elections inspired Republican leader Bob Dole to argue with a straight face that because his party's 43 of 100 senators equaled Clinton's 43 percent of the national popular vote, the GOP had as strong a claim to a mandate as the president—ignoring the obvious fact that Clinton won a clear majority of the two-party vote and a two-thirds majority of the electoral votes (the only ones that count), as well as that Democrats held a strong majority in the Senate.

Below the surface of partisan change, the 1992 congressional elections made an enormous difference in the composition of the chamber. One hundred eight new members were elected to the 435-member House, along with 13 new senators. The number of women in the House rose from 28 to 47 (35 of them Democrats); the African American contingent grew from 25 to 38 (all of them Democrats); and the number of Latinos, including Cuban American Republicans and Mexican American Democrats, increased from 12 to 17. In the Senate, the ranks of women rose from 2 to 6 (5 of them Democrats), including the first black woman in the history of the chamber, Carol Moseley-Braun of Illinois. Meanwhile, voters in all fourteen states that had ballot measures proposing to limit senators to two six-year terms and House members to either three (as in eight states), four (four states), or six (two states) two-year terms approved the measures, usually by 60 percent or more.

The amount of turnover in 1992 seemed to belie the claim that term limits were needed to bring new faces into Congress. It stood in stark contrast to the stability that marked the 1990 congressional elections just two years earlier, when 90 percent of House members sought and won reelection and only one incumbent senator was defeated. Even then, the average winning percentage for incumbents reelected to the House in 1990 was the lowest since World War II.[95] And several events occurred in 1991 and 1992 that upset the seemingly stable political apple cart.

One was predictable: the redistricting that followed the 1990 census, which caused nineteen House seats from thirteen Rust Belt states to be reallocated to eight Sun Belt states, including California, which gained seven seats; Florida, which gained four; and Texas, which gained three. District boundaries in these twenty-one states obviously needed to be redrawn, but so did the boundaries nearly everywhere else in order to reflect the population movement that had occurred within each state since the 1980 census. One consequence was that multiple members ended up in the same districts and had to run against each other if they wanted to stay in Congress, either in a primary if they were of the same party or in the general election if one was a Democrat and the other a Republican.

As usually occurred in census-year elections, most potentially strong challengers sat out 1990 and waited until 1992, when the effects of reapportionment and redistricting would be clear. In 1990 the field of challengers was remarkably weak: only 10 percent had ever held elective office, the lowest share in the post–World War II era.[96] In 1992 the field was unusually strong, with 24 percent of challengers experienced at seeking and winning office.[97] The recently expanding ranks of women with electoral experience provided a rich talent pool of new candidates. By 1992 women held about 20 percent of statewide offices such as lieutenant governor and state treasurer, 20 percent of city council memberships, 15 percent of state legislative seats, and 10 percent of mayor's offices.[98] All were plausible launching pads for a congressional campaign. And feminist groups were ready as never before to help fund their elections, including the National Organization for Women's political action committee and EMILY's List (Early Money Is Like Yeast).

Compounding the complexities created by the redrawing of district lines in time for the 1992 election, the Supreme Court had recently interpreted amendments added to the Voting Rights Act Amendment in 1982 to require that every southern state create congressional districts dominated by racial and ethnic minorities wherever residential patterns allowed.[99] The GOP did not control most state governments but, realizing that the mandate for states to create "majority-minority" districts would "bleach" surrounding districts of reliably pro-Democratic minority voters, Republicans joined with black and Latino Democrats in the effort to maximize the number of such districts. For the first time since Reconstruction, House districts in Alabama, Florida, North Carolina, South Carolina, and Virginia elected an African American to Congress. These states and the other southern jurisdictions covered by the voting act also elected twenty-two additional Republicans, most of them from previously Democratic districts that were drained of black voters.

A series of events occurred after the 1990 midterm election that threw Congress further into turmoil. In 1991 it became widely known that the House maintained a sort of bank for its members that regularly covered overdrafts—as many as 8,000 or more bad checks each year—without penalty. Two hundred sixty-seven members currently serving in the House were overdrawn at least once, and the ranks of those who wrote 100 or more bad checks included 13.4 percent of Democratic members and 6.6 percent of Republicans.[100] Fifty-two House incumbents, concentrated among the most egregious offenders, retired rather than face the voters in 1992, and nineteen others were defeated in primaries. Both numbers set postwar records. Adding to the incentive to step down was that through a quirk in the law 1992 was the last year that retiring members could convert their campaign funds to personal use.

Senators, who were unaffected by redistricting and had no in-house bank, nevertheless were caught up in the voters' general disgust with privileged congressional behavior. They were tarred with the same brush as their House colleagues by public outrage over congressional pay raises, which had increased the annual salary in both chambers from $77,400 to $125,000 over the past four years. The public anger was so strong that state legislatures hastened to ratify a constitutional amendment requiring that any congressional pay increase be postponed until after the next election. The amendment, which Congress proposed in 1789, had been rattling around the ratification process for 203 years before heightened public awareness led to its approval by the requisite three-fourths of the states in 1992. It entered the Constitution as the Twenty-Seventh Amendment, the only one to be added since the early 1970s.[101]

Adding fuel to the fire, in October 1991 senators came under attack for their handling of President Bush's nomination of Clarence Thomas, a conservative African American, to the Supreme Court. In confirmation hearings that were televised live on all three broadcast networks, the monochromatically white male Senate Judiciary Committee appeared to dismiss the allegations of a former Thomas employee, the African American law professor Anita Hill, who accused him of treating her in sexually offensive ways. In the backlash that followed, especially among Democratic women, eight senators retired and Sen. Alan Dixon was defeated by Moseley-Braun in the Illinois primary. With more women voting for women candidates than in any previous election, more ran and more were elected.[102]

Democrats benefited from what soon was labeled "The Year of the Woman"—more accurately, "The Year of the Democratic Woman." As political scientist Marjorie Randon Hershey observed, "The stereotyping of women as more moral and less tainted by 'politics as usual' put women, the ultimate outsiders, in just the position that most male candidates were trying to attain."[103] But because Democratic Senate candidates had done so well in 1986, the last time these seats were on the ballot, the deck was stacked in the Republicans' favor in 1992. Only fifteen Republican seats were at risk, compared with twenty-one Democratic seats, nine of which were won only narrowly six years earlier.

In elections to both chambers, few incumbents were defeated in November: just 7 percent in the House and 16 percent in the Senate, where two Democratic senators from the South and two Republican senators from the North and West lost. These numbers wildly understated the year's electoral volatility because by November the herd had been culled of vulnerable incumbents, most of whom retired or lost their primaries. One ironic effect of the massive turnover in the membership of both chambers was that the term limits movement, which was animated by the belief that incumbents were nearly invulnerable to challenge, lost its best argument. The movement peaked in 1992 with its victories at the ballot box and receded soon afterward, partly because the new Congress was flooded with new members and partly because in 1995 the Supreme Court ruled in *U.S. Term Limits v. Thornton* that the Constitution denied states the power to impose term limits on members of the federal legislature.[104] After the 1994 midterm election, when many more incumbent members were replaced by newcomers, the effort to impose term limits fizzled completely

Fortunately for Clinton, the results of the congressional elections meant that many members of the Ninety-Third Congress would be, like him, new to Washington and therefore less likely to be locked in to old ways of doing things. Unfortunately, not as many of them would be Democrats as he would have liked, although Clinton had seemed to lump in Democratic members with Republicans when he decried the "brain-dead politics in Washington" in his acceptance speech at the Democratic convention. The sad irony for the new president was that his party's losses in the congressional elections masked the coattails he actually had. Until November the bank scandal and redistricting in the House, the greater number of vulnerable

Democratic seats in the Senate, and the pay increases in both chambers seemed to augur strong Republican gains. Clinton's campaign and election probably kept the Democrats from losing even more seats, but this effect was too subtle to be noticed at the time. All people did notice was that fewer Democrats were in Congress after the election than before it.

With the exception of Republican control of the Senate during the first six years of the Reagan administration, both chambers of Congress had been Democratic for nearly forty years, ever since 1954. Divided government as the normal governing situation in Washington prevailed in this period whenever, as usually was the case, a Republican president was in the White House. Clinton's victory, however middling it was and despite the GOP's modest gains in the congressional elections, brought Democrats the consolation that the election restored united party government in their favor. Their challenge would be to improve on their performance since the last time they controlled both Congress and the presidency, the ill-starred Carter years.

7

REDIVIDING GOVERNMENT
BILL CLINTON AND CONGRESS,
1993–1995

Bill Clinton's inaugural address on January 20, 1993, was filled with bold promises of change. He spoke of "renewal," of the need to "revitalize," and of his intention to "force the spring."[1] An image related to bringing crops out of the ground prematurely, the last of these should have been a cause for concern. As he did after his first election as governor of Arkansas in 1978, Clinton overinterpreted his mandate from the 1992 presidential election. Now as then he was encouraged to do so by his wife, who was also his most valued political adviser. At an early administration retreat, the incoming First Lady—once again bearing the name Hillary Rodham Clinton—dismissed a suggestion that the president establish priorities in his agenda by saying, "Why are we here if we don't go for it?"[2] (See appendix F for the text of Clinton's first inaugural address.)

Unfavorable circumstances were an impediment to the transformational style of leadership to which Clinton aspired, as were some poorly considered decisions by the president-elect himself. Clinton's 43 percent of the national popular vote and hard-to-detect down-ballot coattails offered the furthest thing from the sort of mandate that historically has spurred Congress to follow the president's lead on matters of public policy. A report during the postelection transition period that the annual budget deficit in the coming fiscal year and beyond would be considerably higher than previously forecast—with damaging consequences for interest rates and therefore economic growth—constrained his freedom of action. Throughout the campaign, Clinton said that his economic program "starts with a middle-class tax cut" as a prelude to increased "investments" in education and job training.[3] Now he was told that to rein in the deficit and forestall further interest rate increases from the Federal Reserve Board, he would have to raise taxes and reduce spending. "You mean to tell me that the success of my reelection hinges on the Federal Reserve and a bunch of fucking bond traders?" the president-elect fumed in a January 7 meeting with his economic team.[4] He felt trapped by the need to impress Fed chair Alan Greenspan, a Republican, with his seriousness about deficit reduction, even while acknowledging that he had no choice but to do so.

Republicans in Congress placed further limits on Clinton's ability to lead. "Fifty-seven percent of the Americans who voted in the presidential election voted against Clinton," said Senate minority leader Bob Dole, "and I intend to represent that majority on the floor of the United States Senate."[5] Even if Clinton got the traditional "honeymoon" that greets new presidents, Dole said, he would play the role of "chaperone."[6] As political scientist Frances Lee has shown, ever since the GOP secured a Senate majority in 1980 for the first time in a quarter century and Democratic leader Robert Byrd of West Virginia launched a newly aggressive strategy aimed at winning back control for his party, confrontation had supplanted cooperation as the standard approach of the chamber's minority, whichever party it was.[7] A deal maker by inclination, Dole nevertheless accepted this approach as the GOP's best hope for regaining the Senate majority that Byrd's Democrats won in the 1986 midterm elections. The forty-three Republicans in the chamber could not pass legislation of their own devising, but with the power of the filibuster at their disposal, they could keep many objectionable elements of the president's program from being enacted.

Although Republicans lacked the ability to either enact or obstruct in the filibuster-free House of Representatives, their de facto leader, minority whip Newt Gingrich, was determined to throw as many roadblocks in Clinton's path as possible in pursuit of his goal of making the GOP the chamber's majority party for the first time in four decades. In Gingrich's case, unlike Dole's, personal temperament and partisan strategy were as one. In the nine House leadership contests that took place from 1980 to 1988, not a single candidate who favored a confrontational approach to the Democratic majority was chosen. From 1989 to 1992 such candidates—notably Gingrich himself in 1989—won six of nine contests, including all three held right after Clinton's election in 1992.[8]

As governor, Clinton had grown accustomed to working with his fellow state chief executives across party lines. In dealing with the overwhelmingly Democratic Arkansas legislature, he never had to worry about effective Republican opposition. The legislature was part-time, consisting of members who earned their living in other ways and met for just one three-month session every two years; only about one-tenth of its members were Republicans. Washington, well stocked with Republicans both partisan and powerful, would be different in ways for which Clinton was not entirely prepared.

Congressional Democrats posed additional problems for Clinton. More than two-thirds of House Democrats and half of Senate Democrats had never served with a Democratic president. Their experience was rooted in opposition, not cooperation. Few supported Clinton for the party's presidential nomination, and most resented his criticisms during the campaign of their "midnight pay raise" in 1989 and their misuse of the House bank and post office.[9] Only a minority considered themselves Clinton-style New Democrats or thought they owed their election to him. Most represented safe Democratic constituencies and therefore had no incentive to abandon their party's traditional liberalism. Virtually all won a higher share of the vote than Clinton, providing them with further confirmation that no change in approach was necessary. The ranks of liberal Democratic women and ethnic and racial minorities rose substantially in the 1992 elections, moving the party's caucus several degrees to the left.

"I didn't run for president to be a bare-fanged partisan," Clinton said, but that was how Republican legislators intended to portray him and what many of his fellow Democrats in Congress wanted him to be.[10] Even before he took office, House Democratic leaders backed him down from his preelection promises to pursue campaign finance reform, welfare reform, and a reduction in congressional staffs. When added to the new president's lack of a popular vote majority, these concessions "left Clinton without the strength of his own convictions to govern from a majority standpoint," according to deputy domestic policy adviser Bruce Reed.[11] The new president was determined not to repeat the mistake of his most recent Democratic predecessor, Jimmy Carter, by getting off on the wrong foot with his party on Capitol Hill. But in ceding control of his first-term agenda to conventionally liberal Democratic congressional leaders, "I've lashed myself to Congress like Ahab to Moby Dick," Clinton soon lamented.[12]

In addition to being constrained by circumstances, Clinton created problems for himself. "What's typical of talented governors of small states," observed William Galston, whom Clinton appointed as Reed's fellow deputy domestic policy aide, "is that they are head and shoulders above the other politicians in their state and they can—through force of intellect and character and a loyal, dedicated staff—move the political system of those states."[13] Rather than focus on ability or even loyalty when choosing most of the cabinet, Clinton appointed department heads to placate his party's various constituency groups: feminists, racial and ethnic minorities, environmentalists, unions, and so on. He wanted a cabinet that "looks like America," Clinton declared, but his mix of women, African Americans, Latinos, and liberals consisted mainly of wealthy lawyers.[14] Italian Americans, Irish Americans, and other European ethnics, long the mainstay of the Democratic coalition, were noticeably absent. Even George Stephanopoulos, one of Clinton's more left-leaning aides, acknowledged that "our appointees are generally more liberal than our vision."[15]

Focused on fending off what he called the "bean counters" in his party who were pressuring him on cabinet appointments, Clinton waited until late in the transition to cobble together his White House office out of the raw material of his campaign staff and Arkansas associates. "I hardly spent any time on the White House staff," he later rued; the result was "too many young people in this White House who are young but not wise."[16] Among the president's major aides, only national security adviser Anthony Lake had ever worked in the White House. "If you added up all the years of White House experience of all the people in the Clinton White House . . . , it's not clear to me you would have gotten to twenty-five," said Galston.[17] Never having run a large operation or served in Washington, Clinton needed a disciplined, experienced staff. Eventually he got one, but for more than a year he lurched from one oversized, unruly, inconclusive, and leak-prone staff meeting to another, fostering a media image of a president in over his head. "The kind of free-form, nonhierarchical, hardworking but fun-loving kind of atmosphere that was successful during the campaign persisted in the White House during the first year," observed chief speechwriter David Kusnet, "with much less success."[18]

EARLY STUMBLES

Faced with these challenging circumstances, some of his own making, the newly inaugurated president stumbled badly out of the gate. Although he had promised to "focus on the economy like a laser beam," he was instantly caught up in a cultural firestorm over his intention to issue an executive order to lift the existing ban on gays and lesbians serving in the military.[19] It quickly became apparent that if he did, Congress would overturn his decision with veto-proof majorities in both houses. "People couldn't understand it," Sen. Edward M. Kennedy said of the president's decision to lead with the issue. "I think it's fair to say it was probably the opening of the antagonism towards Clinton."[20] Clinton soon backed off, issuing instead a "don't ask, don't tell" order that required gay and lesbian service members to remain closeted. "I got the worst of both worlds," he realized. "I lost the fight"—making him appear both weak and the furthest thing from a "different kind of Democrat"—"and the gay community was highly critical of me" for compromising.[21] News accounts of additional lapses in judgment by the president, ranging from a much-maligned $200 onboard haircut as *Air Force One* sat on a runway at the Los Angeles airport to the trashing of his first two loosely vetted choices for attorney general, Zoë Baird and Kimba Wood, for employing illegal immigrants as nannies, left the country incredulous.

Clinton's first year in office was not bereft of success, but the benefits proved to be long-term while the costs were immediate. Citing the estimated $350 billion budget shortfall for fiscal year 1993 that he inherited from the Bush administration, Clinton substituted a tax hike for his campaign promise of a middle-class tax cut. The $241 billion increase, some of it targeted at high earners but much of the rest falling on everyday purchases of gasoline, was part of an overall plan to cut $496 billion from the deficit in five years that also included $255 billion in spending reductions. Congressional Republicans marched in lockstep against Clinton's economic program and were able to defeat his $16 billion short-term stimulus package, which he offered as a hedge against the economic contraction that might result from shrinking the budget deficit. As for the larger budget proposal, enough Democrats defected that it passed by the narrowest majority possible against unified Republican opposition. The final vote in August was 218–216 in the House and 50–50 in the Senate, with Vice President Al Gore casting the tie-breaking vote. Interest rates did come down, eventually fueling an economic boom, but at the time most voters only saw that the candidate who promised them lower taxes and new federal programs had morphed into the president who raised their taxes and reduced existing programs. The new reality of a deficit-reducing Democratic president ran so counter to voters' long-standing impressions of the party that it was slow to sink in.

Clinton's other first-year legislative achievements were similarly problematic in the political short term. Because he merely inherited the Family and Medical Leave Act from congressional Democrats, who previously had

A weary Bill and Hillary Clinton about a month before their health care reform proposal was defeated in Congress. Courtesy of the William J. Clinton Presidential Library.

passed it only to be thwarted by a veto from President George Bush, Clinton received little personal credit when the bill became law in February. Conversely, because he inherited the North American Free Trade Agreement (NAFTA) from Bush, Clinton's endorsement of it in the fall alienated the labor unions on whom many Democratic candidates relied for money and organization. "We have $10 million that we'd like to spend on television ads promoting your health care plan," AFL-CIO president Lane Kirkland told the president. "Of course, if you insist on going ahead with NAFTA, we're going to take the $10 million and spend it on opposition to that."[22] On September 14 every former president and secretary of state stood by Clinton in the White House to lend their voices to his in support of the trade agreement. Bush was so impressed by Clinton's "eloquent statement" that he quipped, "Now I understand why he's on the inside looking out while I'm on the outside looking in."[23] But a quarter century of Democratic futility in presidential elections meant that most of these ex-presidents and secretaries were Republicans. When the House approved NAFTA on November 20, Republican members supported it by 132 to 43 and Democratic members—including majority leader Richard Gephardt and majority whip

David Bonior—opposed it by 157 to 102. The Senate soon added its approval, also relying on Republican rather than Democratic votes.

Pointing out that no president in the history of polling had crossed the 50 percent disapproval mark among voters as early in his term as Clinton, *Time* featured him on its June 7, 1993, cover as "The Incredible Shrinking President." The story merely confirmed what Clinton's campaign pollster, Stan Greenberg, told him in a memo: "we look parochial, small, and overwhelmed" to the point that 55 percent of Americans think the president is in "over his head."[24]

The doubts about character that plagued Clinton during the election were reinforced by congressional and independent counsel investigations into his and Hillary Rodham Clinton's decade-old investment in the Arkansas real estate deal known as Whitewater. So focused was the press on the alleged scandal that by March 1994 there had been more stories in major newspapers on Whitewater than on health care reform, crime policy, and welfare reform combined.[25] When files relating to Whitewater were found to have been removed from the office of deputy White House counsel Vince Foster after he committed suicide on July 20, 1993, Democrats joined Republicans in demanding that Clinton instruct Attorney General Janet Reno (his third choice for the office) to appoint a special prosecutor. Yielding to pressure, Clinton did so on January 11, 1994. Reno quickly chose a respected Republican, Robert Fiske, who concluded after about five months that neither of the Clintons had committed a crime. Even as he was issuing his report, however, Congress revived the Independent Counsel Act, which had expired in December 1992. The act required that independent counsels be appointed not by the attorney general but by a three-judge federal panel. In August the panel replaced Fiske with a former Reagan-appointed appellate court judge, Kenneth Starr, who relaunched the investigation.

In addition to the doubts about Clinton's character, doubts about his competence in foreign policy beset him during the early stages of his presidency. They seemed confirmed in October 1993 when, in the largest firefight since the Vietnam War, eighteen American soldiers were killed, seventy-four wounded, and one captured in Mogadishu, Somalia, as part of an ill-conceived effort to track down a rebel warlord. Congress threatened to cut off funding for the mission, which somehow had morphed from humanitarian assistance to nation building. Grudgingly, Clinton agreed to limit involvement to protecting American forces and securing supply lines for relief aid.

Just one week after the disastrous "Black Hawk down" debacle in Mogadishu, about a hundred armed thugs chanting "Another Somalia!" in Port-au-Prince, Haiti, were able to turn away the battleship USS *Harlan County*. The ship was carrying lightly armed troops whose mission was to train a new civilian police force while underscoring Clinton's desire to see the military junta step down in favor of the democratically elected president, Jean-Bertrand Aristide. "We had sent the ship out with zero military support," lamented national security adviser Lake, resulting in a "total fuck-up."[26] "I can't believe we're getting pushed around by these two-bit pricks," complained Clinton.[27] One consequence of the embarrassing failure of the two humanitarian missions, Lake recalled, was that the president "decided not to intervene militarily in Rwanda, even though there was a genocide, because we were so scared by Somalia."[28] The Rwandan civil war in spring 1994 resulted in the rapid slaughter of about 800,000 Tutsis by the rival Hutus. Similarly, after pledging during the election campaign that he would intervene in the former Yugoslavia to end Serbia's pursuit of its "ethnic cleansing" strategy of rape, concentration camps, and forced evacuation in neighboring Bosnia and Croatia, Clinton backed off his promise to lift the arms embargo on Bosnia and strike Serbian enclaves with airpower. Faced with domestic reluctance to get involved from Congress, the Pentagon, and public opinion, Clinton retreated when the British and French complained that such actions would endanger their peacekeeping forces in the region.

HEALTH CARE

Early in 1993 Clinton made a strategic choice to focus on health care reform, a secondary theme of his election campaign but one that congressional Democrats supported. In doing so he necessarily downplayed welfare reform, a primary campaign theme that they despised. On September 23 Clinton gave an effective nationally televised prime-time speech to Congress outlining in broad strokes the plan whose development Hillary Rodham Clinton oversaw after the president chose her for that role during the transition. The initial response to his promise to "guarantee all Americans a comprehensive package of benefits over the course of an entire lifetime" was positive.[29] An ABC News poll found that four times as many Americans thought that to do nothing about health care would be more dangerous than to adopt the Clintons' plan.[30]

The plan, which was developed by a large task force behind closed doors without the involvement of Congress or the cabinet, did not stand up well to the intense public scrutiny that followed the initial rollout. Funded by a new payroll tax on workers and businesses, it was complicated (the bill was 1,342 pages long) and costly (an estimated $50 to $100 billion per year). Worse, it left the vast majority of Americans who were satisfied with their existing health insurance worried that they would have to pay more for lower-quality, less-available care. "Ambitious, idealistic, and highly logical" as the plan was, wrote Stephanopoulos, it was also "inflexible, overly complex, and highly susceptible to misinterpretation." But the First Lady's unique closeness to the president meant that "inside the White House, her position stifled healthy skepticism."[31] Staff and cabinet members "worried about the Rube Goldberg quality of the plan—but they were reluctant to take on Mrs. Clinton."[32] "You make your point once to the president's wife and if it is not accepted you don't press it," said one cabinet member.[33]

Liberals supported the Clintons' proposal, but in recent years many left-leaning groups had become Washington-based, staff-dominated organizations whose efforts were focused on litigation and lobbying.[34] Such groups did not have the vibrant local chapters that conservative organizations such as the National Federation of Independent Business and the Christian Coalition had. They also lacked the large network of talk radio stations featuring conservative hosts, who roused their millions of listeners in opposition to all things Clinton. As recently as 1960 there were just two all-talk stations; the AM dial was dominated by music, and most radios lacked FM. By 1995 FM dials were common, music had migrated there, talk filled the resulting AM vacuum, and there were 1,130 talk stations. Seventy percent of their listeners were conservatives who tuned in because they distrusted the mainstream media. Rush Limbaugh alone reached 20 million people on 650 stations. In alliance with the health insurance and pharmaceutical industries, grassroots conservative groups energized by daily doses of talk show rhetoric waged an effective campaign to fan doubts about the Clinton plan.[35]

The Clintons dug in, resisting suggested changes in their proposal that would modify it to extend coverage to all but about 5 percent of Americans. In his January 25, 1994, State of the Union address, the president threw down a gauntlet to Congress, brandishing a pen and promising to "veto the legislation" unless it "guarantees every American private health insurance that can never be taken away."[36] By summer, polls showed that twice as many voters feared adopting Clinton's proposal more than preserving the status quo.[37] Locked in by his all-or-nothing pledge, which he later rued as "an unnecessary red flag to my opponents in Congress," the president had no choice but to accept defeat when the bill died for lack of support in late September 1994.[38]

THE 1994 MIDTERM ELECTION

Politically, Clinton faced the same challenge Richard Nixon had when he began his presidency: to build on the 43 percent he received in his initial election by bringing voters who cast their ballots for an independent candidate—George C. Wallace in 1968, Ross Perot in 1992—into his coalition.[39] Nothing seemed less likely heading into the 1994 midterm election. Even though Clinton focused on reducing the federal deficit that his independent rival had complained so much about in the course of winning 18.9 percent of the popular vote, Perot sneered that the president's budget plan was just more "tax and spend" and bought a half hour of airtime on NBC to say so.[40] Clinton himself worried that voters regarded him as "a knee-jerk liberal whose mask of moderation had been removed."[41] Even the administration-sponsored crime bill, which increased sentences for numerous federal offenses, funded state prison construction, and subsidized the hiring of 100,000 new officers by local police forces, seemed to backfire politically. Clinton refused advice from Speaker Tom Foley and majority leader Gephardt to remove the bill's ban on assault weapons because it would hurt rural Democrats seeking reelection. The bill passed, and when violent crime rates subsequently went down, Clinton trumpeted the news to good political effect in his campaign for reelection in 1996. But in the short term, Clinton later concluded, Foley and Gephardt were right and "I was wrong."[42]

Just how wrong became apparent in the results of the November 8 elections. The Democrats lost 54 House seats and 10 Senate seats, thereby ceding control of both chambers to the Republicans: 230 to 204 in the House and 53 to 47 in the Senate. The GOP's gains were massive and across the board. In addition to retaking Congress for the first time in forty years, Republicans added eleven governorships, raising their ranks from nineteen to thirty, including seven of the eight largest states. They also added about 100 state Senate seats and 370 state House seats, enabling them to increase the number of states in which they controlled both chambers from eight to nineteen—one more than the Democrats.[43] In Congress, Gingrich became Speaker of the House and Dole became majority leader of the Senate.

As Foley had feared, the National Rifle Association mobilized its grassroots membership against Clinton's gun control policy so effectively that he, among other Democrats from rural districts, was defeated—the first

House Speaker to be denied reelection since 1862. Other factors contributed to the Republicans' triumph, including Gingrich's effort to unite nearly all the party's House candidates behind a ten-point Contract with America, a series of conservative promises that he vowed to pursue if the GOP won the election.[44] The list of what Gingrich called "60 percent issues" because of their poll-tested popularity was as notable for what it did not include—controversial social issues such as abortion and public school prayer, for example—as for what it did, including deregulation, a balanced budget amendment to the Constitution, and term limits on members of Congress.[45] The Republicans' success in uniting behind a common congressional platform belied the adage that "all politics is local." Gingrich saw that as conservative southern Democratic voters shifted toward the Republican Party and liberal northeastern Republicans enlisted with the Democrats, a national campaign spanning hundreds of districts and all fifty states could be the formula for victory.

More than anything else, the midterm election was a rebuke of Clinton, whose strenuous campaigning for his party's candidates was, if anything, counterproductive. The very voters he promised to bring in to the Democratic Party when he ran in 1992—the "forgotten middle class," southern whites, and Perot supporters—swung hard to the GOP. For the first time since Reconstruction, the Republicans won a majority of southern governorships and seats in Congress. Perot voters, who went narrowly Democratic in the 1992 congressional elections, backed GOP candidates by 67 percent to 33 percent in 1994. "It's over, I think, for President Clinton, no matter how hard he tries," said ABC White House correspondent Sam Donaldson, one of a chorus of pundits who wrote off Clinton's chances for reelection.[46]

REBOUND

With interest rates down, inflation and unemployment low, the budget deficit declining, and the economy growing at a 4 percent annual rate, Clinton's economic plan was working as 1995 began. But most Americans did not see that yet. Nearly two years of presidential missteps and negative press coverage had sown such widespread doubts about Clinton's competence that voters believed the national economy was getting worse even as their personal circumstances improved. A majority thought the deficit had risen and the recession had not ended, and they disapproved of the president's overall handling of the economy. Clinton benefited as a candidate in 1992 when all that many voters saw in Bush's deficit reduction plan was a president who promised not to raise their taxes making them pay more for fewer services. Clinton suffered as president in 1994 when they thought they saw the same betrayal in him. The luxury he had that Bush did not was an additional two years for the larger benefits of his economic policies to became impossible to ignore before he had to run for reelection.

Clinton had been in this situation fourteen years earlier. During his first term as governor of Arkansas, he overreached and paid the price politically. He learned from the experience and came back stronger than ever two years later. "My daddy never had to whip me twice for the same thing," Clinton said then.[47] "We got the living daylights beat out of us," he conceded now.[48] Liberal Democrats like Senator Kennedy told Clinton that he needed to double down on his party's progressive agenda in order to rally the support of African Americans, unions, gays and lesbians, women, and teachers in his bid for reelection.[49] Heeding a December *Los Angeles Times* poll showing that two-thirds of Democratic voters wanted to see Clinton's nomination for a second term challenged, some party operatives began to "whisper conspiratorially" about replacing him with Gore at the head of the ticket.[50] Gore squelched that effort.[51]

Confident that voters would appreciate the benefits of his economic policies if they could overcome their lack of faith in his character and leadership, Clinton returned to his centrist New Democrat roots rather than moving leftward. Indeed, the foundations of Clinton's 1996 reelection strategy were built on the ashes of the Democrats' heavy midterm losses in 1994. "It was clear by the fall of 1994 that the American people had decided that the '92 campaign had been a bait-and-switch operation," according to Galston—baited with innovative centrist promises and then switched to conventional liberal policies. "He'd been listening to advice from advisers who were oriented toward congressional Democrats. . . . The fact that the New Democratic strategic course had never gotten a careful examination during the first two years was not lost on the president. I don't think he felt very happy about it."[52] With Democrats no longer serving as House speaker, Senate majority leader, or committee chairs in either chamber, Clinton no longer felt as constrained by them as he had during his first two years.

Clinton also counted on Gingrich and the Republicans to overreach. During the first phase of the modern era of divided government, Republican presidents Nixon, Gerald Ford, Ronald Reagan, and Bush faced a Democratic Congress. As a result of the 1994 elections, divided government took the form of a Democratic president and a Republican Congress for the first time since 1947. Clinton had already had two years to make his mis-

takes and learn from them. Now Republicans on Capitol Hill—especially
in the House, none of whose GOP members had ever been in the majority—would have to adapt to their new position of responsibility. The hubris
and inexperience that led Clinton to overinterpret his 1992 mandate as the
dawn of a new Democratic era threatened to lead the GOP, convinced by its
triumph in 1994 that the party's defeat two years earlier had been a fluke,
to overinterpret theirs. Gingrich somehow persuaded himself that the 1994
elections were the most important since 1860, when Abraham Lincoln was
elected president.[53]

During the first half of 1995, Clinton gradually adopted a two-pronged
strategy for reelection, the elements of which were firmly in place by the
end of the year. The first prong was to preempt any challenge to his renomination at the Democratic convention by raising so much money that no
credible opponent would dare to take him on. "We'll raise the money faster
than it's ever been done in American politics," Democratic fund-raiser
Terry McAuliffe told Clinton. He kept his promise with a series of early
events, first in New Jersey ("to stifle all talk of [Sen. Bill] Bradley challenging
Clinton"), and then in Little Rock, Chicago, Miami, Denver, San Francisco,
and Los Angeles.[54] By September, McAuliffe and the president had raised
the legal maximum of $43.2 million. In addition, eight states canceled their
Democratic presidential primaries in order to discourage potential challengers. Among those who thought about running before backing off were
Bradley, fellow senators Bob Kerrey of Nebraska and Robert Casey of Pennsylvania, Gephardt, and Rev. Jesse Jackson. Clinton's success in this effort
made him the first Democratic presidential candidate since FDR in 1936
not to face opposition for his party's nomination. His campaign treasury
was full, and he would not have to spend a penny of it fending off a primary
opponent.

Hoping to revive the impression created during the 1992 campaign that
he represented a fresh approach to governing, Clinton also resurrected his
New Democrat message of "opportunity, responsibility, and community."
In translating this message into action, Clinton adopted political strategist
Dick Morris's goals of "triangulation" in policy and, in presidential style, a
more dignified, statesmanlike demeanor.[55] Morris was a mostly Republican
political operative who nonetheless answered Clinton's distress call after he
lost his first bid for reelection as governor of Arkansas in 1980. Now, in the
aftermath of a similarly devastating defeat, Clinton summoned him again.

Morris persuaded Clinton that it was important not only to stake out a
position in the political center but also to find new issues that would allow

him to rise above the conventional left-right political spectrum and offer a "third way." The baseline of the new political triangle would be occupied at opposite ends by liberal Democrats and conservative Republicans, with Clinton hovering at a point above and between them. As Morris urged Clinton to embrace, and thereby neutralize, Republican issues such as crime, taxes, welfare, and the budget, the president displayed a renewed commitment to middle-class concerns. "I had discovered the middle class in [my] presidential campaign," Clinton said, "and forsaken them as president."[56] He would forsake them no longer.

Part of triangulation involved claiming the Republicans' emphasis on values as his own. For Democrats, most cultural issues were matters of rights—abortion, affirmative action, nondiscrimination against gays and lesbians, and so on. Republicans were much more likely to focus on values, especially those relating to family, faith, and neighborhood. Clinton was personally comfortable with Morris's advice to take a series of executive actions that were more about values than rights, including school uniforms, curfews for teenagers, cell phones for community watch groups, a voluntary rating system for television programs, and encouragement for student religious groups in public schools. Individually, these measures were small. Together, they added up. In some cases, such as discouraging youth smoking and requiring that V-chips be installed in new televisions so parents could keep their kids from watching violent or sexually suggestive programs, Republicans' ties to industry left them stuck on the other side.

"The government does hugely complicated things that the public is just never going to get," reflected Clinton's press secretary Joe Lockhart. "So he wanted to have the government start doing things that people would get. . . . He wanted a simple thing every day, and he wanted the public to go to bed every night saying, 'That's a pretty good idea.'"[57] "Clinton is the first president to use executive actions the way a painter uses a brush," wrote presidential historian Michael Beschloss, "to slowly, carefully fill in parts of his own public image."[58]

Clinton's adoption of the triangulation strategy animated his approach to the defining controversy of his third year as president: the battle with the 104th Congress over the fiscal year 1996 budget.[59] Fresh from their triumph in the midterm election, the Gingrich-led Republicans went beyond the promises of the Contract with America by committing themselves to cut taxes by $245 billion and domestic spending by $270 billion over five years. Congressional Democrats opposed them on both counts, aiming most of their fire at the proposed spending reductions.

Clinton initially angered these Democrats—a markedly more urban, liberal, minority, and coastal group after the party's loss of southern and rural seats in 1994—by boldly embracing the Republicans' goal of a balanced budget in seven years. But he won back their support by insisting that core Democratic programs such as Medicare, Medicaid, educational funding, and environmental enforcement be left substantially unaltered. "You know what was really important?" observed National Economic Council director Robert Rubin. "When [the Republicans] put out whatever their budget was, they had that proposal for a $270 billion reduction in Medicare and a $270 [sic] billion tax cut, which was already headed on its way to the most affluent. I remember George [Stephanopoulos] saying we can frame our whole political strategy around this. . . . [George] turned out to be exactly right, because it symbolized for people a whole approach to—it had symbolic value."[60]

Politically, Clinton's approach to the budget seamlessly wove together the triangulation strategy of appealing to the broad center of the American electorate with a base strategy of defending his party's most valued policies. But Gingrich, who thought Bush erred by caving in to the Democrats on the budget in 1990, was determined not to do so this time. Dole's desire to win the Republican presidential nomination in 1996 against more conservative rivals like Sen. Phil Gramm of Texas convinced him he had no choice but to follow Gingrich's lead. Ideologically, Dole was boxed in. According to Rubin's deputy, Gene Sperling, "In a leadership meeting during the second shutdown [Dole] said it was time to cut a deal and get this over with. [House majority leader Richard] Armey just pointed at Dole and said, 'Mr. President, that man does not speak for us.'"[61] As Clinton rightly perceived, Dole's deference to Gingrich made him seem like a "second banana," the farthest thing from a presidential image.[62] Within his own chamber's Republican caucus, Dole also had to worry about the influence of newly elected "Gingrich senators," confrontational conservatives like those who had just chosen Trent Lott of Mississippi as majority whip against Dole's preferred candidate, the more moderate incumbent, Alan Simpson of Wyoming.[63]

The public, roused by millions of dollars worth of under-the-radar pro-administration television ads financed by the Democratic National Committee, sided with the president. To keep reporters from noticing, the ads ran outside New York and Washington while reaching 125 million viewers three times per week. When the Republicans tried to impose their own budget on Clinton, he refused to yield. The president then persuaded the voters that Gingrich, Dole, and the Republican Congress were responsible for the

Senate majority leader Bob Dole, Vice President Al Gore, President Bill Clinton, and Speaker of the House Newt Gingrich shake hands in the midst of the difficult 1995–1996 budget negotiations. Courtesy of the William J. Clinton Presidential Library.

two federal government shutdowns that began in late 1995 in the absence of a budget agreement. The first lasted from November 14 to November 19. The second stretched three weeks, from December 16 to January 6. What Clinton knew that Gingrich did not was that voters would always blame the GOP when the government shuts down because for decades Republican rhetoric had been so relentlessly antigovernment. Polls showed that by a two-to-one margin they did so in this case, with devastating effects on Gingrich's popularity and collateral damage for Dole.[64] "I think I'm beating them to death on the politics," Clinton privately told author Taylor Branch.[65]

The shutdowns were a political triumph for Clinton. Having trailed Dole in trial heat polls throughout 1995, he now took the lead. Still, although running ahead of his main rival at the start of the election year was better than the alternative, it was no guarantee of success. Four of Clinton's six predecessors—Lyndon B, Johnson in 1968, Gerald Ford in 1976, Carter in 1980, and Bush in 1992—led the other's party's front-runner at the start of their reelection years. None ended up winning.[66]

Even worse in the longer term for the president was that the seeds of later problems were sown when the shutdowns forced the White House to operate with a much-reduced staff. Interns filled the gap, including a new college graduate named Monica Lewinsky who was working in the chief of staff's office. Lewinsky set her sights on the president soon after starting work in July 1995. Her first chance to be alone with Clinton came on November 15, when she flashed her scanty undergarment at him. He summoned her later that night for what turned out to be the first of nine sexual encounters in the Oval Office, including one in which the president left physical evidence of his passion on a dress that Lewinsky was wearing. In April 1996 the deputy chief of staff, Evelyn Lieberman, had Lewinsky transferred to the Defense Department to discourage similar meetings. A period of phone sex and occasional encounters began that continued until Clinton ended the affair in May 1997. While working at the Pentagon, Lewinsky was befriended by another employee, Linda Tripp, who surreptitiously recorded some of their conversations about Lewinsky's liaisons with Clinton. In January 1998 Tripp shared them with Kenneth Starr, the independent counsel.

Clinton already was dealing with a sexual harassment lawsuit filed in May 1994 by Paula Jones, a former Arkansas state employee who alleged that he exposed himself to her in a Little Rock hotel room in 1991. On January 9, 1996, a federal appeals court ruled that the suit could proceed while Clinton was still president, a decision that the Supreme Court affirmed on May 27, 1997.[67] On January 17, 1998, with discovery proceedings under way and the president under oath, Jones's lawyers asked him about alleged sexual encounters with other women, including Lewinsky. Clinton lied. After hearing Tripp's recordings, Starr secured permission from Attorney General Reno to broaden his investigation. Within a few days, the Lewinsky affair and the president's lies about it, which persisted for months, became public.

The combination of Jones's lawsuit, Congress's renewal of the independent counsel statute, and the affair with Lewinsky set in motion the train of events that led to Clinton's impeachment by the House of Representatives in December 1998. But none of this was known when Congress returned to Washington in January 1996 for the second session of the 104th Congress. The president, having outmaneuvered the Republicans the previous year, now co-opted their most popular theme, declaring in the State of the Union address—the first by a Democratic president to a Republican Congress in forty-eight years—that "the era of big government is over."[68] This line was no mere rhetorical flourish. In his 1993 address, Clinton had said, "I believe the government must do more."[69] Now, reversing course, he withstood furious criticism from liberal members of his party and vowed to pursue his 1992 campaign promise to "end welfare as we know it," thereby "recreating the Nation's social bargain with the poor" by requiring responsibility in return for opportunity.[70] As with his pursuit of a balanced budget, the president hoped that doing so would neutralize an issue that Republicans long had used to club Democrats for being devoted to giveaway programs.

Clinton also trumpeted the prospects for achieving the sorts of savings and reductions in bureaucratic red tape that Republicans regularly blamed Democrats for not caring about through the administration's "reinventing government" (REGO) program. This initiative was originally championed by journalist David Osborne and former city manager Ted Gabler, who argued that the failure of traditional bureaucracies to solve basic social and economic problems demonstrated the need for an alternative to standard, centralized administration.[71] A prominent feature of Clinton's New Democrat agenda, REGO was the centerpiece of the National Performance Review, which Gore chaired on the president's behalf. The vice president's reports, the second of which was issued with much fanfare in September 1995, featured a set of proposals that saved the government $108 billion over five years by trimming 252,000 jobs from the federal civil service, overhauling federal procurement laws, updating the government's information systems, and even eliminating a few programs and subsidies.

Hoping to strengthen his credentials as an effective, independent executive, Clinton also began to present himself to the voters as statesmanlike rather than partisan or political. After the April 19, 1995, bombing of the Oklahoma City federal office building by domestic terrorist Timothy McVeigh, the president had his first opportunity since the midterm election to do so. McVeigh's bombs killed 168 people, including 19 children, and wounded 780 others—making it the worst terrorist attack on American soil in history at that time. Clinton's effort to give meaning to the moment was successful. Empathetic by nature, his years as governor had provided numerous occasions to display dignity and compassion in communities disrupted by tornados and other natural disasters. Now, one observer recorded, in the aftermath of the traumatic bombing Clinton "exhibited the take-charge determination as well as the on-key rhetoric that Americans expect of their president in times of trouble."[72] "There is nothing patriotic about hating your country or pretending that you can love your country but despise your government," the president told an audience at Michigan State University.[73]

Clinton's presidential surefootedness in Oklahoma City was not an isolated event. Political scientist Paul Light has pointed out that presidents typically undergo a "cycle of increasing effectiveness" that comes with experience in office.[74] Adhering to the pattern of his long tenure as governor of Arkansas, Clinton put his on-the-job training as president to good use. His deportment mirrored his growth. Out went the much-photographed (and much-ridiculed) jogging shorts, public confession of his preference for "boxers" over "briefs," and "furtive" salutes on formal military occasions that made him look "as if he were being caught at something he wasn't supposed to do."[75] In came (after sessions spent studying videotapes of Reagan, who inaugurated the practice of presidents returning military salutes) a straight, shoulders-back posture, dignified attire, and, with some coaching, crisp salutes. In addition, the White House staff, hastily thrown together late in the transition period that followed the 1992 election and predictably chaotic during the first two years of his presidency, began to function more effectively after Clinton appointed longtime Washington insider Leon Panetta as chief of staff.[76] One important change on which Panetta insisted was to alter Morris's status from back-channel adviser to the president to full member of the team. Panetta had seen how slow the Bush campaign was to get off the ground in advance of the 1992 election because the campaign functioned separately from the White House. He would not allow Clinton to repeat that mistake.[77]

In foreign policy, the president gained confidence as commander in chief when he discovered that the American people respected him for having the courage to make the unpopular decisions that extended American assistance to Haiti, Mexico, and Bosnia. In September 1994, recovering from his earlier stand-down in Haiti, the president ordered American forces to intervene if the military government headed by Raoul Cedras did not cede power to Aristide. Cedras fled. When Mexico's economy stood on the brink of collapse in January 1995, Clinton authorized the Treasury Department to prop up the peso until the crisis passed. In November, he again overruled public opinion and strong congressional opposition by sending 20,000 troops on a peacekeeping mission in Bosnia. Privately, the president likened the political credit he earned by making these controversial decisions to "telling your children to go to the dentist—they don't want to go, but they know you're right."[78]

Clinton's resolve to uphold American responsibilities in the world, coming on the heels of his confrontation with Congress over the budget, appeared to belie his reputation as an irresolute amateur who lacked a clear set of principles. The president really was, as Clinton insisted in the aftermath of the 1994 elections, "still relevant."[79] "I'm the big rubber clown doll you had as a kid," he told Gingrich, "and every time you hit it, it bounces back up. That's me—the harder you hit me, the faster I come back up.[80] Or, as political adviser James Carville put it even more colorfully, "Hell, you work for Bill Clinton, you go up and down more times than a whore's nightgown."[81]

As the 1990s reached the halfway mark, Americans had already tried out three of the four possible combinations of united and divided government. At the start of the decade, Republican president George Bush served with a Democratic Congress. In 1992, the voters elected Democratic presidential candidate Bill Clinton and preserved the Democrats' majority in both legislative chambers. Two years later they matched Clinton with a Republican Congress.[82] Only one combination remained untried on the eve of the 1996 election. Would the Republicans be given a chance to run a united party government: president, Senate, and House of Representatives?

THE ELECTION OF 1996

No modern presidential election campaign awaits the start of the election year. As described in chapter 7, in the aftermath of his party's crushing defeat in the midterm election, President Bill Clinton spent most of 1995 smothering potential challenges to his renomination by raising campaign funds preemptively, restoring his reputation as a New Democrat with a variety of creatively centrist executive actions, and branding his potential Republican rivals as pawns of their party's increasingly unpopular Speaker of the House, Newt Gingrich. Sen. Bob Kerrey of Nebraska, a Democratic rival in 1992 and a frequent critic of the president, was among those who seriously considered running against Clinton again before deciding to back off. He chose instead to build up credits within the party by heading the Democratic Senatorial Campaign Committee. Bill Bradley of New Jersey fueled speculation that he might challenge Clinton when he announced his retirement from the Senate in August 1995. Clinton thought that Bradley was positioning himself to run as an independent.[1] But, like Kerrey, Bradley decided that he was young enough to wait until 2000, when Clinton would not be on the ballot and he could seek the nomination without dividing the party and assuring a Republican victory. Kerrey never did run again but Bradley did, losing the 2000 nominating contest to Vice President Al Gore.

Three additional potential challengers to Clinton's renomination were sidelined for other reasons. Mario Cuomo was defeated in his bid for a fourth term as governor of New York in 1994. House Democratic leader Richard Gephardt bore the stigma of his party's lost control of that chamber for the first time in forty years. As for Jesse Jackson, after hinting on the Sunday morning talk show *Face the Nation* that he might run against Clinton, he opted instead to continue his lucrative television career as host of his own program for CNN, *Both Sides Now.*

The advantages Clinton derived from his uncontested renomination were several. No Democratic opponents toured the country criticizing the president and tearing away at his popularity, as Democrat Edward Kennedy did to President Jimmy Carter in 1980 and Republicans Ronald Reagan and Pat Buchanan did to Presidents Gerald Ford and George Bush in 1976 and 1992, respectively. Nor, as the political scientist Linda Fowler has pointed out, did Clinton have to worry about defending his left flank in contested Democratic primaries and caucuses in which the electorate would be skewed toward ideological liberals.[2] He could continue moving toward the center knowing that he would always be liberal voters' and activists' better alternative to whomever the Republicans nominated. "Any Democrat running could have drained us of our resources," said campaign aide Doug Sosnik. "If you look at what we did in '96 to Dole, it was based on our ability to avoid a primary and thus get ready in '95, so that when there was a Republican nominee, we could flatten him."[3]

Clinton benefited even more from the booming economy. As 1996 approached, the so-called misery index—the sum of the unemployment and inflation rates—reached its lowest point since 1969. The proliferation of new technologies rooted in the spread of personal computers accounted for much of the boom, as did the end of the Cold War and the 1990 budget agreement between President George Bush and Congress. But Clinton's tough budgetary decisions during his first year in office, however politically costly in the short term, made a difference as well, one that voters began to notice. The low interest rates that reduced deficits were fueling the massive capital investments by businesses and individuals that made the computing revolution possible.

THE REPUBLICAN FIELD FORMS

As Clinton locked down his party's support for a second term, several contenders for the 1996 Republican presidential nomination spent much of 1995 laying the foundation for their own campaigns, jostling each other for primacy within the party while doing their best to discredit the president against whom one of them would run in the fall. On paper, Dan Quayle was a presumptively strong candidate by virtue of having been vice president for four years. But Quayle, distracted by potentially serious problems with blood clots in his lungs, did little to build the organization or raise the money needed to mount a campaign. He decided not to run, thinking at age forty-seven that he would have several more opportunities in the future.

Former Joint Chiefs of Staff chair and national security adviser Colin Powell also considered seeking the Republican nomination before deciding not to. As the most popular figure to emerge from the 1991 Persian Gulf War, Powell was widely admired in ways that transcended party. A September 1995 Gallup poll showed him leading Clinton by 15 percentage points.[4] But Powell was smart enough to know that the moment he became a political candidate his reputational bubble would burst. In particular, conservative activists would recoil once his pro-choice, pro–affirmative action positions became widely known. Powell's wife was strongly opposed to his running, certain that as an African American with a serious chance to become president, he would be a target for assassination. On November 8, after completing a five-week book tour that benefited enormously from the speculation that he might run, Powell announced that although he was a Republican (he had privately been one since 1988), he would not be a candidate.

Pete Wilson, who was reelected governor of California in 1994, was another possible contender who ultimately decided to pass. Wilson had seemed headed for defeat when he decided to tie his gubernatorial candidacy to Proposition 187, a ballot measure aimed at denying undocumented immigrants access to nonemergency services, notably state health care and public education. Wilson's appeal was based on being governor of the nation's largest state, one that Republican presidential candidates had been able to count on in six consecutive elections before Clinton won it in 1992. But Wilson was little known outside California, and his pro-choice and pro–gay rights stances were unacceptable to most Republican voters. He entered the race on June 15, 1995, underwent an unexpectedly slow recovery from throat surgery that made it hard for him to speak, and was embarrassed by news reports that his anti-immigrant stance had not kept him from hiring an undocumented housekeeper and failing to pay his share of her Social Security taxes. Cutting his losses—his campaign was already deeply in debt—Wilson withdrew on September 29.

Even with Quayle, Powell, and Wilson on the sidelines, the Republican field did not lack for contenders.[5] Former Tennessee governor and US secretary of education Lamar Alexander had been planning to run for president ever since George Bush was defeated for reelection in 1992. In imitation of his successful campaign for governor, Alexander donned a red-and-black flannel shirt, walked across New Hampshire (a considerably shorter hike than in Tennessee), and excitedly advertised himself as "La-mar!" He formally entered the race in February 1995, spooking Clinton, who regarded Alexander as the candidate most like himself: a moderate southerner and political outsider who as governor of his state had stressed education. "He's too much like me," Clinton said.[6] But Alexander's plan to run as an outsider (he claimed that his time in Washington was "long enough to be vaccinated but not infected") on a platform of term limits for members of Congress was undermined by the results of the midterm election.[7] If, as Alexander argued, the absence of term limits caused Congress to become ossified, how to explain the massive turnover in 1994 that over-threw the Democratic majority in both chambers? Would Republicans still want to change the rules now that they were in charge?

Pat Buchanan entered the race one month after Alexander, hoping to translate the support he received as a protest candidate in 1992 and his continuing visibility as a talk show regular into an actual nomination. Bu-chanan was a more authentic outsider than Alexander, never having held any elective office. As in 1992, he promoted an "America First" agenda that characterized immigration as a threat to national unity and NAFTA as "a sellout of the American worker."[8] Only the end of a half century of war against Germany and Japan and the Cold War with the Soviet Union made Buchanan's revival of the pre–World War II isolationist slogan politically possible. Even so, his America First stance set him apart from all of his rivals within the party. Buchanan calculated that if he could hang on to the roughly 25 percent of the vote he received in his one-on-one race against Bush, he would win some primaries in the multicandidate field that was forming for 1996.

Buchanan's main challenger in the ultimate-outsider lane not only had never held elective office but had never served in government at all: Steve Forbes, the editor of *Forbes* and heir of the magazine's billionaire founder. Forbes's preferred candidate to carry the banner for his proposal to replace the graduated income tax with a 17 percent flat tax was Jack Kemp. But in September Kemp decided not to run. Like Quayle he simply did not want to endure the endless fund-raising gauntlet necessary to compete. Forbes announced his own candidacy, making a virtue of his inexperience. "I am running because I believe this nation needs someone . . . who can unlock the stranglehold that the political class has on American life," he declared.[9] Forbes immediately blanketed the airwaves in Iowa and New Hampshire with self-financed campaign ads. A typical New Hampshire voter saw his commercials thirty-four times per week.

Neither Alexander, Buchanan, nor Forbes was taken as seriously by national political reporters and GOP leaders as Sen. Phil Gramm of Texas. A free market economic conservative, Gramm was Buchanan's opposite on issues of trade and immigration. He was elected to the House of Representatives as a conservative Democrat in 1978, switched parties in 1983, resigned, ran and won as a Republican, and was elected to the Senate in 1984. Gramm often said that he had "the most reliable friend you can have in American politics, and that is ready money."[10] He proved it on February 23, 1995, the eve of his announcement, when he raised an unprecedented $4.1 million at a campaign event in Dallas. With twenty-nine primaries "front-loaded" into the six weeks between February 20 and March 26—an artifact of more states moving their events from later to earlier on the calendar—the Gramm campaign's deep pockets were regarded as an unusually valuable asset. Forbes, spending his own money, would be able to match him, but not Buchanan or Alexander.

The leading Republican contender, Senate majority leader Bob Dole, also raised a great deal of money and hired a large and experienced campaign staff in 1995. He began the year in a stronger position than the president. Clinton's approval rating in an early January *Washington Post* poll was 45 percent compared with Dole's 62 percent. Still more dramatic was the contrast between their disapproval ratings. Twice as many voters—51 percent—disapproved of Clinton as disapproved of Dole: 25 percent.[11]

Dole clearly had thrived during Clinton's first two years as Senate minority leader. But he found that preparing to run for president as majority leader, his status after the midterm election posed difficult challenges. The responsibilities of the new job tied him down in Washington more than would otherwise have been the case. Even more important, they tied him to Gingrich, who emerged from 1994 as the architect of the Republican triumph in the midterm. "If he had let one ounce of light between him and the House leadership," said Dole aide Sheila Burke, "we would have spent every waking day defending Dole from the accusation that he had dumped on the House."[12] With Gingrich driving legislative strategy, Dole felt he had no choice but to support the speaker's brinksmanship in the budget fight that led to the two late 1995 government shutdowns—even though Dole's every inclination was to compromise. Starting in October, Democratic Party advertising on Clinton's behalf yoked Dole with the increasingly unpopular Gingrich as if they were equally committed obstructionists. In the ads' voice-over narration, "Dole Gingrich" was spoken as if it was one word, as in "the DoleGingrich cuts in Medicare."[13] "If Dole wins and Gingrich runs

Congress, there'll be nobody there to stop them," warned one Clinton ad.[14] "Dumbest thing Newt ever did was shut down the government," Dole later reflected. "If there was ever any doubt about Clinton's reelection—probably wasn't much—there wasn't after that. Dumb, dumb, dumb."[15]

As difficult as it was for Dole to run for president while leading the Senate, he found it even harder as a moderate, pragmatic conservative to navigate the shoals of an increasingly conservative Republican Party. Awkwardly— because inauthentically—Dole tried to compensate by overcorrecting. On April 7, 1995, the day he announced his candidacy for president, he publicly signed the same pledge never to raise taxes that he refused to endorse in 1988. He then claimed, "I was there, fighting the fight, voting against Medicare—one of twelve—because we knew it wouldn't work."[16] After refusing to "pick out a group and discriminate against them for political gain," Dole returned a $1,000 campaign donation from the pro–gay rights Log Cabin Republicans—and then said he should not have done that.[17] Flailing in a July appearance before the Republican National Committee, Dole said, "I am willing to be another Ronald Reagan. If that's what you want."[18] The net effect of Dole's difficulties within the Senate and within his party was that conservatives did not think he was authentically conservative while moderate voters thought he was too far to the right.

An additional obstacle confronted Dole: his age, compounded by his dry, even crotchety demeanor. Clinton admired Dole, unlike the other Republican contenders who in his view "didn't have any tall." But he thought that Dole's campaign was based on one idea: "I've been around a long time and deserve to be president."[19] From 1994 to 1996, memos from campaign advisers to Dole noted the political challenge that his longevity posed. On March 31, 1994, for example, friend and adviser Bill Lacy summarized "the case the media and our opposition will make about you" by placing "Bob Dole is a dinosaur" and "He's too old" first and second on the list. Two years later, reporting on the fourteen focus groups he conducted in seven states during the last week of April 1996, campaign pollster Bob Ward wrote that "Dole's age" was "the most frequently mentioned negative in these groups." Lacy hastened to add that Reagan overcame the same concerns in 1980, and Ward implausibly claimed that Dole's age "could be turned into an advantage by carefully telling the Dole story" as "the quintessentially American story." But less partisan pollsters like Andrew Kohut found that "old" was the word that most often came to mind when voters were asked to describe Dole.[20] "Dole's Birthday Renews Age-Old Old-Age Debate"—a not unusual story—appeared on the front page of the Washington Post on

July 21, 1995, the eve of Dole's seventy-second birthday.[21] Pledging to serve only one term—an idea Dole considered—would only draw attention to the fact that he would be eighty-one at the end of a second term.[22] Nor did Dole's nationally televised response to Clinton's highly successful State of the Union address on January 23, 1996, do him any good. His "wooden, almost funereal" demeanor was reinforced by dark lighting and an uninspired text.[23]

PRIMARIES AND CAUCUSES

By the end of 1995, Dole had accumulated more endorsements from Republican officeholders and raised more money ($24.6 million, compared with $20.8 million for Gramm) than the other candidates. In 1988 he had seen how much more important were the endorsements Bush received from Republican governors, who serve full-time in their states, than the ones Dole received from his fellow senators. In 1995, well before the first votes were cast, Dole lined up support from all but four of his party's thirty-one governors.[24] Throughout the year he led nearly every poll of Republican voters with 45 to 50 percent support compared with second-place Gramm's 10 to 13 percent. When Powell was included, Dole ran about even with him.[25]

But the severe front-loading of the nominating process in 1996 went beyond states moving up their primaries and caucuses to earlier in the year in order to have their votes counted before the contest was effectively settled. Republicans in Iowa, traditionally the first state on the delegate selection calendar, decided to further press their advantage by reviving the Iowa straw poll at their annual convention in August 1995 after taking a hiatus in 1991. Florida Republicans scheduled a straw poll of their own in November. As Dole, like a general fighting the last war, focused on getting ready for the actual Iowa caucuses and New Hampshire primary in February 1996, his performance in both "preseason" straw polls was disappointing. Gramm literally tied him for first in Iowa's poll, in which each had 2,582 votes, and he defeated Gramm by only 33 percent to 26 percent in the Florida poll. Buchanan finished a strong third in Iowa with 18 percent to Dole's and Gramm's 24 percent, and Alexander did the same in Florida with 23 percent.

Forbes and, especially, Buchanan had their own days in the sun before Iowa held its actual caucuses on February 12. For most states—notably California and New York, which moved their primaries from June to March—front-loading meant advancing closer to the front of the line. Alaska and Louisiana decided to jump it altogether by holding their caucuses two weeks (Alaska) and one week (Louisiana) ahead of Iowa. Republicans in Iowa, normally the first caucus state, and New Hampshire, the first primary state, made clear that they would punish any candidate who competed in either of these new contests. Dole and Alexander took their admonitions to heart but not Buchanan and Forbes, who dominated the lightly attended Alaska caucuses on January 27 with 33 percent and 30 percent of the vote, respectively. Buchanan competed again in Louisiana, where his rival was Gramm. So confident was Gramm of victory in his home state's eastern neighbor that he boasted, "I have to win here in Louisiana" and predicted that he would sweep all twenty-one delegates.[26] Instead, Buchanan won thirteen delegates to Gramm's eight. The evangelical Christians who made up much of the small caucus electorate were more drawn to Buchanan's cultural conservatism than Gramm's fiscal conservatism.

Gramm was the big loser in these early contests, and he soon dropped out after finishing fifth in the Iowa caucuses. Buchanan was the big winner. As for Dole, he was glad to see his seemingly most credible opponent go down but clearly was going to have to fight for a nomination he had hoped to win more easily. This meant fending off attacks from his Republican rivals for several more weeks and spending money to defeat them that he would rather use to launch his campaign against Clinton.

Dole's campaign strategy was a mirror image of the one George Bush deployed against him in 1988: survive the most brightly spotlighted early contests in Iowa and, eight days later, New Hampshire and then rely on his campaign's deep pockets and national organization to prevail soon afterward when multiple states voted on the same day. Junior Tuesday (March 5) featured eight primaries in which 208 delegates would be chosen. One week later, on Super Tuesday, seven states would choose 362 delegates. A corollary of Dole's strategy, which had worked for Bush in 1988, was to secure enough endorsements from white evangelical leaders and state Republican officials in South Carolina to win its March 2 primary no matter what happened in Iowa and New Hampshire.

Sure enough, Dole stumbled out of the gate in Iowa, as Bush had, and nearly broke stride in New Hampshire, as Bush had not. Buchanan and Alexander, neither of whom was nearly as well financed or organized on a national basis as Dole, each tried to catch lightning in a bottle by concentrating their time and resources in these two states. Alexander did reasonably well, finishing third in Iowa with 18 percent and an even closer third in New Hampshire with 23 percent. Buchanan did exceedingly well. He finished second in Iowa with 23 percent, holding the victorious Dole to 26 percent in a neighboring state that as a Kansan he should have dominated. Riding that momentum, Buchanan defeated Dole in New Hampshire by 27 percent to 26 percent. "You watch the establishment," Buchanan crowed, "all the knights and barons when we ride in at the castle, pulling up the drawbridge. All the peasants are coming with pitchforks."[27] New Hampshire proved to be an extremely close call for Dole, who told an aide, "If I finish third, I'll drop out."[28]

Like Dole, however, Alexander and Buchanan also were fighting a previous war. In the more spread-out, less primary-intensive Democratic nominating contest of 1976, the little-known former governor of Georgia, Jimmy Carter, had enough time to build on his success in Iowa and New Hampshire by raising the money and building the organization he needed to wage a national campaign in an extended series of contests. But the front-loading of the primary process that accelerated into 1996 took this strategy off the table. As in 1992, when Buchanan's impressive showing in New Hampshire gave him a quick surge of momentum, he once again lacked the resources to sustain it. The southern primaries, clustered in early March, were as much a firewall for Dole as they had been for Bush. In heavily evangelical South Carolina, Dole enjoyed the support of the Christian Coalition (which had calculated that he would win the nomination) and nearly every elected Republican official, including the former and current governor and the state GOP's towering figure, Sen. Strom Thurmond. Dole easily defeated Buchanan by 45 percent to 29 percent.

Unlike Buchanan, Forbes had money to spend, nearly all of it his own. Under federal campaign finance laws as modified by the Supreme Court in the 1976 case of *Buckley v. Valeo*, Forbes could free himself from spending limits by eschewing federal matching funds (which all the other candidates took) and relying on his personal fortune.[29] Outspending everyone on television and radio in organizationally important Iowa, New Hampshire, and South Carolina, states with legions of political activists and operatives who were richly experienced from previous presidential campaigns, did Forbes little good: he finished fourth, fourth, and a distant third, respectively. Delaware, which added a new primary to the calendar on February 24, and Arizona, which scheduled its contest for February 27, were a different story. In neither state were there cadres of veteran primary combatants from earlier nominating contests. In both, therefore, Forbes's massive media spending filled a political vacuum. He outpaced Dole by 33 percent to 27 percent in Delaware and 33 percent to 30 percent in Arizona. But because Dole disdained these primaries as sideshows, Forbes's victories were not treated as defeats for him. Losing South Carolina would have been much worse, but that was never in the cards. To an even greater extent than Buchanan, Forbes (13 percent) and Alexander (10 percent) foundered there.

Dole's victory in South Carolina was the first in an unbroken winning streak that encompassed every other remaining primary on the calendar, all of which he won by double digits. After Super Tuesday, Dole essentially had the nomination wrapped up. (See the results of the Republican primaries and caucuses in appendix D.) But his success was costly, both literally and figuratively. Having spent nearly all of the $29.6 million he raised from donors and the $13.5 million he received in federal matching funds in order to win the nomination, Dole's campaign was essentially broke until after the Republican convention in August. Because he agreed, like all the other candidates except Forbes, to accept federal funding, Dole was forbidden to raise and spend any more until he received his next cash infusion from the government when he became the official nominee of his party. During this nearly five-month hiatus, Clinton was able to spend much of his $28.3 million in donations and $13.4 million in matching funds to continue building himself up and tearing Dole down. Although Clinton faced no primary opponents, the law treated his candidacy for the nomination of his party the same as if he did.

Equally damaging to Dole's prospects in the general election were the attacks his Republican rivals made on him during the nominating campaign. Buchanan branded Dole as part of the establishment against whom his army of pitchfork-wielding peasants was revolting. In many of Forbes's widely viewed campaign ads, he tarnished Dole as a Washington insider with a long record of embracing tax increases and resisting congressional term limits. The Democrats' defeated nominee in 1984, Walter Mondale, wryly observed, "In 1984 they had us killing each other for months and then they delivered me, the cadaver. It looks like the Republicans have the same strategy."[30] Nor, in the course of winning the nomination, had Dole managed to develop a compelling message of his own. "Once Clinton's perceived as a liberal, the election's over," he told an aide, dismissing the idea that he needed to articulate a vision for the country.[31] Lapsing frequently into legislative shorthand and droll asides that only fellow insiders understood, Dole's positive message essentially boiled down to his long experience in government. "I've been tested and tested," he often said. The subtext of this message, of course, was that he was old, especially when he accompanied it with remarks like, "The Internet is a good tool to use to get on the Net" (a particularly odd comment by the candidate whose campaign was the first to have a website).[32] Dole's age was the last thing of which voters needed to be reminded.

No senator in history had been nominated by his party while serving as the chamber's majority leader, which did not stop Dole from fooling himself into thinking he could regain the initiative against Clinton by "running from the Senate floor," thereby showing the country that he was "a doer, not a talker." But as political scientist William Mayer observed, "Dole found that many of the tactics he had used so effectively to thwart the Clinton agenda in 1993 and 1994 were now being used against him by Senate Democrats."[33] Taking advantage of the rule that allowed just forty-one senators to keep legislation from coming to a vote—as Dole had when he led the chamber's forty-three Republicans in the 103rd Congress—he now found himself stymied by the Senate's forty-seven Democrats. His responsibilities as leader also tied him down in Washington when he could have been campaigning around the country.

On May 15, Dole impulsively announced that on June 11 he would resign not just as majority leader but from the Senate entirely. A dramatic move in and of itself, the decision was unmoored from any strategy to take advantage of his new status as an outsider. The Clinton campaign ran ads suggesting that Dole was a quitter. Meanwhile, the president continued to crank out modest but popular executive actions concerning truancy, teenage smoking, domestic violence, and other matters. Dole and his fellow Republicans hoped that Clinton would continue to veto the welfare reform measures they kept enacting, but in July the president signed the Personal Responsibility and Work Opportunity Reconciliation Act, taking an issue away from the GOP and fulfilling his 1992 campaign promise to "end welfare as we know it."[34] Signing the version of the act that he vetoed in December 1995 would have been popular with voters but might have triggered a primary challenge fueled by angry liberal Democrats. Unhappy as they were when he signed the third version in mid-1996, it was too late to do anything about it. As for Dole, having left the Senate he was unable to claim even a portion of credit for the bill.

Compounding Dole's problems, his successor as majority leader, Trent Lott, was much more interested in preserving his party's control of the Senate than in electing Dole. To assure that Republican members had a record of accomplishment heading into the November election, Lott worked with Clinton and the Democrats to pass not just welfare reform but also other popular bills raising the minimum wage and assuring the portability of health insurance coverage when people change jobs. The latter was a measure cosponsored by Senator Kennedy, a Democrat, and Dole's erstwhile colleague from Kansas, Republican Nancy Kassebaum. At a post-election gathering of campaign strategists, the one thing Republicans and Democrats could agree on was that congressional "Republicans threw Dole overboard," in George Stephanopoulos's phrase. Or, as Dole's communications director, John Buckley, put it, "They aimed the torpedoes at the hull and then started throwing water at it," fully aware that his candidacy was going down no matter what they did.[35]

THE CONVENTIONS

Dole made better use of his next opportunity to regain the initiative, the four-day Republican National Convention in San Diego, which began on August 12. Although he and Jack Kemp had never gotten along—Dole once said of Kemp that "he never met a deficit he didn't like" and Kemp rejoined that Dole "never met a tax he didn't hike"—Dole not only brought his former rival onto the ticket on the eve of the convention but also called for a Kemp-style across-the-board 15 percent income tax cut.[36] What Kemp offered was energy, exuberance, and a strong following among Republican conservatives—none of which Dole had in abundance. The boldness of the surprise choice, announced by Dole on August 10, captured the imagination of the press corps and the delegates, both of which were essential to fulfilling Dole's hope that an enthusiastic, united, positive convention would help convince the country to give him a fresh look.

In addition to energizing his party, Dole wanted to use the convention to convey a sense of the GOP as a big tent, under which Republicans with differing opinions on issues could live in harmony. In contrast to the 1992 convention, when Pat Buchanan was the featured speaker on the first night, Dole invited Colin Powell to deliver the main address. The second night's program reinforced Powell's theme of moderation and diversity by spotlighting the one African American Republican of Congress, Rep. J. C. Watt of Oklahoma, along with a woman governor (Christine Todd Whitman of New Jersey), a woman senator (Kay Bailey Hutchinson of Texas), and a woman representative (Susan Molinari of New York). Elizabeth Dole, the candidate's wife and a former secretary of transportation, gave an appealing speech about her husband on Wednesday night. Breaking all tradition, she left the podium and teleprompter behind and took to the convention floor with a handheld microphone.

Other aspects of the convention were less effective. Dole's hope of modifying the pro-life plank contained in recent party platforms by adding

Reelection-seeking incumbents Bill Clinton and Al Gore stride off a campaign bus featuring their "21st Century" campaign theme. Courtesy of the William J. Clinton Presidential Library.

language acknowledging the differences among Republicans on the issue foundered when his leading evangelical supporters told him that would be unacceptable.[37] And his acceptance speech on the final night of the convention, uncharacteristically eloquent and well delivered as it was, underscored the idea that Dole was a candidate of the past. "Let me be the bridge to an America that only the unknowing call myth," he declared. "Let me be the bridge to a time of tranquility, faith, and confidence in action. And to those who say it was never so, I say you're wrong. And I know because I was there."[38] Dole may as well have said, let me take you back to a time when I was young. Columnist E. J. Dionne compared his campaign to "a slightly grainy black-and-white movie."[39]

The Republican convention gave the ticket the customary but temporary bounce in the polls. Postconvention surveys showed Dole trailing Clinton by 5 percentage points or less instead of by 15 points. So ephemeral were Dole's gains, however, that they vanished by the time the Democrats convened in Chicago on August 26.[40] Meanwhile, Clinton realized that in offering himself as a bridge to the past, "Dole had inadvertently given me the central message of the 1996 campaign."[41] The president would promise to be "a bridge to the twenty-first century," which was just four years away.

Gore previewed the theme in his acceptance speech on Wednesday night. "Dole offered himself as a bridge to the past," Gore said. "Tonight Bill Clinton and I offer ourselves as a bridge to the future." Then Clinton pounded home the metaphor in his speech on Thursday, invoking "bridge" references more than twenty times before he was done.

PEROT

As soon as the national conventions made them the official nominees of their parties, Clinton and Dole each received $62 million from the federal government to spend on the general election campaign. The same campaign finance law that funded the two major parties' nominees also entitled Ross Perot to $29 million on the strength of his popular vote share in 1992. To make use of these funds, however, he would have to abandon his stance as a pure independent and form a political party.

Perot's reputation suffered lasting damage from his peckish, uninformed performance in a nationally televised debate with Vice President Al Gore about NAFTA in November 1993. But in less visible and more politically effective ways, Perot stayed connected with his core supporters through the state chapters of his nonpartisan United We Stand America organization. In 1995, as a prelude to launching a new party, he invited the Republican candidates (all of whom came) and President Clinton (who declined) to a national United We Stand gathering in Dallas on August 11. Not surprisingly, Perot's supporters deemed them all unsatisfactory, and on September 25 he said on *Larry King Live* that he planned to "start the process of starting a new party."[42] Eschewing personal ambition, Perot declared that he was looking for a "George Washington II" to lead the party into the election.

Theoretically, anyone could compete for the Reform nomination for president. But when former Colorado governor Richard Lamm announced his intention to do so on July 9, 1996, Perot hopped into the race two days later. Through an elaborate process that involved sending ballots in August to 1.13 million Reform Party members (basically, anyone who signed a petition), Perot prevailed over Lamm by 65 percent to 35 percent. The luster of his nomination was dimmed somewhat when only 4 percent of party members—fewer than 50,000—actually voted.

Perot now needed to find a vice presidential candidate in order to meet state ballot requirements. Running at about 5 percent in the polls against Clinton and Dole, with no prospect of being allowed to participate in the fall debates, Perot found it impossible to attract a running mate with political stature. Former Oklahoma governor David Boren and Rep. Marcy Kaptur of Ohio were among those who turned him down. On September 10, Perot settled on Pat Choate, an author who shared his protectionist, anti-NAFTA views on international trade.

THE CAMPAIGN

Heading into the fall campaign, the election clearly was Clinton's to lose. The economy not only was strong, but voters had come to realize it was strong. The world was generally at peace. To the extent that Clinton's actions in Haiti, Mexico, Bosnia, and elsewhere furthered that end, voters credited him. As for the broad center of the American electorate, Clinton occupied it. What at the time had seemed politically disastrous for the president—the loss of Congress to the Republicans in 1994—turned out to be a blessing in disguise. Gingrich led his party to the far right, dragging a reluctant Dole along in his wake. Congressional Democrats were, on average, more liberal than ever as a result of their loss of southern seats in the midterm election. But as the minority party they no longer had the votes to impose their orthodoxy on the president. In all, Clinton's record of peace, prosperity, and moderation offered the perfect combination for an incumbent seeking reelection on the basis of his first-term record.[43] It enabled him to continue offering gauzy rhetoric about building a bridge to the future without having to be very specific about what he planned to do if he won. In terms used by political scientists, Clinton could rely on voters to cast their ballots retrospectively rather than prospectively. In poker terms, he had a pat hand.

Strategically, Clinton's focus was less on winning the election for his party than on securing a strong personal victory. This was not unusual for a reelection-seeking president. Eisenhower in 1956, Nixon in 1972, and Reagan in 1984 all ran similarly self-focused campaigns for a second term, which is one reason why all three saw their party lose seats in the Senate even as they were winning by a landslide. An additional consideration for Clinton was that he did not want to begin his second term without ever having won a majority of the national popular vote. As in 1992, Perot's presence in the race made this more difficult than if Clinton had been running against just Dole. Also, having suffered politically during his first two years from the presence of a Democratic Congress and benefited during his second two years from the presence (if mostly as a foil) of a Republican Congress, Clinton's lack of enthusiasm for seeing the 1996 congressional elections go the Democrats' way was understandable. In any event, Clinton definitely was not willing to closely link his campaign to theirs or ease up on his personal fund-raising for the sake of making more money available for Democratic candidates further down the ballot.

In political scientist Daniel Galvin's assessment, Clinton spent his first four years in office as a "party predator" rather than a "party builder." The party on which he preyed was his own. Clinton did little to "provide campaign services" to the Democratic Party or to "build human capital," "mobilize voters," or "support internal activities" on the party's behalf. Far from helping to "finance party operations," he took soft money donated to the Democratic Party—that is, money that by law was meant to fund state-by-state party-building activities such as voter registration and getting people to the polls—and used it to finance his massive pre–election year advertising campaign.[44]

Getting more than 50 percent of the popular vote was psychologically important to Clinton, but he was well aware that electoral votes were the only ones that counted. Confident that he could hold on to nearly all of the thirty-two states and 370 electoral votes he carried in 1992, Clinton hoped to expand the map by adding states where he came within 5 percentage points of Bush in 1992: Arizona, Florida, North Carolina, South Dakota, Virginia—even Texas.[45] If, without losing any of the states he did win in that election, Clinton could gain even 30 of the 95 electoral votes in those six states, it would take him to 400, the traditional benchmark for a landslide. This would be hard, however, because of his vulnerability in the eleven states with 107 electoral votes that he won by less than 5 points against Bush.[46] It would be even harder if he tethered himself to congressional Democrats. When Clinton buried one reference to electing a Democratic Congress in his acceptance address at the Democratic convention, it triggered voters' most negative reaction of any line in the speech, pollster Stan Greenberg found.[47]

Unlike Clinton, Dole floundered in his quest for a strategy, lurching instead from tactic to tactic. At various times he stressed his tax cut plan, his support for family values, and his opposition to affirmative action. Without settling on one line of attack against Clinton, he tried out several: the president was too liberal, his administration was corrupt, he was responsible for an increase in teenage drug use, and so on. In one speech, inadvertently displaying his campaign's themelessness, Dole proclaimed: "It all boils down to one word: Trust. . . . That's what the election is all about. Trust." He then added: "It's about leadership. It's about family. It's about business. It's about the next century."[48] Attacking welfare, a stock-in-trade for previous Republican presidential candidates, was no longer an available tactic for Dole now that his fellow partisans in Congress had passed and the president signed the welfare reform act.[49] Dick Morris, Clinton's political consultant until fired in a prostitution scandal at the Democratic convention, surely exaggerated when he advised the president that to veto the bill would cost him the election, but there is no doubt that signing it contributed to his victory by taking the issue off the table for Dole.[50]

Eventually, as the campaign neared its end, Dole found a focus: the public's distrust of Clinton's character. Polls in early September showed that most Americans regarded the president as neither "honest and trustworthy" nor grounded in "high personal and moral ethical standards."[51] Fortuitously for Dole, in early October news reports began appearing that highlighted improper foreign contributions to the Clinton reelection campaign, particularly by the Indonesian Lippo Group. John Huang, a Democratic National Committee fund-raiser and former Lippo employee, was the channel for many of these donations. Video appeared of Gore raising $140,000 at a Buddhist temple near Los Angeles in April 1996, an implausible setting for a donors' event with an even less plausible set of monk-robed contributors.

At last, Dole had caught a break. His "Where's the outrage?" lament finally found an audience. Indeed, voters who said they made up their mind during the last week of the campaign preferred him to Clinton by 41 percent to 35 percent, according to the Voter News Service national exit poll. But these late deciders amounted to only 17 percent of the electorate. Dole also earned 84 percent support from those who identified "honesty and trust" as "the candidate quality that mattered most." But only one in five voters identified that as the most important quality they wanted in a president.[52]

In terms of an electoral vote strategy, Dole found himself in the same position as other severely trailing candidates. Like Michael Dukakis in 1988 and George Bush in 1992, Dole tried to thread a needle that would enable him to win a majority in the Electoral College even as he was losing the national popular vote. He wrote off all but twenty-nine mostly small and medium-sized states that, taken, together, had 278 electoral votes, only 8 more than the 270 required for victory. In some of them, Clinton had double-digit leads.[53] Initially, Dole's strategy relied on carrying four northeastern states with a combined 49 electoral votes: Connecticut, Delaware, New Jersey, and Pennsylvania. But in mid-October, right after his second debate with Clinton, it became obvious that Dole wasn't going to win any of them (he ended up losing all four by landslides). In desperation, he turned instead to California with its 54 electoral votes.[54] California had an anti–affirmative action

President Bill Clinton and Republican nominee Bob Dole face off in one of their two debates in 1996. Courtesy of the William J. Clinton Presidential Library.

proposition on the ballot whose coattails Dole hope to ride. The proposition passed by 9 percentage points, but Dole lost the state anyway, by 13 points, after sinking $4 million into an advertising campaign. Throwing another Hail Mary pass as the clock ticked down, Dole sent his campaign manager, Scott Reed, to Dallas in late October to ask Perot to withdraw in his favor. Perot dismissed the move as "weird and totally inconsequential."[55]

Dole's chances of victory were slim. Perot's were none. His only hope for a strong showing on a par with 1992 was to be allowed once again to participate in the presidential debates. Relatedly, Perot hoped that Choate, a skilled polemicist, would be invited to the vice presidential debate where, as a veteran talk show performer, he presumably would be more at home than James Stockdale was in 1992. But the Commission on Presidential Debates determined that the Perot-Choate ticket had no "realistic chance" to win based on its meager showing in the polls, and neither Clinton nor Dole wanted to include either one of them. Deprived of the debate platform and audience, Perot relied on the same old playbook—a few speeches, an occasional appearance on *Larry King Live*, and paid thirty-minute infomercials focused on campaign finance reform, the budget deficit, and foreign trade.

Dole was hardly an enthusiastic debater, but he realized that as the underdog he had to seize every opportunity he could to occupy the national spotlight. Working in his favor was the natural reluctance of incumbent presidents to prepare. No candidate enjoys debate practice and Clinton, like Bush before him, had the perfect excuse to cut it short: he had a job to do and, besides, what topic could come up that he hadn't already been dealing with for the past four years? Clinton's negotiators were able to keep the number of debates to two, on October 6 and 16. At their insistence, the second debate had the town hall format in which Clinton excelled in 1992. They also agreed to a single debate on October 9 between Gore and his vice presidential challenger, Jack Kemp.

Clearly, Dole and Kemp needed to carry the attack to Clinton if the debates were to change any minds. But Dole, aware of the reputation as a "hatchet man" that he earned from his first debate appearance when running for vice president in 1976, felt constrained from going negative for fear of reinforcing that image. Asked by the moderator of the first debate, Jim Lehrer, if there were "significant differences in the more personal area that are relevant to this election," Dole declined to take advantage of the "lob" that Lehrer intentionally sent his way and instead hit it into the net.[56] "I don't like to get into personal matters," Dole said. One week later, Kemp eschewed the running mate's essential job of hitting the opposition hard so that the head of the ticket can take the high road. Kemp not only passed up his own invitation from Lehrer to go on the attack at the start of the debate but also tied Dole's hands in the upcoming second presidential debate by saying, "It is beneath Bob Dole to go after anyone personally."[57] "It looked like a fraternity picnic there for a while," Dole commented sourly.[58] Meanwhile, Clinton and Gore reiterated their campaign themes of peace, prosperity, and moderation. Viewers regarded them as having won all three debates even though neither uttered a memorable phrase.[59]

Part of Dole's challenge was to convince voters that his age should not concern them. On September 18 a distressing event occurred when, campaigning in California, he fell three and a half feet off a narrow stage. Dole was unhurt and carried on with his speech but not before photographers captured the image of a distressed candidate struggling to rise without the use of his war-injured right arm. Trumpeting Dole's immediate recovery from the fall, campaign spokesman Nelson Warfield said, "This should put to rest the age question once and for all."[60] But merely to mention Dole's age was to draw attention to it. The pictures spoke louder than Warfield's words to voters who already worried that Dole might be too old to serve. Similarly, when Clinton turned a debate question about Dole's age into an attack on "the age of his ideas," there it was again: that word. Dole later joked that people were taking his "Dole in '96" campaign signs and changing them to "Dole *is* 96."[61] But with polls consistently showing that about one-third of voters regarded Dole's age as a cause for concern, it was no joke on Election Day.[62]

The late-breaking reports of shady foreign donations to the Clinton campaign provided a last-minute boost not only to Dole's campaign but to Perot's as well. The corrupting influence of money in politics had been a theme of his from the beginning. In contrast to 1992, Perot now aimed most of his rhetorical fire at Clinton, even calling on him to resign on October 28.[63] As for Dole, in fourteen Gallup polls conducted in September and October, he surpassed 40 percent only once and held Clinton below 50 percent only twice. With Election Day approaching on November 5, victory was out of reach, but Dole might at least be able to bring himself up—and Clinton down—into the 40s.

THE RESULTS

The electoral map in the 1996 presidential election closely resembled the 1992 map. Only five states voted differently from one election to the next. As he had against Bush, Clinton essentially swept the Northeast, the industrial Midwest, and the Pacific Coast. In the South, he hung on to Arkansas, Louisiana, and Tennessee while adding Florida and losing Georgia—a net gain of 12 electoral votes. In the West, he added Arizona, whose 8 electoral votes nearly offset his loss of Colorado (8 votes) and Montana (3 votes). Other than Indiana, Dole carried only southern and thinly populated western and Plains states. The net effect was that Clinton earned 379 electoral votes, 11 more than in 1992, to Dole's 159. Perot once again carried no states, rising as high as 14.2 percent only in Maine. Nor, in contrast to his previous performance, did he finish second in even one state.

Perot's 8.4 percent of the national popular vote was far from insubstantial. Other than George Wallace in 1968, he outpolled every other third-party candidate in almost three-fourths of a century (since Robert LaFollette in 1924). No other independent challenger had ever drawn this much support in two different elections. But impressive though it was, Perot's 1996 tally was well under half the 18.9 percent he received in 1992. More of those who voted for him in 1992 cast their ballots for Dole (44 percent) than for Perot (33 percent), with Clinton receiving 22 percent. As in 1992, about as many of those who voted for Perot in 1996 would have supported Clinton as Dole if Perot had not been on the ballot. Most Perot supporters said they would not have voted at all.[64] (See the state-by-state results of the presidential election in appendix E.)

Dole won 40.7 percent of the national popular vote, 3.3 points more than Bush had but nowhere close to his Democratic rival. Clinton received 49.2 percent, a 6.2-point increase over his own previous share. But he fell short of his ambition of winning a clear majority. Voter turnout was also disappointingly low, falling to 49 percent of the voting age population, the first time since 1924 that less than half of the voting age population participated in a presidential election. Dole's and Perot's success among voters who decided late in the campaign, after news accounts of Clinton's fund-raising infelicities appeared, took away from his support.

In addition to late deciders, the exit poll found that Dole did well with certain groups of white voters, who made up 83 percent of the electorate. He prevailed with men (+11 points over Clinton), Protestants (+17 points), the affluent (+10 points among those making $75,000 or more), married women (+2 points), and the relatively small minority of voters for whom taxes (+54 points), the budget deficit (+25 points), and the candidates' honesty and trustworthiness (+76 points) were important considerations. He also carried Asian Americans (+5 points) and kept his fellow Republicans (+67 points) and conservatives (+51 points) united behind him.[65]

Unfortunately for Dole, Clinton did well with everyone else. The president's greatest strength was among African Americans (+72 points over Dole) and Latinos (+51 points); working (+21 points) and unmarried (+28 points) women; Catholics (+16 points), Jews (+62 points), and adherents of "other religions" (+37 points); gays, lesbians, and bisexuals (+43 points); all age-groups but especially voters younger than thirty (+19 points); those with incomes below $30,000 (+21 points); liberals (+67 points) and moderates (+24 points); members of union households (+29 points); Democrats (+74 points) and independents (+8 points); and those who regarded Social Security and Medicare (+41 points), the economy and jobs (+34 points), education (+62 points), having "a vision for the future" (+64 points), and "cares about people like me" (+55 points) as the most important issues and qualities at stake in the election. Compared with his performance in 1992, Clinton's biggest gains were among women, Latinos, liberals, moderates, union households, and young people. He lost support among white men, Protestants, and older voters.

For all the personal disappointment that attended his failure to exceed 50 percent, Clinton's victory was significant. He was the first Democrat to be elected to a second term since Franklin D. Roosevelt—and only the fourth Democrat in history to win reelection. (Andrew Jackson and Woodrow Wilson were the others.) Of his seven immediate predecessors in the

White House—John F. Kennedy, Lyndon B. Johnson, Richard Nixon, Gerald Ford, Jimmy Carter, Ronald Reagan, and George Bush—Clinton was the only one besides Reagan who was on track to serve two full terms.

CONGRESS

During the general election campaign, Clinton detached himself from congressional Democrats, and congressional Republicans detached themselves from Dole. Both strategies were politically astute. Clinton was handily reelected and the 105th Congress was as Republican after the election as the 104th Congress was before it. The Democrats gained nine seats in the House while losing two in the Senate—a countervailing 2 percent partisan swing in both chambers.

Political scientists James Ceaser and Andrew Busch have argued that in 1996 "Bill Clinton well understood that he was a much more popular president with a Republican Congress than he had been with a Democratic Congress."[66] In his pursuit of the largest possible reelection majority, Clinton not only separated himself from his party's congressional candidates but also soaked up much of the money from Democratic donors that might otherwise have helped them in their races. Well into the fall campaign, riding high in polls that pointed to a strong popular vote majority, Clinton modified this approach, appearing with some Democratic candidates in close contests. Even then he "typically made few comments about them," observed political reporter Richard Cohen.[67] And he regretted doing even that much when the late-breaking campaign finance scandal placed his effort to win a personal majority in jeopardy.

Congressional Republicans bailed on Dole even more completely than Clinton did on congressional Democrats. Led by Lott, Dole's replacement as the Senate Republican leader, they decided that for the majority party to go into the election without any record of accomplishment would be politically fatal. In July and August, legislation concerning welfare, health care, and wages that had been buried ever since the GOP took control of Congress suddenly was allowed to come forth. As the year unfolded, Republican National Committee chair Haley Barbour winked to his party's candidates for Congress that they should wage their campaigns on the assumption that Clinton would win the presidential election. "If Clinton is reelected, heaven forbid," Barbour said in a news conference, "the last thing the American people want is for him to have a blank check in the form of a liberal Democratic Congress."[68] A Republican ad soon appeared showing a fortune-teller gazing into a crystal ball as a voice intoned, "What would happen if the Democrats controlled Congress *and* the White House?" The answer: tax increases, socialized medicine, and other dire consequences.[69] Corporate political action committees and other large donors, dreading the restoration of a united Democratic government, aligned their preferences with their spending by backing Republican congressional candidates unreservedly.

Rather than nationalizing the election, as the Republicans did in 1994 with the Contract with America, the GOP now encouraged its candidates to tailor their campaigns to the individual states and districts they represented. Forty-seven of the seventy-three freshman Republicans in the House had been elected in 1994 with less than 55 percent of the vote. As ripe targets for the Democrats, they could not afford to tether their campaigns to a weak presidential candidate. With encouragement from party leaders not to do so, few did and all but twelve were reelected.

In the end, the Republicans secured a 224 to 207 majority in the House and a 55 to 45 majority in the Senate. The Republicans' two-seat gain in Senate elections was all the more impressive because they were defending nineteen seats to the Democrats' fifteen. Working in their favor was that, frustrated by their loss of majority status, more than half of the Democratic senators whose seats were up for reelection retired—a first in the eight decades–long, post–Seventeenth Amendment era in which senators are elected by the people rather than the state legislatures. The job had become less desirable. Every veteran Democrat chaired one or more Senate committees or subcommittees until 1994; with the GOP in charge, none of them did. As Senate Democratic campaign chair, Kerrey did himself little good by recruiting several wealthy political novices to replace them based on their ability to fund their own campaigns.

The Republicans were able to win three of the eight Democratic open seat elections. Two of these were in the South, where the GOP continued to gain ground by winning previously Democratic seats in Alabama (Jeff Sessions) and Arkansas (Tim Hutchinson). Four Republicans also retired, but the party held on to all four of their vacant positions and only one incumbent Republican was defeated, Sen. Larry Pressler of South Dakota. In Texas, Sen. Phil Gramm's failed candidacy for president did not keep him from being reelected to a third term by a 15-point margin.

Retirements also impeded the Democrats' efforts to regain the House. As in the Senate, with majority control now in the hands of the GOP, the power and perquisites House Democrats grew accustomed to wielding during the previous four decades were gone. Twenty-nine of them, most of whom represented conservative southern districts, decided that serving in the minority was not worth another campaign and left the House. Nine of their seats went Republican, compared with the four that Democrats won when Republicans retired. The lack of majority status also had a dampening effect on the Democrats' ability to recruit strong candidates to run against Republican incumbents. Only 22 percent of Democratic challengers had won elective office before, considerably less than the 36 percent average that marked previous elections in which the minority party took back control of the chamber.[70] Minority status put the Democrats at a competitive disadvantage in fund-raising. For the first time in years, corporate and trade association donors interested in currying favor with whichever party controlled the House were able to place their bets on the GOP, the party they preferred on policy grounds but previously had not backed unreservedly for fear of losing influence.

Equally depressing for Democrats other than Clinton, their fortunes in the states continued to decline, shrinking the farm system from which future congressional candidates typically rise. When soft money donations whose legal purpose was to help state parties build themselves up were diverted to Clinton's reelection instead, the cost became apparent in the state legislative elections. After losing 148 seats to the Republicans in 1992 and 470 in 1994, the Democrats lost another 53 in 1996. Fortunately for them, perhaps, only eleven governorships were on the ballot, most of them in small states. Although they broke even in these elections—losing West Virginia to the Republicans but gaining New Hampshire—this still left them with only seventeen governors to the GOP's thirty-two.

In historical terms, Clinton's absence of coattails was remarkable. As political scientist Gary Jacobson has observed, "The idea that the Democrats could win the White House by 8 million votes without winning control of Congress would have been unthinkable only a few years ago."[71] Indeed, until Clinton, no Democratic presidential candidate in history had ever been elected without his party controlling at least one chamber. But in 1996 voters were content with the divided government the election perpetuated. In a postelection Pew survey, 53 percent said they were glad Clinton won and 65 percent were glad the Republicans retained control of Congress. For the first time since 1936, a Democratic president won a second term. For the first time since 1928, a Republican Congress was reelected.

BILL CLINTON AND A NEW ERA OF
DE FACTO DIVIDED GOVERNMENT

Bill Clinton was a part of every presidential election in which he was old enough to vote. In pre–Twenty-Sixth Amendment 1968, when twenty-one was the minimum age for voters, the twenty-two-year-old, newly minted Georgetown University graduate spent the summer before embarking for Oxford as a Rhodes scholar working for the Democratic ticket in Arkansas. He was successful in helping his boss, J. William Fulbright, get reelected to the Senate even as independent presidential candidate George C. Wallace was winning the state's six electoral votes and incumbent Republican governor Winthrop Rockefeller was securing a second term—split-ticket voting at its most extreme. In 1972 Clinton and Hillary Rodham took time off from their studies at Yale Law School to run Democratic presidential nominee George McGovern's campaign in Texas. Four years later, while waging his own successful campaign for Arkansas attorney general, Clinton helped lead Democratic candidate Jimmy Carter's effort in his home state.

In 1980 Clinton's bid to be reelected governor of Arkansas suffered collateral damage when President Carter, also seeking a second term, "screwed" him (Clinton's word) by sending thousands of Cuban deportees to Fort Chaffee in Arkansas.[1] In 1984, once again his state's governor, Clinton gave a successful prime-time speech at the Democratic National Convention. Soon after, he began planning to seek the 1988 presidential nomination, only to abandon the effort when it became clear that at a time of media hypervigilance about candidates' sexual histories, his own would be embarrassingly scrutinized. Clinton's only public role was to deliver what nearly all viewers thought was a boring and overlong nominating speech for Gov. Michael Dukakis at the Democratic National Convention.

THE 2000 ELECTION

Clinton, of course, did run and win in 1992. Constitutionally, the Twenty-Second Amendment made his reelection in 1996 the last of his own campaigns for president, although in a sense his successful effort to fend off removal from office when the House voted to impeach him in 1998 was a kind of "third presidential campaign."[2] (See the text of Clinton's second inaugural address in appendix G.) In 2000, at age fifty-four, Clinton made clear that he would have "run again in a heartbeat if I could," but that option was not available.[3] Nor did he pursue the course that John Quincy Adams, John Tyler, and Andrew Johnson did—return home and run for Congress. Instead he supported Hillary Clinton's successful bid for a Senate seat from New York, the first of her four campaigns for senator and president.

Clinton described Al Gore, his vice president and the Democratic Party's nominee for president in 2000, as "the next best thing."[4] It was a two-edged description. Clinton condescendingly thought voters would be settling for Gore since they could not have him. But he also regarded that outcome as the country's best available option and wanted to do everything he could to see Gore elected. With Republican nominee George W. Bush ending every speech by pledging, in scarcely veiled contrast to Clinton, that he would "uphold the honor and dignity of the office to which I have been elected, so help me God," only Gore's election would vindicate Clinton's own record as president.[5] And hadn't Gore said on the day of Clinton's impeachment that he "will be regarded in the history books as one of our greatest presidents"?[6]

To Clinton, it seemed obvious that Gore's best strategy was to run on the administration's record in office—"essentially for a third term," as he told author Taylor Branch.[7] In his speech to the Democratic convention, Clinton urged voters to ask themselves, "Are we better off than we were eight years ago? . . . Are we going to keep the progress and prosperity going?"[8] For four years the economy had grown at an annual rate of at least 4 percent and Clinton's job approval ratings stayed above 60 percent—the highest and most consistent ratings for a second-term president in the history of polling. In addition, unemployment fell during every year of Clinton's presidency, eventually dropping below 4 percent; the average annual rate of inflation during the Clinton years was the lowest since the early 1960s; and the enormous budget deficits that Clinton inherited from his predecessor became substantial budget surpluses. In a CBS/*New York Times* poll taken one month before the election, nine in ten voters said they would "describe the condition of the U.S. economy" as "very good" or "somewhat good."[9]

Employing various historically based statistical models that forecast the national popular vote in presidential elections, seven political scientists at the September 2000 meeting of the American Political Science Association were unanimous in predicting that Gore would win by a margin of anywhere from 6 to 20 percentage points.[10] Their assumption was that Gore would run a competent campaign, embracing the administration's record of accomplishment while asking voters to judge him on the basis of his own straight-laced character, not Clinton's rakish one. For most politicians, this would have been an easy road to navigate. As Clinton himself told Gore, "Al, there's not a single person in the country who thinks you messed around with Monica Lewinsky."[11]

Instead, Gore ham-handedly distanced himself from both Clinton the president and Clinton the person. On June 16, 1999, the day he announced his candidacy, Gore told the prime-time ABC News program *20/20* that he regarded Clinton's affair with Lewinsky as "inexcusable."[12] He chose as his vice presidential running mate Sen. Joseph Lieberman of Connecticut, who had publicly condemned Clinton's behavior as "immoral" and "harmful."[13] Attuned to a New Age adviser's recommendation that he challenge the president in order to shed his vice presidential image as a "beta male" and replace Clinton as the nation's "alpha male," Gore went overboard.[14] Telling the voters in his acceptance speech at the Democratic convention that "I stand here tonight as my own man" was appropriate and politically beneficial.[15] Rejecting Clinton's repeated offers to campaign for him, which party leaders pleaded with Gore to accept, was not.[16]

Even worse, instead of emphasizing the national prosperity that marked the Clinton-Gore years, Gore ran a populist-sounding "they're for the powerful, we're for the people" campaign more appropriate for a candidate challenging an incumbent in economic hard times than for a vice president seeking to extend his party's control of the presidency in good times. Gore's strongest political advantage in 2000 was his ability to ask the voters: If eight years of Democratic rule has produced peace and prosperity, why elect a Republican? Yet as *Slate* editor Michael Kinsley summarized the theme of the Gore campaign, "You've never had it so good, and I'm mad as hell about it."[17] In his three nationally televised debates with Bush, Gore never mentioned Clinton, part of the generally abysmal performance that cost him the lead he had going into the debates.

"We made a campaign decision to associate ourselves with Clinton and the Clinton economy and to use it in the last month," pollster Stan Greenberg commented.[18] "The only problem is that Gore didn't do it." "We might have blown it," another Gore aide said near the end of the campaign. "We didn't remind people of how well off they are."[19] "More than anything else," political scientist Gary Jacobson concluded, "Gore's inability to exploit his biggest asset, the Clinton economy, effectively cost him a clear-cut victory."[20]

THE 2008 ELECTION

Clinton was a Democratic rock star after leaving the White House in 2001. Not only did his administration's eight years in office look even better to his fellow partisans in hindsight than they had at the time, but the contrast Democrats drew between him and President George W. Bush, as well as their deepening resentment of Gore for losing the 2000 election by separating himself from Clinton, cast a gauzy glow around the former president.

Clinton's role in 2004 was relatively modest. He remained aloof from the Democratic nominating contest and, in any event, spent much of the spring and summer touring the country to promote his newly published memoir, *My Life*. In early September, at about the time he planned to start campaigning actively for his party's presidential nominee, Sen. John Kerry of Massachusetts, Clinton was admitted to the hospital for what turned out to be quadruple-bypass, open-heart surgery. He offered advice to Kerry in phone calls from his hospital room. Whatever disappointment Clinton may have felt over the Democrat's defeat by Bush was tempered by the knowledge that it cleared the deck for Hillary Clinton to seek the party's presidential nomination four years later.

Senator Clinton's main opponent in 2008 was Barack Obama, a relatively junior senator from Illinois but a serious contender to become the first African American president in history. Although in his own presidential campaigns Bill Clinton worked hard to bring white southerners, blue-collar workers, and moderates back into the Democratic fold, his strongest support as president came from African Americans. Defending Clinton from efforts to impeach him in 1998, celebrated novelist Toni Morrison actually described him as "our first black president." "Clinton displays almost every trope of blackness: single-parent household, born poor,

The outgoing president in a rare campaign appearance for 2000 Democratic presidential nominee Al Gore, who worked to separate his candidacy from Clinton. Courtesy of the William J. Clinton Presidential Library.

working-class, saxophone-playing, McDonald's-and-junk-food-loving boy from Arkansas," she wrote."[21]

Convinced that his hold on black voters was stronger than Obama's, Clinton overruled Hillary Clinton's campaign advisers and insisted on making a major personal effort to win the South Carolina primary, the first on the calendar whose Democratic electorate was dominated by African Americans. A rusty campaigner, Clinton blundered severely. Furious at the media for what he regarded as its softball coverage of Obama and hardball coverage of his wife concerning their positions on the Bush administration's war in Iraq, Clinton erupted at a campaign event. In a red-faced, finger-wagging tirade, he said, "Give . . . me . . . a . . . break. This whole thing is the biggest fairy tale I've ever seen."[22] Construed narrowly, "this whole thing" was the idea that Obama had consistently opposed the war since its inception. Construed broadly, as many listeners did, it seemed to demean Obama's right to be taken seriously as a possible president. "To call that dream a fairy tale, which Bill Clinton seemed to be doing, could very well be insulting to some of us," said Rep. Jim Clyburn, the leading black politician in the state.[23]

When Obama won the primary by 55 percent to 27 percent based on his four-to-one majority among African American voters, Clinton testily dismissed the victory. "Jesse Jackson won South Carolina in '84 and '88. Jackson ran a good campaign. And Obama ran a good campaign," he said, giving the impression that any African American could win the state. When Sen. Edward Kennedy told the former president that he was endorsing Obama, Clinton angrily replied, "The only reason you're endorsing him is because he's black."[24] And when Obama commented that "Ronald Reagan changed the trajectory of America in a way that . . . Bill Clinton did not," both Clintons erupted, violating the basic political axiom that campaigns should be about the candidate, not the candidate's spouse.[25] "Two months earlier, Bill Clinton had been the best loved Democrat in the country," concluded election chroniclers John Heilemann and Mark Halperin. "Now, in something like a heartbeat, he'd been transformed into a figure of derision and scorn."[26]

THE 2016 ELECTION

Clinton mended his relationship with President Obama, who brought Hillary Clinton into his administration as secretary of state. In 2012 the former president gave a brilliantly effective speech on the current president's behalf at the Democratic National Convention, cut a widely viewed ad for Obama, and filled in for him on the campaign trail during the four days he spent dealing with the devastation caused by Hurricane Sandy. Obama, a strong orator himself, admiringly called Clinton his "Secretary of Explaining Stuff." But the 2016 election, in which Hillary Clinton once again was a candidate, revealed even further deterioration in her husband's reputation.

Since Bill Clinton was first elected in 1992, the Democratic Party had become considerably more liberal. At that time, about 25 percent of Democratic voters identified as liberals, the same percentage who said they were conservatives. (The rest—nearly half—were self-described moderates.) By 2016, a quarter century later, the liberals' share had risen to 50 percent.[27] The party's leftward movement was even more pronounced among grassroots party activists.[28] One consequence was that major policy changes that occurred during the Clinton presidency—notably, welfare reform, the crime bill, financial deregulation, and the basic strategy of "triangulation"—came to be regarded by many Democrats not as achievements but as cave-ins to conservatives. The surprisingly effective nomination campaign that Sen. Bernie Sanders of Vermont, a self-described "democratic socialist," waged against Hillary Clinton brought all of these resentments to the surface. Even the television series *The West Wing*, once treasured on the left as a kind of alt-history of the early 2000s in which a Clinton-style president was in office, came under attack as insufficiently orthodox.[29]

A certain unfairness toward President Clinton marked these criticisms. The political momentum in late twentieth-century American politics was all on the right. Four of the five presidential elections from 1972 to 1988 were Republican landslides. Clinton stopped that trend in its tracks in 1992. All eleven Supreme Court appointments in the quarter century prior to his election were made by Republican presidents. Clinton added two liberal justices to the Court during his first two years in office. Congress went Republican in 1994 for the first time in forty years, led by the party's hard-charging conservative wing. Clinton nonetheless was able to stem the GOP tide by winning reelection two years later. During his two terms as president he rode the conservative Republican tiger, in political scientist Walter Dean Burnham's phrase, and went some way toward taming it.[30]

In 2016 Hillary Clinton overcame Sanders's challenge and was nominated to run against Republican Donald Trump, whose nationalist rhetoric and celebrity businessman background were prefigured by the 1992 campaigns waged by Pat Buchanan and Ross Perot, respectively. Like both of his predecessors from that election, Trump decried trade agreements, Middle East wars, office-holding experience, and a system allegedly rigged against the white working class. But once again changing attitudes toward her husband's record shadowed her candidacy. Not just left-wing economic and social policies but also concerns about sexual misconduct against women had risen to new heights on the Democratic Party's agenda. In 1998 Gloria Steinem and many other feminists defended President Clinton against such allegations. Monica Lewinsky's "relationship with President Clinton has never been called unwelcome," Steinem wrote. "There is no evidence to suggest that Ms. Lewinsky's will was violated."[31] By 2016 feminist Democrats were more numerous and less forgiving of a powerful fifty-year-old man's affair with a twenty-two-year-old low-level employee.

In a bizarre twist, Trump was able to turn clear evidence of his own misogyny against Hillary Clinton by invoking the former president. On October 8, a 2005 recording surfaced of Trump saying that when it came to beautiful women, "I just start kissing them. . . . And when you're a star, they let you do it. . . . Grab 'em by the pussy. You can do anything."[32] Two days later, in his second debate with Hillary Clinton, Trump brought four Clinton accusers to the debate hall in St. Louis, paraded them before the media, and sat them in the audience just a glance away from the former president.

Asked in the debate to comment on his loose talk about sexual assault, Trump said, "That was locker room talk." But, he added, "If you look at Bill Clinton, far worse. Mine are words and his was action. . . . There's never been anybody in the history of politics in this nation who's been so abusive to women." Feminists did not vote for Trump, but by invoking Bill Clinton he managed to deflect what otherwise might have been a fatal blow to his candidacy.[33]

Clinton also complicated his wife's candidacy on June 27, when he ambled across the runway at the Phoenix airport from his parked aircraft to a plane carrying Attorney General Loretta Lynch. The visit raised suspicions that their discussion might concern the Justice Department's investigation of Hillary Clinton's use of a private e-mail server to conduct State Department business. Although FBI director James Comey, who was leading the investigation, did not think it did, he decided he "needed to visibly step away from Loretta Lynch" and take the highly unusual step of personally announcing the results.[34] On July 5 Comey declared that "although we did not find clear evidence that Secretary Clinton or her colleagues intended to violate laws concerning the handling of classified information, there is evidence that they were extremely careless in their handling of very sensitive, highly classified information."[35] Both the criticism and the decision not to prosecute gave new energy to Trump's tweets about "Crooked Hillary" and his crowds' chants of "Lock her up," contributing to her defeat in the election.

DE FACTO DIVIDED GOVERNMENT SINCE CLINTON: A NEW ERA

Changes since 1992 in Bill Clinton's standing with the American people in general and the Democratic Party in particular parallel changes in the nature of divided government during this period. Whether divided (chapter 3), united (chapter 6), or redivided (chapter 7) in form, a new era in American politics and governance has emerged. Divided government traditionally required that the president's party lack a majority in one or both houses of Congress. During the Clinton years, the parties began conducting themselves nearly all the time as if the government were divided. Governance in the modern era typically takes the shape of "de facto divided government."

As discussed at length in chapter 1, for much of American history divided government in the traditional, formal sense was an unusual occurrence. For more than a century after Zachary Taylor's election in 1848, the voters gave every newly elected president a Congress controlled by his own party to work with. Starting in 1968, however, divided government became the norm, and always in a particular form: a Republican president and a wholly or partially Democratic Congress.

Clinton's election in 1992 seemed at the time like an exception to this pattern. Congress remained Democratic and the presidency became so. The Republicans' capture of Congress in 1994 also seemed exceptional. For the first time since 1946, the voters paired a Republican Congress with a Democratic president. But in contrast to that Harry S. Truman–era election, which was undone when congressional Democrats regained control after just two years, the voters preserved divided government in its new form for the remaining six years of the Clinton presidency. In 2000 they endorsed yet another seemingly unusual combination by electing Republican George W. Bush and a Republican Congress, an arrangement they confirmed in the 2002 midterm election and the 2004 presidential election.[36] In 2006, however, voters paired Bush with a Democratic Congress in a midterm election the president described as a "thumping."[37]

The accumulation of exceptions to a rule is the best evidence that the rule no longer applies. The fourteen years that separated the 1992 and 2006 elections saw every possible manifestation of divided and united party government: a Democratic president and Democratic Congress, a Democratic president and Republican Congress, a Republican president and Republican Congress, and a Republican president and Democratic Congress. In 2008 Democrat Barack Obama was, like Clinton, elected with a Democratic Congress that lasted for only the first two of his eight years in office. (He called the voters' rebuke of his party in the 2010 midterm a "shellacking.")[38] In 2016 and 2018, Republican Donald Trump repeated the pattern: a Congress controlled by his party during his first two years but not after the first midterm election, which Trump nonetheless blithely characterized as a "tremendous success" while attributing the Republicans' loss of the House to their insufficient devotion to him.[39]

Are there subtle patterns in what appears on the surface to be the patternless quarter century of politics and government ushered in by Clinton's elections in 1992 and 1996? Certainly none that are as apparent as the one that characterized the first two-thirds of the twentieth century, when united party government prevailed for fifty-four of sixty-eight years (79 percent of the time) or during the period that began in 1968, when government was divided for twenty of twenty-four years (83 percent of the time, and always in the form of a Republican president and a Democratic House, Senate, or both). Political scientist Byron Shafer aptly describes the era ushered in by Clinton's first election as one of "partisan volatility" and "kaleidoscopic variation"—a "succession of partisan outcomes, unified and split, with either party holding Congress and either party holding the presidency."[40]

Nonetheless, the political era that Clinton's victory in 1992 inaugurated has discernibly distinctive qualities. Every president elected since 1992—Clinton, Bush, Obama, and Trump—has had to serve with a Congress not controlled by his party for part of his tenure. But only part. Each of these four presidents was able to avoid the experience of recent predecessors Richard Nixon, Gerald Ford, and George Bush by serving at least some of his time with a Congress of his own party. In every case, that period overlapped with their first two years in office, usually lasting no longer than that.

The result of this volatility is that the old pattern of sometimes united, sometimes divided government has given rise to another: divided government in fact even when united in form. Under de facto divided government, when new presidents take office with their party in control of Congress, the expectation is no longer that the party's hold on the House and Senate will remain secure. As a result, far from giving each new president the traditional "honeymoon," the opposition congressional party's every incentive is to generate maximum dissatisfaction with the administration right off the bat, in hopes that voters will turn against the incumbent president and party in the midterm election.[41]

Consequently, what seemed exceptional during Clinton's first two years—the openly expressed intention of Senate Republican leader Bob Dole and House Republican whip Newt Gingrich to obstruct the president from the very beginning—has become familiar. As measured by success at the ballot box, this strategy worked well against Clinton in 1994, as did a similar approach by Republican legislators against Obama in 2010. Senate Republican leader Mitch McConnell said, "The single most important thing we want to achieve is for President Obama to be a one-term president." House minority leader Eric Cantor told his party's caucus, "We're not here to cut deals and get crumbs and stay in the minority."[42] Democrats were just as quick to embrace their role as the "party of no" when Trump became president. They reaped the harvest of this approach in the 2018 midterm. The only exception to this pattern—congressional Democrats' willingness to work with George W. Bush on education reform legislation even before the September 11, 2001, terrorist attacks on New York and Washington briefly united the country—seemed to demonstrate the new rule when the GOP maintained and even expanded its congressional majority in 2002.

No opposition party in Congress is likely to embrace that approach again any time soon.

Aggravating the severely confrontational stance of the opposition party is the polarization between Republicans and Democrats that has accelerated since Clinton's elections, both in Congress and in the electorate. In Congress, the ideological distance between Republican and Democratic members has grown steadily for more than four decades. By 2017, not a single Democratic senator or representative was more conservative than the most liberal Republican member.[43] As late as the 1980s, the Republican caucus in both chambers included a significant liberal wing centered in the Northeast. The Democrats' ranks included numerous southern conservatives. That ceased to be the case after conservative Democratic voters in the South moved into the Republican Party and northeastern liberal Republicans became Democrats.

From Progressive Era thinkers like Woodrow Wilson and Henry Jones Ford in the 1900s to President Franklin D. Roosevelt in the 1940s, the American Political Science Association in the 1950s, and grassroots activists in both the Republican and Democratic parties in the 1960s, the dream of "responsible party" competition between a conservative GOP and a liberal Democratic Party flourished. Stripped of internal ideological divisions, the two parties would present the voters with clear alternatives in each election, and whichever party won would then be able to enact its promised agenda.[44] All of these reformers assumed that united party government would continue to be the normal governing situation as it had been for decades, a necessary condition if the winning party was to be able to keep its promises to the electorate. In this assumption they clearly were wrong.

Nor did advocates of ideologically unified parties anticipate that healthy competition between Republicans and Democrats would give way to mutual loathing among both leaders and followers. In 2012 Republican Mitt Romney wrote off "the 47 percent . . . who believe they are victims." Four years later, Democrat Hillary Clinton went him 3 percent better when she said, "You could put half of Trump's supporters into what I call a basket of deplorables. The racist, sexist, homophobic, xenophobic, Islamophobic— you name it."[45] Neither Romney nor Clinton was a harshly partisan political leader. Both were running for an office still nominally called president of the *United* States. Yet as political scientists Marc Hetherington and Jonathan Weiler have shown, since 1980 the proportion of self-identified Republicans and Democrats who "hate" the other party (that is, who score it below 20 on a 100-point favorability scale) has risen from about 10 percent to about 50 percent. Nearly half the members of both parties would also be "somewhat" or "very" concerned if their son or daughter married a member of the other party—up from about 5 percent when that question was asked in 1960.[46] Recent presidents' job approval rating by members of their own party regularly exceeds 85 percent even as their rating by opposition party members often falls below 10 percent—a much greater contrast than in the not-too-distant past.[47] Once thought to be an elites-only separation that left most voters stranded in the political center without a comfortable home in either party, it is now the case that "polarization in Washington reflects polarization within the public, especially . . . the attentive, informed, and active citizens" whose numbers, political scientist Alan Abramowitz has shown, have been steadily growing.[48]

New, ideologically driven forms of media—talk radio, cable news channels, websites, and social media—have been accelerants fanning the flames of division. Until these new media began arising in force starting in the late 1980s, "the nightly [television] news and morning papers, building on each other's reporting and amplifying their findings, combined to form a single voice," observe historians Kevin Kruse and Julian Zelizer.[49] The three broadcast networks that dominated the television airwaves all made money by reaching the largest and therefore most politically diverse audience possible, as did the newspapers that loomed large in every town and city and the wire services that provided them with national news. The business model for the media ushered in by cable and the web involved segmenting the market and dominating a particular slice of it. Ideology replaced neutrality as the key to profitability.[50]

Underlying the recent efflorescence of mutual partisan loathing has been the supplanting of economic issues by cultural issues as the main line of cleavage between Republicans and Democrats. As president, Nixon's campaign to win over the white southerners and blue-collar workers who supported Wallace in 1968 succeeded by focusing on the "social issue"—crime, drugs, law and order, busing, school prayer, and so on—while leaving alone the entitlement programs on which many of these voters depended. Reagan and his Republican successors, culminating in Trump, built on these efforts. In reaction, the Democrats embraced the identity politics of gender, race and ethnicity, and sexual orientation. Economic disagreements lend themselves to "split the difference" compromises on taxes and spending that members of both political parties can live with. Cultural issues, many of which involve fundamental values, are less prone to compromise and more likely to inflame partisans on different sides against each other.

The growing cultural differences between the parties are closely tied to geography, with more voters living in like-minded communities that reinforce their political predispositions. As a rough-and-ready measure of these differences, political analyst David Wasserman has identified culturally conservative, mostly rural counties as those with a Cracker Barrel Old Country Store and culturally liberal, mostly urban and upscale suburban counties as those with a Whole Foods Market. When Clinton was elected in 1992, he carried 40 percent of Cracker Barrel counties and 61 percent of Whole Foods counties, a 21-point "culture gap." Trump won in 2016 by carrying 76 percent of Cracker Barrel counties and 22 percent of Whole Foods counties—a culture gap that had grown to 54 points after rising in every intervening election.[51]

Cooler, more strategic calculations have also accelerated the trend toward partisan polarization. As political scientist Frances Lee has shown, in the modern era battles for control of the presidency, the House, and the Senate have all become more closely fought, as measured by the absence of landslide presidential elections starting in 1992, the frequency of turnover in partisan control of the House that began in 1994, and, dating back even further, both parties' realistic chance of winning control of the Senate in every election since 1980. "When party control seemingly hangs in the balance," Lee writes, "members and leaders of both parties invest more effort in enterprises to promote their own party's image and undercut that of the opposition."[52] Not coincidentally, the only era to rival the current one for close partisan competition—the late nineteenth century—was also the only one to match contemporary levels of ideological separation between the parties in Congress.[53] Ideology aside, the prospect of winning or losing control of an elected branch generates a "harder-edged, more forceful style of partisanship" that includes "nonideological appeals accusing the other party of corruption, failure, or incompetence."[54]

In terms of governance, the consequences of divided government—whether formal or de facto—have been dysfunctional bordering on corrosive. Shutdowns of the federal government, once unheard of, have become a familiar occurrence. Under Reagan, George Bush, and Clinton, shutdowns happened occasionally, but only when the other party controlled one or both houses of Congress. In 2018 budgetary stalemates between Trump and Congress shut down the government for thirty-five days starting on December 22, breaking the record set by Clinton and Congress in 1995–1996. Although both chambers had Republican majorities, united Democratic opposition and Senate Democrats' use of the filibuster kept Trump and his party from working their will. Even when the president and his fellow Republicans formed a united majority in the Senate in favor of a budget, forty-one Democratic senators could prevent it from coming to a vote, emulating the GOP's approach when Clinton and Obama were in office.

A different kind of budget-related problem has more recently emerged from divided government. As late as the Clinton presidency, budgetary policy was shadowed by a concern for deficits. Republicans and Democrats clashed over policy priorities—domestic programs for Democrats, defense and tax cuts for Republicans—but all acknowledged that a concern about the size of the overall deficit needed to shape their efforts. Since then, each party has implicitly agreed to let the other have its way: a short-term win-win approach with risky long-term consequences. "Reagan proved that deficits don't matter," Vice President Richard Cheney blithely observed in 2004.[55] Spending in all areas—and, consequently, budget deficits—soared. Even as Trump and Congress locked horns in early 2018 over the president's proposal to spend money building a wall along the nation's southern border, for example, they readily agreed to raise both domestic and defense spending for fiscal year 2019 by 10 percent after cutting taxes substantially. Despite a booming economy like the one that produced surpluses during Clinton's second term, the deficit rose to $1 trillion per year during Trump's presidency, increasing the national debt to nearly $25 trillion by 2020. Following their parties' lead, the share of the public who were concerned about the deficit shrank from about three-fourths in 2013 to about one-half in 2019.[56]

More generally, political scientist Sarah A. Binder has shown, issues on the national agenda increasingly are muzzled, never coming to a vote in Congress. The result has been that liberal and, soon after, conservative groups began pursuing their policy goals on matters such as abortion, race, the environment, gun rights, and campaign finance through litigation rather than legislation.[57] In addition, presidents have made increasing use of unilateral executive actions. Clinton, Bush, and Obama typically did so only after their party lost control of Congress and the legislative door to policy change was slammed shut. Trump did so from the beginning. Despite taking office with a Republican majority in both houses, he quickly determined that the filibuster rule in the Senate would allow the Democrats to smother administration-sponsored legislation in its cradle. At the close of his first hundred days as president, Trump bragged that he had signed more executive orders than any president since Truman.[58] The ideological polarization of the two parties, initially in Congress and among party activists and increasingly among voters, has left the center of the political spectrum, which many Republican and Democratic legislators once inhabited, barren ground.

A major casualty of divided government, whether formal or de facto, has been the reputation of the third branch of government, the judiciary, for standing apart from partisan politics. Judicial appointments have become political footballs in the battle between presidents and opposition-party senators, so much so that by 2019 many Democrats regarded three of the five Republican-appointed justices on the Supreme Court as illegitimate: Clarence Thomas and Brett Kavanaugh because of allegations of sexual misconduct made against them in sworn Senate testimony, and Neil Gorsuch because he filled a seat that Senate Republicans denied to Obama nominee Merrick Garland by refusing even to consider his appointment.

From 1900 to 1968, during the era of united party government, only three of forty-five Supreme Court nominations (7 percent) were rejected by the Senate. Two of these rejections were of Democratic president Lyndon B. Johnson's nominations of Abraham Fortas and Homer Thornberry in October 1968, a moment when the Republicans firmly expected to win control of the presidency but not the Senate in the following month's election. Twenty-nine Supreme Court appointments—nearly two-thirds of them—during the first two-thirds of the twentieth century actually were approved viva voce, without controversy.

This degree of comity is remarkable considering that during this long era each party almost always held more than one-third of Senate seats, the requisite number needed at the time to sustain a filibuster. (The two-thirds requirement for invoking cloture to end a filibuster was reduced to three-fifths in 1975.) Yet both parties assumed that because united government was the norm, their presidents would sometimes be in the position of nominating justices. To reject a Supreme Court nominee when the other party controlled the White House would be to invite retaliation in kind when the tables were turned. A shared desire to avoid this form of mutually assured destruction led Republican and Democratic senators alike to confirm virtually all presidential nominations to the Court. With regard to lower court nominations, senators' norm of mutual deference promoted the "blue-slip" tradition of senatorial courtesy, under which the Senate would reject any nominee who was objectionable to either senator from a nominee's home state and confirm any nominee of whom those senators approved.

Since 1969, six of twenty-four Supreme Court nominations (25 percent) have failed. No nominee has been approved by voice vote, and even confirmed nominees in the twenty-first century have drawn an average of thirty-eight dissenting votes. When Obama nominated Judge Garland in March 2016 to fill the vacancy on the court left by the death of Justice Antonin Scalia, Senate Republicans refused to hold committee hearings on the grounds that Obama was in his final year as president. They were able to cite Obama's vice president, Joseph Biden, in support of their stance. On June 25, 1992, then Senate Judiciary Committee chair Biden said that if, as seemed possible at the end of the Supreme Court's 1991–1992 term, a justice retired, President Bush should "not name a nominee until after the November election is completed." Much to Obama and Biden's dismay, Senate Republicans christened this the "Biden Rule."

Still worse, as political scientist John Anthony Maltese has shown, the "selling of Supreme Court nominees" has become indistinguishable from overtly partisan battles about public policy.[59] In 2016, as a way of uniting the Republican Party behind his candidacy, Trump issued two lists of potential Supreme Court justices and promised to choose his nominees from them. The lists were generated by the Federalist Society and the Heritage Foundation, two conservative organizations. Candidates for the Democratic presidential nomination in 2020 even proposed packing the court with additional justices, an idea previously regarded as buried forever after Franklin D. Roosevelt's notoriously unsuccessful effort to do so in 1937. Meanwhile, Senate majority leader Mitch McConnell said that his objection to considering Supreme Court nominations in an election year would not apply to a Trump nominee if a vacancy occurred in 2020. Such actions have placed the legitimacy of the judicial system, dependent as it is on public trust in its nonpartisanship, in jeopardy

Although no Supreme Court nomination since 1969 has been rejected when the Senate was controlled by the president's party, de facto divided government has come to prevail in other judicial confirmations.[60] In 2003, with the Senate in Republican hands, Democrats filibustered President George W. Bush's appellate court nomination of Miguel Estrada, the first filibuster of a lower court nominee in history and the first of several that soon followed. In 2013, with the Senate under Democratic control, Senate Republicans filibustered many of Obama's appellate and district court appointments, including four of his five nominees to the court of appeals for the District of Columbia, generally regarded as the second-most-important court in the country. In 2017, Senate Democrats made clear that they would do the same to Trump's first Supreme Court nominee, Neil Gorsuch.

Changing the rules of a game to generate a preferred outcome is playing with fire, but that is exactly what has happened with regard to judicial nominations. In 2013 Senate majority leader Harry Reid persuaded his fellow Democrats to change the chamber's rules to bar any use of the filibuster in lower court confirmations. In 2017 Senator McConnell, Reid's successor as majority leader, persuaded his fellow Republicans to forbid filibusters against Supreme Court nominations as well. He also made clear that senatorial courtesy would no longer apply to appellate court judgeships, breaching the blue-slip tradition that since 1979 had denied Senate approval to every nominee to whom both of a state's senators objected and all but three whom even one found unacceptable.[61] In all cases, these power plays came in response to power plays by the other party. But their purpose was to generate particular outcomes in ways that made the Senate as an institution more majoritarian and less deliberative.

Perhaps the gravest consequence of divided government's routinization, whether formal or de facto, has been the acceleration of "politics by other means"—that is, means other than elections. Because neither the Democratic Party nor the Republican Party has been able to develop a stable majority in the electorate, political scientists Benjamin Ginsberg and Martin Shefter argue, "contending forces are increasingly relying on such institutional weapons of political struggle as legislative investigations, media revelations, and judicial proceedings to weaken their political rivals and gain power for themselves."[62] The pursuit of Nixon's Watergate crimes by Congress, the courts, and the media was an exceptional event at the time. Since then, they note, "character assassination has become a routine aspect of American politics." In February 2018 *Politico* compiled a list of forty-six political scandals that since 1973 had been characterized by various national leaders as "worse than Watergate," many of them accompanied by some combination of media frenzy, congressional investigation, and prosecution.[63] The ranks of fallen or wounded political leaders include senators, party leaders in the House of Representatives, cabinet members, presidential aides, and presidents. "You'd be in jail" if he were elected, Trump threatened Hillary Clinton in their second presidential debate.[64] Ideological news sources, notably cable channels Fox News and MSNBC, along with multiple online sites, have fueled these efforts. Conservative talk radio, which emerged as a tool for Republican politicians, became an enforcer of right-wing orthodoxy against so-called RINOs: Republicans In Name Only.

Organized efforts have been made to impeach every president since Clinton, who was in fact impeached along partisan lines, only to be vindicated—again along partisan lines—by the Senate.[65] Even before they took office, the legitimacy of George W. Bush's election was disputed, as was

Barack Obama's constitutional eligibility as a spuriously accused natural-born citizen of Kenya. In Trump's case impeachment talk moved at warp speed from left-wing media to an organized petition drive funded by a billionaire investor to the halls of Congress—all within four months of his taking office. With 70 percent of Democratic voters saying they wanted the House of Representatives to impeach the president, Rep. Al Green of Texas declared in May 2017 that he intended to introduce an impeachment resolution.[66] In October he did so and soon forced the first in a series of votes on the House floor, earning the support of fifty-eight Democrats, a number that grew in subsequent roll calls. Grassroots pressure from Democratic activists to impeach Trump accelerated into 2019, overlapping with the traditional process of removing an unpopular president: the 2020 election. On the basis of new evidence of Trump's misdeeds, in October 2019 a nearly unanimous majority of House Democrats voted to launch a formal impeachment inquiry over the objections of every Republican member.

GOOD NEWS, BAD NEWS: TWO CLINTON COUNTEREXAMPLES

For those concerned about governance in the modern era, the Clinton presidency offers reason for both encouragement and discouragement. On the one hand, of the four most recent presidents, only he was able to make divided government work, albeit for just two of the six years that he served alongside a Republican Congress. In 1996 Clinton and the congressional Republican majority faced their first reelection campaign after a year of gridlock. Both parties approached the election realizing that without a record of accomplishment both were at risk of defeat.

Although a major theme of Clinton's 1992 presidential campaign was "ending welfare as we know it," he was initially stymied in this effort less by congressional Republicans than by congressional Democrats. During the transition period that followed the election, Clinton "committed to [Democratic leaders] Tom Foley, George Mitchell, and Dick Gephardt, at a dinner in Little Rock, that he would not go for welfare reform," Clinton campaign chair Mickey Kantor recalled, "because they didn't want him to do so."[67] The 1994 midterm election altered that equation. "The day after the election he stopped taking orders from Democrats in Congress," according to deputy domestic policy adviser Bruce Reed. "Welfare reform was something the Republicans wanted to do. So we had one area in common, one item that was at the top of their agenda and the top of our agenda."[68]

The road to enactment was not smooth. Republicans pushed for—and passed—two bills that were more severe than Clinton was willing to sign. He vetoed both. Dole, running for president, preferred having the issue to having a bill. But, Reed recalled, "eventually, in June of '96, House Republicans panicked, and the class that had been elected in the '94 elections realized that they were in danger of facing the electorate without having enacted a single item from the Contract [with America] into law."[69] Speaker Gingrich agreed to drop a few of the most objectionable elements from the bill; Senate majority leader Trent Lott, similarly motivated, agreed; and both chambers passed the welfare reform act (formally the Personal Responsibility and Work Opportunity Act) in August. Overruling objections from liberals in his administration and party, Clinton signed it. The desire of both the Democratic president and the Republican Congress to create a record on which to run in 1996 also facilitated the passage of bills to increase the minimum wage, make health insurance portable for people changing jobs, and grant the president a line-item veto.

After succeeding in their bids for reelection in 1996, Clinton and Congress returned once again to the issue of the budget deficits that had animated fiscal policy making for nearly a decade. The accumulated deficits from fiscal years 1970 to 1997 had raised the national debt by 1400 percent, from $381 billion to $5.369 trillion. Massive tax cuts, steep defense spending increases, and soaring entitlement outlays all contributed to the persistence of large deficits in good times and bad. In an influential article, political scientist Mathew D. McCubbins traced a causal link between divided government and increasing deficits.[70] Six years later, journalists George Hager and Eric Pianin argued that partisan warfare made politicians' oft-repeated promise to balance the budget a "mirage" in a book of that title.[71] Gary Jacobson concluded that divided government offered voters the budget-busting benefits they wanted more than a balanced budget: lower taxes from whichever branch of government the Republicans controlled and generous middle-class entitlements and other popular domestic programs from the branch controlled by the Democrats.[72]

Nonetheless, in 1997 the Republican Congress passed and the Democratic president signed the Balanced Budget Act. Of critical importance, observed National Economic Council director Gene Sperling, both parties "decided to reach an agreement that would pass with support from a majority of both parties. This meant being willing to acknowledge each other's priorities. We didn't want a capital gains tax cut, but that was very important to them. They'd sworn they'd never approve a new entitlement program, but that's what SCHIP [State Children's Health Insurance Program] was."[73] Aided by a booming economy, surpluses accumulated totaling $569 billion in fiscal years 1998–2002, the first time since the 1920s that the federal government ran a surplus for four consecutive years.

This two-year record of accomplishment, spanning two Congresses and two presidential terms, demonstrated that divided government need not mean legislative stalemate, even in the modern era. Discouragingly, neither of Clinton's successors who approached reelection with an opposition-controlled House—Obama in 2012 and Trump in 2020—attempted as he did to refocus his legislative priorities on overlapping areas of their political agendas. Trump, for example, placed rebuilding the nation's infrastructure of roads, bridges, tunnels, waterworks, airports, and train tracks—a goal he claimed to share with congressional Democrats—on the back burner while emphasizing the highly divisive issue of building a wall on the nation's southern border.

Yet even Clinton's successful efforts to work fruitfully across party lines did not last. The parties already were becoming more ideologically polarized by the 1990s. In addition, Democrats and Republicans were ambitious to retake the other's branch, with Democrats not content to concede Congress and the Republicans unwilling to forfeit the presidency. What hastened the breakdown of cooperation in the immediate aftermath of the welfare reform and balanced budget acts was the revelation in January 1998 that Clinton had been having an affair with White House intern Monica Lewinsky. The ensuing scandal handed the Republicans a political weapon they could not resist using to impeach the president. Clinton survived and even maintained his popularity with the voters. His party gained seats in the midterm election, the first time this had happened in the sixth year of a president's tenure since 1834, when Andrew Jackson was midway through his second term. But legislative stalemate marked Clinton's final two years in office. A similar pattern had marked the first two years of Reagan's second term, when the Republican president and Senate and the Democratic House enacted major legislation concerning tax reform, immigration reform, and budget balancing, only to succumb to stalemate after the Democrats pursued new revelations about what came to be called the Iran-Contra scandal.

In sum, de facto divided government in the aftermath of Republicans' newfound control of Congress and Democrats' gaining of the presidency emerged in the 1990s in no settled form. Confrontation from 1993 to 1995 yielded to cooperation in 1996 and 1997 only to revert to confrontation in 1998. Arguably, each swing from one extreme to the other in the relationship can be explained with reference to the distinctive challenges posed by divided government: the hostile years in terms of heightened political and policy antagonism between the parties and the cooperative years in terms of their shared desire to show voters that they could govern despite their differences. Since Clinton's presidency, the hostility has only continued to grow. Whether cooperation can sometimes overcome it is an open question.

APPENDIX A

1992 REPUBLICAN PRIMARY RESULTS (%)

Date	State	George Bush	Pat Buchanan	Uncommitted	Others
Feb. 18	New Hampshire	53.2	37.5		0.5
Feb. 25	South Dakota	69.3		30.7	
Mar. 3	Colorado	67.5	30.0		
	Georgia	64.3	35.7		
	Maryland	70.2	29.9		
Mar. 7	South Carolina	66.9	25.7		7.1
Mar. 10	Florida	68.1	31.9		
	Louisiana	62.0	27.0		9.7
	Massachusetts	65.6	27.7	3.8	2.1
	Mississippi	72.3	16.7		10.6
	Oklahoma	69.6	26.6		2.6
	Rhode Island	63.0	31.8	2.8	2.1
	Tennessee	72.6	22.2	2.0	3.1
	Texas	69.8	23.9	3.5	2.5
Mar. 17	Illinois	76.4	22.5		1.2
	Michigan	67.2	25.0	5.3	2.4
	Connecticut	66.7	21.9	9.1	2.3
Apr. 7	Kansas	62.0	14.8	16.6	4.2
	Minnesota	63.9	24.2	3.1	5.8
	Wisconsin	75.6	16.3	1.8	3.5
Apr. 28	Pennsylvania	76.7	23.2		0.1
May 5	Washington, DC	81.5	18.5		
	Indiana	80.1	19.9		
	North Carolina	70.7	19.5	9.8	
May 10	Montana	71.6	11.8	16.6	
May 12	Nebraska	81.4	13.5		1.5
	West Virginia	80.5	14.6		4.9
May 19	Washington	67.0	10.2		20.8
	Oregon	67.1	19.0		2.2
May 26	Idaho	63.5	13.1	23.4	
	Kentucky .	74.5		25.5	
May 27	Arkansas	83.1	11.9	5.0	
June 2	Alabama	74.3	7.6	18.1	
	California	73.6	26.4		
	Ohio	83.3	16.7		
	New Jersey	77.5	15.0		7.5
	New Mexico	63.8	9.1	27.1	

1992 DEMOCRATIC PRIMARY AND CAUCUS RESULTS (%)

Date	State	Bill Clinton	Jerry Brown	Paul Tsongas	Bob Kerrey	Tom Harkin	Uncommitted	Others
Feb. 10	Iowa (caucuses)	2.8	1.6	4.1	2.4	76.6	11.9	
Feb. 18	New Hampshire	24.8	8.2	33.2	11.1	10.2		2.1
Feb. 23	Maine (caucuses)	15.1	30.8	29.3	3.0	5.0	16.7	0.9
Feb. 25	South Dakota	19.1	3.9	9.6	40.1	25.2		1.1
Mar. 3	Colorado	26.9	28.8	25.6	12.3	2.5	2.2	1.1
	Georgia	57.2	8.1	24.0	4.9	2.1	3.8	
	Idaho (caucuses)	11.6	4.6	28.8		29.6	17.5	
	Maryland	35.8	8.8	43.4	5.1	6.2		0.8
	Minnesota (caucuses)			19.2		26.7		
Mar. 7	Utah (caucuses)	18.2	28.4	33.8	10.6	4.0	2.3	0.7
	Washington (caucuses)	13.8	19.3	32.0	6.1	7.5	20.4	0.8
	Arizona (caucuses)	29.2	27.5	34.4		7.6	1.3	
	South Carolina	62.9	6.0	18.3	0.5	6.6	3.1	
	Wyoming (caucuses)	28.6	23.1	11.7		14.3	22.3	0.9
Mar. 8	Nevada (caucuses)	26.5	34.8	19.7	1.0	0.5	17.6	
Mar. 10	Florida	50.8	12.2	34.8	1.1	1.2		
	Hawaii (caucuses)	51.5	13.6	14.3	0.4	12.7	7.5	
	Louisiana	69.5	6.6	11.1	0.8	1.1		8.0
	Massachusetts	11.0	14.6	66.4	0.7	0.5	1.5	0.9
	Mississippi	73.1	9.6	8.1	0.9	1.3	6.2	0.7
	Missouri	45.1	5.7	10.2			39.0	
	Oklahoma	70.5	16.7		3.2	3.4		5.6
	Texas	65.6	8.0	19.2	1.4	1.3		2.9
Mar. 17	Illinois	51.7	14.7	25.8	0.7	2.0	4.5	0.7
	Michigan	50.7	16.6	25.8	0.6	1.1	4.8	0.4
	North Dakota (caucuses)	37.0	7.7	10.5	1.2	7.0	26.5	

Date	State							
Mar. 24	Connecticut	35.6	37.2	19.5	0.7	1.1	3.1	2.7
Mar. 31	Vermont	17.2	47.4	9.7			25.7	
Apr. 2	Alaska (caucuses)	30.9	33.1	1.3			34.7	
Apr. 7	Kansas	51.3	13.0	15.2	1.4	0.6	13.8	1.2
	Minnesota	31.1	30.6	21.4	0.6	2.0	5.6	3.1
	New York	40.9	26.2	28.6	1.1	1.2		2.0
	Wisconsin	37.2	34.5	21.8	0.4	0.7	2.0	1.7
Apr. 11	Virginia (caucuses)	52.0	12.0				36.0	
Apr. 28	Pennsylvania	56.5	25.7	12.8	1.6	1.7		1.7
May 5	Delaware (caucuses)	20.8	19.5	30.2			29.6	
	Indiana	63.3	21.5	12.2	3.0			
	North Carolina	54.1	10.4	8.3	0.9	0.9	15.4	
	Washington, DC	73.9	7.2	10.4			8.5	
May 12	Nebraska	45.5	21.0	7.1		2.8	16.4	2.3
	West Virginia	74.2	11.9	6.9	1.0	0.9		1.5
May 19	Oregon	45.1	31.2	10.5				3.8
	Washington	42.0	23.1	12.8	1.0	1.3		0.7
May 26	Idaho	49.0	16.7				29.1	5.2
	Kentucky	56.1	8.3	4.9	0.9	1.9	28.0	
May 27	Arkansas	68.1	11.0				18.0	2.9
June 2	Alabama	68.2	6.7				20.2	4.8
	California	47.5	40.2	7.4	1.2			3.8
	Montana	46.8	18.5	10.7			24.0	
	New Jersey	63.3	19.8	11.2				1.9
	New Mexico	52.9	16.9	6.2		1.8	19.4	2.8
	Ohio	61.2	18.9	10.6	2.4			1.7

1992 GENERAL ELECTION RESULTS

	Popular Vote								Electoral Vote	
	Bill Clinton		George Bush		Ross Perot		Others*		Bill Clinton	George Bush
State	Votes	%	Votes	%	Votes	%	Votes	%	Votes	Votes
Alabama	690,080	40.9	804,283	47.7	183,109	10.9	10,588	0.6	0	9
Alaska	78,294	30.3	102,000	39.5	73,481	28.4	4,731	1.8	0	3
Arizona	543,050	36.5	572,086	38.5	353,741	23.8	18,129	1.2	0	8
Arkansas	505,823	53.2	337,324	35.5	99,132	10.4	8,374	0.9	6	0
California	5,121,325	46.0	3,630,574	32.6	2,296,006	20.6	83,816	0.8	54	0
Colorado	629,681	40.1	562,850	35.9	366,010	23.3	10,639	0.7	8	0
Connecticut	682,318	42.2	578,313	35.8	348,771	21.6	6,930	0.4	8	0
Delaware	126,054	43.5	102,313	35.8	59,213	20.5	2,040	0.7	3	0
District of Columbia	192,619	84.6	20,698	9.1	9,681	4.3	4,574	2.0	3	0
Florida	2,072,698	39.0	2,173,310	40.9	1,053,067	19.8	15317	0.3	0	25
Georgia	1,008,966	43.5	995,252	42.9	309,657	13.3	7258	0.3	13	0
Hawaii	179,310	48.1	136,822	36.7	53,003	14.2	3,707	1.0	4	0
Idaho	137,013	28.4	202,645	42.0	130,395	27.1	12,061	2.5	0	4
Illinois	2,453,350	48.6	1,734,096	34.3	840,515	16.6	22,196	0.4	22	0
Indiana	848,420	36.8	989,375	42.9	455,934	19.8	12,142	0.5	0	12
Iowa	586,353	43.3	504,891	37.3	253,468	18.7	9,895	0.7	7	0
Kansas	390,434	33.7	449,951	38.9	312,358	27.0	4,513	0.4	0	6
Kentucky	665,104	44.6	617,178	41.3	203,944	13.7	6,674	0.4	8	0
Louisiana	815,971	45.6	733,386	41.0	211,478	11.8	29,182	1.6	9	0
Maine	263,420	38.8	206,504	30.4	206,820	30.4	2,755	0.4	4	0
Maryland	988,571	49.8	707,094	35.6	281,414	14.2	7,967	0.4	10	0
Massachusetts	1,318,662	47.5	805,049	29.0	632,312	22.8	17,551	0.6	12	0
Michigan	1,871,182	43.8	1,554,940	36.4	824,813	19.3	23,738	0.6	18	0
Minnesota	1,020,997	43.5	747,841	31.9	562,506	24.0	16,604	0.7	10	0

Mississippi	400,258	40.8	487,793	49.7	85,626	8.7	8,116	0.8	0	7
Missouri	1,053,873	44.1	811,159	33.9	518,741	21.7	7,497	0.3	11	0
Montana	154,507	37.6	144,207	35.1	107,225	26.1	4,644	1.1	3	0
Nebraska	217,344	29.4	344,346	46.6	174,687	23.6	2,906	0.4	0	5
Nevada	189,148	37.4	175,828	34.7	132,580	26.2	8,762	1.7	4	0
New Hampshire	209,040	38.9	202,484	37.7	121,337	22.6	4,354	0.8	4	0
New Jersey	1,436,206	43.0	1,356,865	40.6	521,829	15.6	28,694	0.9	15	0
New Mexico	261,617	45.9	212,824	37.3	91,895	16.1	3,650	0.6	5	0
New York	3,444,450	49.7	2,346,649	33.9	1,090,721	15.8	45,105	0.7	33	0
North Carolina	1,114,042	42.7	1,134,661	43.4	357,864	13.7	5,283	0.2	0	14
North Dakota	99,168	32.2	136,244	44.2	71,084	23.1	1,637	0.5	0	3
Ohio	1,984,942	40.2	1,894,310	38.4	1,036,426	21.0	24,286	0.5	21	0
Oklahoma	473,066	34.0	592,929	42.7	319,878	23.0	4,486	0.3	0	8
Oregon	621,314	42.5	475,757	32.5	354,091	24.2	11,481	0.8	7	0
Pennsylvania	2,239,164	45.2	1,791,841	36.1	902,667	18.2	26,138	0.5	23	0
Rhode Island	213,299	47.0	131,601	29.0	105,045	23.2	3,532	0.8	4	0
South Carolina	479,514	39.9	577,507	48.0	138,872	11.6	6,634	0.6	0	8
South Dakota	124,888	37.1	136,718	40.7	73,295	21.8	1,353	0.4	0	3
Tennessee	933,521	47.1	841,300	42.4	199,968	10.1	7,849	0.4	11	0
Texas	2,281,815	37.1	2,496,071	40.6	1,354,781	22.0	21,351	0.3	0	32
Utah	183,429	24.7	322,632	43.4	203,400	27.3	34,537	4.6	0	5
Vermont	133,592	46.1	88,122	30.4	65,991	22.8	1,996	0.7	3	0
Virginia	1,038,650	40.6	1,150,517	45.0	348,639	13.6	20,859	0.8	0	13
Washington	993,037	43.4	731,234	32.0	541,780	23.7	21,514	0.9	11	0
West Virginia	331,001	48.4	241,974	35.4	108,829	15.9	1,873	0.3	5	0
Wisconsin	1,041,066	41.1	930,855	36.8	544,479	21.5	14,714	0.6	11	0
Wyoming	68,160	34.1	79,347	39.7	51,263	25.7	1,114	0.6	0	3
TOTALS:	44,909,806	43.01	39,104,550	37.45	19,743,821	18.91	665,746	0.64	370	168

*James "Bo" Gritz (Populist): 107,014; Leonara B. Fulani (New Alliance): 73,714; Howard Phillips (US Taxpayer): 43,434; John Hagelin (Natural Law): 39,174; Ron Daniels (Peace and Freedom): 27,961; Lyndon H. LaRouche Jr. (Economic Recovery): 26,333; James Warren (Socialist Workers): 23,096; Drew Bradford (Independent): 4,749; Jack E. Herer (Grassroots): 3,875; J. Quinn Brisben (Socialist): 3,057; Helen Halyard (Workers League): 3,050; John Yiamouylannas (Take Back America): 2,199; Delbert L. Ehlers (Independent): 1,149; Earl F. Dodge (Prohibition): 961; Jim Boren (Apathy): 956; Eugene A. Hem (Third): 405; Isabell Masters (Looking Back): 339; Robert J. Smith (American): 292; Gloria La Riva (Workers World): 181; scattered write-ins: 16,578.

1996 REPUBLICAN PRIMARY AND CAUCUS RESULTS (%)

Date	State	Bob Dole	Pat Buchanan	Steve Forbes	Lamar Alexander	Phil Gramm	Others
Jan. 29	Alaska (caucuses)	17	32	31	1	9	10
Feb. 6	Louisiana (caucuses)		44			42	4
Feb. 12	Iowa (caucuses)	26	23	10	18	9	12
Feb. 20	New Hampshire	26	27	12	22		9
Feb. 24	Delaware	27	19	33	13	2	10
Feb. 27	Arizona	30	27	33	7		2
	North Dakota	42	18	20	6	9	4
	South Dakota	45	29	13	9		4
Mar. 2	South Carolina	45	29	13	10		2
	Wyoming (caucuses)	40	18	17	7		7
Mar. 5	Colorado	43	21	21	10		5
	Connecticut	54	15	20	5		3
	Georgia	41	29	13	14		3
	Maine	46	24	15	7		5
	Maryland	53	21	13	6		6
	Massachusetts	48	25	14	8		4
	Minnesota (caucuses)	41	33	10	5		10
	Rhode Island	64	3	1	19		4
	Vermont	40	17	16	11	1	14
Mar. 7	New York	55	15	30			
Mar. 9	Missouri (caucuses)	28	36	1			9
Mar. 12	Florida	57	18	20	1		5
	Louisiana	48	33	12	2		4
	Mississippi	60	26	8	2		4
	Oklahoma	59	22	14	1		2
	Oregon	51	21	13	7		5
	Tennessee	51	25	8	11		3
	Texas	56	21	13	2	2	4
Mar. 19	Illinois	65	23	5	1	1	5
	Michigan	51	34	5	1		3
	Ohio	66	22	6	3		3
	Wisconsin	53	34	6	2		3
Mar. 26	California	66	18	7	2	1	6
	Nevada	52	15	19	2		1
	Washington	63	21	9	1		5
Apr. 23	Pennsylvania	64	18	8			11

Date	State	Bob Dole	Pat Buchanan	Steve Forbes	Lamar Alexander	Phil Gramm	Others
May 7	Washington, DC	75	9				
	Indiana	71	19	10			
	North Carolina	71	13	4	2		5
May 14	Nebraska	76	10	6	3		3
	West Virginia	69	16	5	3	2	5
May 21	Arkansas	76	23				
May 28	Idaho	66	22				5
	Kentucky	48	33	13	2		4
June 1	Virginia (caucuses)						
June 4	Alabama	76	16				3
	Montana	61	24	7			
	New Jersey	82	11				7
	New Mexico	76	8	6	4		4

| | Popular Vote | | | | | | | | Electoral Vote | |
| | Bill Clinton | | Bob Dole | | Ross Perot | | Other* | | Bill Clinton | Bob Dole |
State	Votes	%	Votes	%	Votes	%	Votes	%	Votes	Votes
Alabama	662,165	43.2	769,044	50.1	92,149	6.0	10,991	0.7	0	9
Alaska	80,380	33.3	122,746	50.8	26,333	10.9	12,161	5.0	0	3
Arizona	653,288	46.5	622,073	44.3	112,072	8.0	16,972	1.2	8	0
Arkansas	475,171	53.7	325,416	36.8	69,884	7.9	13,791	1.6	6	0
California	5,119,835	51.1	3,828,380	38.2	697,847	7.0	373,422	3.7	54	0
Colorado	671,152	44.4	691,848	45.8	99,629	6.6	48,075	3.2	0	8
Connecticut	735,740	52.8	483,109	34.7	139,523	10.0	34,242	2.5	8	0
Delaware	140,355	51.8	99,062	36.6	28,719	10.6	2,709	1.0	3	0
District of Columbia	158,220	85.2	17,339	9.3	3,611	1.9	6,556	3.5	3	0
Florida	2,546,870	48.0	2,244,536	42.3	483,870	9.1	28,518	0.5	25	0
Georgia	1,053,849	45.8	1,080,843	47.0	146,337	6.4	18,042	0.8	0	13
Hawaii	205,012	56.9	113,943	31.6	27,358	7.6	13,807	3.8	4	0
Idaho	165,443	33.7	256,595	52.2	62,518	12.7	7,163	1.5	0	4
Illinois	2,341,744	54.3	1,587,021	36.8	346,408	8.0	36,218	0.8	22	0
Indiana	887,424	41.6	1,006,693	47.1	224,299	10.5	17,426	0.8	0	12
Iowa	620,258	50.3	492,644	39.9	105,159	8.5	16,014	1.3	7	0
Kansas	387,659	36.1	583,245	54.3	92,639	8.6	10,757	1.0	0	6
Kentucky	636,614	45.8	623,283	44.9	120,396	8.7	8,415	0.6	8	0
Louisiana	927,837	52.0	712,586	39.9	123,293	6.9	20,243	1.1	9	0
Maine	312,788	51.6	186,378	30.8	85,970	14.2	20,761	3.4	4	0
Maryland	966,207	54.3	681,530	38.3	115,812	6.5	17,321	1.0	10	0
Massachusetts	1,571,763	61.5	718,107	28.1	227,217	8.9	39,698	1.6	12	0
Michigan	1,989,653	51.7	1,481,212	38.5	336,670	8.8	41,309	1.1	18	0
Minnesota	1,120,438	51.1	766,476	35.0	257,704	11.8	48,022	2.2	10	0

Mississippi	394,022	44.1	439,838	49.2	52,222	5.8	7,775	0.9	0	7
Missouri	1,025,935	47.5	890,016	41.2	217,188	10.1	24,926	1.2	11	0
Montana	167,922	41.2	179,652	44.1	55,229	13.6	4,458	1.1	0	3
Nebraska	236,761	35.0	363,467	53.7	71,278	10.5	5,909	0.9	0	5
Nevada	203,974	43.9	199,244	42.9	43,986	9.5	17,075	3.7	4	0
New Hampshire	246,214	49.3	196,532	39.4	48,390	9.7	8,039	1.6	4	0
New Jersey	1,652,329	53.7	1,103,078	35.9	262,134	8.5	58,266	1.9	15	0
New Mexico	273,495	49.2	232,751	41.9	32,257	5.8	17,571	3.2	5	0
New York	3,756,177	59.5	1,933,492	30.6	503,458	8.0	123,002	1.9	33	0
North Carolina	1,107,849	44.0	1,225,938	48.7	168,059	6.7	13,961	0.6	0	14
North Dakota	106,905	40.1	125,050	46.9	32,515	12.2	1,941	0.7	0	3
Ohio	2,148,222	47.4	1,859,883	41.0	483,207	10.7	43,122	1.0	21	0
Oklahoma	488,105	40.5	582,315	48.3	130,788	10.8	5,505	0.5	0	8
Oregon	649,641	47.2	538,152	39.1	121,221	8.8	68,746	5.0	7	0
Pennsylvania	2,215,819	49.2	1,801,169	40.0	430,984	9.6	58,146	1.3	23	0
Rhode Island	233,050	59.7	104,683	26.8	43,723	11.2	8,828	2.3	4	0
South Carolina	504,051	43.9	573,458	49.9	64,386	5.6	7,562	0.7	0	8
South Dakota	139,333	43.0	150,543	46.5	31,250	9.7	2,700	0.8	0	3
Tennessee	909,146	48.0	863,530	45.6	105,918	5.6	15,511	0.8	11	0
Texas	2,459,683	43.8	2,736,167	48.8	378,537	6.8	37,257	0.7	0	32
Utah	221,633	33.3	361,911	54.4	66,461	10.0	15,624	2.3	0	5
Vermont	137,894	53.4	80,352	31.1	31,024	12.0	9,179	3.6	3	0
Virginia	1,091,060	45.2	1,138,350	47.1	159,861	6.6	27,371	1.1	0	13
Washington	1,123,323	49.8	840,712	37.3	201,003	8.9	88,799	4.0	11	0
West Virginia	327,812	51.5	233,946	36.8	71,639	11.3	3,062	0.5	5	0
Wisconsin	1,071,971	48.8	845,029	38.5	227,339	10.4	51,830	2.4	11	0
Wyoming	77,934	36.8	105,388	49.8	25,928	12.3	2,321	1.1	0	3
TOTALS:	47,400,125	49.2	39,198,755	40.7	8,085,402	8.4	1,591,119	1.7	379	159

*Harry Brown (Libertarian): 485,789; Howard Phillips (US Taxpayers): 184,658; John Hagelin (Natural Law): 113,668; Monica Moorehead (Workers World): 29,083; Marsha Feinland (Peace and Freedom): 25,332; Charles E. Collins (Independent): 8,941; James E. Harris (Socialist Workers): 8,476; "None of These Candidates": 5,608; Dennis Peron (Grassroots): 5,378; Mary Cal Hollis (Socialist): 4,765; Jerome White (Socialist Equality): 2,438; Diane Beall Templin (American): 1,847; Earl F. Dodge (Prohibition): 1,298; A. Peter Crane (Independent Party of Utah): 1,101; Ralph Forbes (America First): 932; John Birrenbach (Independent Grassroots): 787; Isabell Masters (Looking Back): 752; Steve Michael (Independent): 408; scattered write-ins: 24,537.

BILL CLINTON'S FIRST INAUGURAL ADDRESS, JANUARY 20, 1993

My fellow citizens:

Today we celebrate the mystery of American renewal.

This ceremony is held in the depth of winter. But, by the words we speak and the faces we show the world, we force the spring. A spring reborn in the world's oldest democracy, that brings forth the vision and courage to reinvent America.

When our Founders boldly declared America's independence to the world and our purposes to the Almighty, they knew that America, to endure, would have to change. Not change for change's sake, but change to preserve America's ideals; life, liberty, the pursuit of happiness. Though we march to the music of our time, our mission is timeless. Each generation of Americans must define what it means to be an American.

On behalf of our nation, I salute my predecessor, President Bush, for his half-century of service to America. And I thank the millions of men and women whose steadfastness and sacrifice triumphed over Depression, fascism and Communism.

Today, a generation raised in the shadows of the Cold War assumes new responsibilities in a world warmed by the sunshine of freedom but threatened still by ancient hatreds and new plagues.

Raised in unrivaled prosperity, we inherit an economy that is still the world's strongest, but is weakened by business failures, stagnant wages, increasing inequality, and deep divisions among our people.

When George Washington first took the oath I have just sworn to uphold, news traveled slowly across the land by horseback and across the ocean by boat. Now, the sights and sounds of this ceremony are broadcast instantaneously to billions around the world.

Communications and commerce are global; investment is mobile; technology is almost magical; and ambition for a better life is now universal. We earn our livelihood in peaceful competition with people all across the earth.

Profound and powerful forces are shaking and remaking our world, and the urgent question of our time is whether we can make change our friend and not our enemy.

This new world has already enriched the lives of millions of Americans who are able to compete and win in it. But when most people are working harder for less; when others cannot work at all; when the cost of health care devastates families and threatens to bankrupt many of our enterprises, great and small; when fear of crime robs law-abiding citizens of their freedom; and when millions of poor children cannot even imagine the lives we are calling them to lead, we have not made change our friend.

We know we have to face hard truths and take strong steps. But we have not done so. Instead, we have drifted, and that drifting has eroded our resources, fractured our economy, and shaken our confidence.

Though our challenges are fearsome, so are our strengths. And Americans have ever been a restless, questing, hopeful people. We must bring to our task today the vision and will of those who came before us.

From our revolution, the Civil War, to the Great Depression to the civil rights movement, our people have always mustered the determination to construct from these crises the pillars of our history.

Thomas Jefferson believed that to preserve the very foundations of our nation, we would need dramatic change from time to time. Well, my fellow citizens, this is our time. Let us embrace it.

Our democracy must be not only the envy of the world but the engine of our own renewal. There is nothing wrong with America that cannot be cured by what is right with America.

And so today, we pledge an end to the era of deadlock and drift; a new season of American renewal has begun. To renew America, we must be bold. We must do what no generation has had to do before. We must invest more in our own people, in their jobs, in their future, and at the same time cut our massive debt. And we must do so in a world in which we must compete for every opportunity. It will not be easy; it will require sacrifice. But it can be done, and done fairly, not choosing sacrifice for its own sake, but for our own sake. We must provide for our nation the way a family provides for its children.

Our Founders saw themselves in the light of posterity. We can do no less. Anyone who has ever watched a child's eyes wander into sleep knows what posterity is. Posterity is the world to come; the world for whom we hold our ideals, from whom we have borrowed our planet, and to whom we bear sacred responsibility. We must do what America does best: offer more opportunity to all and demand responsibility from all.

It is time to break the bad habit of expecting something for nothing, from our government or from each other. Let us all take more responsibility, not only for ourselves and our families but for our communities and our country. To renew America, we must revitalize our democracy.

This beautiful capital, like every capital since the dawn of civilization, is often a place of intrigue and calculation. Powerful people maneuver for position and worry endlessly about who is in and who is out, who is up and who is down, forgetting those people whose toil and sweat sends us here and pays our way.

Americans deserve better, and in this city today, there are people who want to do better. And so I say to all of us here, let us resolve to reform our politics, so that power and privilege no longer shout down the voice of the people. Let us put aside personal advantage so that we can feel the pain and see the promise of America. Let us resolve to make our government a place for what Franklin Roosevelt called "bold, persistent experimentation," a government for our tomorrows, not our yesterdays. Let us give this capital back to the people to whom it belongs.

To renew America, we must meet challenges abroad as well at home. There is no longer division between what is foreign and what is domestic; the world economy, the world environment, the world AIDS crisis, the world arms race; they affect us all.

Today, as an old order passes, the new world is more free but less stable. Communism's collapse has called forth old animosities and new dangers. Clearly America must continue to lead the world we did so much to make.

While America rebuilds at home, we will not shrink from the challenges, nor fail to seize the opportunities, of this new world. Together with our friends and allies, we will work to shape change, lest it engulf us.

When our vital interests are challenged, or the will and conscience of the international community is defied, we will act; with peaceful diplomacy whenever possible, with force when necessary. The brave Americans serving our nation today in the Persian Gulf, in Somalia, and wherever else they stand are testament to our resolve.

But our greatest strength is the power of our ideas, which are still new in many lands. Across the world, we see them embraced, and we rejoice. Our hopes, our hearts, our hands, are with those on every continent who are building democracy and freedom. Their cause is America's cause.

The American people have summoned the change we celebrate today. You have raised your voices in an unmistakable chorus. You have cast your votes in historic numbers. And you have changed the face of Congress, the presidency and the political process itself. Yes, you, my fellow Americans have forced the spring. Now, we must do the work the season demands.

To that work I now turn, with all the authority of my office. I ask the Congress to join with me. But no president, no Congress, no government, can undertake this mission alone. My fellow Americans, you, too, must play your part in our renewal. I challenge a new generation of young Americans to a season of service; to act on your idealism by helping troubled children, keeping company with those in need, reconnecting our torn communities. There is so much to be done; enough indeed for millions of others who are still young in spirit to give of themselves in service, too.

In serving, we recognize a simple but powerful truth: we need each other. And we must care for one another. Today, we do more than celebrate America; we rededicate ourselves to the very idea of America.

An idea born in revolution and renewed through two centuries of challenge. An idea tempered by the knowledge that, but for fate we, the fortunate and the unfortunate, might have been each other. An idea ennobled by the faith that our nation can summon from its myriad diversity the deepest measure of unity. An idea infused with the conviction that America's long heroic journey must go forever upward.

And so, my fellow Americans, at the edge of the 21st century, let us begin with energy and hope, with faith and discipline, and let us work until our work is done. The scripture says, "And let us not be weary in well-doing, for in due season, we shall reap, if we faint not."

From this joyful mountaintop of celebration, we hear a call to service in the valley. We have heard the trumpets. We have changed the guard. And now, each in our way, and with God's help, we must answer the call.

Thank you, and God bless you all.

BILL CLINTON'S SECOND INAUGURAL ADDRESS, JANUARY 20, 1997

My fellow citizens:

At this last presidential inauguration of the 20th century, let us lift our eyes toward the challenges that await us in the next century. It is our great good fortune that time and chance have put us not only at the edge of a new century, in a new millennium, but on the edge of a bright new prospect in human affairs, a moment that will define our course, and our character, for decades to come. We must keep our old democracy forever young. Guided by the ancient vision of a promised land, let us set our sights upon a land of new promise.

The promise of America was born in the 18th century out of the bold conviction that we are all created equal. It was extended and preserved in the 19th century, when our nation spread across the continent, saved the union, and abolished the awful scourge of slavery.

Then, in turmoil and triumph, that promise exploded onto the world stage to make this the American Century.

And what a century it has been. America became the world's mightiest industrial power; saved the world from tyranny in two world wars and a long cold war; and time and again, reached out across the globe to millions who, like us, longed for the blessings of liberty.

Along the way, Americans produced a great middle class and security in old age; built unrivaled centers of learning and opened public schools to all; split the atom and explored the heavens; invented the computer and the microchip; and deepened the wellspring of justice by making a revolution in civil rights for African Americans and all minorities, and extending the circle of citizenship, opportunity and dignity to women.

Now, for the third time, a new century is upon us, and another time to choose. We began the 19th century with a choice, to spread our nation from coast to coast. We began the 20th century with a choice, to harness the Industrial Revolution to our values of free enterprise, conservation, and human decency. Those choices made all the difference.

At the dawn of the 21st century a free people must now choose to shape the forces of the Information Age and the global society, to unleash the limitless potential of all our people, and, yes, to form a more perfect union.

When last we gathered, our march to this new future seemed less certain than it does today. We vowed then to set a clear course to renew our nation.

In these four years, we have been touched by tragedy, exhilarated by challenge, strengthened by achievement. America stands alone as the world's indispensable nation. Once again, our economy is the strongest on Earth. Once again, we are building stronger families, thriving communities, better educational opportunities, a cleaner environment. Problems that once seemed destined to deepen now bend to our efforts: our streets are safer and record numbers of our fellow citizens have moved from welfare to work.

And once again, we have resolved for our time a great debate over the role of government. Today we can declare: Government is not the problem, and government is not the solution. We, the American people, we are the solution. Our founders understood that well and gave us a democracy strong enough to endure for centuries, flexible enough to face our common challenges and advance our common dreams in each new day.

As times change, so government must change. We need a new government for a new century—humble enough not to try to solve all our problems for us, but strong enough to give us the tools to solve our problems for ourselves; a government that is smaller, lives within its means, and does more with less. Yet where it can stand up for our values and interests in the world, and where it can give Americans the power to make a real difference in their everyday lives, government should do more, not less. The preeminent mission of our new government is to give all Americans an opportunity, not a guarantee, but a real opportunity to build better lives.

Beyond that, my fellow citizens, the future is up to us. Our founders taught us that the preservation of our liberty and our union depends upon responsible citizenship. And we need a new sense of responsibility for a new century. There is work to do, work that government alone cannot do: teaching children to read; hiring people off welfare rolls; coming out from behind locked doors and shuttered windows to help reclaim our streets from drugs and gangs and crime; taking time out of our own lives to serve others.

Each and every one of us, in our own way, must assume personal responsibility, not only for ourselves and our families, but for our neighbors and our nation. Our greatest responsibility is to embrace a new spirit of community for a new century. For any one of us to succeed, we must succeed as one America.

The challenge of our past remains the challenge of our future, will we be one nation, one people, with one common destiny, or not? Will we all come together, or come apart?

The divide of race has been America's constant curse. And each new wave of immigrants gives new targets to old prejudices. Prejudice and contempt, cloaked in the pretense of religious or political conviction are no different. These forces have nearly destroyed our nation in the past. They plague us still. They fuel the fanaticism of terror. And they torment the lives of millions in fractured nations all around the world.

These obsessions cripple both those who hate and, of course, those who are hated, robbing both of what they might become. We cannot, we will not, succumb to the dark impulses that lurk in the far regions of the soul everywhere. We shall overcome them. And we shall replace them with the generous spirit of a people who feel at home with one another.

Our rich texture of racial, religious and political diversity will be a Godsend in the 21st century. Great rewards will come to those who can live together, learn together, work together, forge new ties that bind together.

As this new era approaches we can already see its broad outlines. Ten years ago, the Internet was the mystical province of physicists; today, it is a commonplace encyclopedia for millions of schoolchildren. Scientists now are decoding the blueprint of human life. Cures for our most feared illnesses seem close at hand.

The world is no longer divided into two hostile camps. Instead, now we are building bonds with nations that once were our adversaries. Growing connections of commerce and culture give us a chance to lift the fortunes and spirits of people the world over. And for the very first time in all of history, more people on this planet live under democracy than dictatorship.

My fellow Americans, as we look back at this remarkable century, we may ask, can we hope not just to follow, but even to surpass the achievements of the 20th century in America and to avoid the awful bloodshed that stained its legacy? To that question, every American here and every American in our land today must answer a resounding "Yes."

This is the heart of our task. With a new vision of government, a new sense of responsibility, a new spirit of community, we will sustain America's journey. The promise we sought in a new land we will find again in a land of new promise.

In this new land, education will be every citizen's most prized possession. Our schools will have the highest standards in the world, igniting the spark of possibility in the eyes of every girl and every boy. And the doors of higher education will be open to all. The knowledge and power of the Information Age will be within reach not just of the few, but of every classroom, every library, every child. Parents and children will have time not only to work, but to read and play together. And the plans they make at their kitchen table will be those of a better home, a better job, the certain chance to go to college.

Our streets will echo again with the laughter of our children, because no one will try to shoot them or sell them drugs anymore. Everyone who can work, will work, with today's permanent underclass part of tomorrow's growing middle class. New miracles of medicine at last will reach not only those who can claim care now, but the children and hardworking families too long denied.

We will stand mighty for peace and freedom, and maintain a strong defense against terror and destruction. Our children will sleep free from the threat of nuclear, chemical or biological weapons. Ports and airports, farms and factories will thrive with trade and innovation and ideas. And the world's greatest democracy will lead a whole world of democracies.

Our land of new promise will be a nation that meets its obligations, a nation that balances its budget, but never loses the balance of its values. A nation where our grandparents have secure retirement and health care, and their grandchildren know we have made the reforms necessary to sustain those benefits for their time. A nation that fortifies the world's most productive economy even as it protects the great natural bounty of our water, air, and majestic land.

And in this land of new promise, we will have reformed our politics so that the voice of the people will always speak louder than the din of narrow interests, regaining the participation and deserving the trust of all Americans.

Fellow citizens, let us build that America, a nation ever moving forward toward realizing the full potential of all its citizens. Prosperity and power, yes, they are important, and we must maintain them. But let us never forget: The greatest progress we have made, and the greatest progress we have yet to make, is in the human heart. In the end, all the world's wealth and a thousand armies are no match for the strength and decency of the human spirit.

Thirty-four years ago, the man whose life we celebrate today spoke to us down there, at the other end of this Mall, in words that moved the conscience of a nation. Like a prophet of old, he told of his dream that one day America would rise up and treat all its citizens as equals before the law and in the heart. Martin Luther King's dream was the American Dream. His quest is our quest: the ceaseless striving to live out our true creed. Our history has been built on such dreams and labors. And by our dreams and labors we will redeem the promise of America in the 21st century.

To that effort I pledge all my strength and every power of my office. I ask the members of Congress here to join in that pledge. The American people returned to office a President of one party and a Congress of another. Surely, they did not do this to advance the politics of petty bickering and extreme partisanship they plainly deplore. No, they call on us instead to be repairers of the breach, and to move on with America's mission.

America demands and deserves big things from us, and nothing big ever came from being small. Let us remember the timeless wisdom of Cardinal Bernardin, when facing the end of his own life. He said, "It is wrong to waste the precious gift of time, on acrimony and division."

Fellow citizens, we must not waste the precious gift of this time. For all of us are on that same journey of our lives, and our journey, too, will come to an end. But the journey of our America must go on.

And so, my fellow Americans, we must be strong, for there is much to dare. The demands of our time are great and they are different. Let us meet them with faith and courage, with patience and a grateful and happy heart. Let us shape the hope of this day into the noblest chapter in our history. Yes, let us build our bridge. A bridge wide enough and strong enough for every American to cross over to a blessed land of new promise.

May those generations whose faces we cannot yet see, whose names we may never know, say of us here that we led our beloved land into a new century with the American Dream alive for all her children; with the American promise of a more perfect union a reality for all her people; with America's bright flame of freedom spreading throughout all the world.

From the height of this place and the summit of this century, let us go forth. May God strengthen our hands for the good work ahead, and always, always bless our America.

NOTES

CHAPTER 1. THE VIEW FROM 1988:
THE FIELD OF DEMOCRATS FORMS

1   Michael Nelson, *Resilient America: Electing Nixon in 1968, Channeling Dissent, and Dividing Government* (Lawrence: University Press of Kansas, 2014), 4.

2   The convention of coloring states red (Republican) and blue (Democratic) on election night traces only to 2000. Before then, the television networks' colored maps varied from election to election and usually differed from each other. In 1980, for example, NBC colored the states carried by Reagan blue and, as more and more fell into Reagan's column, anchor David Brinkley compared the map to a "suburban swimming pool." Tom Zeller, "One State, Two State, Red State, Blue State," *New York Times*, February 8, 2004.

3   Samuel L. Popkin, *The Candidate: What It Takes to Win—and Hold—the White House* (New York: Oxford University Press, 2012), 198. See also John Sides, Michael Tesler, and Lynne Vavreck, *Identity Crisis: The 2016 Presidential Campaign and the Battle for the Meaning of America* (Princeton, NJ: Princeton University Press, 2018).

4   "Mondale: Democrats' Chances Slim in 1992," *Southern Illinoisan*, February 24, 1991.

5   Jack Germond and Jules Witcover, *Whose Broad Stripes and Bright Stars: The Trivial Pursuit of the Presidency, 1988* (New York: Warner Books, 1989), 343–344.

6   Michael Nelson, "Constitutional Aspects of the Elections," in *The Elections of 1988*, ed. Michael Nelson (Washington, DC: CQ Press, 1989), 190.

7   For other explanations of divided government, see, for example, Morris Fiorina, *Divided Government* (New York: Macmillan, 1992); and Gary C. Jacobson, *The Electoral Origins of Divided Government: Competition in U.S. House Elections, 1946–1988* (Boulder, CO: Westview Press, 1990).

8   Matt Grossman and David A. Hopkins, *Asymmetric Politics: Ideological Republicans and Group Interest Democrats* (New York: Oxford University Press, 2016), 6. The authors discuss at length the different natures of the two parties identified in their book's title.

9   Walter F. Mondale, with David Hage, *The Good Fight: A Life in Liberal Politics* (New York: Scribner, 2010), 287–288.

10 "Key Sections from Transcripts of Democrats' Debate in Iowa," *New York Times*, February 13, 1984, http://www.nytimes.com/1984/02/13/us/key-sections-from-transcripts-of-democrats-debate-in-iowa.html?pagewanted=all.

11 Mondale, *The Good Fight*, 293.

12 Mondale, 293.

13 Steven M. Gillon, *The Democrats' Dilemma: Walter F. Mondale and the Liberal Legacy* (New York: Columbia University Press, 1992), 354.

14 Mondale, *The Good Fight*, 287.

15 Mondale, 307.

16 Larry Sabato, *PAC Power: Inside the World of Political Action Committees* (New York: W. W. Norton, 1984).

17 Jacob S. Hacker and Paul Pierson, *Winner-Take-All Politics: How Washington Made the Rich Richer—and Turned Its Back on the Middle Class* (New York: Simon & Schuster, 2010), 178.

18 Sam Rosenfeld, *The Polarizers: Postwar Architects of Our Partisan Era* (Chicago: University of Chicago Press, 2018), 249.

19 Adam Bonica et al., "Why Hasn't Democracy Slowed Rising Inequality?," *Journal of Economic Perspectives* 27 (Summer 2013): 114.

20 "1984 Democratic Party Platform," The American Presidency Project, https://www.presidency.ucsb.edu/documents/1984-democratic-party-platform.

21 Randall Rothenberg, *The Neoliberals: Creating the New American Politics* (New York: Simon & Schuster, 1984), 121, 131.

22 Kevin M. Kruse and Julian E. Zelizer, *Fault Lines: A History of the United States since 1974* (New York: W. W. Norton, 2019), 129.

23 Jon F. Hale, "The Making of the New Democrats," *Political Science Quarterly* 110 (Summer 1995): 210.

24 Eric Alterman and Kevin Mattson, *The Cause: The Fight for American Liberalism from Franklin Roosevelt to Barack Obama* (New York: Viking, 2012), 360–361; and Al From, *The New Democrats and the Return to Power* (New York: Palgrave Macmillan, 2012), 2. Bill Clinton wrote the foreword to this book.

25 Arthur M. Schlesinger Jr., "For Democrats, Me-Too Reaganism Will Spell Disaster," *New York Times*, July 6, 1986; and Popkin, *The Candidate*, 185.

26 David E. Price, *Bringing Back the Parties* (Washington, DC: CQ Press, 1984), 289–294.

27 Peter Brown, *Minority Party: Why Democrats Face Defeat in 1992 and Beyond* (Washington, DC: Regnery Gateway, 1991), 25.

28 Eleanor Clift and Tom Brazaitas, *War without Bloodshed: The Art of Politics* (New York: Simon & Schuster, 1996), 27; Gillon, *The Democrats' Dilemma*, 395; and Thomas P. Edsall, "The Not-So-Silent White Majority," *New York Times*, November 17, 2016.

29 Michael S. Dukakis, "Address Accepting the Presidential Nomination at the Democratic National Convention in Atlanta, July 21, 1988," The American Presidency Project, http://www.presidency.ucsb.edu/ws/?pid=25961.

30 Brown, *Minority Party*, 124.

31 Commission on Presidential Debates, "The Second Bush-Dukakis Presidential Debate," October 13, 1988, http://www.debates.org/index.php?page=october-13-1988-debate-transcript.

32 Jim Lehrer, *Tension City: Inside the Presidential Debates, from Kennedy-Nixon to Obama-McCain* (New York: Random House, 2011), 36.

33 Sidney Blumenthal, *Pledging Allegiance: The Last Campaign of the Cold War* (New York: HarperCollins, 1990), 310, 315; and Nelson, "Constitutional Aspects of the Election," 194–195.

34 Brown, *Minority Party*, 125. "What the hell was that, by the way, thousand points of light? What did that mean?" Donald Trump echoed in 2018. Brett Molina, "President Trump Takes Swipe at George H. W. Bush's 'Thousand Points of Light,'" *USA Today*, July 6, 2018.

35 Brown, *Minority Party*, 125–126.

36 Brown, 125–126.

37 Martin P. Wattenberg, "Why Clinton Won and Dukakis Lost: An Analysis of the Candidate-Centered Nature of American Party Politics," *Party Politics* 1 (1995): 251–252.

38 CNN, "Race for the White House: Bush vs. Dukakis," March 20, 2016.

39 Wattenberg, "Why Clinton Won and Dukakis Lost," 247–248.

40 Paul C. Quirk, "The Election," in Nelson, *The Elections of 1988*, 82.

41 David Maraniss, *First in His Class: A Biography of Bill Clinton* (New York: Simon & Schuster, 1995), 49.

42 Bill Clinton, *My Life* (New York: Alfred A, Knopf, 2004), 63.

43 Clinton, 45–47.

44 Clinton, 88.

45 Clinton, 117.

46 Clinton, 144.

47 Maraniss, *First in His Class*, 144.

48 The phrase is from a letter Clinton wrote to the head of the ROTC unit at the University of Arkansas explaining why he would not be reporting as promised. *Frontline*, "Bill Clinton's Draft Letter," December 3, 1969, http://www.pbs.org /wgbh/pages/frontline/shows/clinton/etc/draftletter.html.

49 Clinton, *My Life*, 157.

50 "The Class of '69," *Life*, June 20, 1969, 28–33. Excerpts from Rodham's speech are on page 31, alongside excerpts from the speech at Brown University by Ira Magaziner, her future collaborator on health care reform in the Clinton administration.

51 David Maraniss, *The Clinton Enigma: A Four-and-a-Half-Minute Speech Reveals the President's Entire Life* (New York: Simon & Schuster, 1998), 77.

52 Clinton, *My Life*, 194.

53 Maraniss, *First in His Class*, 349.

54 Clinton, *My Life*, 60.

55 Clinton, 257.

56 William H. Chafe, *Bill and Hillary: The Politics of the Personal* (New York: Farrar, Straus and Giroux, 2012), 68.

57 David Osborne, *Laboratories of Democracy: A New Breed of Governor Creates Models for National Growth* (Boston: Harvard Business School Press, 1990), 90. Clinton wrote the foreword to this book and is featured more than any other governor.

58 Clinton, *My Life*, 265. Clinton added "until 1994" when he signed the bill renewing the independent counsel statute.

59 Maraniss, *First in His Class*, 388. See also Clinton, *My Life*, 275–279.

60 Osborne, *Laboratories of Democracy*, 91.

61 Clinton, *My Life*, 287.

62 John Brummett, *Highwire: From the Backwoods to the Beltway—The Education of Bill Clinton* (New York: Hyperion, 1994), 68.

63 Brummett, 295. In view of the violent behavior from which Clinton protected his mother from his stepfather, this is an especially interesting turn of phrase.

64 Michael Kruse, "What It Took," *Politico*, November 4, 2016, https://www.politico .com/magazine/story/2016/11/2016-longreads-election-hillary-rodham -clinton-first-woman-president-214416.

65 Brummett, *Highwire*, 436.

66 Ernest Dumas, ed., *The Clintons of Arkansas: An Introduction by Those Who Know Them Best* (Fayetteville: University of Arkansas Press, 1993), 101.

67 Osborne, *Laboratories of Democracy*, 93.

68 Brown, *Minority Party*, 67.

69 Maraniss, *The Clinton Enigma*, 60.

70 Matt Bai, *All the Truth Is Out: The Week Politics Went Tabloid* (New York: Alfred A. Knopf, 2014), 107.

71 Bai, 147, 157; and Paul Taylor, *See How They Run: Electing the President in an Age of Mediaocracy* (New York: Alfred A. Knopf, 1990), 53.

72 Ben Bradlee, *A Good Life: Newspapering and Other Adventures* (New York: Simon & Schuster, 1995), 495.

73 Taylor, *See How They Run*, 73. See also Larry S. Sabato, *Feeding Frenzy: How Attack Journalism Has Transformed American Journalism* (New York: Free Press, 1991), 171–177. A biographer of Barbara Bush suggests that her husband and her assistant Jennifer Fitzgerald had a "surreptitious romance" that lasted more than twelve years. Susan Page, *Matriarch: Barbara Bush and the Making of an American Dynasty* (New York: Twelve, 2019), 241–243.

74 Carl Bernstein, *A Woman in Charge: The Life of Hillary Rodham Clinton* (New York: Alfred A. Knopf, 2007, 177.

75 Brummett, *Highwire*, 233.

76 Robert D. Novak, *The Prince of Darkness: 50 Years of Reporting in Washington* (New York: Crown Forum, 2007), 440–441.

77 Maraniss, *The Clinton Enigma*, 96–97.

78 Maraniss, 96.

79 Maraniss, *First in His Class*, 443.

80 Arthur M. Schlesinger Jr., *Journals, 1952–2000* (New York: Penguin, 2007), 638–639.

81 Marshall Frady, *Jesse: The Life and Pilgrimage of Jesse Jackson* (New York: Random House, 1996), 295.

82 PBS, "The Contenders: 16 for 16: The Originals," October 4, 2016.

83 Frady, *Jesse*, 308.

84 Frady, 343.

85 Frady, 350.

86 Frady, 14.

87 Frady, 342.

88 Frady, 342.

89 Frady, 47.

90 Frady, 383.

91 Blumenthal, *Pledging Allegiance*, 204.

92 PBS, "The Contenders: 16 for 16: The Originals."

93 Frady, *Jesse*, 14–15.

94 Roger Simon, *Show Time: The American Political Circus and the Race for the White House* (New York: Random House, 1998), 140.

95 Robin Toner, "Dukakis Avoids Taking Stand on No. 2 Post," *New York Times*, June 23, 1988, http://www.nytimes.com/1988/06/23/us/dukakis-avoids-taking -a-stand-on-no-2-post.html.

96 Frady, *Jesse*, 39.

97 John J. Piney Jr., *After Reagan: Bush, Dukakis, and the 1988 Election* (Lawrence: University Press of Kansas, 2019), 23–24.

98 Tali Mendelberg, *The Race Card: Campaign Messages, Implicit Messages, and the Norm of Equality* (Princeton, NJ: Princeton University Press, 2001), 135.

99 David Maraniss and Ellen Nakashima, *The Prince of Tennessee: Al Gore Meets His Fate* (New York: Simona & Schuster, 2000), 43.

100 Popkin, *The Candidate*, 21.

101 Maraniss and Nakashima, *The Prince of Tennessee*, 106.

102 Anthony J. Badger, *Albert Gore, Sr.: A Political Life* (Philadelphia: University of Pennsylvania Press, 2019).

103 John Eisendrath, "The Longest Shot: Measuring Al Gore Jr. for the White House," *Washington Monthly*, November–December 1986, 43; and James Reston, "The Media and the Election," *New York Times*, March 15, 1987.

104 Bill Turque, *Inventing Al Gore: A Biography* (Boston: Houghton Mifflin, 2000), 182–187.

105 Maraniss and Nakashima, *The Prince of Tennessee*, 206.

106 Turque, *Inventing Al Gore*, 204.

107 Germond and Witcover, *Whose Broad Stripes and Bright Stars*, 225.

108 Germond and Witcover, 157.

109 Maraniss and Nakashima, *The Prince of Tennessee*, 26.

110 Walter R. Mears, *Deadlines Past: Forty Years of Presidential Campaigning: A Reporter's Story* (Kansas City, MO: Andrews McMeel, 2003), 230.

111 Mears, 230.

112 William D. Cohan, *Four Friends: Promising Lives Cut Short* (New York: Flatiron Books, 2019), 284–285.

113 Blumenthal, *Pledging Allegiance*, 209.

114 Robert S. McElvaine, *Mario Cuomo: A Biography* (New York: Scribner, 1988), 19.

115 McElvaine, 89.

116 McElvaine, 63.

117 McElvaine, 124.

118 McElvaine, 335. The term is Walter Olson's.

119 Dan Balz, Emily Langer, and Phillip Bump, "Mario Cuomo, 3-Term New York Governor, Dies," *Washington Post*, January 2, 2015, https://www.washingtonpost

.com/local/obituaries/mario-cuomo-ny-governor-spoke-loudly-for-liberal-ideals/2015/01/01/953d2602-9223-11e4-a412-4b735edc7175_story.html?utm_term=.62c5917eb0cc.

120 Mario Matthew Cuomo, "1984 Democratic National Convention Keynote Address," http://www.americanrhetoric.com/speeches/mariocuomo1984dnc.htm.

121 McElvaine, *Mario Cuomo*, 92.

122 Mario Cuomo, "Religious Belief and Public Morality: A Catholic Governor's Perspective," http://archives.nd.edu/research/texts/cuomo.htm.

123 McElvaine, *Mario Cuomo*, 10–11.

124 McElvaine, 151.

125 McElvaine, 208.

126 McElvaine, 209.

127 McElvaine, 20.

128 McElvaine, 402.

129 Peter Goldman, Tom Mathews, and the *Newsweek* Special Election Team, *The Quest for the Presidency: The 1988 Campaign* (New York: Simon & Schuster, 1989), 54.

CHAPTER 2. THE VIEW FROM 1988:
THE FIELD OF REPUBLICANS FORMS

1 Sidney M. Milkis and Michael Nelson, *The American Presidency: Origins and Development, 1776–2018* (Washington, DC: CQ Press, 2020), 478.

2 Nolan McCarty, Keith T. Poole, and Howard Rosenthal, *Polarized America: The Dance of Ideology and Unequal Riches* (Cambridge, MA: MIT Press, 2006), 11.

3 Sean M. Theriault, *Party Polarization in Congress* (New York: Cambridge University Press, 2008), 30.

4 Sam Rosenfeld, *The Polarizers: Postwar Architects of Our Partisan Era* (Chicago: University of Chicago Press, 2018), chap. 3.

5 Barry Goldwater, *The Conscience of a Conservative* (Shepherdsville, KY: Victor, 1960).

6 Jon Meacham, *Destiny and Power: The American Odyssey of George Herbert Walker Bush* (New York: Random House, 2015), 135.

7 Raymond Tatalovich, *The Politics of Abortion in the United States and Canada: A Comparative Study* (Armonk, NY: M. E. Sharpe, 1997), 154.

8 Donald T. Critchlow, *The Conservative Ascendancy: How the Republican Right Rose to Power in Modern America*, 2nd ed. (Lawrence: University Press of Kansas, 2011), 150.

9 Kevin M. Kruse and Julian Zelizer, *Fault Lines: A History of the United States since 1974* (New York: W. W. Norton, 2019), 103.

10 "Jimmy Carter Acceptance Speech: Our Nation's Past and Future," 4President, July 15, 1976, http://www.4president.org/speeches/carter1976acceptance.htm.

11 See especially Jude Wanniski, *The Way the World Works: How Economies Fail—and Succeed* (New York: Basic Books, 1978).

12 Michael Nelson, "Lost Confidence: The Democratic Party, the Vietnam War, and the 1968 Election," *Presidential Studies Quarterly* 48 (September 2018): 570–585.

13 Critchlow, *The Conservative Ascendancy*, chap. 4.

14 Lyman A. Kellstedt, Corwin E. Smidt, and Paul M. Kellsted, "Religious Tradition, Denomination, and Commitment: White Protestants and the 1988 Election," in *The Bible and the Ballot Box*, ed. James L. Guth and John C. Green (Boulder, CO: Westview Press, 1991), 140, 142.

15 Donald T. Critchlow, *Phyllis Schlafly and Grassroots Conservatism: A Woman's Crusade* (Princeton, NJ: Princeton University Press, 2005), 217–239.

16 Daniel K. Williams, *God's Own Party: The Making of the Christian Right* (New York: Oxford University Press, 2010), 115, 155–158.

17 Jill Lepore, *These Truths: A History of the United States* (New York: Ecco, 2018), 664.

18 Kenneth L. Woodward, *Getting Religion: Faith, Culture, and Politics from the Age of Eisenhower to the Era of Obama* (New York: Convergent Books, 2016), 381.

19 Woodward, 85.

20 Kruse and Zelizer, *Fault Lines*, 94.

21 Michael Tomasky, *If We Can Keep It: How the Republic Collapsed and How It Might Be Saved* (New York: W. W. Norton 2019), 106; and Frances FitzGerald, *The Evangelicals: The Struggle to Reshape America* (New York: Simon & Schuster, 2017), 290. Falwell's earlier antipolitics sermon, "Ministers and Marchers," is discussed on pp. 284–286.

22 Williams, *God's Own Party*, 5, 7.

23 Critchlow, *The Conservative Ascendancy*, 176.

24 Sidney Blumenthal, *Pledging Allegiance: The Last Campaign of the Cold War* (New York: HarperCollins, 1990), 100.

25 FitzGerald, *The Evangelicals*, 332, 335.

26 Jacob S. Hacker and Paul Pierson, *Winner-Take-All Politics: How Washington Made the Rich Richer—and Turned Its Back on the Middle Class* (New York: Simon & Schuster, 2010), 149.

27 Michael Nelson, "How the GOP Conquered the South," in *Race and Ethnic Relations*, ed. John Kromkowski (Dubuque, IA: McGraw-Hill, 2007), 35–39.

28 V. O. Key Jr., *Southern Politics in State and Nation* (New York: Alfred A. Knopf, 1949), 5.

29 For a fuller treatment of Bush's pre–vice presidential life and career, see Michael Nelson, "George Bush: Texan, Conservative," in *41: Inside the Presidency of George H. W. Bush*, ed. Michael Nelson and Barbara A. Perry (Ithaca, NY: Cornell University Press, 2014), 27–47.

30 Herbert S. Parmet, *George Bush: The Life of a Lone Star Yankee* (New York: Scribner, 1997), 96. Robert Welch, who headed the John Birch Society, estimated that the United States was "50–70 percent Communist-controlled"—and rising. Godfrey Hodgson, *The World Turned Right Side Up: A History of the Conservative Ascendancy in America* (Boston: Houghton Mifflin, 1996), 61.

31   Hugh Heclo, "George Bush and American Conservatism," in Nelson and Perry, *41: Inside the Presidency of George H. W. Bush*, 49.

32   Quoted in John C. Topping Jr., John R. Lazarek, and William H. Linder, *Southern Republicanism and the New South* (Cambridge, MA: Ripon Society, 1966), 111.

33   Parmet, *George Bush*, 96–97.

34   George Bush, "The Republican Party and the Conservative Movement," *National Review*, December 1, 1965.

35   Rosenfeld, *The Polarizers*, 105.

36   The idea that Bush was a Republican moderate during his years in the House of Representatives prevails in every book about him. See, for example, Timothy Naftali, *George H. W. Bush* (New York: Times Books, 2007), 16–20; Tom Wicker, *George Herbert Walker Bush* (New York: Viking, 2004), 20–21; Parmet, *George Bush*, chap. 7; and John Robert Greene, *The Presidency of George Bush* (Lawrence: University Press of Kansas, 2000), 18.

37   Quoted in Parmet, *George Bush*, 134.

38   David M. Kennedy, *Birth Control in America: The Career of Margaret Sanger* (New Haven, CT: Yale University Press, 1970). For example, Margaret Sanger came to believe that "working class misery was attributable not to economic and political dislocation, but to the fecundity of the working class itself. In that view, ... the artificial restriction of fertility was seen as an instrument with which the dominant classes could check threatened social disruption" (112–113).

39   See, for example, Rowland Evans and Robert Novak, "Young Texas Congressman Bush Gets Nixon Look as Running Mate," *Washington Post*, June 5, 1968; Robert B. Semple, "Nixon Considering a Moderate on Ticket," *New York Times*, June 30, 1968; and "Reagan Avows Candidacy Agnew for Nixon," *New York Times*, August 6, 1968.

40   George Bush, *All the Best, George Bush: My Life in Letters and Other Writings* (New York: Scribner, 1999), 117–118.

41   Evans and Novak, "Young Texas Congressman Bush Gets Nixon Look as Running Mate."

42   Meacham, *Destiny and* Power, 135.

43   Meacham, 135.

44   Tom Wicker, "Mr. Nixon on the Stump," *New York Times*, October 29, 1970.

45   James E. Anderson, Richard W. Murray, and Edward F. Farley, *Texas Politics: An Introduction*, 2nd ed. (New York: Harper & Row, 1975), 74.

46   Meacham, *Destiny and Power*, 173–174.

47   Parmet, *George Bush*, 169.

48   Richard B. Cheney Oral History, Miller Center, University of Virginia, George H. W. Bush Presidential Oral History Project, March 16–17, 2000, https://millercenter.org/the-presidency/presidential-oral-histories/richard-b-cheney-oral-history-secretary-defense.

49   Meacham, *Destiny and Power*, 195–196.

50   "The Presidents: George H. W. Bush," American Experience, Public Broadcasting System, December 4, 2018, https://www.pbs.org/wgbh/americanexperience/films/bush/.

51 Meacham, *Destiny and Power*, 204.

52 Meacham, 209, 211.

53 Jeffrey A. Engel, *When the World Seemed New: George H. W. Bush and the End of the Cold War* (Boston: Houghton Mifflin, 2017), 25.

54 Richard Ben Cramer, *What It Takes: The Way to the White House* (New York: Random House, 1992), 791.

55 Wicker, *George Herbert Walker Bush*, 136. Twelve years earlier, CBS News anchor Walter Cronkite remarked that despite his impressive national political debut at the 1968 Republican convention, Reagan was probably too old to mount another campaign for president. Michael Nelson, *Resilient America: Electing Nixon in 1968, Channeling Dissent, and Redividing Government* (Lawrence: University Press of Kansas, 2014).

56 Jack S. Germond and Jules Witcover, *Blue Smoke and Mirrors: How Reagan Won and Why Carter Lost the Election of 1980* (New York: Viking, 1981), 117.

57 Meacham, *Destiny and Power*, 235.

58 Meacham, 225, 227.

59 James A. Baker III, *"Work Hard, Study . . . and Keep Out of Politics": Adventures and Lessons from an Unexpected Political Life* (New York: Putnam, 2006), 89.

60 Baker, 95.

61 Jules Witcover, *The American Vice Presidency: From Irrelevance to Power* (Washington, DC: Smithsonian Books, 2014), 449.

62 Germond and Witcover, *Blue Smoke and Mirrors*, 183–188.

63 Jim Wooten, "One Campaign Too Many," in Arthur Grace, *Choose Me: Portraits of a Presidential Race* (Hanover, NH: Brandeis University Press, 1989), 17.

64 Meacham, *Destiny and Power*, 251, 255.

65 Meacham, 292.

66 Baker, *"Work Hard, Study . . . and Keep Out of Politics,"* 149, 157.

67 Milkis and Nelson, *The American Presidency*, chap. 17.

68 Joe Klein, *Politics Lost: From RFK to W: How Politicians Have Become Less Courageous and More Interested in Keeping Power Than in Doing What's Right for America* (New York: Broadway Books, 1996), 100.

69 David R. Runkel, *Campaign for President: The Managers Look at '88* (Dover, MA: Auburn House, 1989), 184.

70 Meacham, *Destiny and Power*, 297.

71 Craig Fuller Oral History, Miller Center, University of Virginia, George H. W. Bush Presidential Oral History Project, May 12, 2004, https://millercenter .org/the-presidency/presidential-oral-histories/craig-fuller-oral-history-chief -staff-vice-president.

72 John H. Sununu Oral History, Miller Center, University of Virginia, George H. W. Bush Presidential Oral History Project, June 8–9, 2000, https://miller center.org/the-presidency/presidential-oral-histories/john-h-sununu-oral -history-062000-white-house-chief.

73 Milkis and Nelson, *The American Presidency*, chap. 17.

74 Michael Nelson, "Evaluating the Presidency," in *The Presidency and the Political System*, 8th ed., ed. Michael Nelson (Washington, DC: CQ Press, 2006), 1–27.

75 Maureen Dowd, "Washington Talk: White House," *New York Times*, May 12, 1989, http://www.nytimes.com/1989/05/12/us/washington-talk-white-house .html.

76 George F. Will, "George Bush: The Sound of a Lapdog," *Washington Post*, January 30, 1986, https://www.washingtonpost.com/archive/politics/1986/01/30 /george-bush-the-sound-of-a-lapdog/9322b0c0-c006–4709–99fc-4283fcb 35ea8/?utm_term=.18b62fcab1a6.

77 "George Bush: Fighting the Wimp Factor," cover; and Margaret Garrard Warner, "Bush Battles the 'Wimp Factor,'" *Newsweek*, October 19, 1987, http:// www.newsweek.com/bush-battles-wimp-factor-207008.

78 Walter Pincus, "Bush 'Out of the Loop' on Iran-Contra?," *Washington Post*, September 24, 1992, https://www.washingtonpost.com/archive/politics/1992 /09/24/bush-out-of-the-loop-on-iran-contra/4ee467ab-8531-46e5-8da5-ff7bd 97a6609/?utm_term=.450903fe2c22.

79 Hendrik Hertzberg, *Politics: Observations and Arguments, 1966–2004* (New York: Penguin, 2004), 179, 177.

80 Peter Goldman, Tom Mathews, and the *Newsweek* Special Election Team, *The Quest for the Presidency: The 1988 Campaign* (New York: Simon & Schuster, 1989), 200.

81 Meacham, *Destiny and Power*, 319–320.

82 John Dickerson, *Whistlestop: My Favorite Stories from Presidential Campaign History* (New York: Twelve, 2016), 78.

83 Robertson chose not to run again in future elections, deciding instead to use the vast mailing list he accumulated as a candidate to form a grassroots successor to the Moral Majority called the Christian Coalition in 1989.

84 "Are you proud of your son?" the Barbara Bush character was asked in one skit, to which she answered, "He's not my son, he's my husband." Susan Page, *Matriarch: Barbara Bush and the Making of an American Dynasty* (New York: Twelve, 2019), 210.

85 Meacham, *Destiny and Power*, 328.

86 CNN, "Race for the White House: Bush vs. Dukakis," March 20, 2016.

87 Alexander P. Lamis, *The Two-Party South* (New York: Oxford University Press, 1984). Lamis identified Atwater as the source of the statement in the 1990 edition of his book. The full interview in which he said it can be heard at https://www.thenation.com/article/exclusive-lee-atwaters-infamous-1981 -interview-southern-strategy/.

88 Doug Rossinow, *The Reagan Era: A History of the 1980s* (New York: Columbia University Press, 2015), 246.

89 Meacham, *Destiny and Power*, 341.

90 Joel K. Goldstein, *The White House Vice Presidency: The Path to Significance, Mondale to Biden* (Lawrence: University Press of Kansas, 2016), 272.

91 Ronald Reagan, "Remarks at the Republican National Convention in New Orleans, Louisiana, August 15, 1988," https://reaganlibrary.archives.gov/archives /speeches/1988/081588b.htm.

92 George Bush, "Address Accepting the Presidential Nomination at the Republican National Convention in New Orleans, April 18, 1988," The American Presidency Project, http://www.presidency.ucsb.edu/ws/?pid=25955.

93 Meacham, *Destiny and Power*, 339, 159; and Sununu Oral History, https://miller center.org/the-presidency/presidential-oral-histories/john-h-sununu-oral -history-062000-white-house-chief.

94 Richard Darman, *Who's in Control? Polar Politics and the Sensible Center* (New York: Simon & Schuster, 1996), 92.

95 Richard Darman Oral History, Miller Center, University of Virginia, George H. W. Bush Presidential Oral History Project, July 19, 2000, https://millercenter .org/the-presidency/presidential-oral-histories/george-h-w-bush.

96 Arthur M. Schlesinger Jr., *Journals, 1952–2000* (New York: Penguin, 2007), 658.

97 Sigmund Rogich Oral History, Miller Center, University of Virginia, George H. W. Bush Presidential Oral History Project, March 8–9, 2001, https://miller center.org/the-presidency/presidential-oral-histories/sigmund-rogich-oral -history-assistant-president.

98 CNN, "Race for the White House."

99 Williams, *God's Own Party*, 221; and Paul C. Quirk, "The Election," in *The Elections of 2008*, ed. Michael Nelson (Washington, DC: CQ Press, 1989), 82.

100 "Voter Turnout in Presidential Elections, 1828–2012," The American Presidency Project, http://www.presidency.ucsb.edu/data/turnout.php.

101 Michael Duffy and Dan Goodgame, *Marching in Place: The Status Quo Presidency of George Bush* (New York: Simon & Schuster, 1992), 33.

102 Goldman, Mathews, et al., *Quest for the Presidency*, 218.

103 Richard Ben Cramer, *Bob Dole* (New York: Random House, 1995), 117.

104 Cramer, 134.

105 Williams, *God's Own Party*, 131.

106 Cramer, *Bob Dole*, 146.

107 Cramer, *What It Takes*, 67.

108 Goldman, Mathews, et al., *Quest for the Presidency*, 256.

109 Cramer, *Bob Dole*, xxi.

110 Tomasky, *If We Can Keep It*, 172.

111 Cramer, *What It Takes*, 900.

112 "Dole Tells Bush: 'Quit Lying about My Record,'" *Dispatch*, February 17, 1988, https://news.google.com/newspapers?nid=1734&dat=19880217&id=buob AAAAIBAJ&sjid=71EEAAAAIBAJ&pg=6817,4627023&hl=en.

113 Meacham, *Destiny and Power*, 326.

114 Morton Kondracke and Fred Barnes, *Jack Kemp: The Bleeding-Heart Conservative Who Changed America* (New York: Sentinel, 2015), 320.

115 Kondracke and Barnes, 72.

116 Kondracke and Barnes, 169.

117 Kondracke and Barnes, 260.

118 Goldman, Mathews, et al., *Quest for the Presidency*, 208.

119 Ed Rollins, with Tom DeFrank, *Bare Knuckles and Back Rooms: My Life in American Politics* (New York: Broadway Books, 1996), 182.

120 David Frum, *Dead Right* (New York: Basic Books, 1994), 50.

121 Kondracke and Barnes, *Jack Kemp*, 27, 203.

122 J. Danforth Quayle Oral History, Miller Center, University of Virginia, George H. W. Bush Presidential Oral History Project, March 12, 2002, https://miller center.org/the-presidency/presidential-oral-histories/j-danforth-quayle-oral -history-vice-president-united.

123 Richard F. Fenno Jr., *The Making of a Senator: Dan Quayle* (Washington, DC: CQ Press, 1989).

124 Fenno, 167.

125 Dan Quayle, *Standing Firm* (New York: HarperPaperbacks, 1994), 20.

126 James A. Baker, III, Oral History, Miller Center, University of Virginia, George H. W. Bush Presidential Oral History Project, January 29, 2000, https://miller center.org/the-presidency/presidential-oral-histories/james-baker-iii-oral -history-2011-white-house-chief.

127 Some accounts add Sen. John Danforth of Missouri and Attorney General Richard Thornburgh to the list of finalists.

128 Jack W. Germond, *Fat Man in a Middle Seat: Forty Years of Covering Politics* (New York: Random House, 1999), 215.

129 Meacham, *Destiny and Power*, 337.

130 Goldstein, *White House Vice Presidency*, 197.

131 Bob Woodward and David S. Broder, *The Man Who Would Be President: Dan Quayle* (New York: Simon & Schuster, 1992), 64.

132 Quayle, *Standing Firm*, 10.

133 Blumenthal, *Pledging Allegiance*, 272.

134 Parmet, *George Bush*, 349.

135 Paul Taylor, *See How They Run: Electing the President in an Age of Mediaocracy* (New York: Alfred A. Knopf, 1990), 162.

136 Quayle, *Standing Firm*, 69.

137 Michael Nelson, "Constitutional Aspects of the Elections," in Nelson, *The Elections of 1988*, ed. Michael Nelson (Washington, DC: CQ Press, 1989), 190.

138 Robert D. Novak, *The Prince of Darkness: 50 Years of Reporting in Washington* (New York: Crown Forum, 2007), 452.

139 Williams, *God's Own Party*, 221.

140 Germond, *Fat Man in a Middle Seat*, 241.

141 Runkel, *Campaign for President*, 215.

142 Timothy Stanley, *The Crusader: The Life and Tumultuous Times of Pat Buchanan* (New York: St. Martin's Press, 2012), 56.

143 Patrick J. Buchanan, *Nixon's White House Wars: The Battles That Made and Broke a President and Divided America Forever* (New York: Crown Forum, 2017), chaps. 3 and 4.

144 Stanley, *The Crusader*, 71.

145 Howard Kurtz, *Hot Air: All Talk All the Time* (New York: Basic Books, 1997), 108, 116.

146 Steve Kornacki, *The Red and the Blue: The 1990s and the Birth of Political Tribalism* (New York: Ecco, 2018), 151.

147 Stanley, *The Crusader*, 95.

148 Sidney Blumenthal, "Pat Buchanan and the Great Right Hope," *Washington Post*, January 8, 1987.

149 James Ceaser and Andrew Busch, *Upside Down and Inside Out: The 1992 Elections and American Politics* (Lanham, MD: Rowman & Littlefield, 1993), 45.

150 Novak, *Prince of Darkness*, 435.

151 Patrick J. Buchanan, *Right from the Beginning* (Boston: Little, Brown, 1988), 3–8.

152 Lepore, *These Truths*, 714.

153 Adam Edelman, "Donald Trump Claims He Was Considered to Be George H. W. Bush's Running Mate in 1988," *New York Daily News*, November 8, 2015; and Meacham, *Destiny and Power*, 326.

CHAPTER 3. DIVIDED GOVERNMENT: GEORGE BUSH AND THE DEMOCRATS (AND ROSS PEROT), 1989–1991

1   George J. Church, "A Tale of Two Bushes," *Time*, January 7, 1991, http://content.time.com/time/specials/packages/article/0,28804,2030812_2030725,00.html.

2   Herbert S. Parmet, *George: The Life of a Lone Star Yankee* (New York: Scribner, 1997), 430.

3   Thomas Scully Oral History, Miller Center, University of Virginia, George H. W. Bush Presidential Oral History Project, September 2–3, 1999, https://millercenter.org/the-presidency/presidential-oral-histories/george-h-w-bush.

4   Sean Wilentz, *The Age of Reagan: A History 1974–2008* (New York: HarperCollins, 2008), 286.

5   Stephen Skowronek, *The Politics Presidents Make: Leadership from John Adams to George Bush* (Cambridge, MA: Harvard University Press, 1993).

6   Stephen Skowronek, *Presidential Leadership in Political Time: Reprise and Reappraisal* (Lawrence: University Press of Kansas, 2008), 99.

7   Skowronek, *Presidential Leadership in Political Time*, 99.

8   Walter Dean Burnham, "The Legacy of George Bush: Travails of an Understudy," in *The Election of 1992*, ed. Gerald M. Pomper (Chatham, NJ: Chatham House, 1993), 1–38. John Adams, James Madison, Martin Van Buren, William Howard Taft, and Herbert Hoover preceded Bush in the role of "understudy," according to Burnham. Bush received 37.4 percent of the national popular vote in 1992.

9   *NBC Nightly News*, March 31, 1991.

10 James A. Baker III, *The Politics of Diplomacy: Revolution, War, and Peace, 1989–1992* (New York: Putnam, 1995), 194.

11 Wilentz, *The Age of Reagan*, 154.

12 Jeffrey A. Engel, *When the World Seemed New: George H. W. Bush and the End of the Cold War* (Boston: Houghton Mifflin, 2017), 300.

13 Jon Meacham, *Destiny and Power: The American Odyssey of George Herbert Walker Bush* (New York: Random House, 2015), 381.

14 Jeffrey A. Engel, "When George Bush Believed the Cold War Ended," in *41: Inside the Presidency of George H. W. Bush*, ed. Michael Nelson and Barbara A. Perry (Ithaca, NY: Cornell University Press, 2014), 119.

15 Michael Nelson, "Lost Confidence: The Democratic Party, the Vietnam War, and the 1968 Election," *Presidential Studies Quarterly* 48 (September 2018): 570–585.

16 Ronald Brownstein, "Cuomo Seeks to Deal with Iraq Remarks," *Los Angeles Times*, December 4, 1991, http://articles.latimes.com/1991-12-04/news/mn -268_1_los-angeles-times.

17 Thomas L. Friedman, "Clinton's Foreign Policy Agenda Reaches across Broad Spectrum," *New York Times*, October 4, 1992, http://www.nytimes.com/1992 /10/04/us/1992-campaign-issues-foreign-policy-looking-abroad-clinton -foreign-policy.html?pagewanted=all.

18 Andrew J. Bacevich, *American Empire: The Realities and Consequences of U.S. Diplomacy* (Cambridge, MA: Harvard University Press, 2001), 68.

19 Michael Duffy and Dan Goodgame, *Marching in Place: The Status Quo Presidency of George Bush* (New York: Simon & Schuster, 1992), 200.

20 Duffy and Goodgame, 201.

21 Engel, *When the World Seemed New*, 439.

22 Gallup, "Presidential Approval Ratings—Gallup Historical Statistics and Trends," http://www.gallup.com/poll/116677/presidential-approval-ratings -gallup-historical-statistics-trends.aspx.

23 *The Gallup Poll: Public Opinion 1991* (Lanham, MD: Rowman & Littlefield), 1992), 70–77. See also Charles D. Hadley and Harold W. Stanley, "Surviving the 1992 Presidential Nominating Process," in *America's Choice: The Election of 1992*, ed. William Crotty (Guilford, CT: Dushkin Publishing Group, 1991), 32.

24 William C. Berman, *America's Right Turn: From Nixon to Clinton* (Baltimore: Johns Hopkins University Press, 1994), 153.

25 *NBC Nightly News*, August 2, 1991.

26 Tali Mendelberg, *The Race Card: Campaign Strategy, Implicit Messages, and the Norm of Equality* (Princeton, NJ: Princeton University Press, 2001), 155.

27 Richard Darman, *Who's in Control? Polar Politics and the Sensible Center* (New York: Simon & Schuster, 1996), 92.

28 Samuel L. Popkin, *The Candidate: What It Takes to Win—and Hold—the White House* (New York: Oxford University Press, 2012), 165.

29 Engel, *When the World Seemed New*, 128.

30 Thomas Scully Oral History.

31 Berman, *America's Right Turn*, 83, 285.

32 E. J. Dionne Jr., *Why the Right Went Wrong: Conservatism—From Goldwater to the Tea Party and Beyond* (New York: Simon & Schuster, 2016), 21.

33 Duffy and Goodgame, *Marching in Place*, 70–71, 283.

34 James A. Baker, III, Oral History, Miller Center, University of Virginia, George H. W. Bush Presidential Oral History Project, March 17, 2011, https://miller center.org/the-presidency/presidential-oral-histories/james-baker-iii-oral -history-2011-white-house-chief.

35 John Podhoretz, *Hell of a Ride: Backstage at the White House Follies, 1989–1993* (New York: Simon & Schuster, 1993), 52.

36 James P. Pinkerton Oral History, Miller Center, University of Virginia, George H. W. Bush Presidential Oral History Project, February 6, 2001, https://miller center.org/the-presidency/presidential-oral-histories/james-p-pinkerton -oral-history-deputy-assistant.

37 Wayne P. Steger, "Presidential Renomination Challenges in the 20th Century," *Presidential Studies Quarterly* 33 (December 2003): 827–852.

38 Jack W. Germond and Jules Witcover, *Mad as Hell: Revolt at the Ballot Box, 1992* (New York: Warner Books, 1993), 131, 132.

39 Timothy Stanley, *The Crusader: The Life and Tumultuous Times of Pat Buchanan* (New York: St. Martin's Press, 2012), 135.

40 Patrick J. Buchanan, "A Crossroads in Our Country's History," 4President, December 10, 1991, http://www.4president.org/speeches/buchanan1992 announcement.htm.

41 Charles T. Royer, ed., *Campaign for President: The Managers Look at '92* (Hollis, NH: Hollis Publishing, 1994), 107.

42 Royer, 24.

43 Peter Goldman, Thomas M. DeFrank, et al., *The Quest for the Presidency 1992* (College Station: Texas A&M University Press, 1994), 321.

44 Germond and Witcover, *Mad as Hell*, 127.

45 Dan Balz, "Democrats' Perennial Rising Star Wants to Put New Face on Party," *Washington Post*, June 25, 1991.

46 George Stephanopoulos interview, Pryor Center for Arkansas Oral and Visual History, University of Arkansas, Diane D. Blair Project, December 11, 1992, https://pryorcenter.uark.edu/project.php?thisProject=11.

47 Carl Bernstein, *A Woman in Charge: The Life of Hillary Rodham Clinton* (New York: Alfred A. Knopf, 2007), 188–189.

48 David Maraniss, *First in His Class: A Biography of Bill Clinton* (New York: Simon & Schuster, 1995), 456.

49 Gloria Cabe interview, Pryor Center for Arkansas Oral and Visual History, University of Arkansas, Diane D. Blair Project, April 22, 1993, https://pryorcenter .uark.edu/project.php?thisProject=11.

50 Russell L. Riley, *Inside the Clinton White House: An Oral History* (New York: Oxford University Press, 2016), 19.

51 Clinton discusses his work with the National Governors Association in Bill Clinton, *My Life* (New York: Random House, 2004, 313–350. On the DLC, see Kenneth S. Baer, *Reinventing Democrats: The Politics of Liberalism from Reagan to Clinton* (Lawrence: University Press of Kansas, 2000).

52 William Galston and Elaine Ciulla Kamarck, "The Politics of Evasion: Democrats and the Presidency," Progressive Policy Institute, September 1989, http:// www.progressivepolicy.org/wp-content/uploads/2013/03/Politics_of_Evasion .pdf.

53 Bruce Reed Oral History, Miller Center, University of Virginia, William J. Clinton Presidential Oral History Project, February 19–20, 2004, https://miller

center.org/the-presidency/presidential-oral-histories/bruce-reed-oral-history
-february-2004-domestic-policy.

54   Al From Oral History, Miller Center, University of Virginia, William J. Clinton Presidential Oral History Project, April 27, 2006, https://millercenter.org
/the-presidency/presidential-oral-histories/al-oral-history2006-domestic
-policy-advisor-clinton.

55   Frank Greer Oral History, Miller Center, University of Virginia, William J. Clinton Presidential Oral History Project, October 27–28, 2005, https://millercenter
.org/the-presidency/presidential-oral-histories/frank-greer-oral-history
-media-consultant.

56   Bruce Reed Oral History, February 19–20, 2004; and Al From Oral History,
April 27, 2008.

57   Eli Jay Segal Oral History, Miller Center, University of Virginia, William J. Clinton Presidential Oral History Project, February 8–10, 2006, https://millercenter
.org/the-presidency/presidential-oral-histories/eli-jay-segal-oral-history-chief
-staff-clintons-1992; and Steven Waldman, *The Bill: How the Adventures of Clinton's National Service Bill Reveal What Is Corrupt, Comic, Cynical—and Noble—
about Washington* (New York: Viking, 1995), chap. 1.

58   William Galston Oral History, Miller Center, University of Virginia, William
J. Clinton Presidential Oral History Project, April 22–23, 2004, https://miller
center.org/the-presidency/presidential-oral-histories/william-galston-oral
-history-deputy-assistant-president.

59   Al From Oral History, April 27, 2006.

60   Bruce Reed Oral History, February 19–20, 2004.

61   Patrick J. Maney, *Bill Clinton: New Gilded Age President* (Lawrence: University
Press of Kansas, 2016), 33.

62   Frank Greer interview, Pryor Center for Arkansas Oral and Visual History,
University of Arkansas, Diane D. Blair Project, December 28, 1992, https://
pryorcenter.uark.edu/project.php?thisProject=11.

63   Frank Greer Oral History, October 27–28, 2005.

64   The term is closely associated with Larry S. Sabato, *Feeding Frenzy: How Attack
Journalism Has Transformed American Journalism* (New York: Free Press, 1991).

65   Bruce Reed Oral History, February 19–20, 2004.

66   See Michael Nelson, "Bill Clinton and Welfare Reform: A Perspective from
Oral History," *Congress and the Presidency* 42 (September–December 2015):
243–263.

67   Bruce Reed Oral History, Miller Center, University of Virginia, William J. Clinton Presidential Oral History Project, April 12, 2004, https://millercenter.org
/the-presidency/presidential-oral-histories/bruce-reed-oral-history-april-2004
-domestic-policy.

68   Stanley B. Greenberg, *Middle Class Dreams: The Politics and Power of the New
American Majority* (New Haven, CT: Yale University Press, 1996), 213.

69   By campaign's end, Arkansas ranked first in the nation in per capita campaign
contributions. Diane D. Blair, "The Big Three of Late Twentieth-Century Ar-

kansas Politics: Dale Bumpers, Bill Clinton and David Pryor," *Arkansas Historical Quarterly* 54 (Spring 1995): 53–79.

70 Tom Rosenstiel, *Strange Bedfellows: How Television and the Presidential Candidates Changed American Politics, 1992* (New York: Hyperion, 1993), 47.

71 Germond and Witcover, *Mad as Hell*, 193.

72 Royer, *Campaign for President*, 3.

73 Lisa Belkin, "For Some, a Job Puts a Life in Perspective," *New York Times*, September 28, 2003, http://www.nytimes.com/2003/09/28/jobs/life-s-work-for-some-a-job-puts-a-life-in-perspective.html.

74 Germond and Witcover, *Mad as Hell*, 161.

75 John J. Pitney, Jr., *After Reagan: Bush, Dukakis, and the 1988 Election* (Lawrence: University Press of Kansas, 2019), 121.

76 Royer, *Campaign for President*, 3.

77 Steve Daley, "Ex-Gov. Brown Enters Race, Blasts 2 Parties," *Chicago Tribune*, October 22, 1991, http://articles.chicagotribune.com/1991-10-22/news/9104050270_1_greed-and-corrupt-politics-jerry-brown-democrats-and-republicans.

78 L. Douglas Wilder, *Son of Virginia: A Life in America's Political Arena* (Guilford, CT: Rowman & Littlefield, 2015), 127.

79 Wilder, 131.

80 *NBC Nightly News*, April 14, 1991.

81 Goldman, DeFrank, et al., *Quest for the Presidency 1992*, 57.

82 Germond and Witcover, *Mad as Hell*, 101.

83 Goldman, DeFrank, et al., *Quest for the Presidency 1992*, 58.

84 Royer, *Campaign for President*, 45.

85 Mary Vespa, "A Tornado Named Debra Winger Has a Whirl with Nebraska's Governor—'Rockin' Bob Kerrey," *People*, June 6, 1983, http://people.com/archive/a-tornado-named-debra-winger-has-a-whirl-with-nebraskas-governor-rockin-bob-kerrey-vol-19-no-22/.

86 Germond and Witcover, *Mad as Hell*, 94.

87 Goldman, DeFrank, et al., *Quest for the Presidency 1992*, 81.

88 Steven J. Rosenstone, Roy L. Behr, and Edward H. Lazarus, *Third Parties in America*, 2nd ed. (Princeton, NJ: Princeton University Press, 1996).

89 Steven V. Roberts, "Is It Too Late for a Man of Honesty, High Purpose, and Intelligence to Be Elected President of the United States?," *Esquire*, October 1967, 89ff.

90 Michael D'Antonio, *Never Enough: Donald Trump and the Pursuit of Success* (New York: St. Martin's Press, 2015), 182–183, 245–256; and Michael Kranish and Marc Fisher, *Trump Revealed: An American Journey of Ambition, Ego, Money, and Power* (New York: Scribner, 2016), 275–277, 284–287.

91 Germond and Witcover, *Mad as Hell*, 210–214; and Goldman, DeFrank, et al., *Quest for the Presidency 1992*, 413–418.

92 Gerald Posner, *Citizen Perot: His Life and Times* (New York: Random House, 1996), 181.

93 Meacham, *Destiny and Power*, 210.

94 James A. Baker III, Oral History, Miller Center, University of Virginia, George
H. W. Bush Presidential Oral History Project, January 29, 2000, https://miller
center.org/the-presidency/presidential-oral-histories/james-baker-iii-oral
-history-2000-white-house-chief.

95 Thomas Scully Oral History.

96 *NBC Nightly News*, January 18, 1991.

97 Posner, *Citizen Perot*, 240–241.

98 Larry King, with Mark Stengel, *On the Line: The New Road to the White House*
(New York: Harcourt, Brace, 1993), 18–23.

**CHAPTER 4. THE BATTLE FOR THE 1992 REPUBLICAN NOMINATION
AND THE RISE AND (TEMPORARY) FALL OF ROSS PEROT**

1 James Ceaser and Andrew Busch, *Upside Down and Inside Out: The 1992 Elections and American Politics* (Lanham, MD: Rowman & Littlefield, 1993), 50.

2 Peter Goldman et al., *Quest for the Presidency 1992* (College Station: Texas A&M
University Press, 1994), 4.

3 J. Danforth Quayle Oral History, Miller Center, University of Virginia, George
H. W. Bush Oral History Project, March 12, 2002, https://millercenter.org/the
-presidency/presidential-oral-histories/j-danforth-quayle-oral-history-vice
-president-united.

4 George W. Bush, *41: A Portrait of My Father* (New York: Crown, 2014), 224.

5 Susan Page, *Matriarch: Barbara Bush and the Making of an American Dynasty*
(New York: Twelve, 2019), 230.

6 Colin Powell with Joseph Persico, *My American Journey* (New York: Ballantine,
1995), 560.

7 Charles Kolb, *White House Daze: The Unmaking of Domestic Policy in the Bush
Years* (New York: Free Press, 1994), 271; and Richard W. Waterman, "Storm
Clouds on the Political Horizon: George Bush at the Dawn of the 1992 Presi-
dential Election," *Presidential Studies Quarterly* 26 (1996): 337–349.

8 John Robert Greene, *The Presidency of George H. W. Bush*, 2nd ed. (Lawrence:
University Press of Kansas, 2015), 216.

9 Daniel Galvin, *Presidential Party Building: Dwight D. Eisenhower to George W.
Bush* (Princeton, NJ: Princeton University Press, 2010), 157.

10 A photograph of Untermeyer's memo appears in Hunter S. Thompson, *Better
Than Sex: Confessions of a Political Junkie* (New York: Ballantine, 1994), 35.

11 "Presidential Job Approval—F. Roosevelt (1941)–Trump," The American Presidency Project, http://www.presidency.ucsb.edu/data/popularity.php?pres=41.

12 Samuel L. Popkin, *The Reasoning Voter: Communication and Persuasion in Presidential Campaigns*, 2nd ed. (Chicago: University of Chicago Press, 1994), 240–
241.

13 James A. Baker III Oral History, Miller Center, University of Virginia, George
H. W. Bush Oral History Project, January 29, 2000, https://millercenter.org
/the-presidency/presidential-oral-histories/james-baker-iii-oral-history-2000
-white-house-chief.

14 "The Presidents: George H. W. Bush," American Experience, Public Broadcasting System, 2018: https://www.pbs.org/wgbh/americanexperience/films/bush/.

15 Recently fired White House chief of staff John Sununu, who as governor had been instrumental in Bush's victory in the 1988 New Hampshire primary, was especially dismissive: "Teeter, a good friend but he cannot run a one-car funeral. Malek has the political sense of a doorknob." John H. Sununu Oral History, Miller Center, University of Virginia, George H. W. Bush Oral History Project, June 8–9, 2000, https://millercenter.org/the-presidency/presidential-oral-histories/john-h-sununu-oral-history-062000-white-house-chief.

16 Mary Matalin and James Carville, *All's Fair: Love, War, and Running for President* (New York: Random House, 1994), 165, 191.

17 James A. Baker III Oral History; and Ceaser and Busch, *Upside Down and Inside Out*, 33.

18 James A. Baker III Oral History.

19 "State of the Union: Transcript of President Bush's Address on the State of the Union," *New York Times*, January 27, 1992.

20 Charles T. Royer, ed., *Campaign for President: The Managers Look at '92* (Hollis, NH: Hollis Publishing, 1994), 25.

21 Timothy Stanley, *The Crusader: The Life and Tumultuous Times of Pat Buchanan* (New York: St. Martin's Press, 2012), 161.

22 Jill Lepore, *These Truths: A History of the United States* (New York: W. W. Norton, 2018), 704.

23 Tom Rosenstiel, *Strange Bedfellows: How Television and the Presidential Candidates Changed American Politics* (New York: Hyperion, 1993), 168.

24 Goldman et al., *Quest for the Presidency 1992*, 324.

25 Dan Quayle, *Standing Firm: A Vice Presidential Memoir* (New York: Harper-Paperbacks, 1994), 331–332.

26 James P. Pinkerton Oral History, Miller Center, University of Virginia, George H. W. Bush Oral History Project, February 6, 2001, https://millercenter.org/the-presidency/presidential-oral-histories/james-p-pinkerton-oral-history-deputy-assistant.

27 Matalin and Carville, *All's Fair*, 112–113.

28 Matalin and Carville, 125.

29 Stanley, *The Crusader*, 159; and David F. Demarest Jr. Oral History, Miller Center, University of Virginia, George H. W. Bush Oral History Project, January 28, 2010, https://millercenter.org/the-presidency/presidential-oral-histories/david-f-demarest-jr-oral-history-assistant-president.

30 *The Simpsons*, "Stark Raving Dad: Alternate Version," IMDB, https://www.imdb.com/title/tt0701217/alternateversions.

31 Jack W. Germond and Jules Witcover, *Mad as Hell: Revolt at the Ballot Box 1992* (New York: Warner Books, 1993), 150.

32 Steve Kornacki, *The Red and the Blue: The 1990s and the Birth of Political Tribalism* (New York: Ecco, 2018), 157.

33 Stanley, *The Crusader*, 106.

34 Walter R. Mears, *Deadlines Past: Forty Years of Presidential Campaigning: A Reporter's Story* (Kansas City, MO: Andrews McMeel, 2003), 266.

35 Larry M. Bartels, *Presidential Primaries and the Dynamics of Public Choice* (Princeton, NJ: Princeton University Press, 1988), 35.

36 Kornacki, *The Red and the Blue*, 157.

37 Herbert E. Alexander and Anthony Corrado, *Financing the 1992 Election* (Armonk, NY: M. E. Sharpe, 1995), 33.

38 Goldman et al., *Quest for the Presidency 1992*, 348.

39 Germond and Witcover, *Mad as Hell*, 235.

40 Daniel K. Williams, *God's Own Party: The Making of the Christian Right* (New York: Oxford University Press, 2010), 231.

41 *NBC Nightly News*, March 10, 1992.

42 *CNN Evening News*, May 29, 1992.

43 Andrew Rosenthal, "Bush Encounters the Supermarket, Amazed," *New York Times*, February 5, 1992. In truth, Rosenthal wasn't even present at the event where Bush made the comment. Marlin Fitzwater, *Call the Briefing! A Memoir: Ten Years in the White House with Presidents* (XLibris, 2000), 328.

44 *NBC Nightly News*, June 18, 1992.

45 Gov. Walter Hickel of Alaska, Sen. Lowell Weicker of Connecticut, and Rep. Bernie Sanders of Vermont.

46 Germond and Witcover, *Mad as Hell*, 221.

47 Larry King with Mark Stengel, *On the Line: The New Road to the White House* (New York: Harcourt Brace, 1993), 25–26.

48 *CNN Evening News*, May 18, 1992.

49 *NBC Nightly News*, March 23, 1992; and Henry Muller and Richard Woodbury, "An Interview with Ross Perot," *Time*, May 25, 1992.

50 Muller and Woodbury, "An Interview with Ross Perot."

51 Muller and Woodbury.

52 *NBC Nightly News*, June 25, 1992.

53 Greene, *The Presidency of George H. W. Bush*, 2nd ed., 220.

54 *NBC Nightly News*, April 10, 1992.

55 Gil Troy, *The Age of Clinton: America in the 1990s* (New York: Thomas Dunne, 2015), 69.

56 Muller and Woodbury, "An Interview with Ross Perot."

57 Matalin and Carville, *All's Fair*, 229.

58 Matalin and Carville, 148.

59 Jon Meacham, *Destiny and Power: The American Odyssey of George Herbert Walker Bush* (New York: Random House, 2015), 503.

60 King, *On the Line*, 29–30.

61 Gallup News, "Gallup Presidential Election Trial Heat Trends, 1936–2008," http://news.gallup.com/poll/110548/gallup-presidential-election-trial-heat-trends.aspx.

62 Gerald Posner, *Citizen Perot: His Life and Times* (New York: Random House, 1996), 253–254.

63 Posner, 258.

64 Germond and Witcover, *Mad as Hell*, 367.

65 Posner, *Citizen Perot*, 255.

66 Robert Shogan, "Perot Draws Line on Posts for Gays and Adulterers," *Los Angeles Times*, May 29, 1992.

67 *NBC Nightly News*, May 28, 1992.

68 Ed Rollins with Tom DeFrank, *Bare Knuckles and Back Rooms: My Life in American Politics* (New York: Broadway Books, 1996), 252.

69 FiveThirtyEight, "The Ross Perot Myth," October 8, 2016, https://fivethirty eight.com/features/the-ross-perot-myth.

70 *NBC Nightly News*, May 12, 1992.

71 Howard Kurtz, "Perot Scores Points by Scoring the Media," *Washington Post*, May 23, 1992; *NBC Nightly News*, June 12, 1992; and *NBC Nightly News*, May 28, 1992.

72 Thomas Scully Oral History, Oral History, Miller Center, University of Virginia, George H. W. Bush Presidential Oral History Project, September 2–3, 1999, https://millercenter.org/the-presidency/presidential-oral-histories/george-h -w-bush.

73 Germond and Witcover, *Mad as Hell*, 371.

74 Bill Scher, "Can the Dems Truly Unify?," *Politico*, July 24, 2016, https://www .politico.com/magazine/story/2016/07/can-the-dems-truly-unify-214096.

75 Goldman et al., *Quest for the Presidency 1992*, 368, 375.

76 Fred Steeper memo, July 20, 1992, quoted in Goldman, 703–704.

77 Quayle, *Standing Firm*, 281.

78 Meacham, *Destiny and Power*, 508.

79 Greene, *The Presidency of George H. W. Bush*, 2nd ed., 224.

80 Matalin and Carville, *All's Fair*, 202, 203. According to Quayle's chief of staff, Bill Kristol, the vice president chose Murphy Brown to preempt any accusation that he was targeting poor and unwed black mothers. Nina J. Easton, *Gang of Five: Leaders at the Center of the Conservative Crusade* (New York: Simon & Schuster, 2000), 240.

81 Joel K. Goldstein, *The White House Vice Presidency: The Path to Significance, Mondale to Biden* (Lawrence: University Press of Kansas, 2016), 117.

82 Meacham, *Destiny and Power*, 508.

83 James A. Baker III, Oral History, Miller Center, University of Virginia, George H. W. Bush Presidential Oral History Project, January 29, 2000, https://miller center.org/the-presidency/presidential-oral-histories/james-baker-iii-oral -history-2000-white-house-chief.

84 Meacham, *Destiny and Power*, 509.

85 Quayle, *Standing Firm*, 383.

86 "Bush Angrily Denes a Report of an Affair," *New York Times*, August 12, 1992.

87 Gail Sheehy, *Hillary's Choice* (New York: Ballantine Books, 2000), 204.

88 Quayle, *Standing Firm*, 512.

89 Michael Nelson, "Clinton's Elections: Redividing Government in the 1990s," *Presidential Studies Quarterly* 46 (June 2016): 457–472.

90 Michael Duffy, "The 34% Solution," *Time*, June 1, 1992, 34–35.

91 Matalin and Carville, *All's Fair*, 316–317.

92 Germond and Witcover, *Mad as Hell,* 407; and *Planned Parenthood of Southeastern Pennsylvania v. Casey,* 505 U.S. 833 (1992).

93 Asked about his daughter, Quayle told Larry King he would "support her in whatever decision she made," only to be rebuked by his wife, Marilyn. King, *On the Line,* 40.

94 "Republican Party Platform of 1992," The American Presidency Project, http://www.presidency.ucsb.edu/ws/?pid=25847.

95 Fred Steeper memo, March 16, 1992, quoted in Goldman et al., *Quest for the Presidency 1992,* 650.

96 "Pat Buchanan Speaks at the 1992 Republican National Convention," ABC News, http://abcnews.go.com/Politics/video/archival-video-pat-buchanan -speaks-1992-republican-national-40578648.

97 Meacham, *Destiny and Power,* 511.

98 Quayle, *Standing Firm,* 383.

99 Marilyn Tucker Quayle, "Remarks at the 1992 RNC—August 19, 1992," Archives of Women's Political Communications, Iowa State University, https://awpc .cattcenter.iastate.edu/2017/03/21/remarks-at-the-1992-rnc-aug-19-1992-2/.

100 Barbara Bush, *Barbara Bush: A Memoir* (New York; Scribner, 1994), 482.

101 "1992 Republican Convention: Quayle Text," *Los Angeles Times,* August 21, 1992, http://articles.latimes.com/1992-08-21/news/mn-5796_1_republican -convention.

102 Matalin and Carville, *All's Fair,* 310.

103 George Bush, "Remarks Accepting the Presidential Nominating at the Republican National Convention in Houston," The American Presidency Project, http://www.presidency.ucsb.edu/ws/index.php?pid=21352.

104 Goldman et al., *Quest for the Presidency 1992,* 409.

105 Bush, *41,* 238–239.

106 Royer, *Campaign for President,* 156.

107 Matalin and Carville, *All's Fair,* 301.

CHAPTER 5. THE BATTLE FOR THE 1992 DEMOCRATIC NOMINATION

1 On the 1968 election and its aftermath, see Michael Nelson, *Resilient America: Electing Nixon in 1968, Channeling Dissent, and Dividing Government* (Lawrence: University Press of Kansas, 2014).

2 David Kusnet Oral History, Miller Center, University of Virginia, William J. Clinton Oral History Project, March 19, 2010, https://millercenter.org/the-presi dency/presidential-oral-histories/david-kusnet-oral-history-chief-speechwriter.

3 David Wilhelm interview, Pryor Center for Arkansas Oral and Visual History, University of Arkansas, Diane D. Blair Project, December 12, 1992, http:// pryorcenter.uark.edu/project.php?thisProject=11.

4 Bernard von Bothmer, *Framing the Sixties: The Use and Abuse of a Decade from Ronald Reagan to George W. Bush* (Amherst: University of Massachusetts Press, 2010), 135.

5 William H. Chafe, *Bill and Hillary: The Politics of the Personal* (New York: Farrar, Straus and Giroux, 2012), 133.

6   "Transcript: Bill Clinton and Gennifer Flowers Audio Tapes," Accuracy in Media, March 20, 1992, http://www.freerepublic.com/focus/f-news/1077346/posts.

7   Herbert E. Alexander and Anthony Corrado, *Financing the 1992 Election* (Armonk, NY: M. E. Sharpe, 1995), 31, 33.

8   Walter Mears, *Deadlines Past: Forty Years of Presidential Campaigning: A Reporter's Story* (Kansas City, MO: Andrews McMeel, 2003), 251.

9   Mary Matalin and James Carville, *All's Fair: Love, War, and Running for President* (New York: Random House, 1994), 107; and Amy Chozick, "'90s Scandals Threaten to Erode Hillary Clinton's Strength with Women," *New York Times*, January 20, 2016.

10 Shawn Boburg, "Enabler or Family Defender? How Hillary Clinton Responded to Husband's Accusers," *Washington Post*, September 28, 2016; and Chafe, *Bill and Hillary*, 143–144.

11 Jack W. Germond and Jules Witcover, *Mad as Hell: Revolt at the Ballot Box 1992* (New York: Warner Books, 1993), 186.

12 Carl Bernstein, *A Woman in Charge: The Life of Hillary Rodham Clinton* (New York: Alfred A. Knopf, 2007), 202.

13 Michael Kruse, "The TV Interview That Haunts Hillary Clinton," *Politico*, September 23, 2016, https://www.politico.com/magazine/story/2016/09/hillary-clinton-2016-60-minutes-1992-214275.

14 "Bill Clinton's Draft Letter," *Frontline*, PBS, December 3, 1969, https://www.pbs.org/wgbh/pages/frontline/shows/clinton/etc/draftletter.html. Turning his back on the University of Arkansas as well as the army, he applied to Yale Law School the day before he wrote to Holmes.

15 John Dickerson, *Whistlestop: My Favorite Stories from Presidential Campaign History* (New York: Twelve, 2016), 67.

16 George Stephanopoulos, *All Too Human: A Political Education* (Boston: Little, Brown, 1999), 74.

17 Nigel Hamilton, *Bill Clinton: An American Journey—Great Expectations* (New York: Random House, 2003), 633.

18 Roy M. Neel Oral History, Miller Center, University of Virginia, William J. Clinton Oral History Project, November 14, 2002, https://millercenter.org/the-presidency/presidential-oral-histories/roy-m-neel-oral-history-al-gores-1992-campaign-manager.

19 Frank Greer Oral History, Miller Center, University of Virginia, William J. Clinton Oral History Project, October 27–28, 2005, https://millercenter.org/the-presidency/presidential-oral-histories/frank-greer-oral-history-media-consultant.

20 Bruce Reed Oral History, Miller Center, University of Virginia, William J. Clinton Oral History Project, February 19–20, 2004, https://millercenter.org/the-presidency/presidential-oral-histories/bruce-reed-oral-history-february-2004-domestic-policy.

21 Dickerson, *Whistlestop*, 67.

22 Frank Greer Oral History. The term "feeding frenzy" was coined by Larry S. Sabato in his book *Feeding Frenzy: How Attack Journalism Has Transformed American Politics* (New York: Free Press, 1991).

23 Stanley B. Greenberg, *Dispatches from the War Room: In the Trenches with Five Extraordinary Leaders* (New York: St. Martin's Press, 2009), 46.

24 Thomas P. Edsall, "Black Leader View Clinton Strategy with Mix of Pragmatism, Optimism," *Washington Post*, October 28, 1992.

25 Robert O. Boorstin interview, Pryor Center for Arkansas Oral and Visual History, University of Arkansas, Diane D. Blair Project, November 19, 1992, http://pryorcenter.uark.edu/project.php?thisProject=11.

26 Greenberg, *Dispatches from the War Room*, 50.

27 Germond and Witcover, *Mad as Hell*, 251.

28 Germond and Witcover, 260.

29 Jeff Gerth, "Clintons Joined S & L Operator in an Ozark Real Estate Venture," *New York Times*, March 8, 1992.

30 Dan Balz and Edward Walsh, "Clinton's Wife Finds She's Become Issue," *Washington Post*, March 17, 1992.

31 Bernstein, *A Woman in Charge*, 205.

32 Bernstein, 206.

33 Chafe, *Bill and Hillary*, 137.

34 Germond and Witcover, *Mad as Hell*, 271; and *NBC Nightly News*, April 4, 1992.

35 Peter Goldman et al., *Quest for the Presidency 1992* (College Station: Texas A&M University Press, 1994). New Yorkers did not settle for Clinton's standard disclaimer that he had "never broken a state law."

36 Goldman et al., 241.

37 *NBC Nightly News*, May 4, 1992.

38 Calculated from data in Paul R. Abramson, John H. Aldrich, and David W. Rohde, *Change and Continuity in the 1992 Elections*, rev. ed. (Washington, DC: CQ Press, 1995), 36–38.

39 Matalin and Carville, *All's Fair*, 98; and George Stephanopoulos interview, Pryor Center for Arkansas Oral and Visual History, University of Arkansas, Diane D. Blair Project, December 11, 1992, http://pryorcenter.uark.edu/project .php?thisProject=11.

40 Charles T. Royer, ed., *Campaign for President: The Managers Look at '92* (Hollis, NH: Hollis Publishing, 1994), 42.

41 Russell L. Riley, *Inside the Clinton White House: An Oral History* (New York: Oxford University Press, 2016), 44.

42 Thomas R. Edsall, "Clinton Stuns Rainbow Coalition," *Washington Post*, June 14, 1992.

43 Matalin and Carville, *All's Fair*, 215.

44 Margaret O'Mara, *Pivotal Tuesdays: Four Elections That Shaped the Twentieth Century* (Philadelphia: University of Pennsylvania Press, 2015), 163.

45 Bill Clinton, *My Life* (New York: Alfred A. Knopf, 2004), 330.

46 Nancy McFadden interview, Pryor Center for Arkansas Oral and Visual His-

tory, University of Arkansas, Diane D. Blair Project, October 21, 1992, http://pryorcenter.uark.edu/project.php?thisProject=11.

47 Frank Greer Oral History.

48 Frank Greer Oral History.

49 Dan Balz and E. J. Dionne Jr., "Clinton Secures Party Nomination," *Washington Post*, June 3, 1992. The same was true of Ohio Democratic primary voters who cast their ballots the same day.

50 James Carville interview, Pryor Center for Arkansas Oral and Visual History, University of Arkansas, Diane D. Blair Project, February 4, 1992, http://pryor center.uark.edu/project.php?thisProject=11.

51 Stanley Greenberg Oral History, Miller Center, University of Virginia, William J. Clinton Oral History Project, January 27, 2005, https://millercenter.org/the -presidency/presidential-oral-histories/stanley-greenberg-oral-history -2005-pollster.

52 Michael Takiff, *A Complicated Man: The Life of Bill Clinton as Told by Those Who Know Him* (New Haven, CT: Yale University Press, 2010), 129.

53 Stan Greenberg, James Carville, and Frank Greer memo, April 27, 1992, quoted in Goldman et al., *Quest for the Presidency 1992*, 660; and Stanley B. Greenberg, *Middle Class Dreams: The Politics and Power of the New American Majority* (New York: Times Books, 1995), 224–225.

54 Stephanopoulos, *All Too Human*, 94.

55 Celinda Lake and Stan Greenberg, "Research on Hillary Clinton," May 12, 1992, Pryor Center for Arkansas Oral and Visual History, University of Arkansas, Diane D. Blair Project, "The Clinton Files," *Washington Free Beacon*, n.d., https://www.scribd.com/doc/205858605/The-Clinton-Files (accessed October 14, 2019); and Stephanopoulos, *All Too Human*.

56 Bernstein, *A Woman in Charge*, 208–209.

57 Howard Kurtz, *Hot Air: All Talk All the Time* (New York: Basic Books, 1997), 91.

58 Christine F. Ridout, "News Coverage and Talk Shows in the 1992 Presidential Campaign," *PS: Political Science and Politics* 26 (December 1993): 712–716.

59 Goldman et al., *Quest for the Presidency 1992*, 263–264.

60 Bruce Reed Oral History.

61 Paul Begala interview, Pryor Center for Arkansas Oral and Visual History, University of Arkansas, Diane D. Blair Project, February 2, 1993, http://pryor center.uark.edu/project.php?thisProject=11.

62 Mandy Grunwald interview, Pryor Center for Arkansas Oral and Visual History, University of Arkansas, Diane D. Blair Project, December 20, 1992, http://pryor center.uark.edu/project.php?thisProject=11.

63 Joel K. Goldstein, *The White House Vice Presidency: The Path to Significance, Mondale to Biden* (Lawrence: University Press of Kansas, 2016), 179.

64 Mickey Kantor Oral History, Miller Center, University of Virginia, William J. Clinton Oral History Project, June 28, 2001, https://millercenter.org/the-presi dency/presidential-oral-histories/michael-mickey-kantor-oral-history-us-trade.

65 Roy M. Neel Oral History.

66 Election guru Charlie Cook, for example, wrote a column listing thirteen vice presidential possibilities. None of them was Gore. Charlie Cook, "Clinton Veepstakes May Not Matter, but Here's Our List," *Roll Call*, May 18, 1992.

67 *NBC Nightly News*, July 10, 1992.

68 "Polls," *National Journal*, August 8, 1992, 1862.

69 Germond and Witcover, *Mad as Hell*, 371.

70 Kathleen M. Frankovic, "Public Opinion in the 1992 Campaign," in *The Election of 1992*, ed. Gerald M. Pomper (Chatham, NJ: Chatham House, 1993), 110–131.

71 Royer, *Campaign for President*, 301.

72 Matalin and Carville, *All's Fair*, 240.

73 "The Man from Hope," Independent Video Archive, http://mediaburn.org /video/the-man-from-hope/.

74 Mickey Kantor Oral History.

75 David Wilhelm interview, Pryor Center for Arkansas Oral and Visual History, University of Arkansas, Diane D. Blair Project, December 12, 1992, http:// pryorcenter.uark.edu/project.php?thisProject=11.

76 Bill Turque, *Inventing Al Gore: A Biography* (Boston: Houghton Mifflin, 2000), 255.

77 Stanley Greenberg Oral History.

78 Stuart Rothenberg, "Don't Be Fooled by Convention Bounces," *Washington Post*, July 7, 2016, https://www.washingtonpost.com/news/powerpost/wp/2016/07 /07/dont-be-fooled-by-convention-bounces/?utm_term=.37007f1a22f9.

79 Matalin and Carville, *All's Fair*, 240.

CHAPTER 6. UNITING GOVERNMENT:
THE GENERAL ELECTION FOR PRESIDENT AND CONGRESS IN 1992

1   Charles T. Royer, ed., *Campaign for President: The Managers Look at '92* (Hollis, NH: Hollis Publishing, 1994), 285.

2   Mary Matalin and James Carville, *All's Fair: Love, War, and Running for President* (New York: Random House, 1994), 301.

3   Dee Dee Myers, "New Technology and the 1992 Clinton Presidential Campaign," *American Behavioral Scientist* 37 (November–December 1993): 181. See also *The War Room*, a documentary film directed by Chris Hegedus and D. A. Pennebaker (1993).

4   Samuel L. Popkin, *The Reasoning Voter: Communication and Persuasion in Presidential Campaigns*, 2nd ed. (Chicago: University of Chicago Press, 1994), 257.

5   David Wilhelm interview, Pryor Center for Arkansas Oral and Visual History, University of Arkansas, Diane D. Blair Project, December 12, 1992, http:// pryorcenter.uark.edu/project.php?thisProject=11.

6   George Stephanopoulos interview, Pryor Center for Arkansas Oral and Visual History, University of Arkansas, Diane D. Blair Project, December 11, 1992, http://pryorcenter.uark.edu/project.php?thisProject=11.

7   Calculated from data in Ross Perot, *United We Stand: How We Can Take Back Our Country* (New York: Hyperion, 1992), chap. 4.

8   For a more nuanced view that incorporates other models, see Lynn Vavreck, *The Message Matters: The Economy and Presidential Campaigns* (Princeton, NJ: Princeton University Press, 2009).

9   John Dillin, "Election by Equation: 2 Analysts See a Bush Win," *Christian Science Monitor*, April 22, 1992; and Nathaniel Beck, "Forecasting the 1992 Presidential Election: The Message Is in the Confidence Interval," *Public Perspective*, September–October 1992, https://ropercenter.cornell.edu/public-perspective/ppscan/36/36032.pdf.

10 See, for example, James Q. Wilson, "Realignment at the Top, Dealignment at the Bottom," in *The American Elections of 1984*, ed. Austin Ranney (Durham, NC: Duke University Press, 1985), 308–309.

11 David Wilhelm interview.

12 Mandy Grunwald interview, Pryor Center for Arkansas Oral and Visual History, University of Arkansas, Diane D. Blair Project, December 20, 1992, http://pryorcenter.uark.edu/project.php?thisProject=11.

13 Peter Goldman et al., *Quest for the Presidency 1992* (College Station: Texas A&M University Press, 1994), 504. See also, Darrell M. West et al., "Ads in Presidential Campaigns: The Strategies of Electoral Appeal," *Political Communications* 12 (1995): 272–290.

14 Matalin and Carville, *All's Fair*, 244.

15 Frank Greer Oral History, Miller Center, University of Virginia, William J. Clinton Oral History Project, October 27–28, 2005, https://millercenter.org/the-presidency/presidential-oral-histories/frank-greer-oral-history-media-consultant.

16 Thomas Patterson, *Out of Order* (New York: Alfred A. Knopf, 1993), 113, 169. Marc Hetherington showed that people who watched the news regularly were more likely to think the economy was in bad shape and vote against Bush. Marc J. Hetherington, "The Media's Role in Forming Voters' National Economic Evaluations in 1992," *American Journal of Political Science* 40 (May 1996): 372–395.

17 Paul R. Abramson, John H. Aldrich, and David W. Rohde, *Change and Continuity in the 1992 Elections*, rev. ed. (Washington, DC: CQ Press, 1995), 174.

18 Governor Bill Clinton and Senator Al Gore, *Putting People First: How We Can All Change America* (New York: Times Books, 1992).

19 Elaine Kamarck Oral History, Miller Center, University of Virginia, William J. Clinton Oral History Project, May 7–8, 2008, http://web1.millercenter.org/poh/transcripts/ohp_2008_0507_kamarck.pdf.

20 Mandy Grunwald interview.

21 Jack W. Germond and Jules Witcover, *Mad as Hell: Revolt at the Ballot Box 1992* (New York: Warner Books, 1993), 442.

22 Susan Thomases Oral History, Miller Center, University of Virginia, William J. Clinton Oral History Project, January 6, 2006, https://millercenter.org/the-presidency/presidential-oral-histories/susan-thomases-oral-history-personal-advisor-chief.

23   James A. Baker Oral History, Miller Center, University of Virginia, George
      H. W. Bush Oral History Project, January 29, 2000, https://millercenter.org
      /the-presidency/presidential-oral-histories/james-baker-iii-oral-history-2000
      -white-house-chief.

24   Matthew Robert Kerbel, *Edited for Television: CNN, ABC, and American Presi-
      dential Elections*, 2nd ed. (New York: Westview Press, 1998), 55, 62.

25   Frank Greer Oral History; and Anthony Lake Oral History, Miller Center, Uni-
      versity of Virginia, William J. Clinton Oral History Project, May 21, 2002,
      https://millercenter.org/the-presidency/presidential-oral-histories/anthony
      -lake-oral-history-2002-national-security-advisor.

26   Sigmund Rogich Oral History, Miller Center, University of Virginia, George
      H. W. Bush Oral History Project, March 8–9, 2001, https://millercenter.org
      /the-presidency/presidential-oral-histories/sigmund-rogich-oral-history
      -assistant-president.

27   John H. Aldrich and Thomas Weko, "The Presidency and the Election Cam-
      paign: Framing the Choice in 1992," in *The Presidency and the Political System*,
      4th ed., ed. Michael Nelson (Washington, DC: CQ Press, 1995), 260, 261.

28   Royer, *Campaign for President*, 226.

29   *NBC Nightly News*, August 2, 1992.

30   Popkin, *The Reasoning Voter*, 256.

31   William G. Mayer, "The 1992 Elections and the Future of American Politics,"
      Polity 25 (Spring 1993): 461–474.

32   Russell L. Riley, *Inside the Clinton White House: An Oral History* (New York:
      Oxford University Press, 2016), 75.

33   "The Presidents: George H. W. Bush," American Experience, Public Broad-
      casting System, December 4, 2018, https://www.pbs.org/wgbh/american
      experience/films/bush/.

34   Thomas Scully Oral History, Oral History, Miller Center, University of Virginia,
      George H. W. Bush Presidential Oral History Project, September 2–3, 1999,
      https://millercenter.org/the-presidency/presidential-oral-histories/george
      -h-w-bush.

35   Michael Takiff, *A Complicated Man: The Life of Bill Clinton as Told by Those Who
      Know Him* (New Haven, CT: Yale University Press, 2010), 133.

36   Takiff, 134.

37   Robert O. Boorstin interview, Pryor Center for Arkansas Oral and Visual
      History, University of Arkansas, Diane D. Blair Project, November 19, 1992,
      http://pryorcenter.uark.edu/project.php?thisProject=11.

38   Stanley Greenberg Oral History, Miller Center, University of Virginia, William
      J. Clinton Oral History Project, January 27, 2005, https://millercenter.org/the
      -presidency/presidential-oral-histories/stanley-greenberg-oral-history
      -2005-pollster.

39   Boorstin interview.

40   Goldman et al., *Quest for the Presidency 1992*, 593.

41   Eli Segal Oral History, Miller Center, University of Virginia, William J. Clin-
      ton Oral History Project, February 8–10, 2006, https://millercenter.org/the

-presidency/presidential-oral-histories/eli-jay-segal-oral-history-chief-staff
-clintons-1992.

42 Thomas Scully Oral History.

43 James A. Baker III Oral History, Miller Center, University of Virginia, George
H. W. Bush Oral History Project, January 29, 2000, https://millercenter.org
/the-presidency/presidential-oral-histories/james-baker-iii-oral-history-2000
-white-house-chief.

44 Anthony Corrado, *Let America Decide* (New York: Twentieth Century Fund
Press, 1995), 82.

45 F. Christopher Arterton, "Campaign '92: Strategies and Tactics of the Candidates," in *The Election of 1992*, ed. Gerald M. Pomper (Chatham, NJ: Chatham
House, 1993), 94.

46 Germond and Witcover, *Mad as Hell*, 469.

47 Alan I. Abramowitz, "Bill and Al's Excellent Adventure: Forecasting the 1996
Presidential Election," *American Politics Quarterly* 24 (October 1996): 434–442.

48 J. Danforth Quayle Oral History, Miller Center, University of Virginia, George
H. W. Bush Oral History Project, March 12, 2002, https://millercenter.org
/the-presidency/presidential-oral-histories/j-danforth-quayle-oral-history
-vice-president-united.

49 Alan Schroeder, *Presidential Debates: Risky Business on the Campaign Trail* (New
York: Columbia University Press, 2016), 41.

50 Riley, *Inside the Clinton White House*, 69.

51 Germond and Witcover, *Mad as Hell*, 458.

52 Germond and Witcover, 459.

53 Matalin and Carville, *All's Fair*, 366.

54 Herbert E. Alexander and Anthony Corrado, *Financing the 1992 Election* (Armonk, NY: M. E. Sharpe, 1995), 128–132.

55 Corrado, *Let America Decide*, 78–79.

56 The elections were in 1860, 1912, 1924, 1948, 1968, and 1980. The incumbent
party won only in 1924 and 1948.

57 Matalin and Carville, *All's Fair*, 413.

58 James A. Baker III Oral History, Miller Center, University of Virginia, George
H. W. Bush Oral History Project, March 7, 2011, https://millercenter.org/the
-presidency/presidential-oral-histories/james-baker-iii-oral-history-2011-white
-house-chief.

59 Jon Meacham, *Destiny and Power: The American Odyssey of George Herbert
Walker Bush* (New York: Random House, 2015), 515, 518.

60 "The 1992 Campaign: Transcript of First TV Debate among Bush, Clinton and
Perot," *New York Times*, October 12, 1992, https://www.nytimes.com/1992/10
/12/us/the-1992-campaign-transcript-of-first-tv-debate-among-bush-clinton
-and-perot.html.

61 Bruce Reed Oral History, Miller Center, University of Virginia, William J.
Clinton Oral History Project, February 19–20, 2004, https://millercenter.org
/the-presidency/presidential-oral-histories/bruce-reed-oral-history-february
-2004-domestic-policy.

62 "Campaign '92: Transcript of the Vice Presidential Debate," *Washington Post*, October 14, 1992, https://www.washingtonpost.com/archive/politics/1992/10/14/campaign-92-transcript-of-the-vice-presidential-debate-part-i/e6dceccb-c794-4c12-aa07-2eca78ce5a67/?utm_term=.e516c578dcd3.

63 Newton D. Minow and Craig L. Lamay, *Inside the Presidential Debates: Their Improbable Past and Promising Future* (Chicago: University of Chicago Press, 2008), 159–162.

64 "The 1992 Campaign: Transcript of 2d TV Debate between Bush, Clinton and Perot," *New York Times*, October 16, 1992, https://www.nytimes.com/1992/10/16/us/the-1992-campaign-transcript-of-2d-tv-debate-between-bush-clinton-and-perot.html.

65 Schroeder, *Presidential Debates*, 226.

66 David F. Demarest, Oral History, Miller Center, University of Virginia, George H. W. Bush Oral History Project, January 28, 2010, https://millercenter.org/the-presidency/presidential-oral-histories/david-f-demarest-jr-oral-history-assistant-president.

67 Riley, *Inside the Clinton White House*, 71.

68 Jill Lepore, *These Truths: A History of the United States* (New York: W. W. Norton, 2018), 706.

69 "The 1992 Campaign: Transcript of 3d TV Debate between Bush, Clinton and Perot," *New York Times*, October 20, 1992, https://www.nytimes.com/1992/10/20/us/the-1992-campaign-transcript-of-3d-tv-debate-between-bush-clinton-and-perot.html.

70 Kathleen A. Frankovic, "Public Opinion in the 1992 Campaign," in Pomper, *The Election of 1992*, 110–131.

71 Stanley Greenberg interview, Pryor Center for Arkansas Oral and Visual History, University of Arkansas, Diane D. Blair Project, December 10, 1992, http://pryorcenter.uark.edu/project.php?thisProject=11.

72 Matalin and Carville, *All's Fair*, 449.

73 Germond and Witcover, *Mad as Hell*, 495, 496.

74 Germond and Witcover, 489.

75 Germond and Witcover, 505.

76 Germond and Witcover, 497.

77 Abramowitz, "Bill and Al's Excellent Adventure."

78 Meacham, *Destiny and Power*, 520.

79 "The Bush Years: Family, Duty, Power (Part 4)," CNN, March 17, 2019.

80 For exit poll data, see Paul J. Quirk and Jon K. Dalager, "The Election: A 'New Democrat' and a New Kind of Presidential Campaign," in *The Elections of 1992*, ed. Michael Nelson (Washington, DC: CQ Press, 1993), 78; and Gerald M. Pomper, "The Presidential Election," in Pomper, *The Election of 1992*, 138–139.

81 Lyman Kellstedt et al., "Religious Voting Blocs in the 1992 Elections: The Year of the Evangelical?," *Sociology of Religion* 55 (1994): 307–326.

82 Steven A. Holmes, "An Eccentric but No Joke," *New York Times*, November 5, 1992.

83 Michael (Mickey) Kantor Oral History, Miller Center, University of Virginia, William J. Clinton Oral History Project, June 28, 2002, https://millercenter .org/the-presidency/presidential-oral-histories/michael-mickey-kantor-oral -history-us-trade.

84 E. J. Dionne, "Perot Not Seen as Affecting Vote Outcome," *Washington Post*, November 8, 1991.

85 See, for example, Martin P. Wattenberg, "Why Clinton Won and Dukakis Lost: An Analysis of the Candidate-Centered Nature of American Party Politics," *Party Politics* 1 (1995): 247–252.

86 Dionne, "Perot Not Seen as Affecting Voter Outcome."

87 "Ross Perot Concession Speech, November 3, 1992," https://www.c-span.org /video/?34047-1/ross-perot-concession-speech.

88 Stanley B. Greenberg, *Dispatches from the War Room: In the Trenches with Five Extraordinary Leaders* (New York: St. Martin's Press, 2009), 66.

89 "How reminiscent it all is," wrote Schlesinger, "reminiscent of 1933, of 1961—a momentous reversal of direction for the nation . . . after a decade of passivity and neglect." Arthur Schlesinger Jr., "Memo to the 1993 Crowd: Believe in Yourselves," *Newsweek*, January 10, 1992.

90 William D. Cohan, *Four Friends: Promising Lives Cut Short* (New York: Flatiron Books, 2019), 301–303.

91 Dan B. Thomas and Larry R. Baas, "The Postelection Campaign: Competing Constructions of the Clinton Victory in 1992," *Journal of Politics* 58 (May 1996): 322.

92 Abramson, Aldrich, and Rohde, *Change and Continuity in the 1992 Elections*, 101.

93 Michael Nelson, "The Presidency: Clinton and the Cycle of Politics and Policy," in Nelson, *The Elections of 1992*, 125–152.

94 James MacGregor Burns and Georgia J. Sorensen, *Dead Center: Clinton-Gore Leadership and the Perils of Moderation* (New York: Scribner, 1999), 13.

95 Popkin, *The Reasoning Voter*, 246.

96 Gary C. Jacobson, "Congress: Unusual Year, Unusual Election," in Nelson, *The Elections of 1992*, 153–182.

97 Abramson, Aldrich, and Rohde, *Change and Continuity in the 1992 Elections*, 273.

98 Michael X. Delli Carpini and Ester R. Fuchs, "The Year of the Woman? Candidates, Voters, and the 1992 Elections," *Political Science Quarterly* 108 (Spring 1993), 29–36.

99 *Thornburg v. Gingles*, 478 U.S. 30 (1986).

100 Jacobson, "Congress."

101 Remarkably, the prime mover in getting the amendment ratified was a University of Texas sophomore who discovered it in 1982 while doing research for a paper and then spread the word among members of Congress, one of whom alerted Maine's legislature that the amendment was still eligible for ratification.

102 James Ceaser and Andrew Busch, *Upside Down and Inside Out: The 1992 Elections and American Politics* (Lanham, MD: Rowman & Littlefield, 1993), 7.

103 Marjorie Randon Hershey, "The Congressional Elections," in Pomper, *The Election of 1992*, 177.

104 *U.S. Term Limits v. Thornton*, 514 U.S. 779 (1995).

CHAPTER 7. REDIVIDING GOVERNMENT:
BILL CLINTON AND CONGRESS, 1993–1995

1   William J. Clinton, "Inaugural Address, January 20, 1993," The American Presidency Project, https://www.presidency.ucsb.edu/documents/inaugural-address-51.

2   James MacGregor Burns and Georgia J. Sorensen, *Dead Center: Clinton-Gore Leadership and the Perils of Moderation* (New York: Scribner, 1999), 104.

3   John F. Harris, *The Survivor: Bill Clinton in the White House* (New York: Random House, 2005), 7.

4   Harris, 5.

5   Quoted in Brendan J. Doherty, "Root Canal Politics: Economic Policy Making in the New Administration," in *42: Inside the Bill Clinton Presidency*, ed. Michael Nelson, Barbara A. Perry, and Russell L. Riley (Ithaca, NY: Cornell University Press, 2016), 106.

6   William Saletan, "The Dark Side: What You Need to Know about Bob Dole," *Mother Jones*, January–February 1996, https://www.motherjones.com/politics/1996/01/dark-side-what-you-need-know-about-bob-dole/.

7   Frances E. Lee, *Insecure Majorities: Congress and the Perpetual Campaign* (Chicago: University of Chicago Press, 2016).

8   Calculated from data in Lee, *Insecure Majorities*, 101.

9   Dan Balz and Ronald Brownstein, *Storming the Gates: Protest Politics and the Republican Revival* (Boston: Little, Brown, 1996), 86.

10   Bob Woodward, *The Choice* (New York: Simon & Schuster, 1996), 105.

11   Bruce Reed Oral History, Miller Center, University of Virginia, William J. Clinton Oral History Project, February 19–20, 2004, https://millercenter.org/the-presidency/presidential-oral-histories/bruce-reed-oral-history-february-2004-domestic-policy.

12   Balz and Brownstein, *Storming the Gates*, 104.

13   William Galston Oral History, Miller Center, University of Virginia, William J. Clinton Oral History Project, April 22–23, 2004, https://millercenter.org/the-presidency/presidential-oral-histories/william-galston-oral-history-deputy-assistant-president.

14   Paul Richter and David Lauter, "Education, Energy Picks Appear Set," *Los Angeles Times*, December 21, 1992.

15   George Stephanopoulos, *All Too Human: A Political Education* (Boston: Little, Brown, 1999), 141.

16   Bill Clinton, *My Life* (New York: Alfred A. Knopf, 2004), 467; and Stephanopoulos, *All Too Human*, 324.

17   William Galston Oral History.

18 David Kusnet Oral History, Miller Center, University of Virginia, William J. Clinton Oral History Project, March 19, 2010, https://millercenter.org/the-presidency/presidential-oral-histories/david-kusnet-oral-history-chief-speechwriter.

19 Joe Klein, *The Natural: The Misunderstood Presidency of Bill Clinton* (New York: Doubleday, 2002), 44.

20 Barbara A. Perry, *Edward M. Kennedy: An Oral History* (New York: Oxford University Press, 2019), 123.

21 Clinton, *My Life*, 486.

22 Klein, *The Natural*, 80–81.

23 Elizabeth Drew, *On the Edge: The Clinton Presidency* (New York: Simon & Schuster, 1994), 299.

24 Stanley Greenberg, *Dispatches from the War Room: In the Trenches with Five Extraordinary Leaders* (New York: St. Martin's Press, 2009), 90.

25 William H. Chafe, *The Unfinished Journey: America since World War II* (New York: Oxford University Press, 2011), 497.

26 Klein, *The Natural*, 44.

27 William H. Chafe, *Bill and Hillary: The Politics of the Personal* (New York: Farrar, Straus and Giroux, 2012), 199.

28 Anthony Lake Oral History, Miller Center, University of Virginia, William J. Clinton Oral History Project, May 21, 2002, https://millercenter.org/the-presidency/presidential-oral-histories/anthony-lake-oral-history-2002-national-security-advisor.

29 William J. Clinton, "Address to a Joint Session of the Congress on Health Care Reform, September 23, 1993, https://www.presidency.ucsb.edu/documents/address-joint-session-the-congress-health-care-reform.

30 Steve Kornacki, *The Red and the Blue: The 1990s and the Birth of Political Tribalism* (New York: Ecco, 2018), 269.

31 Stephanopoulos, *All Too Human*, 301–302.

32 Drew, *On the Edge*, 307.

33 Chafe, *Unfinished Journey*, 493.

34 Benjamin Ginsberg and Martin Shefter, *Politics by Other Means: Politicians, Prosecutors, and the Press from Watergate to Whitewater* (New York: W. W. Norton, 2002), 62.

35 Matt Grossman and David A. Hopkins, *Asymmetric Politics: Ideological Republicans and Group Interest Democrats* (New York: Oxford University Press, 2016), 171–172.

36 William J. Clinton, "Address before a Joint Session of Congress on the State of the Union, January 25, 1994," The American Presidency Project, https://www.presidency.ucsb.edu/documents/inaugural-address-51.

37 Kornacki, *The Red and the Blue*, 272.

38 Clinton, *My Life*, 577.

39 Michael Nelson, *Resilient America: Electing Nixon in 1968, Channeling Dissent, and Redividing Government*, rev. ed. (Lawrence: University Press of Kansas, 2014).

40 Drew, *On the Edge*, 167; and Kornacki, *The Red and the Blue*, 241.

41 Clinton, *My Life*, 520.

42 Clinton, 612–613.

43 In twelve states, each party controlled one chamber. Nebraska's legislature is unicameral and nonpartisan.

44 "Republican Contract with America," http://media.mcclatchydc.com/static /pdf/1994-contract-with-america.pdf (accessed September 15, 2019).

45 John Micklethwait and Arian Woodridge, *The Right Nation: Conservative Power in America* (New York: Penguin, 2004), 115–122.

46 Howard Kurtz, *Hot Air: All Talk All the Time* (New York: Basic Books, 1997), 173.

47 Clinton, *My Life*, 295.

48 Clinton, 629.

49 Adam Clymer, *Edward M. Kennedy: A Biography* (New York: William Morrow, 1999), 561.

50 Paul R. Abramson, John H. Aldrich, and David W. Rohde, *Change and Continuity in the 1992 Elections* (Washington, DC: CG Press, 1995), 336.

51 Bill Turque, *Inventing Al Gore: A Biography* (Boston: Houghton Mifflin, 2000), 290.

52 William Galston Oral History.

53 Elizabeth Drew, *Showdown: The Struggle between the Gingrich Congress and the Clinton White House* (New York: Simon & Schuster, 1996), 21.

54 Terry McAuliffe with Steve Kettmann, *What a Party! My Life among Democrats, Presidents, Candidates, Donors, Activists, Alligators, and Other Wild Animals* (New York: St. Martin's Press, 2007), 103.

55 Dick Morris, *Behind the Oval Office: Winning the Presidency in the Nineties* (New York: Random House, 1997).

56 Woodward, *The Choice*, 25.

57 Joseph Lockhart Oral History, Miller Center, University of Virginia, William J. Clinton Oral History Project, September 19–20, 2005, https://millercenter .org/the-presidency/presidential-oral-histories/joseph-lockhart-oral-history -white-house-press-secretary.

58 Burns and Sorensen, *Dead Center*, 274.

59 See Michael Nelson, "Redivided Government and the Politics of the Budgetary Process during the Clinton Years: An Oral History Perspective," *Congress and the Presidency* 43 (September–December 2016): 243–263.

60 Robert Rubin Oral History, Miller Center, University of Virginia, William J. Clinton Oral History Project, November 3, 2005, https://millercenter.org/the -presidency/presidential-oral-histories/robert-rubin-oral-history-director -national-economic.

61 Transcribed by the author at a Presidential Leadership Scholars event at the Clinton Presidential Center, Little Rock, AK, April 8, 2015.

62 Taylor Branch, *The Clinton Tapes: Wrestling History with the President* (New York: Simon & Schuster, 2009), 315.

63 Sean M. Theriault, *The Gingrich Senators: The Roots of Partisan Warfare in Congress* (New York: Oxford University Press, 2013).

64 Kornacki, *The Red and the Blue*, 325.

65 Branch, *The Clinton Tapes*, 300.

66 Harold W. Stanley, "The Nominations: Republican Doldrums, Democratic Revival," in *The Elections of 1996*, ed. Michael Nelson (Washington, DC: CQ Press, 1997), 17.

67 *Clinton v. Jones*, 520 U.S. 681 (1997).

68 William J. Clinton, "Address before a Joint Session of the Congress on the State of the Union, February 4, 1996)," https://www.presidency.ucsb.edu/docu ments/address-before-joint-session-the-congress-the-state-the-union-9. "The era of big government is over" is the only line ever quoted from the speech, even though it was meant to be balanced with: "But the era of every man for himself must never begin." Ann Lewis, a White House staff member, complained that to say "man" would be "sexist." The line was changed to read: "But we cannot go back to the time when our citizens were left to fend for themselves." As Clinton speechwriter Michael Waldman has observed, the new line "was so soggy it simply wasn't quoted." Michael Waldman, *POTUS Speaks: Finding the Words That Defined the Clinton Presidency* (New York: Simon & Schuster, 2000), 117.

69 William J. Clinton, "Address before a Joint Session of Congress on Administration Goals, February 17, 1993," The American Presidency Project, https://www.presidency.ucsb.edu/documents/address-before-joint-session-congress-administration-goals.

70 William Jefferson Clinton, "Remarks on Signing the Personal Responsibility and Opportunity Reconciliation Act," *Weekly Compilation of Presidential Documents*, August 22, 1996, 1484–1489.

71 David Osborne and Ted Gabler, *Reinventing Government: How the Entrepreneurial Spirit Is Transforming the Public Sector* (Reading, MA: Addison-Wesley, 1992).

72 "Victory March," *Newsweek*, November 18, 1996, 48.

73 William J. Clinton, "Remarks at the Michigan State University Commencement Ceremony in East Lansing, Michigan, May 5, 1995," The American Presidency Project, https://www.presidency.ucsb.edu/documents/remarks-the-michigan-state-university-commencement-ceremony-east-lansing-michigan.

74 Paul Light, *The President's Agenda: Domestic Policy Choice from Kennedy to Reagan* (Baltimore: Johns Hopkins University Press, 1991), 37.

75 George Stephanopoulos, "What I Saw," *Newsweek*, March 14, 1999, https://www.newsweek.com/what-i-saw-163892.

76 Howard Kurtz, *Spin Cycle: Inside the Clinton Propaganda Machine* (New York: Free Press, 1998).

77 Woodward, *The Choice*, 141.

78 Woodward, 368.

79 Sidney M. Milkis and Michael Nelson, *The American Presidency: Origins and Development, 1776–2018* (Washington, DC: CQ Press, 2020), 505.

80 Steven M. Gillon, *The Pact: Bill Clinton, Newt Gingrich, and the Rivalry That Defined a Generation* (New York: Oxford University Press, 2008), 115.

81 Evan Thomas et al., *Back from the Dead: How Clinton Survived the Republican Revolution* (New York: Atlantic Monthly Press, 1997), 79–80.

82 James W. Ceaser, and Andrew E. Busch, *Losing to Win: The 1996 Election and American Politics* (Lanham, MD: Rowman & Littlefield, 1997), 1.

CHAPTER 8. THE ELECTION OF 1996

1 Taylor Branch, *The Clinton Tapes: Wrestling History with the President* (New York: Simon & Schuster, 2009), 295.

2 Linda Fowler, "Where Did All the Candidates Go?," in *Toward the Millennium: The Elections of 1996*, ed. Larry J. Sabato (Needham Heights, MA: Allyn and Bacon, 1997), 23.

3 Michael Takiff, *A Complicated Man: The Life of Bill Clinton as Told by Those Who Know Him* (New Haven, CT: Yale University Press, 2010), 246.

4 Harold W. Stanley, "The Nominations: Republican Doldrums, Democratic Revival," in *The Elections of 1996*, ed. Michael Nelson (Washington, DC: CQ Press, 1997), 15.

5 Other potential Republican candidates who declared they were not running included former secretary of defense Richard Cheney and former secretary of state James Baker, Gov. Tommy Thompson of Wisconsin, Rep. Jack Kemp (who ran and lost in 1988), and Speaker of the House Newt Gingrich. In addition to Wilson, two other candidates declared but, getting nowhere, withdrew later in 1995: Sen. Arlen Specter of Pennsylvania and Rep. Robert Dornan of California. Reagan administration assistant secretary of state Alan Keyes, Sen. Richard Lugar of Indiana, and businessman Morry Taylor campaigned into 1996 but without measurable success.

6 Dick Morris, *Behind the Oval Office: Winning the Presidency in the Nineties* (New York: Random House, 1997), 266.

7 James W. Ceaser and Andrew E. Busch, *Losing to Win: The 1996 Election and American Politics* (Lanham, MD: Rowman & Littlefield, 1997), 81.

8 Bob Woodward, *The Choice* (New York: Simon & Schuster, 1996), 146.

9 Ceaser and Busch, *Losing to Win*, 73.

10 William G. Mayer, "The Presidential Nominations," in *The Elections of 1996: Reports and Interpretations*, ed. Gerald M. Pomper (Chatham, NJ: Chatham House, 1997), 27.

11 Steve Kornacki, *The Red and the Blue: The 1990s and the Birth of Political Tribalism* (New York: Ecco, 2018), 272.

12 Institute of Politics, Harvard University, *Campaign for President: The Managers Look at '96* (Hollis, NH: Hollis Publishing, 1997), 53.

13 Evan Thomas et al., *Back from the Dead: How Clinton Survived the Republican Revolution* (New York: Atlantic Monthly Press, 1997), 82.

14 E. J. Dionne Jr., *Where the Right Went Wrong: Conservatism from Goldwater to the Tea Party and Beyond* (New York: Simon & Schuster, 2016), 133.

15 Takiff, *A Complicated Man*, 257.

16 Kornacki, *The Red and the Blue*, 321.

17 Woodward, *The Choice*, 121.

18 Woodward, 219.

19 Branch, *The Clinton Tapes*, 349, 358.

20 Thomas et al., *Back from the Dead*, 5, 217, 250.

21 Blaine Harden, "Dole's Birthday Renews Age-Old Old-Age Debate," *Washington Post*, July 21, 1995.

22 Woodward, *The Choice*, 107.

23 Stanley, "The Nominations," 21.

24 Marty Cohen et al., *The Party Decides: Presidential Nominations before and after Reform* (Chicago: University of Chicago Press, 2008), 218.

25 Paul R. Abramson, John H. Aldrich, and David W. Rohde, *Change and Continuity in the 1996 Elections*, rev. ed. (Washington, DC: CQ Press, 1998), 21.

26 Stanley, "The Nominations," 21.

27 Stanley, 27.

28 Woodward, *The Choice*, 386.

29 *Buckley v. Valeo* 424 U.S. 1 (1976).

30 James MacGregor Burns and Georgia J. Sorensen, *Dead Center: Clinton-Gore Leadership and the Perils of Moderation* (New York: Scribner, 1999), 267.

31 Woodward, *The Choice*, 420; and Jill Lepore, *The Truths: A History of the United States* (New York: W. W. Norton, 2018), 734.

32 Gil Troy, *The Age of Clinton: America in the 1990s* (New York: St. Martin's Press, 2015), 176.

33 Mayer, "The Presidential Nominations," 62.

34 See Michael Nelson, "Bill Clinton and Welfare Reform: A Perspective from Oral History," *Congress and the Presidency* 42 (September–December 2015): 243–263.

35 Institute of Politics, *Campaign for President*, 114–115.

36 Larry J. Sabato, "The Conventions—One Festival of Hope, One Celebration of Impending Victory," in Sabato, *Toward the Millennium*, 98.

37 Daniel K. Williams, *God's Own Party: The Making of the Christian Right* (New York: Oxford University Press, 2010), 239–241.

38 "Text of Robert Dole's Speech to the Republican National Convention, August 15, 1996," CNN, http://www.cnn.com/ALLPOLITICS/1996/conventions/san.diego/transcripts/0815/dole.fdch.shtml.

39 E. J. Dionne, "Mod Squad," *Washington Post*, September 7, 1996.

40 Stanley, "The Nominations," 38.

41 Bill Clinton, *My Life* (New York: Random House, 2004), 724.

42 Gerald Posner, *Citizen Perot: His Life and Times* (New York: Random House, 1996), 334–337.

43 John R. Zaller, "Monica Lewinsky's Contribution to Political Science," *PS: Political Science and Politics* 31 (June 1998): 182–189.

44 Daniel Galvin, *Presidential Party Building: Dwight D. Eisenhower to George W. Bush* (Princeton, NJ: Princeton University Press, 2010), chap. 11. Galvin credits Clinton with becoming a party builder during his second term, after his reelection was secured.

45 Clinton fretted that "guns, gays, and abortion" would cost him votes in Colorado, Nevada, and Georgia. He also worried that his administration's tobacco

policies would reduce his vote in Kentucky and North Carolina, and that the anti–affirmative action proposition on the California ballot would hurt him there. Clinton, *My Life*, 730, 734, 727.

46 The states where Bush held Clinton's margin of victory below 5 points were Colorado, Georgia, Kentucky, Louisiana, Montana, Nevada, New Hampshire, New Jersey, Ohio, Tennessee, and Wisconsin.

47 Elizabeth Drew, *Whatever It Takes: The Real Struggle for Political Power in America* (New York: Viking, 1997), 166.

48 "Dole, in 3-Prong Effort, Seeks to Add Spark to His Campaign," *New York Times*, September 11, 1996.

49 Nelson, "Bill Clinton and Welfare Reform."

50 Morris, *Behind the Oval Office*, 300.

51 Thomas Weko and John H. Aldrich, "The Presidency and the Election Campaign: Framing the Choice in 1996," in *The Presidency and the Political System*, 5th ed., ed. Michael Nelson (Washington, DC: CQ Press, 1998), 284.

52 Michael Nelson "The Election: Turbulence and Tranquility in Contemporary American Politics," in Nelson, *The Elections of 1996*, Nelson, 57.

53 Abramson, Aldrich, and Rohde, *Change and Continuity in the 1996 Elections*, 32.

54 Institute of Politics, *Campaign for President*, 227.

55 Richard L. Berke, "Perot Turns Down Dole Plea to Quit, Calling It "'Weird,'" *New York Times*, October 25, 1996.

56 Alan Schroeder, *Presidential Debates: Forty Years of High-Risk TV* (New York: Columbia University Press, 2000), 140.

57 The text of the 1996 presidential and vice presidential debates may be found at "Presidential Debates, 1960–2016," The American Presidency Project, http:// presidency.proxied.lsit.ucsb.edu/debates.php.

58 Dan Goodgame, "Jack Kemp: From Savior to Scapegoat," *Time*, October 21, 1996.

59 Abramson, Aldrich, and Rohde, *Change and Continuity in the 1996 Elections*, 35–36.

60 Quoted in Josh King, *Off Script: An Advance Man's Guide to White House Stagecraft, Campaign Spectacle, and Political Suicide* (New York: St. Martin's Press, 2016), 170.

61 Takiff, *A Complicated Man*, 295.

62 Scott Keeter, "Public Opinion and the Election," in Pomper, *The Elections of 1996*, 123. The exit poll showed that 34 percent of voters thought "Dole's age would interfere with his ability to serve effectively as president." Larry J. Sabato, "The November Vote—A Status Quo Election," in Sabato, *Toward the Millennium*, 150, 153.

63 Burns and Sorensen, *Dead Center*, 91.

64 Walter J. Stone and Ronald B. Rapoport, "It's Perot, Stupid! The Legacy of the 1992 Perot Movement on the Major-Party System, 1994–2000," *PS: Political Science and Politics* 31 (March 2001): 53; and Sabato, "The November Vote," 151.

65 Unless otherwise indicated, the results of the Voter News Service national exit poll are taken from Nelson, "The Election," 55–57.

66 Ceaser and Busch, *Losing to Win*, 124.

67 Richard E. Cohen, "Campaigning for Congress: The Echo of '94," in Sabato, *Toward the Millennium*, 185.

68 Abramson, Aldrich, and Rohde, *Change and Continuity in the 1996 Elections*, 210.

69 Drew, *Whatever It Takes*, 217.

70 Gary C. Jacobson, "The 105th Congress: Unprecedented and Unsurprising," in Nelson, *The Elections of 1996*, 154.

71 Jacobson, 143.

CHAPTER 9. BILL CLINTON AND A NEW ERA
OF DE FACTO DIVIDED GOVERNMENT

1   David Maraniss, *First in His Class: A Biography of Bill Clinton* (New York: Simon & Schuster, 1995), 388.

2   Jeffrey A. Engel et al., *Impeachment: An American History* (New York: Modern Library, 2018), xiii.

3   Taylor Branch, *The Clinton Tapes: Wrestling History with the President* (New York: Simon & Schuster, 2009), 634.

4   David E. Sanger, "After 'Next Best Thing,' Clinton Carefully Praises Gore," *New York Times*, November 4, 2000.

5   James W. Ceaser and Andrew E. Busch, *The Perfect Tie: The True Story of the 2000 Election* (Lanham, MD: Rowman & Littlefield, 2001), 30.

6   John F. Harris, *The Survivor: Bill Clinton in the White House* (New York: Random House, 2005), 384.

7   Branch, *The Clinton Tapes*, 623.

8   "Transcript of Bill Clinton's Speech to the Democratic National Convention," *New York Times*, September 5, 2008, https://www.nytimes.com/2012/09/05/us/politics/transcript-of-bill-clintons-speech-to-the-democratic-national-convention.html.

9   Kathleen A. Frankovic and Monika L. McDermott, "Public Opinion in the 2000 Election: The Ambivalent Electorate," in *The Election of 2000*, ed. Gerald M. Pomper (New York: Chatham House, 2001), 75.

10 Robert G. Kaiser, "Academics Say It's Elementary: Gore Wins," *Washington Post*, August 31, 2000. "It's not even going to be close," said Michael Lewis-Beck of the University of Iowa as early as May. Robert G. Kaiser, "Is This Any Way to Pick a Winner?," *Washington Post*, May 26, 2000.

11 Harris, *The Survivor*, 389.

12 Sidney Blumenthal, *The Clinton Wars* (New York: Farrar, Straus and Giroux, 2003), 716.

13 Bob Woodward, *Shadow: Five Presidents and the Legacy of Watergate* (New York: Simon & Schuster, 1999), 454.

14 Michael Duffy, "What It Took," *Time*, November 20, 2000, 130.

15 Thomas M. DeFrank, "I'm My Own Man, Says Al," *New York Daily News*, August 18, 2000.

16 David S. Broder, "Gore's Clinton Problem," *Washington Post National Weekly Edition*, October 30, 2000, 4.

17 Michael Kinsley, "The Art of Finger-Pointing," *Slate*, October 30, 2000, http://slate.msn.com/00-10-30/readme.asp.

18 Stanley Greenberg Oral History, Miller Center, University of Virginia, William J. Clinton Oral History Project, October 11, 2007, https://millercenter.org/the-presidency/presidential-oral-histories/stanley-greenberg-oral-history-2007-pollster.

19 "What a Long, Strange Trip," *Newsweek*, November 20, 2000, 126.

20 Gary C. Jacobson, *The 2000 Elections and Beyond* (Washington, DC: CQ Press, 2001), 26.

21 Toni Morrison, "Comment," *New Yorker*, October 5, 1998, https://www.newyorker.com/magazine/1998/10/05/comment-6543.

22 John Heilemann and Mark Halperin, *Game Change: Obama and the Clintons, McCain and Plain, and the Race of a Lifetime* (New York: HarperCollins, 2010), 186.

23 Heilemann and Halperin, 197.

24 Heilemann and Halperin, 219.

25 Dan Balz and Haynes Johnson, *The Battle for America 2008: The Story of an Extraordinary Election* (New York: Viking, 2009), 160.

26 Heilemann and Halperin, *Game Change*, 227.

27 Janie Valencia, "Most Democrats Now Identify as Liberal," *FiveThirtyEight*, January 11, 2019, https://fivethirtyeight.com/features/most-democrats-now-identify-as-liberal/.

28 Alan I. Abramowitz, *The Disappearing Center: Engaged Citizens, Polarization, and American Democracy* (New Haven, CT: Yale University Press, 2010), chap. 3.

29 See, for example, Michael Darer, "There Is No Better Encapsulation of Contemporary White Liberalism Than 'The West Wing.' That's a Bad Thing," *HuffPost*, December 9, 2016, https://www.huffpost.com/entry/there-is-no-better-encapsulation-of-contemporary-white_b_584a59aae4b0151082221a0c; and Emily Todd VanDerWerff, "The West Wing Is 20 Years Old. Too Many Democrats Still Think It's a Great Model for Politics," *Vox*, September 16, 2019, https://www.vox.com/culture/2019/9/16/20857281/the-west-wing-20-anniversary-primetime-podcast-episode-bartlet-biden.

30 Walter Dean Burnham, "Bill Clinton: Riding the Tiger," in *The Election of 1996: Reports and Interpretations*, ed. Gerald M. Pomper (Chatham, NJ: Chatham House, 1997), 1–20.

31 Gloria Steinem, "Feminists and the Clinton Question," *New York Times*, March 22, 1998.

32 David A. Farenthold, "Trump Recorded Having Extremely Lewd Conversation about Women in 2005," *Washington Post*, October 8, 2016.

33 "Full Transcript: Second 2016 Presidential Debate," *Politico*, October 10, 2016, https://www.politico.com/story/2016/10/2016-presidential-debate-transcript-229519.

34 James Comey, *A Higher Loyalty: Truth, Lies, and Leadership* (New York: Flatiron Books, 2018), 180.

35 "Statement by FBI Director James B. Comey on the Investigation of Secretary Hillary Clinton's Use of a Personal E-Mail System," FBI National Press Office, July 5, 2016, https://www.fbi.gov/news/pressrel/press-releases/statement-by-fbi-director-james-b-comey-on-the-investigation-of-secretary-hillary-clinton2019s-use-of-a-personal-e-mail-system.

36 The 2000 election gave Bush a Republican House and, with Vice President Richard Cheney casting tiebreaking votes as president of the Senate, a 51–50 majority in that chamber. In the 2002 midterm elections, the GOP gained two seats in the Senate and eight in the House.

37 Steve Holland, "Bush Admits Republicans Took a 'Thumping,'" Reuters, January 19, 2007, https://www.reuters.com/article/us-usa-elections-bush/bush-admits-republicans-took-a-thumping-idUSN0747831720061108.

38 Kara Rowland, "Obama Concedes 'Shellacking,'" *Washington Times*, November 3, 2010, https://www.washingtontimes.com/news/2010/nov/3/obama-concedes-shellacking/.

39 "Mid-term Elections 2018: Trump Hails 'Tremendous Success,'" BBC News, November 7, 2018, https://www.bbc.com/news/world-us-canada-46125121.

40 Byron E. Shafer, *American Political Patterns: Stability and Change, 1932–2016* (Lawrence: University Press of Kansas, 2016), 177, 180.

41 See Frances E. Lee, *Insecure Majorities: Congress and the Perpetual Campaign* (Chicago: University of Chicago Press, 2016).

42 Kevin M. Kruse and Julian E. Zelizer, *Fault Lines: A History of the United States since 1974* (New York: W. W. Norton, 2019), 297, 298.

43 As measured by DW-NOMINATE scores. George C. Edwards, "No Deal: Donald Trump's Leadership of Congress," *Forum* 15 (October 2017): 456–457.

44 Sam Rosenfeld, *The Polarizers: Postwar Architects of Our Partisan Era* (Chicago: University of Chicago Press, 2018).

45 Molly Moorhead, "Mitt Romney Says 47 Percent of Americans Pay No Income Tax," Politifact, September 18, 2012, https://www.politifact.com/truth-o-meter/statements/2012/sep/18/mitt-romney/romney-says-47-percent-americans-pay-no-income-tax/; and "Clinton: Half of Trump Supporters 'Basket of Deplorables,'" BBC News, September 10, 2016, https://www.bbc.com/news/av/election-us-2016-37329812/clinton-half-of-trump-supporters-basket-of-deplorables.

46 Marc Hetherington and Jonathan Weiler, *Prius or Pickup? How the Answers to Four Simple Questions Explain America's Great Divide* (Boston: Houghton Mifflin, 2018), 128–131. Asked in 2018 if they agreed that members of the other party "are not just worse for politics—they are downright evil," 42 percent of both Democrats and Republicans said yes. Nathan P. Kalmoe and Lilliana Mason, "Lethal Mass Partisanship: Prevalence, Correlates, and Electoral Contingencies" (paper presented at the annual meting of the National Capital Area Political Science Association, January 2019), https://www.dannyhayes.org/uploads/6/9/8/5/69858539/kalmoe___mason_ncapsa_2019_-_lethal_partisanship_-_final_lmedit.pdf.

47   Gary C. Jacobson, *A Divider, Not a Uniter: George W. Bush and the American People*, 2nd ed. (Boston: Longman, 2011), chap. 1. These contrasts persisted throughout the Obama presidency and well into the Trump presidency.

48   Abramowitz, *The Disappearing Center*, x. Hetherington and Weiler argue that since 1992 the Republican-Democrat divide has come to reflect the division between people with "fixed" and "fluid" worldviews. Republicans (fixed) tend to view the world as a dangerous place, and Democrats (fluid) to view it as an inviting one. Hetherington and Weiler, *Prius or Pickup?*, 23.

49   Kruse and Zelizer, *Fault Lines*, 9.

50   James, Poniewozik, *Audience of One: Donald Trump, Television, and the Fracturing of America* (New York: Liveright, 2019), 24, 92.

51   David Wasserman, "Whole Foods vs. Cracker Barrel Culture Gap over Time," https://twitter.com/redistrict/status/796425689360637952?lang=en; and "Senate Control Could Come Down to Whole Foods vs. Cracker Barrel," *FiveThirtyEight*, October 8, 2014, https://fivethirtyeight.com/features/senate -control-could-come-down-to-whole-foods-vs-cracker-barrel/.

52   Lee, *Insecure Majorities*, 2.

53   Geoffrey Skelley, "Are Blowout Presidential Elections a Thing of the Past?," *FiveThirtyEight*, May 28, 2019, https://fivethirtyeight.com/features/are-blowout -presidential-elections-a-thing-of-the-past/.

54   Lee, *Insecure Majorities*, 2, 4.

55   Rebecca Leung, "Bush Sought 'Way' to Invade Iraq?," *60 Minutes*, January 9, 2004, https://www.cbsnews.com/news/bush-sought-way-to-invade-iraq/.

56   Kate Davidson and John Hilsenrath, "How Washington Learned to Love Debt and Deficits," *Wall Street Journal*, June 14, 2019.

57   Sarah A. Binder, *Stalemate: Causes and Consequences of Legislative Gridlock* (Washington, DC: Brookings Institution Press, 2003).

58   Andrew Rudalevige, "The Presidency and Unilateral Power," in *The Presidency and the Political System*, 11th ed., ed. Michael Nelson (Washington, DC: CQ Press, 2018), 471.

59   John Anthony Maltese, *The Selling of Supreme Court Nominees* (Baltimore: Johns Hopkins University Press, 1995).

60   President George W. Bush's abandonment of Harriet Miers's Supreme Court nomination in 2005 came in response to strong objections by Senate Republicans, who controlled that chamber.

61   Carl Hulse, *Confirmation Bias: Inside Washington's War over the Supreme Court from Scalia's Death to Justice Kavanaugh* (New York: Harper, 2019), 186.

62   Benjamin Ginsberg and Martin Shefter, *Politics by Other Means: The Declining Importance of Elections in America* (New York: Basic Books, 1990), x.

63   Taylor Gee and Zach Stanton, "Forty-Six Political Scandals That Were 'Worse Than Watergate,'" *Politico*, February 1, 2018, https://www.politico.com /magazine/story/2018/02/01/46-political-scandals-that-were-worse-than -watergate-216923.

64   "Full Transcript: Second 2016 Presidential Debate."

65 On Article II of the impeachment resolution, for example, House Republicans voted 216 to 12 in favor and Democrats voted 201 to 5 against. In the Senate Republicans voted 50 to 5 in favor and Democrats voted 45 to 0 against.

66 Michael Nelson, *Trump: The First Two Years* (Charlottesville: University of Virginia Press, 2019), chap. 9.

67 Michael (Mickey) Kantor Oral History, Miller Center, University of Virginia, William J. Clinton Oral History Project, June 28, 2002, https://millercenter .org/the-presidency/presidential-oral-histories/michael-mickey-kantor-oral -history-us-trade.

68 Bruce Reed Oral History, Miller Center, University of Virginia, William J. Clinton Oral History Project, April 12, 2004, https://millercenter.org/the-presidency /presidential-oral-histories/bruce-reed-oral-history-april-2004-domestic-policy.

69 Bruce Reed Oral History.

70 Mathew McCubbins, "Government by Lay-Away: Federal Spending and Deficits under Divided Party Control," in *The Politics of Divided Government*, ed. Gary W. Cox and Samuel Kernell (Boulder, CO: Westview Press, 1991), 113–153.

71 George Hager and Eric Pianin, *Mirage: Why Neither Democrats nor Republicans Can Balance the Budget, End the Deficit, and Satisfy the Public* (New York: Crown, 1997).

72 Gary C. Jacobson, *The Politics of Congressional Elections*, 5th ed. (Boston: Longman, 2001), 259.

73 Michael Nelson, "Redivided Government and the Politics of the Budgetary Process during the Clinton Years: An Oral History Perspective," *Congress and the Presidency* 43 (September–December 2016): 257.

BIBLIOGRAPHIC ESSAY

Although no other works about the 1992 and 1996 elections, their historical con-text, and their consequences make the arguments this book makes, many useful accounts have been written by journalists, scholars, and participants.

In the immediate aftermath of every presidential election from 1976 to 2000, political scientist Gerald M. Pomper and colleagues published a book called *The Election of [Year]: Reports and Interpretations* with Chatham House. Starting in 1984, political scientist Michael Nelson and colleagues began publishing a series of post-election books called *The Elections of [Year]* with CQ Press, a series that is slated to continue through at least 2020 with the University of Virginia Press. With different titles from election to election, political scientists James W. Ceaser and Andrew E. Busch, joined in 2008 by John J. Pitney Jr., have authored a book every four years with Rowman & Littlefield. These include *Upside Down and Inside Out: The 1992 Elections and American Politics* (1993) and *Losing to Win: The 1996 Election and American Politics* (1997). After the 1996 election, political scientist Larry J. Sabato and colleagues published the first in a postelection series, *Toward the Millennium: The Elections of 1996* (Needham Heights, MA: Allyn and Bacon, 1997). In addition, two years after each presidential election, political scientists Paul R. Abramson, John H. Aldrich, and David W. Rohde have published books with CQ Press drawing on more recently available survey data. These include *Change and Continuity in the 1992 Elections* (1995) and *Change and Continuity in the 1996 Elections* (1998).

Journalists also have published meritorious postelection books. In the period at the heart of this volume, Jack W. Germond and Jules Witcover authored *Blue Smoke and Mirrors: How Reagan Won and Why Carter Lost the Election of 1980* (New York: Viking, 1981); *Wake Us When It's Over: Presidential Politics of 1984* (New York: Macmillan, 1985); *Whose Broad Stripes and Bright Stars: The Trivial Pursuit of the Presidency, 1988* (New York: Warner Books, 1989); and *Mad as Hell: Revolt at the Ballot Box, 1992* (New York: Warner Books, 1993). A group of *Newsweek* reporters published *The Quest for the Presidency: The 1988 Campaign*, by Peter Goldman, Tom Mathews, and the *Newsweek* Special Election Team (New York: Simon & Schuster, 1989); *The Quest for the Presidency 1992*, by Peter Goldman, Thomas M. DeFrank, Mark Miller, Andrew Murr, and Tom Mathews (College Station: Texas A&M University Press, 1994); and *Back from the Dead: How Clinton Survived the Republican Revolution*, by Evan Thomas, Karen Breslau, Debra Rosenberg, Leslie Kaufman, and Andrew Murr (New York: Atlantic Monthly Press, 1997). On 1988, see also Sidney Blumenthal, *Pledging Allegiance: The Last Campaign of the Cold War* (New York: HarperCollins, 1990).

The transcripts of postelection gatherings of campaign operatives and national political reporters assembled by the Institute of Politics of Harvard University's John F. Kennedy School of Government also provide a valuable resource. These include David R. Runkel, *Campaign for President: The Managers Look at '88* (Dover, MA: Auburn House, 1989); Charles T. Royer, ed., *Campaign for President: The Managers Look at '92* (Hollis, NH: Hollis Publishing, 1994); and Institute of Politics, Harvard University, *Campaign for President: The Managers Look at '96* (Hollis, NH: Hollis Publishing, 1997).

Oral history interviews concerning Clinton's 1992 campaign by political scientist Diane D. Blair and, especially, interviews concerning the Bush and Clinton campaigns and administrations by the University of Virginia's Miller Center are of enormous value to scholars studying these elections and presidencies.

Most of Blair's interviews were conducted in the aftermath of the 1992 election and are archived at the Pryor Center for Visual and Oral History at the University of Arkansas. Among the most useful are those with Paul Begala, Robert Boorstin, Gloria Cabe, James Carville, Stanley Greenberg, Frank Greer, Mandy Grunwald, Nancy McFadden, George Stephanopoulos, and David Wilhelm. Blair's interviews may be accessed at http://pryorcenter.uark.edu/project.php?thisProject=11.

The Miller Center interviews were longer and more comprehensive and were conducted over an extended period in the years after each president left office. (I participated in several of the Clinton-related interviews.) Among the most useful are those with Al From, William Galston, Stanley Greenberg, Frank Greer, Elaine Kamarck, Michael (Mickey) Kantor, David Kusnet, Anthony Lake, Joseph Lockhart, Dee Dee Myers, Roy Neel, Bruce Reed, Robert Rubin, Eli Segal, and Susan Thomases. The Miller Center's Clinton-related oral histories may be accessed at https://millercenter.org/the-presidency/presidential-oral-histories/bill-clinton.

Excerpts from these and other Miller Center Clinton oral history interviews are the basis of Russell L. Riley, *Inside the Clinton White House: An Oral History* (New York: Oxford University Press, 2016). An edited volume that draws extensively on the interviews is Michael Nelson, Barbara A. Perry, and Russell L. Riley, eds., *42: Inside the Bill Clinton Presidency* (Ithaca, NY: Cornell University Press, 2016). Nelson also authored three oral history–based journal articles: "Clinton's Elections: Redividing Government in the 1990s," *Presidential Studies Quarterly* 46 (June 2016): 457–472; "Redivided Government and the Politics of the Budgetary Process during the Clinton Years: An Oral History Perspective," *Congress and the Presidency* 43 (September–December 2016): 243–263; and "Bill Clinton and Welfare Reform: A Perspective from Oral History," *Congress and the Presidency* 42 (September–December 2015): 243–263.

For two different interview-based books on Clinton, see Michael Takiff, *A Complicated Man: The Life of Bill Clinton as Told by Those Who Know Him* (New Haven, CT: Yale University Press, 2010); and Taylor Branch, *The Clinton Tapes: Wrestling History with the President* (New York: Simon & Schuster, 2009).

Among the most valuable Miller Center interviews concerning the Bush presidency are those with James A. Baker III, Richard B. Cheney, David F. Demarest, Craig Fuller, James P. Pinkerton, J. Danforth Quayle, Sigmund Rogich, and John H. Sununu. An edited volume that draws extensively on the interviews is Michael Nelson and Barbara A. Perry, eds., *41: Inside the Presidency of George H. W. Bush* (Ithaca, NY: Cornell University Press, 2014). The Miller Center's Bush-related oral histories may be accessed at https://millercenter.org/the-presidency/presidential-oral-histo ries/george-h-w-bush.

Concerning the candidates, several biographies are worthy of note. The best biography of George Bush is Jon Meacham, *Destiny and Power: The American Odyssey of George Herbert Walker Bush* (New York: Random House, 2015). Others include Herbert S. Parmet, *George Bush: The Life of a Lone Star Yankee* (New York: Scribner, 1997); Timothy Naftali, *George H. W. Bush* (New York: Times Books, 2007); Tom Wicker, *George Herbert Walker Bush* (New York: Viking, 2004); and George W. Bush, *41: A Portrait of My Father* (New York: Crown, 2014). Bush himself did not publish a memoir. Instead, he authored *All the Best, George Bush: My Life in Letters and Other Writings* (New York: Scribner, 1999); and, with Brent Scowcroft, *A World Transformed* (New York: Alfred A. Knopf, 1998).

Treatments of the Bush presidency by scholars and journalists include Jeffrey A. Engel, *When the World Seemed New: George H. W. Bush and the End of the Cold War* (Boston: Houghton Mifflin, 2017); John Robert Greene, *The Presidency of George Bush* (Lawrence: University Press of Kansas, 2000); Greene, *The Presidency of George H. W. Bush*, 2nd ed. (Lawrence: University Press of Kansas, 2015); Michael Duffy and Dan Goodgame, *Marching in Place: The Status Quo Presidency of George Bush* (New York: Simon & Schuster, 1992); and John Podhoretz, *Hell of a Ride: Backstage at the White House Follies, 1989–1993* (New York: Simon & Schuster, 1993).

Accounts of the Bush presidency by administration alumni include James A. Baker III, *"Work Hard, Study . . . and Keep Out of Politics": Adventures and Lessons from an Unexpected Political Life* (New York: Putnam, 2006); Richard Darman, *Who's in Control? Polar Politics and the Sensible Center* (New York: Simon & Schuster, 1996); James A. Baker III, *The Politics of Diplomacy: Revolution, War, and Peace, 1989–1992* (New York: Putnam, 1995); John Sununu, *The Quiet Man: The Indispensable Presidency of George H. W. Bush* (New York: HarperCollins, 2015; and Marlin Fitzwater, *Call the Briefing! A Memoir: Ten Years in the White House with Presidents* (XLibris, 2000).

Useful books about Dan Quayle include Richard F. Fenno Jr., *The Making of a Senator: Dan Quayle* (Washington, DC: CQ Press, 1989); Dan Quayle, *Standing Firm* (New York: HarperPaperbacks, 1994); and Bob Woodward and David S. Broder, *The Man Who Would Be President: Dan Quayle* (New York: Simon & Schuster, 1992).

Barbara Bush's role in her husband's career is the subject of Susan Page, *Matriarch: Barbara Bush and the Making of an American Dynasty* (New York: Twelve, 2019); and Barbara Bush, *Barbara Bush: A Memoir* (New York: Scribner, 1994).

Bill Clinton's prepresidential career is the focus of several books, among them *First in His Class: A Biography of Bill Clinton* by the invaluable David Maraniss (New York: Simon & Schuster, 1995). Others include John Brummett, *Highwire: From the Backwoods to the Beltway—The Education of Bill Clinton* (New York: Hyperion, 1994); and Ernest Dumas, ed., *The Clintons of Arkansas: An Introduction by Those Who Know Them Best* (Fayetteville: University of Arkansas Press, 1993). Clinton's governorship receives particular attention in David Osborne and Ted Gabler, *Reinventing Government: How the Entrepreneurial Spirit Is Transforming the Public Sector* (Reading, MA: Addison-Wesley, 1992); and David Osborne, *Laboratories of Democracy: A New Breed of Governor Creates Models for National Growth* (Boston: Harvard Business School Press, 1990).

The Clinton presidency is chronicled in Patrick J. Maney, *Bill Clinton: New Gilded Age President* (Lawrence: University Press of Kansas, 2016); James MacGregor Burns and Georgia J. Sorensen, *Dead Center: Clinton-Gore Leadership and the Perils of Moderation* (New York: Scribner, 1999); John F. Harris, *The Survivor: Bill Clinton in the White House* (New York: Random House, 2005); Gil Troy, *The Age of Clinton: America in the 1990s* (New York: Thomas Dunne, 2015); Michael Tomasky, *Bill Clinton* (New York: Times Books, 2017); Elizabeth Drew, *On the Edge: The Clinton Presidency* (New York: Simon & Schuster, 1994); Drew, *Showdown: The Struggle between the Gingrich Congress and the Clinton White House* (New York: Simon & Schuster, 1996); Howard Kurtz, *Spin Cycle: Inside the Clinton Propaganda Machine* (New York: Free Press, 1998); Steven M. Gillon, *The Pact: Bill Clinton, Newt Gingrich, and the Rivalry That Defined a Generation* (New York: Oxford University Press, 2008); David Maraniss, *The Clinton Enigma: A Four-and-a-Half-Minute Speech Reveals the President's Entire Life* (New York: Simon & Schuster, 1998); Joe Klein, *The Natural: The Misunderstood Presidency of Bill Clinton* (New York: Doubleday, 2002); Bob Woodward, *Shadow: Five Presidents and the Legacy of Watergate* (New York: Simon & Schuster, 1999); Sean M. Theriault, *The Gingrich Senators: The Roots of Partisan Warfare in Congress* (New York: Oxford University Press, 2013); and Bob Woodward, *The Choice* (New York: Simon & Schuster, 1996), which also discusses Bob Dole.

Accounts of Clinton's presidential campaigns and presidency by Clinton and various associates include Bill Clinton, *My Life* (New York: Random House, 2004); George Stephanopoulos, *All Too Human: A Political Education* (Boston: Little, Brown, 1999); Stanley B. Greenberg, *Dispatches from the War Room: In the Trenches with Five Extraordinary Leaders* (New York: St. Martin's Press, 2009); Terry McAuliffe with Steve Kettmann, *What a Party! My Life among Democrats, Presidents, Candidates, Donors, Activists, Alligators, and Other Wild Animals* (New York: St. Martin's Press, 2007); Dick Morris, *Behind the Oval Office: Winning the Presidency in the Nineties* (New York: Random House, 1997); Michael Waldman, *POTUS Speaks: Finding the Words That Defined the Clinton Presidency* (New York: Simon & Schuster, 2000); Mary Matalin and James Carville, *All's Fair: Love, War, and Running for President* (New York: Random House, 1994); and Sidney Blumenthal, *The Clinton Wars* (New York: Farrar, Straus and Giroux, 2003).

Al Gore's career is the subject of Bill Turque, *Inventing Al Gore: A Biography* (Boston: Houghton Mifflin, 2000); and David Maraniss and Ellen Nakashima, *The Prince of Tennessee: Al Gore Meets His Fate* (New York: Simon & Schuster, 2000). The best treatment of the modern vice presidency is Joel K. Goldstein, *The White House Vice Presidency: The Path to Significance, Mondale to Biden* (Lawrence: University Press of Kansas, 2016).

Hillary Rodham Clinton published *Living History* (New York: Simon & Schuster, 2003) and *Hard Choices* (New York: Simon & Schuster, 2014). She is the subject of Carl Bernstein, *A Woman in Charge: The Life of Hillary Rodham Clinton* (New York: Alfred A. Knopf, 2007); and William H. Chafe, *Bill and Hillary: The Politics of the Personal* (New York: Farrar, Straus and Giroux, 2012).

Campaign books by the candidates in 1992 were published by Governor Bill Clinton and Senator Al Gore, *Putting People First: How We Can All Change America* (New York: Times Books, 1992); and Ross Perot, *United We Stand: How We Can Take Back Our Country* (New York: Hyperion, 1992).

Other books by or about various active or potential candidates in these and other recent elections are useful. On the various Democrats, see Marshall Frady, *Jesse: The Life and Pilgrimage of Jesse Jackson* (New York: Random House, 1996); Robert S. McElvaine, *Mario Cuomo: A Biography* (New York: Scribner, 1988); and L. Douglas Wilder, *Son of Virginia: A Life in America's Political Arena* (Guilford, CT: Rowman & Littlefield, 2015); Adam Clymer, *Edward M. Kennedy: A Biography* (New York: William Morrow, 1999); and Walter F. Mondale, with David Hage, *The Good Fight: A Life in Liberal Politics* (New York: Scribner, 2010).

On Republicans, see Morton Kondracke and Fred Barnes, *Jack Kemp: The Bleeding-Heart Conservative Who Changed America* (New York: Sentinel, 2015); Timothy Stanley, *The Crusader: The Life and Tumultuous Times of Pat Buchanan* (New York: St. Martin's Press, 2012); Patrick J. Buchanan, *Right from the Beginning* (Boston: Little, Brown, 1988); and Richard Ben Cramer, *Bob Dole* (New York: Vintage, 1995). Cramer's book *What It Takes: The Way to the White House* (New York: Random House, 1992) is about 1988 and includes deeply reported profiles of Dole, Richard Gephardt, and other leading figures in both parties.

Ross Perot is the subject of Gerald Posner, *Citizen Perot: His Life and Times* (New York: Random House, 1996), as well as parts of Ed Rollins, with Tom DeFrank, *Bare Knuckles and Back Rooms: My Life in American Politics* (New York: Broadway Books, 1996); and Steven J. Rosenstone, Roy L. Behr, and Edward H. Lazarus, *Third Parties in America*, 2nd ed. (Princeton, NJ: Princeton University Press, 1996).

General treatments of American politics in the period covered by this book include Stephen Skowronek, *Presidential Leadership in Political Time: Reprise and Reappraisal* (Lawrence: University Press of Kansas, 2008); William C. Berman, *America's Right Turn: From Nixon to Clinton* (Baltimore: Johns Hopkins University Press, 1994); Dan Balz and Ronald Brownstein, *Storming the Gates: Protest Politics and the Republican Revival* (Boston: Little, Brown, 1996); Steve Kornacki, *The Red and the Blue: The 1990s and the Birth of Political Tribalism* (New York: Ecco, 2018); Eric Alterman and Kevin Mattson, *The Cause: The Fight for American Liberalism from Franklin Roosevelt to Barack Obama* (New York: Viking, 2012); Kevin M. Kruse and Julian E. Zelizer, *Fault Lines: A History of the United States since 1974* (New York: W. W. Norton, 2019); Sean Wilentz, *The Age of Reagan: A History 1974–2008* (New York: HarperCollins, 2008); Frances E. Lee, *Insecure Majorities: Congress and the Perpetual Campaign* (Chicago: University of Chicago Press, 2016); Benjamin Ginsberg and Martin Shefter, *Politics by Other Means: Politicians, Prosecutors, and the Press from Watergate to Whitewater* (New York: W. W. Norton, 2002); and Byron E. Shafer, *American Political Patterns: Stability and Change, 1932–2016* (Lawrence: University Press of Kansas, 2016).

The political parties in this era—especially the Democratic Party, whose challenges were much discussed—are treated in Daniel Galvin, *Presidential Party Building: Dwight D. Eisenhower to George W. Bush* (Princeton, NJ: Princeton University

Press, 2010); Randall Rothenberg, *The Neo-liberals: Creating the New American Politics* (New York: Simon & Schuster, 1984); Al From, *The New Democrats and the Return to Power* (New York: Palgrave Macmillan, 2012); Peter Brown, *Minority Party: Why Democrats Face Defeat in 1992 and Beyond* (Washington, DC: Regnery Gateway, 1991); Steven M. Gillon, *The Democrats' Dilemma: Walter F. Mondale and the Liberal Legacy* (New York: Columbia University Press, 1992); Kenneth S. Baer, *Reinventing Democrats: The Politics of Liberalism from Reagan to Clinton* (Lawrence: University Press of Kansas, 2000); William Galston and Elaine Ciulla Kamarck, "The Politics of Evasion: Democrats and the Presidency," Progressive Policy Institute, September 1989, http://www.progressivepolicy.org/wp-content/uploads/2013/03/Politics_of _Evasion.pdf.

Campaign finance is the subject of Herbert E. Alexander and Anthony Corrado, *Financing the 1992 Election* (Armonk, NY: M. E. Sharpe, 1995); and Elizabeth Drew, *Whatever It Takes: The Real Struggle for Political Power in America* (New York: Viking, 1997).

The role of the media in the elections is discussed in Paul Taylor, *See How They Run: Electing the President in an Age of Mediaocracy* (New York: Alfred A. Knopf, 1990); Tom Rosenstiel, *Strange Bedfellows: How Television and the Presidential Candidates Changed American Politics, 1992* (New York: Hyperion, 1993); Matthew Robert Kerbel, *Edited for Television: CNN, ABC, and American Presidential Elections*, 2nd ed. (New York: Westview Press, 1998); Larry King, with Mark Stengel, *On the Line: The New Road to the White House* (New York: Harcourt, Brace, 1993); Thomas Patterson, *Out of Order* (New York: Alfred A. Knopf, 1993); and Matt Bai, *All the Truth Is Out: The Week Politics Went Tabloid* (New York: Alfred A. Knopf, 2014).

Televised presidential and vice presidential debates, including those that took place in 1988, 1992, and 1996, are the subject of Alan Schroeder, *Presidential Debates: Risky Business on the Campaign Trail* (New York: Columbia University Press, 2016); Jim Lehrer, *Tension City: Inside the Presidential Debates, from Kennedy-Nixon to Obama-McCain* (New York: Random House, 2011); Anthony Corrado, *Let America Decide* (New York: Twentieth Century Fund Press, 1995); and Newton N. Minow and Craig L. Lamay, *Inside the Presidential Debates: Their Improbable Past and Promising Future* (Chicago: University of Chicago Press, 2008).

Political involvement by evangelical Christians and, more generally, social conservatives is discussed in James L. Guth and John C. Green, eds., *The Bible and the Ballot Box* (Boulder, CO: Westview Press, 1991); Daniel K. Williams, *God's Own Party: The Making of the Christian Right* (New York: Oxford University Press, 2010); Frances FitzGerald, *The Evangelicals: The Struggle to Reshape America* (New York: Simon & Schuster, 2017); Donald T. Critchlow, *The Conservative Ascendancy: How the Republican Right Rose to Power in Modern America*, 2nd ed. (Lawrence: University Press of Kansas, 2011); and Critchlow, *Phyllis Schlafly and Grassroots Conservatism: A Woman's Crusade* (Princeton, NJ: Princeton University Press, 2005). The political effects of race in this era are discussed in Tali Mendelberg, *The Race Card: Campaign Strategy, Implicit Messages, and the Norm of Equality* (Princeton, NJ: Princeton University Press, 2001); and Stanley B. Greenberg, *Middle Class Dreams: The Politics and Power of the New American Majority* (New Haven, CT: Yale University Press, 1996).

Various journal articles and book chapters treat different aspects of these elections. These include Margaret O'Mara, *Pivotal Tuesdays: Four Elections That Shaped the Twentieth Century* (Philadelphia: University of Pennsylvania Press, 2015), chaps. 7 and 8; Eleanor Clift and Tom Brazaitas, *War without Bloodshed: The Art of Politics* (New York: Simon & Schuster, 1996), chap. 1; Walter R. Mears, *Deadlines Past: Forty Years of Presidential Campaigning: A Reporter's Story* (Kansas City, MO: Andrews McMeel, 2003), chaps. 9 and 10; Wayne P. Steger, "Presidential Renomination Challenges in the 20th Century," *Presidential Studies Quarterly* 33 (December 2003): 827–852; Diane D. Blair, "The Big Three of Late Twentieth-Century Arkansas Politics: Dale Bumpers, Bill Clinton and David Pryor," *Arkansas Historical Quarterly* 54 (Spring 1995): 53–79; Richard W. Waterman, "Storm Clouds on the Political Horizon: George Bush at the Dawn of the 1992 Presidential Election," *Presidential Studies Quarterly* 26 (1996): 337–349; Marc J. Hetherington, "The Media's Role in Forming Voters' National Economic Evaluations in 1992," *American Journal of Political Science* 40 (May 1996): 372–395; John H. Aldrich and Thomas Weko, "The Presidency and the Election Campaign: Framing the Choice in 1992," in *The Presidency and the Political System*, 4th ed., ed. Michael Nelson (Washington, DC: CQ Press, 1995), 251–270; Thomas Weko and John H. Aldrich, "The Presidency and the Election Campaign: Framing the Choice in 1996," in *The Presidency and the Political System*, 5th ed., ed. Michael Nelson (Washington, DC: CQ Press, 1998), 275–296; William G. Mayer, "The 1992 Elections and the Future of American Politics," *Polity* 25 (Spring 1993): 461–474; Lyman A. Kellstedt, John C. Green, James L. Guth, and Corwin E. Smidt, "Religious Voting Blocs in the 1992 Elections: The Year of the Evangelical?," *Sociology of Religion* 55 (Fall 1994): 307–326; Josh King, *Off Script: An Advance Man's Guide to White House Stagecraft, Campaign Spectacle, and Political Suicide* (New York: St. Martin's Press, 2016), chaps. 9 and 10; Christine F. Ridout, "News Coverage and Talk Shows in the 1992 Presidential Campaign," *PS: Political Science and Politics* 26 (December 1993), 712–716; Dee Dee Myers, "New Technology and the 1992 Clinton Presidential Campaign," *American Behavioral Scientist* 37 (November–December 1993): 181–184; Dan B. Thomas and Larry R. Baas, "The Postelection Campaign: Competing Constructions of the Clinton Victory in 1992," *Journal of Politics* 58 (May 1996): 309–331; Michael X. Delli Carpini and Ester R. Fuchs, "The Year of the Woman? Candidates, Voters, and the 1992 Elections," *Political Science Quarterly* 108 (Spring 1993): 29–36.

On divided government and other aspects of contemporary American politics, see Alan I. Abramowitz, *The Disappearing Center: Engaged Citizens, Polarization, and American Democracy* (New Haven, CT: Yale University Press, 2010); Marc Hetherington and Jonathan Weiler, *Prius or Pickup? How the Answers to Four Simple Questions Explain America's Great Divide* (Boston: Houghton Mifflin, 2018); Sarah A. Binder, *Stalemate: Causes and Consequences of Legislative Gridlock* (Washington, DC: Brookings Institution Press, 2003); Morris Fiorina, *Divided Government* (New York: Macmillan, 1992); Gary C. Jacobson, *The Electoral Origins of Divided Government: Competition in U.S. House Elections, 1946–1988* (Boulder, CO: Westview Press, 1990); Matt Grossman and David A. Hopkins, *Asymmetric Politics: Ideological Republicans and Group Interest Democrats* (New York: Oxford University Press, 2016);

Jacob S. Hacker and Paul Pierson, *Winner-Take-All Politics: How Washington Made the Rich Richer—and Turned Its Back on the Middle Class* (New York: Simon & Schuster, 2010); Nolan McCarty, Keith T. Poole, and Howard Rosenthal, *Polarized America: The Dance of Ideology and Unequal Riches* (Cambridge, MA: MIT Press, 2006); Sean M. Theriault, *Party Polarization in Congress* (New York: Cambridge University Press, 2008); and E. J. Dionne Jr., *Why the Right Went Wrong: Conservatism—From Goldwater to the Tea Party and Beyond* (New York: Simon & Schuster, 2016).

For election data for president, Congress, and governor, see *Congressional Quarterly's Guide to U.S. Elections* (Washington, DC: CQ Press), any edition published after 1996. For poll data, search the Gallup poll website (http://www.gallup.com) for data on issues, trial heats, exit polls, presidential approval ratings, and other relevant survey results. For a broad range of data on American government and politics, see the biennial editions of Harold W. Stanley and Richard G. Niemi, *Vital Statistics on American Politics* (Washington, DC: CQ Press), published in odd-numbered years. Television commercials are archived at the Museum of the Moving Image website, on "The Living Room Candidate" page (http://www.livingroomcandidate.org). The Vanderbilt Television News Archive (https://tvnews.vanderbilt.edu/) has been recording and making available both regular and special news broadcasts since 1968. The American Presidency Project at the University of California, Santa Barbara (https://www.presidency.ucsb.edu/), is an invaluable source of presidential speeches, documents, data, video, and other primary materials.

1992 election, 91–92, 119, 127, 143, 153
1996 election, 203
United Auto Workers, 9
united party government, 5, 162, 182, 215, 217, 221. *See also* divided government
United States v. Weinberger, 152
United We Stand America, 196
United We Stand: How We Can Take Back Our Country (Ross Perot), 136, 139
Untermeyer, Chase, 99
U.S. Term Limits v. Thornton, 161

Van Buren, Martin, 2, 34, 265n8
vice presidency, 2, 4, 66
concern about, 80–81, 149
1968 election, 46
1976 election, 57–58
1980 election, 48–49, 61
1984 election, 126
1988 election, 26–27, 30, 59, 62, 63–64, 126
1992 election, 109, 111–112, 126, 130–131
1996 election, 194
as steppingstone to the presidency, 2, 7, 49–50, 50–51, 66
Vietnam war, 15, 28, 36–37, 39, 62, 64, 67, 73, 119, 131, 141, 148, 169
Viguerie, Richard, 68, 100
Voles, Lorraine, 92
Voter News Service, 156
voter turnout, 26, 56, 156, 157, 203
voting patterns, 1980 and 1984 elections, 41
voting patterns, 1988 election, 12, 13, 26
voting patterns, 1992 election
demographic, 125, 153–154
geographical, 153
ideology and issues, 154–155
partisan, 154
voting patterns, 1994 election, 173
voting patterns, 1996 election
demographic, 203
geographical, 202

ideology and issues, 203
retrospective vs. prospective voting, 197
Voting Rights Act Amendments of 1982, 159
Voting Rights Act of 1965, 37, 43–44

Waldman, Michael, 287n68
Wallace, George C., 42, 43, 67, 69, 81, 94, 147, 155, 157, 172, 202, 207, 218
Wallace, Henry A., 7, 94
Wall Street Journal, 120–121
Walmart, 19, 136, 150
Walsh, Lawrence, 152
Waltons, The, 104
Wanniski, Jude, 39
Ward, Bob, 188
Warfield, Nelson, 201
Washington, Harold, 24
Washington Monthly magazine, 29
Washington Post, 20, 24, 109, 112, 124, 142, 187, 188–189
Wasserman, David, 219
Watergate scandal, 47, 58, 67, 118, 223
Watson, Thomas, 143
Watt, J. C., 194
Wattenberg, Martin, 12
Weicker, Lowell, 272n45
Weiler, Jonathan, 217–218, 294n48
Weinberger, Caspar, 152
Weko, Thomas, 140
Welch, Robert, 259n30
welfare reform, 28
Clinton presidency and, 165, 169, 176, 179–180, 193, 204, 224–225, 226
as issue in 1992 election, 85, 86, 126, 129, 130, 139, 151, 179–180
1996 election, 193, 225
West, politics of, 56, 153, 202
West Wing, The, 213
Weyrich, Paul, 68
Whig Party, 1
White, Frank, 18
Whitewater scandal, 124, 169
Whitman, Christine Todd, 194
Whole Foods Market, 219